Empirical Asset Pricing Models

Jau-Lian Jeng

Empirical Asset Pricing Models

Data, Empirical Verification, and Model Search

palgrave
macmillan

Jau-Lian Jeng
School of Business and Management
Azusa Pacific University
Stevenson Ranch, CA, USA

ISBN 978-3-030-08932-0 ISBN 978-3-319-74192-5 (eBook)
https://doi.org/10.1007/978-3-319-74192-5

Cover illustration: © Kitschstock / Alamy Stock Photo
Cover design by Ran Shauli

Printed on acid-free paper

This Palgrave Macmillan imprint is published by Springer Nature
The registered company is Springer International Publishing AG
The registered company address is: Gewerbestrasse 11, 6330 Cham, Switzerland

Preface

This book discusses several issues concerning the construction of empirical asset pricing models, including: (1) the setting of essential properties in asset pricing models of stock returns, (2) the statistical inferences that can be applied to verify the necessary properties of empirical asset pricing models, and (3) the model search approach where any model can be considered as only a tentative approximation for asset returns given their time-changing nature.

The main aim of the book is to verify that statistical inferences and time series analysis for asset returns should not be confined to the verification of certain structures or variables based simply on statistical significance alone. These statistical verifications can only be meaningful if the intent or hypothesis for the model is related to the properties developed in the theoretical setting of asset pricing models where systematic components of asset returns are considered.

Blaming the existing models for their deficiency or lack of forecasting superiority is not necessarily a solid way to refute the theories. In fact, unless we have some solid understanding of the ultimate mechanism of stock returns, it is premature to claim the depletion of current existing theories based only on predictability or forecasting. A rigorous justification must originate from more profound alternatives that may belittle the currently existing theoretical framework. Profitability (through forecasting, for instance) can't even be a unique determinant for the validity of empirical models on asset returns.

Speculative profits (through forecasting) may result from technical analysis where no theoretical background of financial economics (or anything else) is discussed at all. Superiority in forecasting with certain proposed models or mechanisms may prevail with short-term horizons among different data sets. Yet, it is not surprising to find that this advantage quickly resolves over time which entails the needs to update and modify the presumed models continuously. Thanks to their properties, this is precisely why financial markets are sufficiently interesting to attract enormous resources in exploring the quintessence of their evolving mechanism. What is really essential for empiricists is how to accommodate this possibly time-changing nature of stock returns, and to strive for the pricing kernels with meaningful interpretation of them.

Part I of this book covers the essential properties of theoretical asset pricing models, especially when linear (factor-pricing) models are of interest. Since the focus of the book is on empirical asset pricing models, only discrete-time models are discussed. From the theoretical issues, the conventional specification tests are also discussed with their possible implications for the models of interest. This leads to the discussion of model searching with various model selection criteria where emphases are mainly of reduction of dimensionality and predictability.

Given the pitfalls of these model selection criteria, Part II provides an alternative methodology where various justifications of the cross-sectional properties of stock returns is emphasized and additional model searching is devised with the specification tests provided. Hence the aim of this book is to reconsider the necessary cautions involved in the analyses of empirical asset pricing models and to provide some alternatives. The book may be used as a technical reference for researchers, graduate students, and professionals who are interested in exploring the possible alternatives that may provide more tractable methods for empirical asset pricing models for various applications in the future.

Stevenson Ranch, CA, USA Jau-Lian Jeng

Acknowledgments

This book is dedicated to my family and my parents for their support with encouragement and patience regarding my stubborn and unrelenting pursuit of academic goals—even when the environment for the pursuit didn't seem appealing or yielding. I would like to thank, in particular, the editorial assistance of Sarah Lawrence and Allison Neuburger at Palgrave Macmillan. Many thanks are also offered to Dr. Jack Hou for his encouragement, comments, and reviews. Above all, I thank especially the one who said "…I am!" for giving me the inspiration that has endured over the decades of my exile and to recognize my limits.

INTRODUCTION

Ever since the pioneering work of the capital asset pricing model, theoretical and empirical discussion on the pricing kernel of asset returns has been huge in the financial economics literature. Although many alternative methodologies and theories have been devised, the difficulty in empirical application of asset pricing models still remains unresolved in many areas such as model instability over different time horizons, variable selection on proxies for factors, and (possibly) applicable robust statistical inferences. It is likely that we will discover that an empirical asset pricing model, once selected, can only apply to a certain time period before the model validity quickly disappears when an extended time horizon or data set is considered.

Unfortunately, this phenomenon seems to prevail in many data sets (domestic or foreign) that are applied. The disappointing results in turn lead to the pervasive discontent with the theoretical foundation of asset pricing models. Emphasis on (time series) predictability becomes the norm for model validity for empirical asset pricing models. With the keen demand for validating empirical asset pricing models, statistical verification (with predictability and specification tests) when certain proxies or variables of interest are used becomes the mainstream for financial time series modeling on asset returns.

Essentially, emphases in finding the common features or characters of asset returns (in an attempt to reduce the dimensionality, for instance) through statistical significance should be dealt with using additional caution since these features, once identified, may only prevail tentatively (or contempornaeously) over the selected time horizon.

Part I surveys (a) the quintessential issues of asset pricing models as the pricing kernels for asset returns and (b) the conventional specification tests that consider the possible reduction of dimensionality with statistical significance, which leads to (c) the importance of model searching for the normal (or expected) returns where model selection criteria are applied. Although various specification tests or model selection criteria have been developed for empirical asset pricing models, few of them emphasize the prerequisite that these included variables (in empirical asset pricing models) should satisfy the systematic properties of pricing kernels such as non-diversifiability so that the separation between normal (or expected) returns and abnormal returns or idiosyncratic risks can be well stated.

In essence, empirical asset pricing models must fulfill a set of more restrictive conditions whereas statistical significance in explanatory power (such as p-value) on certain (pre-)selected variables can only be considered as exploratory. After all, as the purpose of empirical asset pricing models is to identify the intrinsic structure that governs the (possibly time-changing) core or pricing kernel of asset returns, statistical inference of the significance of certain variables or structures is not entirely sufficient.

Developments on the conventional studies in testing empirical asset pricing models focus mainly on asymptotic arguments of time series data. However, for the validity of any empirical asset pricing model, the focus should be on whether the set of selected variables or proxies by which one attempts to explain the pricing kernel of asset returns constitutes the cross-sectional (asymptotic) commonality among the asset returns or not. It appears, if experience in empirical finance is applied, that identification of some statistically significant explanatory variables for asset returns is not too difficult to provide.

The difficulty, however, is whether these identified variables or proxies truthfully reveal the essential (cross-sectional) commonality of asset returns or not. What is misleading in many empirical findings is that the essence of asset pricing models as pricing kernels was sacrificed when statistical verification of the significance and predictability of explanatory variables in the presumed models is advocated through time series data.

Notice that this empirical verification (of predictability) is mostly (if not all) based on known or collected time series data. As a matter of fact in empirical finance, even if the verification is carried out through out-of-sample time series data, these data are usually known in advance. In other words, the models are fitted with a given training sample of presumed time horizon. And then, time series forecastability is verified with the left-over data in the data set which the modeler has already obtained. The major dilemma lies in the trade-offs as to whether the model specification on empirical asset pricing models is to find something that may help to describe the (short-run) dynamics of asset returns or to identify the quintessence of pricing kernels when short-run predictability could be sacrificed.

Although these trade-offs are not immediately clear-cut, given the notorious time-changing nature of financial markets, it is unlikely that there exists an omnipotent model that encompasses all others across all time horizons. To the best that can be shown, the winning model (through statistical verification or otherwise) only represents a tentative explanation or approximation for the underlying pricing kernel of asset returns. Time changes everything.

Hence, even with the contemporaneous model that encompasses all other competitive alternatives, the empirical result only shows the current notion for the underlying determinant of asset returns. What is more critical, however, is whether the tentative model obtained helps us understand more about the pricing kernel of the asset returns or not. And perhaps more essentially, it helps us to modify diligently the model(s) for different time horizons or data sets.

In Chap. 1 of Part I, the discussions focus on the conventional linear models for asset returns. Given the enormous volume of literature on asset pricing models, this book only surveys and develops the discussions on parametric model building and variable selection. The recent developments on semi-parametric (factor) modeling for asset pricing are also briefly discussed.

Starting from the capital asset pricing model (CAPM), the methods for reduction of dimensionality are covered where factor-pricing models are typical examples. It is not too difficult to find that the empiricist in applied finance may criticize these models as somewhat useless in the usage of profit-taking transactions. Nonetheless, from the perspectives of the financial economist, this is precisely the result of a properly working market mechanism where the advantage in any attempt at speculative opportunity should quickly resolve to zero. Does this mean that these theories are all useless in empirical application? We can only be sure if we have some better theories to explain the mechanism of capital markets and the ultimate determinants for pricing kernels of stock returns.

Although many alternative approaches such as the nonlinearity and behavioral assumptions are developed, the question to ask is "Are these alternative approaches good enough to substitute for the original models we have?" or "Are they competitive enough to provide better insights for the pricing mechanism of stock returns?" Up to the current date, these known alternatives (or models), although rigorous and promising, remain as supplementaries, but they are inadequate as substitutes for existing theories on the pricing kernels of stock returns.

For empirical asset pricing models, the basic criteria for model building are: (1) the procedures for identifying a (or a group of) proper model(s) should be easy to implement in statistical inferences (or with other analytical tools); (2) these candidate models must have well-established theoretical foundations to support the findings; and (3) they provide further directions to cope with the developing status of information and model searching.

Chapter 2 in Part I, for instance, will discuss the methodologies that are currently applied in empirical asset pricing models on asset returns. The chapter includes up-to-date coverage on theoretical setting and model specification tests developed for empirical asset pricing models. However, it is not difficult (in empirical application) to find that these identified, presumed to be economic, variables may not necessarily provide better specification and forecasts than the application of simple time series modeling of asset returns. Chapter 3 in Part I surveys the model selection criteria in determining the number of factors of asset returns. Chapter 4 in Part II discussed alternative methods for detecting hidden systematic factors without assuming that there exists a correct factor structure. Chapter 5 considers model search in empirical asset pricing models.

As such, the search for empirical asset pricing models cannot be succinctly accomplished with the in-sample statistical inferences over some limited time horizons or data sets. Various model specification tests have been developed toward robust methods in (dynamic) asset pricing models. However, it seems that most analyses emphasize the asymptotic properties from time series perspectives. One possible reason for this is that the shadow of forecastability still plays an essential role in the robustness of empirical asset pricing models. Nevertheless, what is essential in such models is the strength of (cross-sectional) coherence or association for these identified economic variables/factors that possibly describes the intrinsic mechanism or pricing kernel of asset returns.

Given the evolving nature of these pricing kernels, forecastability of presumed models over an out-of-sample time horizon is usually limited. Instead, tractability is the goal for empirical asset pricing models: that model specification should emphasize the capability and properties of the underlying intrinsic mechanism of asset returns (or so-called pricing kernels) to administer and accommodate the model search when various available information is applied. The interest of study should be on what method (or methods) is (are) to apply in the search for empirical asset pricing models which is often perceived as evolving through time where many data sets have been applied to trace them. Hence, a model search for empirical asset pricing models should focus on the fundamental properties that any pricing kernel (based on any available information) should prevail in addition to the statistical significance of certain (economic) variables identified or their forecastability.

Contents

PART I

Asset Pricing Models: Discussions and Statistical Inferences

CHAPTER 1

Asset Pricing Models: Specification, Data and Theoretical Foundation

The author surveys and discusses linear asset pricing models with the intent to identify some sets of variables or factors with reduced dimensionality to approximate the core or pricing kernel of asset returns. A theoretical foundation may start with discussion on factor pricing models where asset returns are projected onto some lower-dimensional sets of factors that possibly explain the major variations of asset returns. The aim is to identify major determinants for the fluctuations of asset returns where these determinants satisfy some systematic properties that ensures their indispensable roles.

Controversies begin with questions of measurability of factors and their justification. Classical issues such as the measurability of market portfolio in the capital asset pricing model (CAPM) and selection of market indices, for instance, all incur the problems of measurability and representation for the verification of a theoretical framework. Developments and extensions of arbitrage pricing theory (APT) and multi-factor asset pricing models do not make the hope of attaining robust asset pricing models any brighter.

Statistical inferences do not always mediate the severity of problems mentioned if caution regarding their limitations is not taken into account. Given that all measurable factors presumed for asset pricing models may contain some measurement errors, it is unlikely that empirical asset pricing models will resolve the difficulty of completeness in model justification. At their best extent, empirical asset pricing models can only mimic the systematic patterns or properties of asset returns that provide the tractability

J.-L. Jeng, *Empirical Asset Pricing Models*,
https://doi.org/10.1007/978-3-319-74192-5_1

and direction where the pursuit of economic explanations on asset returns may be feasible.

For instance, the earlier study by Fama and MacBeth (1973) with two-path regressions of asset returns (although these may be considered biased or inconsistent in some statistical properties) is an example of where justification of presumed factor(s) in asset pricing models should undertake further cautious verification in their systematic properties rather than statistical inferences based on significance levels (such as *p*-values) for any proposed/identified regularity of the data. Even then, work on empirical asset pricing models only provide a direction where further contemporaneous elaborations or searches are needed for model developments on asset returns. Statistical properties are indeed very important for the justification of empirical results. However, the quintessence of empirical asset pricing models in asset returns is to identify the intrinsic mechanism and its role that determines the coherence of these returns in the capital market.

Statistical inference does indeed help. However, statistical verification of empirical asset pricing models should offer the direction or tractability (and plausibility) for the searching of models. In fact, the tractability of model searching should involve optimal usage of available information which provides the common essentiality that may prevail (in all asset returns, for instance) and allow the evolving nature of the models through applications of various data sets.

In particular, statistical analyses must be accompanied with theoretical properties or reasonings developed under economic/financial theories. Statistical inferences and econometrics provide rigorous verification through the extended study of rigorous layouts on the time-series and cross-sectional properties of data steams. However, those works are never exhaustive. To provide some helpful insights on empirical asset pricing models, innovative thoughts that incorporate new theoretical frameworks for analytical issues and explanation are needed. Otherwise, empirical asset pricing models may simply fall into being criticized as measurement without theory as stated in Koopmans (1947).

Although there are also limits for theories (such as that they can't be treated purely as insights that will provide accurate guidance in decision making or anything else) those developments may offer conceivable hypotheses for empirical work that results in confirmation or rebuttal. Whether statistical inferences from empirical data are confirmatory or not, the introduction of economic theory improves our understanding of the alternatives to underlying schemes of interest. Likewise, innovation of thought may result from such refutations. This is discussed in Wolpin (2013) for the risk of inferences without theory, although Rust (2014) mentions that there are also limits to using theory, pronouncing that it is essential to incorporate (economic) theory into test and empirical work to improve the theories instead of purely relying on randomized experiments and asking the data to speak for themselves.

1.1 Theories, Asset-Pricing Models, and Reduction of Dimensionality

Given that there is a vast amount of literature covering the discussions on the asset pricing model, this section will only survey some basic theoretical developments that are well-known in the field. If loosely defined, these models can be denoted as rational pricing models that attempt to provide basic pricing regularity for security returns. These theoretical developments offer further possibilities to extend the asset pricing models for modification for up-dated information. Even though theories don't necessarily predict the stock returns better than a crystal ball in any short period of time, the rigors of these theoretical works lay down the foundation for extended studies that may accommodate more closely the evolving nature of the capital market.

The aim (for the theoretical foundation), however, is not simply for the search for further extensions to try to cope with the results of empirical findings. It is not surprising that one may discover these empirical findings sometimes even contradict each other when various data, time horizons, test statistics, and/or sampling schemes are applied. Empirical findings (when using statistical inferences or otherwise) are only tools or devices for attempting to identify possible features or characteristics of security returns, for instance. However, these empirical findings are not necessarily so universal as to describe the ultimate or intrinsic regularities of the systems of interest. They are only indications which may depict certain features (of the system of interest) that require attention.

Hence, if the results (at any stage of empirical asset pricing models) are identified, it is necessary that one reflects on the theoretical foundation for the justification of rationality in modeling. And that reflection is not to forge theories to match the data. Although scientific analyses do require the steps from hypotheses/theoretical developments to refutation with data verification, the modification of theoretical work afterward (whether the refutation confirms or rejects the initial hypotheses) should strive for the provision of improvement in understanding (of the system of interest) and not for alteration of theoretical work simply so as to coordinate it with the empirical results.

Many theoretical models and empirical works have provided various insights in the finance and economics literature over recent decades. In spite of the huge volume of articles and research, the intent (of contribution in asset pricing) seems oftentimes to encourage the adaptation to fashionable or contemporary trends of thought. However, reviewing the past literature indicates that the inspiration of epoch-breaking research doesn't just follow such fashions. These advancements, either empirical or theoretical, rarely keep trace of those trends or fashion with further empirical examplification or alternative data sets. Instead, the contribution is of various perspectives and inspiration that incur different schools of thought. Reviewing the past literature for CAPM (or APT) shows that these contributions are not simply dedications to tradition or technicality. Instead, they involve ingenuity and path-breaking thoughts.

1.1.1 Market Model and Capital Asset Pricing Model (CAPM)

Typical asset pricing models start from discussions of one-factor model such as CAPM. The model requires the parameter "beta" to describe the association between market/systematic risk and the rates of return for stocks/portfolios. Much empirical verification and evidence is shown to identify the linear trade-offs of these two. The conventional CAPM begins with a simplified analysis such that, for all assets (or portfolios), the expected rates of return can be expressed as a simple linear model such that for $i = 1, \ldots, n$,

$$E[R_i] = R_f + \beta_i[E(R_m) - R_f],$$

or, in terms of excess returns,

$$E[r_i] = E[R_i] - R_f = \beta_i E[R_m - R_f],$$

where R_f stands for the risk-free rate and $\beta_i = \frac{\mathrm{Cov}(R_i,R_m)}{\sigma_m^2}$ as the systematic risk, R_m stands for the rate of return of the market portfolio. In brief, the asset's risk premium depends on the systematic risk and the market premium $E(R_m) - R_f$. In applying the CAPM onto the stock return data, conventional studies consider the time series regression model as

$$r_{it} = \alpha_i + \beta_i r_{mt} + \epsilon_{it}, \quad i = 1, \ldots, n,\ t = 1, \ldots, T,$$

where $r_{it} = R_{it} - R_{ft}$ is the excess return of asset i at time t, and $r_{mt} = R_{mt} - R_{ft}$. The time series regression will give the estimates for the "betas" of the excess returns of included assets. Accordingly, if the theory holds true, the intercept in the time series regression should be close to zero. Ideally, if the market portfolio is correctly identified then the theory should result in the second-pass regression, such that for $i = 1, \ldots, n$,

$$\bar{r}_i = \gamma_o + \gamma_1 \hat{\beta}_i + \eta_i,$$

where $\bar{r}_i$ is the (time-series) average excess return for asset i, and $\hat{\beta}_i$ is the estimate of beta for asset i from the first-pass regression. Under the model CAPM, the coefficient γ_o should be equal to zero, and γ_1 is the coefficient for the market premium.

However, since the market indices may not precisely represent the market portfolio and the cross-sectional dependence, and since heteroskedasticity may make the conclusion of second-pass regression misleading, Fama and MacBeth (1973) has developed the "grouping" portfolios as applying the estimates of "betas" from the time series regressions so as to consider the second-pass regression such that

$$\bar{r}_p = \mu + \gamma \overline{\beta}_p + \upsilon_p,$$

where $\bar{r}_p$ is the average excess return for portfolio p, and $\overline{\beta_p}$ is the average betas of the assets included in the portfolio p. The reason for regrouping the assets' excess returns and betas into portfolios (according to predetermined characteristics) is to reduce the impact from the errors-in-variables problem since the market indices chosen for the market portfolio in time series regressions may contain measurement errors. In particular, in Fama and MacBeth (1973), a scheme of "rolling" estimates for the betas is implemented over different subperiods of the time series data which possibly reduces the impacts from time-varying coefficients in "betas" when time series regressions are applied.

Regardless of the theoretical appeals that the market-wise risk should be compensated by a suitable risk premium for the risky assets, the empirical findings show that a single market risk premium seems insufficient to explain the risk premiums of asset returns, especially when Chen et al. (1986) show that some other economic variables in addition to market index returns may contribute explanations for asset returns, it is conceivable to see that the development of theoretical modeling toward multi-factor extension will follow logically.

1.1.2 Linear Factor Pricing Models and Arbitrage Pricing Theory

Earlier works on a linear factor pricing model can be found in Ross (1976) and Chamberlain and Rothschild (1983). Grinblatt and Titman (1985) extend the approximate factor structure of Chamberlain (1983) to show that it can be transformed into the exact factor structure in Ross (1976) and vice versa. Following from the works of Grinblatt and Titman (1985) and others, Reisman (1988) applies the Hahn-Banach theorem for the well-defined return space with continuous functionals to establish a similar pricing model. All these theoretical results are based on the existence of a well-defined (approximate) factor structure of return processes.

Intuitively, in a one-factor case, it is easy to see that the return processes can be projected to the factor as

$$r_i = E[r_i] + b_i f + e_i,$$

where r_i is the excess return for asset i, e_i is the idiosyncratic risk, and f is the systematic factor, $E[e_i] = E[f] = \text{Cov}[e_i, f] = 0$. Under no arbitrage condition, the expected premium for asset i should be expressed as

$$E[r_i] \approx \gamma\, b_i.$$

Reisman (1992) extends the analysis to consider the "beta" when defined on the reference variable(s), which establishes a similar result. That is, given the beta $\tilde{b}_i$ (with respect to the reference variable g), it is feasible (if the factor structure is correct) to write

$$\tilde{b}_i \approx \text{Cov}(f, g) b_i.$$

Hence, as long as $\text{Cov}(f, g) \neq 0$, it can be shown that $\gamma b_i \approx \lambda \tilde{b}_i$, where

$$\lambda = \frac{\gamma}{\text{Cov}(f, g)}.$$

Rewrite the above equations as

$$E[r_i] - \lambda \tilde{b}_i = (E[r_i] - \gamma b_i) + \left(\gamma b_i - \lambda \tilde{b}_i\right)$$

which is equivalent to stating that $E[r_i] \approx \lambda \tilde{b}_i$. That is, there exists a pricing functional for expected premiums when using the reference variables.

Following Chamberlain and Rothschild (1983), Reisman (1992), the excess returns for all assets are projected onto the set of factors (or reference variables) $\{f_1, \ldots, f_k\}$such that

$$r_i = \alpha_i + \sum_{j=1}^{k} \beta_{ij} f_j + \epsilon_i,$$

where the $\{\epsilon_i\}_{i=1,\ldots,n}$ represent the idiosyncratic risk of the return processes. The factor structure (with k factors) will hold if the eigenvalues of the covariance matrix of $\{\epsilon_i\}_{i=1,\ldots,n}$ are all bounded from above. Given the factor structure (and under the continuity assumption), it is feasible for the expected returns (or risk premiums) to be expressed as

$$E[r_i] \approx \sum_{j=1}^{k} \beta_{ij} \phi(f_j),$$

where $\phi(f_j)$ is the risk premium of factor $j, j = 1, 2, \ldots, k$, where the pricing errors are square-summable even when the number of assets n increases.

From empirical perspectives, the arbitrage pricing theory extends the conventional models (such as CAPM) into multi-factor space to explain the possible risk premiums of assets. The merit of the model is that the possible explanatory variables (such as reference variables in Reisman 1992) can be extended to higher dimensions, particularly when the number of assets grows large. The difficulty, however, is that there is no indication as to what the "true factors" are and that these factors are usually unobservable. Although proxies or reference variables can be applied to express the risk premiums, there is no justification (or selection rule) as to which set of proxies or reference variables can be considered as optimal. Besides, given that the "true factors" are not observable, little is known of the correlations or associations of the "true factors" and proxies (or reference variables). In fact, as indicated in Lewellen et al. (2010), the cross-sectional regressions in using the proxies for factors may overstate the fittedness of models even when the factors and proxies are only slightly related.

Another question concerns how many factors are needed for these asset returns. Although statistical inferences such as factor analysis seems feasible for identifying the factors, it is usually limited to finite (cross-sectional) dimensions. Expansions in both the cross-sectional and time-series dimensions will require additional analyses (such as Bai and Ng (2002), Bai (2003), and many others) where conventional factor analysis cannot apply. An additional difficulty is that the factors and factor loadings are not identifiable. Any nonsingular linear transform on factors and their loadings will suffice as the same model for describing the return processes. Likewise, empirical applications on these factor-oriented models require extra caution when interpreting estimated results.

1.2 Predictability or Tractability?

Stock return predictability is almost always an issue that attracts much research, using different schemes, data, time periods, and methods. Although there are various studies that cover all possible issues in this field, controversies are bountiful. Different empirical results and claims are covered in much financial literature. The main question still concerns what and how the information of asset returns can be considered when derived from this kind of evidence. For simplicity, the discussions on the forecastability and predictability are used interchangeably. The difference between these two concepts is outlined in Clements and Hendry (1999), namely that forecasts may require additional information on data generating mechanisms and processes while predictability is related to feasible (and possibly lagged) information sets.

When a newer asset pricing model or device is developed, it is usually (and pervasively) assumed that the model will most likely improve the forecastability of asset returns in empirical applications. In addition, the new finding or concept may easily turn into fashionable research when pronounced in the finance literature or elsewhere. More explicitly, various research articles published attempt to find any possible mechanism (including time series models and economic/business attributes such as dividend yields, inflation rates, or earning forecasts) to assess stock return predictability. These earlier studies may have conveyed the notion that predictability is an essential tool for checking the validity of model specification, particularly on asset returns or empirical asset pricing models. However, the proving or disproving of stock return predictability should be to assist the understanding of the underlying systems and to provide better guidance in formatting or modeling the data. It's not merely a demonstration of empirical findings. There are a few issues to be discussed here:

1. Is predictability a necessary result of a good asset pricing model?
2. Is the empirical evidence of finite sample predictability (from the models or other variables) really a reliable source for verification so that stock returns can be traced down accordingly? Are these findings only the confirmations of scholarly trends, or simply the echoes of common knowledge?
3. What role should theoretical asset pricing models play?

For the first issue, according to Clements and Hendry (1999), the unpredictability (for a stochastic process ν_t) is defined as

$$D_{\nu_t}(\nu_t|I_{t-1}) = D_{\nu_t}(\nu_t),$$

where $D_{\nu_t}(\nu_t|I_{t-1})$, and $D_{\nu_t}(\nu_t)$ stand for the conditional and unconditional distribution of ν_t, respectively. That is to say, the (un)predictability is defined upon the available information set I_{t-1}. Choices over different information may cause the empirical results to differ from each other.

Hence, based on the definition, when $\mathscr{I}_{t-1} \subset I_{t-1}$, it is possible to have $D_{\nu_t}(\nu_t|\mathscr{I}_{t-1}) = D_{\nu_t}(\nu_t)$, while $D_{\nu_t}(\nu_t|I_{t-1}) \neq D_{\nu_t}(\nu_t)$—even though the correct information set I_{t-1} may not be known or feasible. In other words, (un)predictability depends on the content of the relevant information sets applied.

Unless justification can be shown on the inclusion relation of the various content of (possibly overlapping) information sets in empirical practices, proofs or disproofs of the predictability of asset returns or asset pricing models (in using different information sets) fall short of being insights into understanding the pricing kernel of asset returns. One of the possible reasons is that these verifications are usually based on different information sets over time horizons, data sources, and constructions of relevant variables. In addition, the notion of (un)predictability can also be considered as time-varying such that for time index $H \geq 1$,

$$D_{\nu_t}(\nu_t|I_{t-1}) = D_{\nu_t}(\nu_t), \quad t = 1, \ldots, T,$$
$$D_{\nu_t}(\nu_t|I_{t-1}) \neq D_{\nu_t}(\nu_t), \quad t = T+1, \ldots, T+H,$$

or,

$$D_{\nu_t}(\nu_t|I_{t-1}) \neq D_{\nu_t}(\nu_t), \quad t = 1, \ldots, T,$$
$$D_{\nu_t}(\nu_t|I_{t-1}) = D(\nu_t), \quad t = T+1, \ldots, T+H.$$

More explicitly, empirical results for predictability of asset returns over different time horizons may vary. Therefore, empirical verifications of (un)predictability for asset returns or asset pricing models across different time horizons may not be identical. As a matter of fact, if the underlying data generating mechanism of asset returns is time-varying, different empirical results of (un)predictability are likely to appear. Likewise, developments in assessing this time-varying nature of asset returns versus asset pricing models need to consider both the detection of the possible time frames for the parameters of interest and the tracking methods (or modelings) for these parameters, too.

For the second issue on empirical verification of asset pricing models, the so-called predictability in many empirical studies is actually discovered from the already known observations collected, in contrast to pure simulations. That is, the empirical results (of predictability) are usually formed from the statistics of so-called in-sample and out-of-sample observations of historical data. Notwithstanding that dividing the historical data into in-sample and out-of-sample observations is subjective and arbitrary, it is rarely feasible that one would simply apply the proposed methods or hypothesized models on the real-time observations from the day-to-day transactions and wait for the results to show. In other words, the entire verification of predictability when using historical data is more likely "in-sample" by the researchers' selection through prior knowledge or otherwise. Random simulations may provide more robust results. However, different schemes of replication may also affect the results of verification. More explicitly, even with high-frequency trading and technology where real-time observations are available in a short period of time, this so-called predictability may vary and/or vanish over different time periods.

Various methods have been designated to the search, including the high-end technology of financial econometrics. However, since any investor will almost always endeavor to pursue speculative profits once the technology is discovered, it is inconceivable that the findings will be published and become enunciable. Hence, it is perhaps not too surprising to say that if one successfully develops a predictive mechanism that belittles others in the market, one should keep it completely confidential.

In particular, under the pavilion of contemporaneous financial econometrics, predictability is essential in either the model verifications or the empirical applications. Unfortunately, even though predictability is only the verification of the model's validity, the provision of some empirical studies may lead to misunderstanding and the attempt to search for the possibility of speculative profits with better forecasts. More strikingly, overemphasis on the predictions and forecasts may lead the financial modeling toward tracking asset returns with devices or mechanisms of short-term validity where no plausible explanation (in financial economics or otherwise) may be feasible. In fact, this kind of emphasis and motivation (for new tracking methods) may simply destroy the validity of verifying model specification (with predictability) since the devised mechanism is only for "tracing and chasing the prey". More specifically, it is not merely due to the possibility of a time-varying pricing mechanism that the theoretical models may not perform better in predictions or forecasts. As a matter of fact, this lack of soundness in predictability simply shows that all models are only approximations for the data generating mechanism. Namely, theoretical models are not developed solely for predictability. Developing models or hypotheses in asset pricing models is to improve the search for understanding and approaches toward some better direction for decision making, if not more.

Thirdly, notice that the ultimate objective of asset pricing models is to identify effectively a tractable explanation for the pricing mechanism (and perhaps on its changing nature) based on the accessible information. Emphasis should be on the continuous effort and work (of finance professionals or academics) of searching for the determinants of the pricing mechanism of stock returns with rigor and explanation—provided that the underlying system of asset returns is almost always evolving through different time periods, regimes, systems, or economies. The goal, however, is to search for any tractable mechanism from which important economic/business decisions can be made. And that (out-of-sample) predictability of the model is only one dimension of the possible statistical properties that may validate the plausibility of the proposed or devised mechanism.

Unfortunately, given the empirical evidence that shows the time series predictability in various aspects, it seems that the fashion leads to finding some plausible alternative theories or else to accommodate the outcomes from empirical studies. In other words, the model search becomes finding theoretical explanations for whatever the empirical statistics may show. This approach could be misleading and counter-productive since one may be attempting to find some plausible excuses for the empirical findings when the past theories (or models) do not hold up completely. The focus for empirical asset pricing models should be on finding the guidelines and theoretical reasonings that may assist the search for the governing structure of asset returns. One should not rely on the empirical findings from various data series, and then develop some plausible ways to accommodate the systems observed empirically.

Although it is not legitimate to take whichever side as favoring predictability or against predictability, it is necessary to stress that the main purpose for empirical asset pricing models is not merely to achieve predictability through any meticulous methodology devised. Discovering the evidence of stock return predictability from various sources is useful indeed. Justification of (say) the profitability of certain devised strategies in considering the long-term predictability of security returns may help us to understand the essence of investments. Yet, verification of these findings can only provide some snapshots within the evolving path of financial markets and the functioning of their participants. How to include these time-changing qualities and to run the empirical asset pricing models to acquire increased plausibility on security returns is far more important.

In short, the provision of a rigorous and/or theoretical analytical apparatus for explaining or forecasting security returns is not to provide any forecast-dominating model or scheme. (In essence, there may be no such ubiquitous model for security returns.) Rather the provision is to offer some guidelines and expectations for pursuing the search for descriptions and rationales that may provide traits in understanding data generating mechanisms. Shmueli (2010) for instance discusses this issue in greater detail.

Explicitly Shmueli (2010) states that statistical models can be used in several essential categories: explanatory modeling, predictive modeling, and descriptive modeling. In essence, the predictability and explanatory power of a model can be considered as two-dimensional requirements for any scientific approach to model building.

As stated in Shmueli (2010), "...the predictive qualities of a model should be reported alongside its explanatory power so that it can be fairly evaluated in terms of its capabilities and compared to the other models. Similarly, a predictive model might not require causal explanation in order to be scientifically useful; however, reporting its relation to causal theory is important for purpose of theory building."

Shmueli (2010) provides a simple example that shows that when a misspecified model is chosen and compared to the so-called true model of the data source, it can be seen that, although the misspecified model suffers from a larger bias in estimating coefficients, the predictive errors of the misspecified model can be less than that of the correct model when some conditions are provided. In that way, if one is emphasizing only predictability, it is easy to choose the misspecified model instead of the true one.

For instance, if a correctly specified statistical model is given as

$$\underline{y} = x_1\beta_1 + x_2\beta_2 + \underline{\varepsilon}, \tag{1.2.1}$$

where unbiased estimation for the model is provided on the correctly specified model such that

$$\mathrm{Var}(\hat{y}) = \sigma^2 \underline{x}'(X'X)^{-1}\underline{x}, \tag{1.2.2}$$

and $\underline{x} = (\underline{x}_1', \underline{x}_2')'$ is the vector of x_1, x_2, and X is the design matrix of $\underline{x}$. The prediction error can be expressed as

$$\begin{aligned} &E(\underline{y} - \hat{\underline{y}})'(\underline{y} - \hat{\underline{y}}) \\ &\quad = \sigma^2(1 + \underline{x}'(X'X)^{-1}\underline{x}). \end{aligned} \tag{1.2.3}$$

For an incorrectly specified model such as

$$\underline{y} = x_1\gamma_1 + \underline{\nu}, \tag{1.2.4}$$

the bias is equal to

$$x_1\gamma_1 - (x_1\beta_1 + x_2\beta_2) = x_1(x_1'x_1)^{-1}x_1'(x_1\beta_1 + x_2\beta_2) - (x_1\beta_1 + x_2\beta_2), \tag{1.2.5}$$

where $\mathrm{Var}(\hat{y}){=}\sigma^2 x_1'(x_1'x_1)^{-1}x_1$. This gives the prediction error of the misspecified model as

$$\begin{aligned} &E(\underline{y} - \underline{\hat{y}})'(\underline{y} - \underline{\hat{y}}) \\ &\quad = (x_1(x_1'x_1)^{-1}x_1'x_2\beta_2 - x_2\beta_2)^2 \\ &\quad + \sigma^2(1 + x_1(x_1'x_1)^{-1}x_1'). \end{aligned} \tag{1.2.6}$$

According to Shmueli (2010), although the misspecified model can have a larger variance when combining the bias and variance, the forecast error can be smaller for the misspecified model under suitable conditions. In other words, if one only emphasizes predictability as the main purpose of empirical asset pricing models, it is likely that the misspecified model (or models) may win the prize. Yet, the underlying model specification does not provide a more insightful analysis for the asset returns.

Hence, this shows that solely using forecast errors to consider model searching for asset returns may be misguided especially when the data are very noisy or subject to a time-varying nature. The task for financial modeling lies on whether the purpose of the model search is to obtain the fundamental and determining features of asset returns or to obtain the possible temporal traces for tentative assessments in asset returns. If the intent is solely on predictability, then searching for any possible device (in time-series dynamics or applications with inter-science technology, for instance) to improve forecasts should suffice. On the other hand, if the researcher is to identify the necessary explanatory role of empirical asset pricing models that may enhance understanding or determination of asset returns, overemphasis on predictability or forecasting could be misleading.

1.2.1 Short-Term Forecastability with Asset Pricing Models

For empirical asset pricing models, the depth of explanatory contribution in theory and adaptability in changing circumstances is critical for the validity of modeling. Likewise, a distinction in the objectives of modeling needs further elaboration in finance, economics, social science, and so on. The contribution of asset pricing models (or theories) should be on the rationales that lead to empirical verification which may enhance the understanding of the mechanism of asset returns. The intent, of which the prescribed hypotheses (or work) are merely for coping with the empirical results, may perhaps veer too keenly toward pragmatism and be less deep for making a significant contribution to an essential explanation.

The literature survey in this section covers some recent contributions on the predictability of security returns. However, given the vast number of studies in this field, it is unlikely to absorb them all. The following sections attempt to summarize some critical empirical results and enlist some possible traits on improvements needed.

Earlier studies on the predictability of stock returns (for instance) can be seen in Pettit and Westerfield (1974) who investigated the predictability of both the CAPM and market model, respectively. In their approach, the CAPM is expressed as

$$E(R_{it}) = R_{ft}(1 - \beta_i) + \beta_i E(R_{mt}), \tag{1.2.7}$$

where $E(R_{it})$ represents the ex ante expected rate of return for asset i, R_{ft} is the risk-free rate at time t, and $E(R_{mt})$ is the expected rate of return for the market portfolio, and β_i is defined as the responsiveness of R_{it} on R_{mt}. Given this, the ex post realized rate of return can be expressed in the following regression as

$$R_{it} = R_{ft}(1 - \beta_i) + \beta_i R_{mt} + \epsilon_{it}, \tag{1.2.8}$$

where R_{it} is the realized (ex post) rate of return for asset i, R_{mt} is the realized (ex post) rate of return for market portfolio, ϵ_{it} is a mutually uncorrelated error term that is orthogonal to R_{mt}. Hence, if the CAPM holds, the above equation shows that the conditional expectation of R_{it} (based on R_{mt}, R_{ft}, and β_i) will be shown as

$$E[R_{it} | R_{ft}, R_{mt}, \beta_i] = R_{ft}(1 - \beta_i) + \beta_i E(R_{mt}). \tag{1.2.9}$$

And hence, the period $T + 1$ forecast can be expressed as

$$E[R_{i,T+1} | R_{m,T+1}, R_{f,T+1}, \hat{\beta}_i] = R_{f,T+1}(1 - \hat{\beta}_i) + \hat{\beta}_i R_{m,T+1}. \tag{1.2.10}$$

For the market model

$$R_{it} = \alpha_i + \beta_i R_{mt} + \varepsilon_{it}, \tag{1.2.11}$$

the conditional expectation is expressed as

$$E[R_{it}|\alpha_i, \beta_i, R_{mt}] = \alpha_i + \beta_i R_{mt}, \tag{1.2.12}$$

and hence the one-period forecast can be expressed as

$$E[R_{iT+1}|\hat{\alpha}_i, \hat{\beta}_i, R_{mT+1}] = \hat{\alpha}_i + \hat{\beta}_i R_{mT+1}. \tag{1.2.13}$$

One method that Pettit and Westerfield (1974) apply is the cross-sectional regression of actual returns on the conditional returns as specified above. For instance, to verify the predictability of CAPM, the regression will be expressed as

$$R_{i,T+1} = a_o + a_1 \hat{E}[R_{i,T+1}|R_{m,T+1}, \hat{\beta}_i, R_{f,T+1}] + e_{i,T+1}, \tag{1.2.14}$$

where $E[e_{i,T+1}] = E[e_{i,T+1}, e_{j,T+1}] = E[e_{i,T+1}|R_{m,T+1}, \hat{\beta}_i, R_{f,T+1}] = 0$, for all $i \neq j$, $i, j = 1, 2, \ldots, n$. The verification then is to see if $a_o = 0$, and $a_1 = 1$, if the CAPM holds according to Pettit and Westerfield (1974).

One of the difficulties in Pettit and Westerfield (1974) is that the rejection of tests applied to Eq. (1.2.14) can possibly be due to many reasons such as model specification errors (in CAPM), time-varying coefficients, measurement errors (in betas), or the evolving nature of stock returns where all models are subject to tentative explanatory power only. In other words, rejection of the restrictions of coefficients in Eq. (1.2.14) is not sufficient to verify the validity (or invalidity) of using CAPM (or the market model) to predict the stock returns. In addition, measurement errors in independent variables may also cause the estimates to be inconsistent. By rewriting the above equation with introduction of measurement errors, the specification becomes

$$\begin{aligned} R_{i,T+1} = a_o + a_1 \hat{E}[R_{i,T+1}|R_{m,T+1}, \hat{\beta}_i, R_{f,T+1}] \\ - \left\{R_{m,T+1}\left(\hat{\beta}_i - \beta_i\right) - \left[\left(\hat{\beta}_i - \beta_i\right) R_{f,T+1}\right]\right\} + \zeta_{i,T+1}, \end{aligned} \tag{1.2.15}$$

where $E(\zeta_{i,T+1}) = E\left[\zeta_{i,T+1}, \zeta_{j,T+1}\right] = E\left[\zeta_{i,T+1} E\left(R_{i,T+1}|\Pi_t\right)\right] = 0$, and Π_t stands for the past information applied.

To verify the statistical properties of the regression models, Pettit and Westerfield (1974) applied the monthly data from the New York Stock

Exchange (NYSE) from January 1926 through June 1968. The difficulty, however, is that the sample selection and ranking of portfolios formed may introduce arbitrariness into the empirical results. Although the setting is for the predictability of asset returns in using asset pricing models, the verifications are actually for the model specification by hypothesis testing. The poor results of predictability are, in fact, confirmatory for the possible time variation of either the parameters or the data generating mechanism of the asset returns.

Even if the results are positive, verification of predictability of stock returns in using certain explanatory variables does not necessarily justify that the model (or models) found can be applied to all time horizons or schemes. Given the predictability shown in statistical significance in specification tests, it is still based on selected samples (in both time-series and cross-sectional settings) obtained by the researchers subjectively or according to the availability of data. Hence, the findings of predictability could result from the a priori information already known to the researchers or from the preliminary data analyses that had been conducted.

Essentially speaking, if predictability (for security returns) is of concern, there are several issues of serious investigation. Namely, one must determine the statistical measure(s) of predictability is(are) to be applied so that justification will be objective. Or, for instance, a robust statistical inference must be devised to identify the predictability where the verification is immune from the possible empirical data selection or time horizons. In addition, the candidate set of models and instrumental variables must be determined to consider the compatibility of competitive specification. Furthermore, if certain superior comparative predictability may exist, concerns on the possible cause of predictability should also be taken into account. More explicitly, the verification of predictability must consider whether the tentative predictability is a consequence of data snooping, data collection and selection, or other spurious reasons.

Ferson and Harvey (1991) provide analysis for the predictable components of monthly common stock and bond portfolio returns. They show that most predictability is associated with sensitivity to economic variables in some rational multi-beta asset pricing models, especially through time-varying risk and risk premiums. Similar to an earlier methodology, the conditional version of asset pricing models is applied. For instance, the conditional CAPM model is introduced as

$$E[R_{it}|Z_{t-1}] = \gamma_o(Z_{t-1}) + b_{im,t-1}\gamma_m(Z_{t-1}), \tag{1.2.16}$$

where R_{it} is the rate of return for asset i between time $t-1$ and t, $b_{im,t-1}$ is the (conditional) beta, $\gamma_m(Z_{t-1})$ is the market premium, $\gamma_o(Z_{t-1})$ is the expected return for all portfolios with market beta equal to zero, and Z_{t-1} is the conditioning information available up to time $t-1$. Notice that the $b_{im,t-1}$ is defined as the conditional covariance between the return and market portfolio divided by the conditional variance of the market portfolio.

Some noticeable differences between Eqs. (1.2.13) and (1.2.14) are that (1) time-varying coefficients are assumed, and (2) these variations are conditional on the available information Z_{t-1}. This model maintains the rational expectation scenario such that the prediction error of actual return from Eq. (1.2.14) is an error term that is orthogonal to the information set Z_{t-1}. In particular, the risk premiums $\gamma_o(Z_{t-1})$ and $\gamma_m(Z_{t-1})$ are time-changing with the conditioning information Z_{t-1}.

A two-pass regression method similar to Fama and MacBeth (1973) is then applied to the cross-sectional regression such as for n assets for month t,

$$r_{it} = \lambda_{ot} + \lambda_{mt}\beta_{im,t-1} + e_{it}, \quad i = 1, 2, \ldots, n, \tag{1.2.17}$$

where $r_{it} = R_{it} - R_{ft}$ represents the excess return of asset i, and R_{ft} is the one-month T-bill rate, $\beta_{im,t-1} = b_{im,t-1} - b_{fm,t-1}$ and $b_{fm,t-1}$ is the conditional beta of Treasury bills, conditional on information available at time $t-1$. According to Ferson and Harvey (1991), predictability should be due to the component related to risk. The component that is not related to risk should be unpredictable. This framework is also generalized to the multi-beta setting as

$$E[R_{it}|Z_{t-1}] = \gamma_o(Z_{t-1}) + \sum_{j=1}^{k} b_{ij,t-1}\gamma_j(Z_{t-1}), \tag{1.2.18}$$

where $b_{ij,t-1}$ are conditional betas of R_{it} on state variable j, $j = 1, 2, \ldots, k$. Accordingly, the cross-sectional regression is given as

$$r_{it} = \lambda_{ot} + \sum_{j=1}^{k} \lambda_{jt}\beta_{ij,t-1} + e_{it}, \quad i = 1, 2, \ldots, n, \tag{1.2.19}$$

where $\beta_{ij,t-1} = b_{ij,t-1} - b_{fj,t-1}$, are the conditional betas of the excess returns, $j = 1, 2, \ldots, k$, λ_{jt} is (according to Ferson and Harvey 1991) a "mimicking portfolio" return whose conditional expected value is an estimate of risk premium $\gamma_j(Z_{t-1})$ for state variable j. As stated earlier, the component $\sum_{j=1}^{k} \lambda_{jt}\beta_{ij,t-1}$ represents the part of return associated with risk, and the $\lambda_{ot} + e_{it}$ represents the part unrelated to risk.

In particular, Ferson et al. (2003) explain the predictive regressions for stock returns from the perspective and concept of spurious regressions as in Yule (1926) and Granger and Newbold (1974). Although the stock returns are not necessarily the nonstationary time series of persistent memory as those well known data series such as gross national products (GNP) or others, Ferson et al. (2003) consider that the incumbent expected rates of return for stock returns can be of persistent memory over time, where the idiosyncratic noises (although subject to little serial dependence) are of larger variance. Their claim is that such a setting will provide less time-series memory (as is usually found) for the stock returns while the expected rate of return is the main cause for the spurious regression. Through their simulation results, the predictability of many regressions (using various predictor variables) may be spurious due to the neglected persistence of memory in expected rates of returns.

However, it is easy to see that if indeed the expected rate of return (as an incumbent component of the stock's rate of return) is of some persistent memory, the correlogram of the stock's rate of return may still contain persistence even though the variance of the idiosyncratic component is relatively large (see Granger and Marmol 1998). Based on their simulations, Ferson et al. (2003) claim that, due to the spurious regressions, many empirical results for predictability of stock returns with various instrumental variables fail when later time periods are applied. In fact, these results of empirical predictability of stock returns may not necessarily be the cause of misleading empirical asset pricing models or spurious unobservable components of asset returns.

Any model identified with given time series data (or with instrumental variables) for any time period, to the best extent, can only be considered as an approximation for the underlying pricing mechanism of asset returns. A common practice in building empirical asset pricing models is to maintain the model(s) that forecasts better and discards the rest.

Unfortunately, all models may become obsolete over time even if the contemporaneous model seems to perform beautifully at that point in time. When the economy or market evolves with new information or conditions, it is not difficult to discover that these models may become less reliable. The (instrumental/predictive) variables that are once statistically significant can thus be treated merely as some "plausible" explanatory variables for the asset returns. Hence, concerns over the choices of variables or models should not be merely to identify the statistical significance over the current available time periods or information sets applied. Likewise, it is necessary (and as a precaution) that all empirical asset pricing models must be examined carefully to verify the existence and the cause of predictability.

Especially when using empirical asset pricing models or time series specification to predict security returns, most of the empirical results are actually provided by applying the existing historical data where modelers may already have some prior knowledge. The so-called out-of-sample performance measure is actually constructed by separating the historical observations into training samples and the test samples for comparing predictability. The sizes of these samples are sometimes essential for the empirical results of comparison. In addition, the measurement interval or window for security return is also of question. There is no consensus that such verification of predictability should be based on daily, weekly, or longer-term returns. Besides, due to the availability of data and in using the existing historical price data, it is also subjective to select the time periods to test the predictability.

For instance, Cooper and Gulen (2006) apply simulations to determine (1) the impact from the size of test samples and (2) the predictability of security returns as if the comparison is performed in real time. It has been discovered that most of the empirical evidence of time series predictability is perhaps subject to data snooping. Cooper et al. (2005) use simulations for the ex ante predictability of the cross-section of security returns by checking whether a real-time investor could use book-to-market equity, firm size, and one-year lagged returns to generate portfolio profits during the 1974–1997 period. Their findings indicate that there is a marked difference between ex post and ex ante predictability and suggest that the existing evidence of the predictability of stock returns in the literature could be exaggerated. The in-sample predictability seems to perform well in the data set. However, there is no substantial out-of-sample predictability.

Cooper et al. (2005) apply the NYSE, Amex, and NASDAQ nonfinancial firms to the Center for Research in Security Prices (CRSP) monthly stock returns and Compustat annual industrial files from 1963 to 1997. Similar to Fama and French (1992), these authors calculate the book-to-market equity ratio by dividing the book value of a firm's equity at fiscal year end $t-1$ from Compustat by the market value from CRSP at the end of December of year $t-1$. Size, then, is defined as the market value of a firm's equity from CRSP at the end of June of year t. In addition, the stock's momentum is defined as its 1-year lagged return. The 1-year-lagged holding period return is defined as from the beginning of July of year $t-1$ to the end of May of year t.

Another concern for the empirical findings is whether the return predictability is consistent with the rational pricing of security returns or not. Kirby (1998) provides the analysis that the overall predictability of returns is consistent with the circumstances where predictability is rational. However, an essential issue is how this predictability of returns (in rationality) may help us understand and modify the specifications of empirical asset pricing models.

Even more complicated and controversial is the technical issue of predictability of security returns. Various empirical results are shown with complexities of techniques and different data sets. Yet, the findings are still incapable of improving the empirical asset pricing models on model specifications or alternative directions.

Simin (2008) examines the time-series forecast errors of conditional and unconditional asset pricing models for portfolios and individual security returns. The conditional models seem to produce higher mean squared errors than unconditional models for step-ahead prediction. His conclusion is that the relatively high variance of security returns may ruin the step-ahead predictability of asset pricing models. Basically, Simin (2008) examines the predictability of asset pricing models on monthly returns by using the following set of equations with time-varying coefficients. Specifically,

$$\begin{aligned} E[r_{it+1}|Z_t] &= \alpha_{it+1} + \beta'_{it+1}E[r_{pt+1}|Z_t], \\ \alpha_{it+1} &= a_{io} + a'_{i1}Z_t, \\ \beta_{it+1} &= b_{io} + b'_{i1}Z_t. \end{aligned} \tag{1.2.20}$$

The dimension of the coefficients $a_{io,}, a_{i1}$, b_{io}, and b_{i1} are determined by the proposed conditional models, Z_t represents the instrumental variables in applications of forecasts. For instance, with the conditional version of the Fama-French model, b_{io} is $3x1$, b_{i1} is $Lx3$ where L is the number of instrumental variables and r_{pt} is a $3x1$ vector of excess market return, the return of portfolios high minus low (HML), and small minus big (SMB). For the unconditional version, the set of Z_t is set to a null set.

Simin (2008) applies different possible time-series specification of the system of equations, particularly on both the specification of α_{it+1} and $E[r_{pt+1}|Z_t]$. The forecasts are generated using the one-month step-ahead forecasts (in a 61-month rolling window) based on the parameters estimated with the 60-month training sample rolled over the time horizon.

Both unconditional and conditional expectation are applied to perform the forecasts. For the unconditional expectation, the time-series average for r_{pt} is used for the forecast. The conditional expectation is performed when using the regression of r_{pt} on Z_{t-1} over the past 60 months to obtain the coefficients and multiply those to the newly available observation of Z_t.

Four possible candidates of the benchmark returns are used: the historical average of asset returns, the historical average return of the market index, a constant, and the conditional mean of the market index. Two metrics are applied to consider predictability: the square root of the mean square forecast error and the test of conditional predictive ability (CTP) by Giacomini and White (2006).

The advantage of using the mean square error is that it is quadratic and can be decomposed into two components: the variance of forecast error and the bias. Namely, for the forecast $\hat{r}_t$ and forecast error $e_t = r_t - \hat{r}_t$,

$$\text{MSFE}(\hat{r}_t) = E[(r_t - \hat{r}_t)^2] = \text{Var}(e_t) + [\text{bias}]^2.$$

And the conditional predictive ability of Giacomini and White (2006) under the null hypothesis as equal predictive ability is defined as

$$H_o : E[\hat{u}_{1,t+1}^2 - \hat{u}_{2,t+1}^2 | F_t] = 0,$$

where $\hat{u}_{i,t+1}$ is the forecast error of model i, $i = 1, 2$, respectively. Denote $\Delta U_{m,t+1}$ as the difference of squared error loss functions of both models when m observations are used in the estimating window. Then, under the null hypothesis, $\{\Delta U_{m,t+1}, F_t\}$ is a martingale difference sequence, which implies the null hypothesis can be stated as $E[h_t \Delta U_{m,t+1}] = 0$, for all F_t-measureable functions h_t.

Giacomini and White (2006) show that the test statistic can be calculated as nR^2, where n is the number of forecasts, and R^2 is the uncentered multiple correlation coefficient from regressing $\Delta U_{m,t+1}$ on h_t'. The α level rejects the null hypothesis of equal conditional predictive ability when nR^2 is greater than $(1 - \alpha)$ quantile of the χ^2distribution. In the applications of Giacomini and White (2006), Simin (2008) applies $h_t = (1, \Delta U_{m,t})'$ where rejection of the null hypothesis does not specify which model provides the better forecasts. Hence, the decision rule is based on the fitted values of regression of $\Delta U_{m,t+1}$ on h_t'. The proportion of when the times of fitted values are positive determines which forecast method will be chosen.

In estimating the theoretical model such as unconditional CAPM, Simin (2008) also provides a proposition as whether to include an intercept in estimating parameters from historical data. Following the conventional approach, the estimation of (say) CAPM will usually include the intercept when the model is fitted with the historical data of excess returns. The intercept, however, is not included in the forecast of CAPM given that the theory suggests the intercept should be equal to zero or suppressed.

As stated in Simin (2008), if the intercept is nothing but a drift that is not used for forecasting, suppressing the intercept when estimating the parameters may provide a lower mean-squared forecast error (MSFE). For instance, since the intercept when estimating the CAPM (or other asset pricing model) is not needed for forecasting, and as theory indicates that the intercept is equal to zero, it is better not to include the intercept in the estimation. And hence, suppressing the intercept as the theory indicates, will result in a lower MSFE.

Notice that the claim only states that if the theory indicates no intercept should be included, estimating the asset pricing models with an intercept and performing forecasts without using the intercept (since the theory considers the intercept should be equal to zero) will not have a lower MSFE. In other words, the claim only considers that if the model(s) indicates that there is no need to include an intercept, then inclusion of an intercept in estimating the model will not produce a better forecast under the validity of the model(s). In other words, if the theory (such as CAPM) holds true, there is no improvement of forecast errors when including the intercept in estimating the coefficients by using historical returns and other economic variables.

However, the claim doesn't state that, when estimating parameters of any empirical asset pricing model, inclusion of an intercept in the model will produce some inferior forecasts. The following proposition of Simin (2008) implicitly assumes the validity of the theoretical models (such as CAPM) which excludes the intercept when the forecasts are performed.[1]

Proposition (Simin 2008): Let r_p be the pth period return to be predicted. Define two sets of prediction errors $\hat{e} = r_p - \hat{r}_p$, and $\tilde{e} = r_p - \tilde{r}_p$ where $\hat{r}_p = X_{1,p}'\hat{a} + X_{2,p}'\hat{b}$ with $\hat{a}, \hat{b}$ are estimated from the regression

$r_t = X_{i,t}\hat{a} + X_{2,t}\hat{b} + v_t$, while $\tilde{r}_p = X'_{2,p}\tilde{b}$ where $\tilde{b}$ is estimated from the restricted regression $r_t = X_{2,t}\tilde{b} + u_t$.

Let $\mathbf{r}_{T\times1}$ represent a $T \times 1$ vector of $\{r_t\}_{t=1,2,\ldots,T}$ where $p > T$ and $X = (X_1, X_2)$as a $T \times K$ matrix, A is a $K_1 \times 1$ vector, and B is a $K_2 \times 1$ vector, where $K = K_1 + K_2$. And let ϵ (a $T \times 1$ vector) of $\{\epsilon_t\}_{t=1,2,\ldots,T}$ be the error term of the regression model

$$\mathbf{r}_{T\times1} = X_1 A + X_2 B + \epsilon_{T\times1}, \tag{1.2.21}$$

where $\epsilon_t \sim (0, \sigma^2)$ for all t, and $E[\epsilon_t \epsilon_s] = 0$, for $t \neq s,\ t,\ s = 1, \ldots, T$. Then $E[\text{MSE}(\hat{e}) - \text{MSE}(\tilde{e})] \geq 0$.

In the empirical verification, Simin (2008) collects (monthly returns of) 25 size and book-to-market portfolios from January 1931 to December 2004. The so-called instrumental variables (for forecasts) include a dummy for the month of January, a one-month T-bill rate from the CRSP file, the dividend yield of the Standard & Poor 500 index, the spread between lagged Moody's Composite Average of Yields on Corporate Bonds and the U.S. one-month T-bill rate from the CRSP file, and the difference between Moody's BAA and AAA rated corporate bond yields. However, when estimating time-varying coefficients where the market index return is replaced with conditional expectation with instrumental variables, Simin (2008) uses the 90-day bid for the T-bill rate; the dividend yield of the NYSE, AMEX, and NASDAQ composite; the spread between the five-year and one-month discount Treasury yield, and the bond default premium from the Ibbotson as a measure of instrument junk.

The market indices applied are the value-weighted NYSE, NASDAQ, and AMEX market indices. All returns are in excess of 30-day Treasury bill returns. For the multifactor models, the SMB and HML spread portfolio returns are applied, similar to Fama and French (1996). Although the selection of data files is pervasive, the returns are collected from 25 size and book-to-market portfolios.

Based on the above instrumental variables selected, Simin (2008) discovers that the theoretical models perform poorly on the forecasts with both the square root of the mean squared forecast error (RMFSE) and the test of conditional predictive ability (CTP). In particular, the conditional models are worse than the unconditional models, where the specifications of time-varying parameters are not more helpful. This also indicates that incorrect specifications of the dynamics of time-varying coefficients may actually introduce more biases in forecasts.

As denoted by Lo and MacKinlay (1990), grouping or sorting of asset returns (with some predetermined criteria) into (say) size portfolios may produce the data snooping problems. Hence, interpretations of the findings of Simin (2008) require additional caution, such as (1) the estimations and tests of parameters may induce bias due to data snooping, and hence the forecasts with biased coefficients may be inefficient; (2) modeling of time-varying coefficients may include additional specification errors if ad hoc assumptions are made on the dynamics of these coefficients; (3) possible measurement errors in the instrumental variables are not discussed explicitly.

In fact, the issue that known theoretical models do not perform better in forecasts indicates that all models devised are only conjectural explorations of the pricing kernel of securities, given the contemporaneous information. The merits of theoretical models are not merely to improve the forecasts. They are to show the directions and plausible accessions to enhance the understanding of the price formation of financial securities.

1.2.2 Predicting Stock Returns Using Other Relevant Variables

1.2.2.1 Predictive Regressions with Macroeconomic and Individual Economic Variables

Being disappointed with the empirical results of predictability when using theoretical asset pricing models, many studies have attempted and provided empirical evidence that some economic variables may offer predictability on stock returns. Although the issue is more related with specification tests for explanatory variables for stock returns, the identification of these variables is essential since the information for the economic variables are usually available with time lags. If properly identified, the predictability of stock returns when using these variables can be assessed accordingly.

Instead of using asset pricing models for forecasting, Chen et al. (1986) consider the innovations of macroeconomic variables as possible explanatory variables for risks rewarded in the stock market. In the empirical evidence stated, the macroeconomic variables, such as the spread between long and short interest rates, expected and unexpected inflation rates, industrial production,[2] and yield spread between high and low-rated bonds are significantly priced in stock returns.

Similar to Fama and MacBeth (1973), a two-pass regression method is applied. That is, during the first-pass estimation, some time series regressions are applied to obtain estimates of the "betas" of these prescribed economic variables. The second-pass cross-sectional regression is then applied to see if these betas of economic variables are actually priced in the stock returns. To reduce the possible errors-in-variable problems (of betas) in the time series regression, these security returns are grouped into portfolios according to the firm sizes.

However, the method of Chen et al. (1986) does not consider the (time-series) memory conditions of these identified economic variables. For instance, either the yield spreads or term structure of interest rates can be of persistent memory such that the typical *t* statistics applied in the regression of stock returns on these prescribed variables are not of the traditional distribution. Hence, the size of these empirical tests may be distorted. Another questionable issue is that the grouping of stock returns into portfolios according to firm sizes may not be robust enough to reduce the impact of the errors-in-variable issue.

In a series of studies by Fama and French (1992, 1995, 1996), in the explanation of stock returns it is shown that a three-factor model with market excess return, the return of longs in high book-to-market stocks and shorts in low book-to-market stocks, and the return of longs in small stocks and shorts in big stocks contributes fairly well to the dynamics of stock returns.

He and Ng (1994), following Fama and French (1992) (who already proclaimed that size and book-to-market value of equity are the only important variables explaining stock returns), examine the possibility that the variables such as size and book-to-market value of equity may proxy the macroeconomic risks identified in Chen et al. (1986). However, He and Ng (1994) consider the influence from size and book-to-market value of equity toward risk factors of Chen et al. (1986) by including these two additional variables into the return regressions using macroeconomic variables. They discover that, upon inclusion of the size and book-to-market value of equity, the macroeconomic variables lose their contribution to the explanatory power for stock returns. Their study nevertheless is questionable.

First of all, the loss of explanatory power in macroeconomic variables may be due to the redundancy of including extra variables in regressions since these variables are closely related to each other. Hence, the regression results do not justify the causality direction of size and book-to-market ratio onto these macroeconomic variables unless additional specification tests (in time series) can be shown. In other words, it is hard to justify that the size and book-to-market ratio actually explain the macroeconomic variables (as risk factors) simply based on the specification test on regressions of all presumed variables simultaneously. More specifically, these variables (that is, size and book-to-market ratio and other macroeconomic variables in Chen et al. (1986)) are all included in the regressions of stock returns and then conventional specification tests are performed to see if the coefficients of these variables are statistically significant or not.

Secondly, these is no consideration of model selection criteria or tests for variable selection in their study. As a result, no decision rule (or optimality condition) is implemented to see which model may dominate the others. To the best extent of their results, the findings can only show that the model with size and book-to-market ratio and that of macroeconomic variables as in Chen et al. (1986) are competitive candidates. It is possible that both sets of explanatory variables are associated with the underlying hidden factors for stock returns. However, it is not clear that the findings are sufficient to justify which set of variables outperforms the other.

Petkova (2006) extends the study to analyze the correlations among the Fama-French HML and SMB factors with innovations of the aggregate dividend yield, term spread, default spread, and one-month Treasury-bill yield. It is shown that these correlations (except for Treasury-bill spread) are significant. In other words, the empirical success of the Fama-French model is consistent with the Intertemporal Capital Asset Pricing Model (ICAPM) in explaining investment opportunities. The approach of Petkova (2006) can be described as a system of equations where for all assets i, $i = 1, 2, \ldots, n$,

$$E[R_i] = \gamma_m \beta_{im} + \sum_{j=1}^{k} \gamma_{ij} \beta_{ij}, \tag{1.2.22}$$

represents the cross-sectional model of the expected rates of return, and

$$R_{it} = \alpha_i + \beta_{im} R_{mt} + \sum_{j=1}^{k} \beta_{ij} u_{jt} + \epsilon_{it}, \tag{1.2.23}$$

is the time-series regression of asset i's excess return on the excess return of market portfolio R_{mt} and the other innovation variables $\{u_{jt}\}_{j=1,2,\ldots,k}$ that are obtained from the unexpected components of some state variables such as dividend yield and term spread. These innovations are the error terms of the vector autoregressive (VAR) of the state variables that are considered as proxies for changes in the investment opportunity set as claimed in Petkova (2006). A first-order VAR system is formed to specify the dynamics of these demeaned state variables such as

$$Z_t = AZ_{t-1} + u_t, \quad (1.2.24)$$

where Z_t is a $k \times 1$ vector of state variables, u_t is a $k \times 1$ vector of innovations $\{u_{jt}\}_{j=1,2,\ldots,k}$.

The analyses then are to find whether these innovations compared with Fama-French factors contribute explanations on asset excess returns. In the empirical evidence provided, these innovations are able to pick up the explanatory power on the asset returns as well as Fama-French factors. The cross-sectional regression (1.2.20) with factor loadings estimated from the time series regressions (1.2.21), these innovations are statistically significant.

In addition, when the two sets of factor loadings are included together in the cross-sectional regressions of asset excess returns, the Fama-French factors become insignificant. Judging from the results, Petkova (2006) concludes that the innovations from the state variables (which represent the change of investment opportunities) are consistent with the ICAPM.

However, it is questionable that in getting the innovations from state variables, the dynamic specification of Eq. (1.2.22) is limited to a constant-coefficient first-ordered VAR system. As discussed in many other studies, the VAR system (over stock returns or economic variables) may be subject to jumps or other structural asymmetries over various time horizons, even though these innovations are orthogonalized. Secondly, there is no justification over model selection or search that these state variables are sufficient to assess the assets' excess returns through a time series regression of Eq. (1.2.21).

1.2.2.2 Predictive Time Series Regressions of Stock Returns

Since most articles demonstrate the empirical evidence derives from different techniques with various variables and time periods, Welch and Goyal (2008) use monthly and yearly or longer-period returns to re-examine the empirical evidence for each variable (of selected explanatory variables) in a simple linear format as

$$R_t = \gamma_o + \gamma_1 x_{t-1} + \epsilon_t, \tag{1.2.25}$$

where R_t is the equity premium, and x_{t-1} is the predictive variable that includes dividend price ratio, dividend yield, earning price ratio, various interest rates and spreads, the inflation rate, the book-to-market ratio, volatility, the investment-capital ratio, the consumption, wealth, and income ratio, and aggregate or net equity issuing activity, respectively. A significant γ_1 represents the predictability of the variable selected.

By using the same methods, time periods, and estimation frequencies, their findings suggest that most models are unstable or spurious. Most models are even insignificant for in-sample periods (from 1926 to 2005) and even those that are still significant fail the simple regression diagnostics. They show that most models perform poorly over the 30-year in-sample periods and for the out-of-sample periods.

An especially interesting issue in Welch and Goyal (2008) is that they find many models with significant statistics are based often on the years up to the Oil Shock of 1973–1975. Nevertheless, their study does not consider the possible instability of coefficients for the predictive regressions. Another question for their predictive regressions is that, for example, the predictors such as dividend yield and interest rates (and their spreads) are usually of long memory (in time series). Specification tests based on conventional statistics of the coefficient γ_1 may not be robust enough to have the proper size.

For instance, the empirical work by Torous et al. (2004) investigates the possible predictability of the economic variables by considering their near-integrated time series properties. The reason is because the economic variables such as dividend yields, book-to-market ratio, default spread, term spread, and short-term interest rates can be subject to persistence in memory as the roots for their autoregressive time series models are near to unity. Although the empirical tests result differently over various time periods, most of these economic variables are near-integrated. The difficulty is that if such a property is ignored, the statistical inferences in using conventional statistics can be misleading as their sizes (of tests) can be distorted.

The findings of Welch and Goyal (2008) are similar to the study of Bossaerts and Hillion (1999) where they apply statistical model selection criteria to determine the time series dynamics of international excess stock returns. In particular, as mentioned in Bossaerts and Hillion (1999), the nonstationarity of time series models for the (economic) variables of interest may have influences on the finite-sample statistics for excess stock returns. Given this, identification for the time series dynamics of the excess stock returns and the relevant explanatory variables is essential. With applications of model selection criteria, they discover ample evidence for in-sample predictability for international excess stock returns.

However, when the time series dynamics are applied to the extended samples with out-of-sample time horizons of five years beyond the original "training" sample, none of the time series models identified originally offers any significant predictability. These results also lead Bossaerts and Hillion (1999) to point out that either (1) the parameters of interest in the original models are time-changing where their evolutions are unknown, or (2) the time series models could be nonlinear. Nevertheless, these model selection criteria are supposed to pick up the "best" linear models of all. At least, their applications to the out-of-sample time horizon should reveal their relative superiority in forecasts. Yet, the findings are quite disappointing.

This shows that although nonstationarity of these time series can be of concern, it may constitute only one of the time series properties for the stock returns data. As such, complexity may be incurred in the excess stock returns and any identification of possible in-sample regularity can only represent a close-call approximation for the underlying system. Given the evolving nature of stock returns, the modelers thus should place more emphasis on the continuing model search than on the sole exhibition (or proclamation) of certain identified regularity based on the sampled data.

Campbell and Thompson (2008) argue that the predictive regression will perform better than historical average returns if weak restrictions (based on investment theory) are imposed on the signs of the coefficients and return forecasts. Similar to Welch and Goyal (2008), Campbell and Thompson (2008) apply monthly data to predict monthly or annual returns on the S&P 500 index. Since more concise data in CRSP start from 1927, the monthly returns prior to that year are subject to construction using dividend payments, the imputations of which the authors consider may be suspicious. Hence, they apply the CRSP data period for the out-of-sample forecast while using the earlier for initial regression. However, differing from the previous study, the consumption, wealth, and income ratios may be considered as being in some cointegrating relationship as in

Lettau and Ludvigson (2001). Hence, these three variables are included together in the forecasting Eq. (1.2.15).[3]

To consider the comparison with the forecasts of historical average returns, Campbell and Thompson (2008) apply the entire history of stock returns to calculate the average. In addition, they provide an out-of-sample $\mathcal{R}_{\mathcal{O}f}^2$ to assess the performance. Specifically, the out-of-sample $\mathcal{R}_{\mathcal{O}s}^2$ is defined as

$$\mathcal{R}_{\mathcal{O}s}^2 = 1 - \frac{\sum_{t=1}^{T}(R_t - \hat{R}_t)^2}{\sum_{t=1}^{T}(R_t - \overline{R}_t)^2},$$

where $\hat{R}_t$ is the fitted value of predictive regression of stock returns estimated up to time $t-1$, and $\overline{R}_t$ is the historical average of stock returns estimated up to time $t-1$. Hence, if $\mathcal{R}_{\mathcal{O}s}^2 > 0$, this implies that the predictive regression when using the predictive variable produces less average mean squared prediction errors. Similar results as in Welch and Goyal (2008) and some mixed evidence are shown in their study.

In particular, Campbell and Thompson (2008) find that if additional sign restrictions for the coefficients of predictive regressions are imposed, the opposite results may appear. This claim seems appealing in practice since a more informative model (with restrictions of coefficients) should perform better in either the goodness of fit or the in-sample/out-of-sample predictability if the restrictions hold.

When performing the predictive regressions, Campbell and Thompson (2008) apply the sign restriction by setting the coefficients of predictive regressions equal to zero if the fitted signs turn out to be different from what the theoretically expected signs ought to be as the full samples are used. Furthermore, they also set the forecasts of equity premium to zero as if investors would presumably rule out the negative equity premium in their expectations. The empirical results from these applications (of sign restrictions) offer improvements for forecasts afterward.

However, the concern is that these sign restrictions are provided according to the hypotheses or conjectures from theoretical reasoning or presumptions. In particular, these restrictions are imposed after the fitted regressions are performed and violation of theoretical hypotheses are found from empirical statistics. And verification on the improvement of forecasts is provided when sign restrictions are imposed afterward even though the empirical data do not display this.

This practice may be questionable since the usual procedures (in econometrics) should be to use the time series data (in the training sample period or others) in performing specification tests on these coefficients to verify the hypotheses of sign restrictions first. If they hold true, then setting the sign restrictions for the predictive regressions to perform comparisons of (out-of-sample) predictability will be legitimate. If the hypotheses of sign restrictions do not hold, additional tests or studies should be considered to examine the cause or reason for the violations in sign restrictions before applying them to verify forecasts. In contrast, setting the sign restrictions to improve forecasts without further justification being performed from the existing data may suffer from the criticism of data manipulation.

On the other hand, the study of Deetz et al. (2009) examines the out-of-sample performance of asset allocation strategies in the German stock market by using conditional multi-factor models to forecast expected returns, and future variance and covariance. They discover that the performance of conditional multi-factor models outperform the unconditional multi-factor models and the passive buy-and-hold strategy. Nevertheless, they also find that the strategy that uses a simple sample mean as a return forecast is superior. In other words, a more sophisticated model is not always better (in predictability or otherwise).

Notice that, however, the results of Deetz et al. (2009) are based on the performance of portfolios associated with different asset pricing models of interest. They are not based on the verification of model reliability. This also shows that the wonders of empirical asset pricing models are trapped in the dilemma (so to speak) of whether to choose predictability for asset allocation or to seek for a plausible explanation with rigorous theories and models.

For the earlier discussion on time series properties of stock returns, Boudoukh et al. (1994) re-examine the autocorrelation patterns of short-term security returns. In the finance literature with empirical findings, there is empirical research that provides evidence of short horizon portfolios being significantly autocorrelated and highly cross-serially correlated.

In doing so, Boudoukh et al. (1994) consider the so-called three schools of thought, as follows. (1) There are the loyalists who consider the markets rationally apply information where the significant autocorrelations are not due to fundamentals. Instead, these result from measurement errors, institutional structure (such as the trading mechanism), and micro-structure effects. (2) There are the revisionists who also consider the markets to be rational. Yet, the autocorrelations are caused by the time-varying economic risk premium. Given that these premiums have a conditional format, past information, such as past market returns and past size returns, can induce a variation of the risk premium. (3) There are the heretics who consider the market as not rational. Thus, these autocorrelations are shown since the investors either overreact or only partially adjust to the information provided to the market.

When examining the autocorrelations of the short-horizon stock returns, Boudoukh et al. (1994) show that existing evidence seems to overstate these patterns. For instance, for the cross-serial correlations, Boudoukh et al. consider the nontrading and risk characteristics of small firms, and show that the effect of nonsynchronous tradings could be a significant determinant of the magnitude of autocorrelations (in portfolio returns). In examining the cross-serial correlations with the contemporaneous correlation between returns of different firms, it is easy to see that

$$\text{corr}(R_{it}, R_{jt-1}) = \text{corr}(R_{it}, R_{jt}) \times \text{corr}(R_{it}, R_{it-1}),$$

they discover that the implied autocorrelations obtained from using the above relation and those actual estimates do not differ much from each other. Hence, the cross-serial correlations can be a result of contemporaneous correlation from different firms of various sizes. In other words, even if the large-firm returns do not contain any more information than that in the small firms, there could be a significant amount of cross-predictability.

In addition, the study considers the week autocorrelations of portfolio returns ending on different days of the week. It appears that these weekly returns show some seasonality. However, there are several points that Boudoukh et al. (1994) consider: (1) holiday or market closures are more likely to occur on some days than others, which hence may possibly cause the bias in the estimates; (2) some extreme observations occur over the sample period from 1962 to 1990; (3) nonstationarities may be present in the data—in other words, the discovered seasonality may not be stationary.

Another possible cause of the autocorrelations is based on the possibility of nonsynchronous trading. As shown in Boudoukh et al. (1994), let s_{it} be the fraction of the trading period before the close during which security i does not trade. The autocorrelation for some portfolios can be shown as

$$\text{corr}\left(R_{pt}, R_{pt-1}\right) \approx \frac{\sum_{i=1}^{n}\sum_{j=1,\neq i}^{n} E[\max(s_{it} - s_{jt}, 0)]}{\sum_{i=1}^{n}\sum_{j=1,\neq i}^{n} 1 - E[\max(s_{it}, s_{jt})] + E[\min(s_{it}, s_{jt})]}.$$

By using simulations, Boudoukh et al. (1994) find that even with a slight likelihood of nontrading over the weekdays, this will induce higher autocorrelations. That is, there exists a small probability of trading very infrequently that may spuriously increase the autocorrelations. Hence, findings over the seasonality or autocorrelations (of portfolio returns) do not suffice to show that the market is inefficient, where the predictability is simply the result of institutional factors.

1.2.2.3 Combinations of Forecasts

In contrast to earlier studies, Rapach et al. (2010) suggest that the combinations of forecasts will produce statistically and economically significant out-of-sample gains in forecastability relative to the historical average because the combinations of forecasts incorporate information of various economic variables that link with the real economy and, thus, reduce forecast volatility. Rapach et al. (2010) reason that with individual predictive regressions, although the individual economic variables (such as dividend yields) may provide information for the individual equity returns, they sometimes may contain "false" signals that cause additional noises and produce implausible forecasts for equity returns. Due to the structural instability of time series models or of individual economic variables of equity returns, the combinations of forecasts may reduce the risk of instability associated with the individual predictive regression models. Rapach et al. apply similar recursive methods on the individual forecasts through the predictive regression as

$$r_{t+1} = \alpha_i + \beta_i x_{i,t} + \epsilon_{t+1},$$

where r_{t+1} is the stock market index return in excess of the risk-free interest rate, $x_{i,t}$ is a predictive variable of interest, and ϵ_{t+1} is the disturbance term. As with earlier studies, they perform the out-of-sample forecasts $\hat{r}_{i,t+1}$ in using recursive estimation windows. With the sample of T observations, the first m observations are considered as in-sample observations. The out-of-sample period will consist of q observations, where the recursive estimation method is applied to the above equation with the expanding dimension $m + k$, $k = 1, 2, \ldots$ for the entire out-of-sample period.

The main difference in the study of Rapach et al. is the combinations of forecasts in using the weighted average of individual forecasts such as

$$\hat{r}_{c,t+1} = \sum_{i=1}^{n} \omega_{i,t}\hat{r}_{i,t+1}.$$

Two classes of weights are applied in forming the combinations of forecasts. The first class uses simple averaging schemes: mean, median, and trimmed mean. The second set of weights considers the performance of the historical forecasting of individual models over the out-of-sample period by the discount mean square prediction error (DMSPE). Specifically, the weight is calculated as

$$\omega_{i,t} = \frac{\phi_{i,t}^{-1}}{\sum_{j=1}^{n} \phi_{j,t}^{-1}},$$

where $\phi_{i,t} = \sum_{s=m}^{t-1} \theta^{t-1-s} \left(r_{s+1} - \hat{r}_{i,s+1}\right)^2$, and θ is the discount factor. Intuitively, the weighting scheme in the DMSPE assigns more weight to individual predictive regression forecasts when having a lower MSPE over the out-of-sample period. For the combinations of forecasts, the first q_o observations from the out-of-sample periods are considered as the initial holdout period. For the combination methods, the combination forecasts are formed over the post-holdout, out-of-sample period, which results in $q - q_o$ observations of forecasts to evaluate.

For the forecast evaluations, Rapach et al. (2010) consider several possible statistics in assessing performance. One is the out-of-sample R^2 (denoted as R_{os}^2) to compare the forecasts such as $\hat{r}_{t+1}$ and $\bar{r}_{t+1}$, for combinations of forecasts and historical average, respectively. The R_{os}^2 is defined as

$$R_{os}^2 = 1 - \frac{\sum_{k=q_o+1}^{q}(r_{m+k} - \hat{r}_{m+k})^2}{\sum_{k=q_o+1}^{q}(r_{m+k} - \bar{r}_{m+k})^2}.$$

Therefore, $R_{os}^2 > 0$, if the combinations of forecasts $\hat{r}_{m+k}$ outperforms the historical average $\bar{r}_{m+k}$. Another statistic (Rapach et al. 2010) apply is the MSPE-adjusted statistic. That is, by first calculating f_{t+1}

$$f_{t+1} = (r_{t+1} - \bar{r}_{t+1})^2 - \left[(r_{t+1} - \hat{r}_{t+1})^2 - (\bar{r}_{t+1} - \hat{r}_{t+1})^2\right],$$

then regress $\{f_{s+1}\}_{m+q_o}^{T-1}$ on a constant. The t-statistic on the constant will approximate to a standard normal distribution where a p-value, one-sided (upper tail) test can be performed. With all 15 economic variables collected and individual forecasts performed, Rapach et al. (2010) discover that the combinations of forecasts show successfully in comparison with the historical average. In other words, the finding supports the hypothesis that (macro)economic variables do contribute to the predictability of equity premiums.

1.2.3 Predictability Using Long-Term Returns

For the predictability of long-term security returns, the findings are also mixed. In particular, when various methods are applied to incorporate the possible instability of parameters with jumps and other economic variables, the results of predictability (or none) are still subject to the time horizons selected for study. An important issue that follows from the discussions on predictability of stock returns is whether the portfolios based on this finding of (long-term) predictability result in profitable performance or not. For instance, Bekaert and Hodrick (1992) seek to characterize predictable components in excess returns on the equity and foreign exchange markets. In using the VAR of lagged excess returns, dividend yields, and forward premiums, the results show one-step-ahead predictability and provide calculations of long-horizon statistics including variance ratios.

Ferson and Korajczk (1995) examine whether the possible predictability of security returns is driven by the premiums of economy-wide risk factors, given that the empirical evidence declares more predictability of return variance and less susceptible market frictions over a longer time horizon. In particular, Ferson and Korajczk apply both the one-factor and multi-beta pricing models (up to five factors) with conditional expectation versus the asymptotic principal components to consider the predictability. For instance, the specification of predictive models can be expressed as

$$E[R_{i,t+1}|Z_t] = \lambda_o(Z_t) + \sum_{j=1}^{k} \beta_{ijt}\lambda_j(Z_t),$$

$$i = 0, \ldots, n, t = 0, \ldots, T-1,$$

where R_{it+1} is the rate of return for asset i between time t and $t+1$, and Z_t is a vector of instruments available at time t, β_{ijt} is the conditional beta of asset i for factor j based on the information up to time t, in the k-factor models. $\lambda_j(Z_t)$, $j = 1, \ldots, k$, are the factor premiums of the k factors conditional on Z_t. In addition, the conditional betas are defined in the factor model as

$$R_{i,t+1} = \alpha_{it} + \sum_{j=1}^{k} \beta_{ijt} F_{j,t+1} + u_{i,t+1},\ i = 0, \ldots, n,\ \ t = 0, \ldots, T-1,$$

where $E[u_{i,t+1}|Z_t] = E[u_{i,t+1}F_{j,t+1}|Z_t] = 0$ for all i, j, and t. The regression tests are applied on the equation (with conditional expectations) as

$$r_{it} = \alpha_{io} + \sum_{p=1}^{L} \alpha_{ip} Z_{p,t-1} + \sum_{j=1}^{K} \beta_{ij} F_{jt} + u_{it}, \qquad t = 1, \ldots, T,$$

where $r_{it} = R_{it} - R_{ft}$, and R_{ft} is the return of a one-month Treasury bill. In assessing the predictability, Ferson and Korajczk (1995) consider the variance ratio as

$$\begin{aligned} \mathrm{VR1}_i &= \frac{\mathrm{Var}\left[E\left(\sum_j \beta_{ij} F_{jt} | Z_{t-1}\right)\right]}{\mathrm{Var}[E(r_{it}|Z_{t-1})]} \\ &= \frac{\mathrm{Var}[Z'_{t-1}\gamma_i \beta_i]}{\mathrm{Var}[Z'_{t-1}\delta_i]}, \end{aligned}$$

for the assessment of predictable variance in returns that are attributed to the model.

The sample period is from 1926 to 1989 for monthly stock returns of individual firms listed on the NYSE and the American Stock Exchange (AMEX). Ten value-weighted portfolios are created by the CRSP according to the size deciles of the NYSE and AMEX samples. In addition, 12 portfolios are created according to the two-digit Standard Industrial Classification code. For returns of longer horizons such as quarterly and annual returns, arithmetic returns (based on the monthly returns) are formed. Based on these data, Ferson and Korajczk (1995) discovered that the regression tests show that the majority of test results reject the null hypothesis as having no predictability (for both industrial portfolios and size portfolios), even in the sub-periods. What Ferson and Korajczk (1995) discovered is that a large fraction of the predictability in returns is explained by the models across all of the investment horizons.

Barberis (2000) also investigated long-run investment profitability when considering returns that are predictable. In doing this, even when considering the possible estimation risk when the parameters of interest were subject to uncertainty over time, it was found that there was sufficient predictability of security returns for investors to consider a long-term portfolio. However, it was also discovered that such an estimation risk must be taken into account, otherwise there is a likelihood for the long-horizon investors to over-allocate to stocks.

One of the questions raised by these studies that provide evidence on the predictability of stock returns (via profitability, for instance) is, if a certain long-term profitability of an investment strategy is proven, why does the market still allow such an incident to persist even though investors (who use alternative perspectives and henceforth lose money) will not modify their perspectives and follow through? That is to say, if a particular strategy or investment portfolio that recognizes long-run predictability and applies that to the long-term portfolio, and if the portfolio enjoys profitability (whether through the simulations or real-time data), why is there little discussion on how and why the market may allow such a profitability to prevail continuously over the long run?

On the other hand, profitability in long-run investments should be weighed against the extent of the long-run risk. Assessing the long-horizon returns as predictable should be plausibly related to the mechanism of capital markets. In other words, the contemporaneous asset pricing models should reformat the logic of explaining and incorporating this phenomenon into the theoretical foundations.

As a result, discussions (or debates) over the (un)predictability of stock returns should be concluded in the form of a more subtle question. That is: Have we learnt more about the fundamentals of stock returns? In other words, the investigations of whether the stock returns are predictable or not shouldn't stop at the proclamation of empirical findings alone. The critical issue concerns how this research can lead and assist us toward a more rigorous understanding of the determinants of stock returns. In fact, provided that the underlying economy is evolving, it is reasonable (if not too demanding) to state that the system of the capital market may run faster than the research (academic or empirical) can keep up with. Nevertheless, one should always beware that research is still incomplete.

Notes

1. In fact, it is rather intuitive to see the claim. If the theory requires no intercept in the model, inclusion of the intercept is redundant in estimations when the theory holds.
2. This should be denoted as the industrial production growth rate since the variable is calculated as the inter-temporal difference of the logarithms of industrial production.
3. Since the dependent variable is equity premium, it is usually of short memory. It would be more appropriate to consider Eq. (1.2.15) with the error-correction model, given that these regressors are long-memory and of a cointegrating relationship.

References

Bai, J. 2003. Inferential Theory for Factor Models of Large Dimensions. *Econometrica* 71: 135–171.

Bai, J., and S. Ng. 2002. Determining the Numbers of Factors in Approximate Factor Models. *Econometrica* 70: 191–221.

Barberis, N. 2000. Investing for the Long Run when Returns Are Predictable. *Journal of Finance* 55: 225–264.

Bekaert, G., and R.J. Hodrick. 1992. Characterizing Predictable Components in Excess Returns on Equity and Foreign Exchange Markets. *Journal of Finance* 47: 467–509.

Bossaerts, P., and P. Hillion. 1999. Implementing Statistical Criteria to Select Return Forecasting Models: What Do We Learn? *Review of Financial Studies* 12: 405–428.

Boudoukh, J., M.P. Richardson, and R.F. Whitelaw. 1994. A Tale of Three Schools: Insights of Autocorrelations of Short-Horizon Stock Returns. *Review of Financial Studies*, 7: 539–573.

Campbell, J.Y., and S.B. Thompson. 2008. Predicting Excess Stock Returns Out of Sample: Can Anything Beat the Historical Average? *Review of Financial Studies* 21: 1509–1531.

Chamberlain, G. 1983. Funds, Factors, and Diversification in Arbitrage Pricing Models. *Econometrica* 51: 1305–1323.

Chamberlain, G., and M. Rothschild. 1983. Arbitrage, Factor Structure, and Mean-Variance Analysis on Large Asset Markets. *Econometrica* 51: 1281–1304.

Chen, N.-F., R. Roll, and S.A. Ross. 1986. Economic Forces and the Stock Market. *Journal of Business* 59: 383–403.

Clements, M.P., and D.F. Hendry. 1999. *Forecasting Non-stationary Economic Time Series*. Cambridge: MIT Press.

Cooper M., and H. Gulen. 2006. Is Time-Series-Based Predictability Evident in Real Time? *Journal of Business* 79: 1263–1292.

Cooper M., R.C. Gutierrez Jr., and B. Marcum. 2005. On the Predictability of Stock Returns in Real Time. *Journal of Business* 78: 469–489.

Deetz, M., T. Poddig, I. Sidorovitch, and A. Varmaz. 2009. An Evaluation of Conditional Multi-Factor Models in Active Asset Allocation Strategies: An Empirical Study for the German Stock Market. *Financial Markets and Portfolio Management* 23: 285–313.

Fama, E.F., and K.R. French. 1992. The Cross-Section of Expected Stock Returns. *Journal of Finance*, 47: 427–465.

Fama, E.F., and K.R. French. 1995. Size and Book-to-Market Factors in Earnings and Returns. *Journal of Finance* 50: 131–155.

Fama, E.F., and K.R. French. 1996. Multifactor Explanations of Asset Pricing Anomalies. *Journal of Finance* 51: 55–84.

Fama, E.F., and J.D. MacBeth. 1973. Risk, Return and Equilibrium: Empirical Tests. *Journal of Political Economy* 81: 607–636.

Ferson, W.E., and C.R. Harvey. 1991. The Variation of Economic Risk Premiums. *Journal of Political Economy* 99: 385–415.

Ferson, W., and R.A. Korajczyk. 1995. Do Arbitrage Pricing Models Explain the Predictability of Stock Returns? *Journal of Business* 68: 309–349.

Ferson, W.E., S. Sarkissian, and T. Simin. 2003. Spurious Regressions in Financial Economics. *Journal of Finance* 58: 1393–1413.

Giacomini, R., and H. White. 2006. Tests of Conditional Predictive Ability. *Econometrica* 74: 1545–1578.

Granger, C.W.J., and F. Marmol. 1998. The Correlogram of a Long Memory Process Plus a Simple Noise, Discussion Paper, 97-29. University of California, San Diego.

Granger, C.W.J., and P. Newbold. 1974. Spurious Regressions in Economics. *Journal of Econometrics* 4: 111–120.

Grinblatt, M., and S. Titman. 1985. Approximate Factor Structures: Interpretations and Implications for Empirical Tests. *Journal of Finance* 40: 1367–1373.

He, J., and K.K. Ng. 1994. Economic Forces, Fundamental Variables, and Equity Returns. *Journal of Business* 67: 599–609.

Koopmans, T.C. 1947. Measurement Without Theory. *Review of Economics and Statistics* 29: 161–172.

Kirby, C. 1998. The Restrictions on Predictability Implied by Rational Asset Pricing Models. *Review of Financial Studies* 11: 343–382.

Lettau, M., and S. Ludvigson. 2001. Consumption, Aggregate Wealth, and Expected Stock Returns. *Journal of Finance* 56: 815–849.

Lewellen, J., S. Nagel, and J. Shanken. 2010. A Skeptical Appraisal of Asset Pricing Tests. *Journal of Financial Economics* 96: 175–194.

Lo, A.W., and A.C. MacKinlay. 1990. Data Snooping Biases in Tests of Financial Asset Pricing Models. *Review of Financial Studies* 3: 431–467.

Petkova, R. 2006. Do the Fama-French Factors Proxy for Innovations in Predictive Variables? *Journal of Finance* 61: 581–621.

Pettit, R.R., and R. Westerfield. 1974. Using the Capital Asset Pricing Model and the Market Model to Predict Security Returns. *Journal of Financial and Quantitative Analysis* 9: 579–605.

Rapach, D.E., J.K. Strauss, and G. Zhou. 2010. Out-of-Sample Equity Premium Prediction: Combination Forecasts and Links to the Real Economy. *Review of Financial Studies* 23: 821–862.

Reisman, H. 1988. A General Approach to the Arbitrage Pricing Theory. *Econometrica* 56: 473–476.

Reisman, H. 1992. Reference Variables, Factor Structure, and the Approximate Multibeta Representation. *Journal of Finance* 47: 1303–1314.

Ross, S.A. 1976. The Arbitrage Theory of Capital Asset Pricing. *Journal of Economic Theory* 13: 341–360.

Rust, J. 2014: The Limits of Inference with Theory: A Review of Wolpin (2013). *Journal of Economic Literature* 52: 820–850.

Shmueli, G. 2010. To Explain or to Predict? *Statistical Science* 25: 289–310.

Simin, T. 2008. The Poor Predictive Performance of Asset Pricing Models. *Journal of Financial and Quantitative Analysis* 43: 366–380.

Torous, W., R. Valkanov, and S. Yan. 2004. On Predicting Stock Returns with Nearly Integrated Explanatory Variables. *Journal of Business* 77: 937–966.

Welch, I., and A. Goyal. 2008. A Comprehensive Look at the Empirical Performance of Equity Premium Prediction. *Review of Financial Studies* 21: 1455–1508.

Wolpin, K.I. 2013. *The Limits of Inference Without Theory*. Cambridge: MIT Press.

Yule, G.U. 1926. Why Do We Sometimes Get Nonsense Correlations Between Time Series? A Study in Sampling and the Nature of Time Series. *Journal of the Royal Statistical Society* 89: 1–63.

CHAPTER 2

Statistical Inferences with Specification Tests

The author discusses the methodologies that are currently applied to empirical asset pricing models on asset returns, including up-to-date coverage on theoretical setting and model specification tests. For instance, factor analysis and (asymptotic) principal component analysis are provided for searching for these pricing cores or kernels of asset returns. Unfortunately, these earlier studies incur the difficulty of observability of these factors and of (economic) interpretation of the principal components. In essence, the application of multi-factor asset pricing models with observed/presumed factors becomes an alternative in the search for the systematic components of asset returns.

Various model specification tests are devised to verify the essentiality of the included variables. However, due to the evolving nature of the intrinsic mechanism of asset returns, later studies that attempt to connect these observable economic variables to factor(s) (or principal components) are still concerned with questions of statistical verification and empirical evidence. In particular, it is not difficult to find that these identified economic/presumed variables may not necessarily provide better specification and forecasts than the application of the simple time series modeling of asset returns.

Studies on statistical inference for security returns are not merely to verify some time-series (or cross-sectional) properties such as serial dependence, heteroskedasticity, and skewness for the data analysis. The essence should be on what may have caused these properties and how they

J.-L. Jeng, *Empirical Asset Pricing Models*,
https://doi.org/10.1007/978-3-319-74192-5_2

may help in the further development of understanding (of security returns versus financial markets) and decision making. Due to the vast amount of research articles in this field of study, this chapter only covers those that are essential for the discussions of the model specification of empirical asset pricing models.

2.1 Data Sources, Anomalies, and Various Econometric Issues

2.1.1 Data Sources

It is easy to find that, in empirical finance, various data sources are applied to either testing the validity of asset pricing models or searching for any anomaly in return series that may refute the theoretical models devised. The empirical results from these various applications of data sources, however, provide conflicting evidence on the validity of the asset pricing models of interest. This in turn creates the dilemma that one (as an empiricist or finance professional, for instance) may ask whether it is the theorists who help to provide some explanation for guidance in decision making or whether it is the data sources.

Various econometric developments are provided through a sophisticated methodology to generalize the possible allowances on the data generating mechanisms (including the dependence conditions of data such as mixing and conditional heteroskedasticity) to provide more robust statistical inferences. Nevertheless, regardless of how robust the devised methodology may be, statistical inferences can only assist in the understanding of or the approximation to the data mechanism. Methodologies can never replace the initiative from theoretical reasoning which precedes the data collection and sample statistics. Likewise, caution should be applied when using empirical verification on certain hypotheses when developing empirical asset pricing models.

The other important issue to discuss is the way that the data set is constructed (or the procedure one chooses to use for the data sources), which may create issues of various consequences in the statistical verification of asset pricing models. Lo and MacKinlay (1990) referred to the data-snooping problem introduced by Aldous (1989) in testing asset pricing models. Since most asset pricing models are generally performed on the portfolios of asset returns so as possibly to reduce the cross-sectional dimension and measurement errors, the selection and grouping of these asset returns may introduce additional subjectivity.

Lo and MacKinlay (1990) introduce formal analyses for the data-snooping biases and demonstrate in their findings that using prior information only marginally correlated with the statistics of interest can distort inferences dramatically. One of the major concerns is that most empirical verifications of theoretical models are performed on the *grouped* data such as portfolios of asset returns. Different schemes or groupings of constructed portfolios may influence the statistical inferences when the standard tests of significance are applied.

To formalize the analysis, Lo and MacKinlay (1990) consider some bivariate vectors $[X_i, \hat{\alpha}_i]'$, $i = 1, \ldots, n$, for some n securities where X_i represents the vector of firm characteristics for each security i, and $\hat{\alpha}_i$ represents the estimated parameter (such as the intercept in testing the conventional capital asset pricing model (CAPM) model) for security i in the equation such that

$$R_{it} - R_{ft} = \hat{\alpha}_i + (R_{mt} - R_{ft})\beta_i + \epsilon_{it},$$

for security $i = 1, \ldots, n$.

If the main concern is that if $\hat{\alpha}_i = \alpha_i + \zeta_i$ where $\alpha_i = 0$ in the null hypothesis, then spurious correlation between X_i and ζ_i may cause the induced order statistics to provide biases of tests. Given this, the data-snooping bias (due to grouping or sorting) may be present in the test of both individual securities and portfolios. Now suppose that the sample of n securities is chosen by sorting the X_i's. The sampling will provide the sequence

$$\begin{pmatrix} X_{1.N} \\ \hat{\alpha}_{[1,N]} \end{pmatrix}, \begin{pmatrix} X_{2,N} \\ \hat{\alpha}_{[2,N]} \end{pmatrix}, \ldots, \begin{pmatrix} X_{N,N} \\ \hat{\alpha}_{[N,N]} \end{pmatrix},$$

where $X_{1.N} < X_{2.N} < \cdots < X_{N.N}$, $X_{i.N}$ represents the ith order statistics from the sample of N observations $\{X_i\}_{i=1,2,\ldots,N.}$ In other words, the statistics $\{\hat{\alpha}_{[j,N]}\}$ is the induced order statistic corresponding to the $X_{j,N}$, where $X_{j,N}$ is the jth order in $\{X_i\}_{i=1,2,\ldots,N.}$. For instance, if X_i represents the firm size, then $\hat{\alpha}_{[j,N]}$ will be the estimated $\hat{\alpha}$ of the j-th smallest of the N firms. Hence, the concern is whether the induced ordering of $\hat{\alpha}_i$ will cause bias in statistical hypothesis tests or not.

According to the result of asymptotic sampling theory by Yang (1977), the test statistics based on the induced order statistics can be shown as follows. Let the vectors $[X_i, \hat{\alpha}_i]'$, $i = 1, \ldots, N$, be independently and identically distributed and let $1 < i_1 < i_2 < \cdots < i_n < N$ be sequences of integers such that as $N \to \infty$, $\frac{i_k}{N} \to \xi_k \in (0, 1), k = 1, 2, \ldots, n$. Then

$$\lim_{N\to\infty} \Pr(\hat{\alpha}_{[i_1,N]} < a_1, \ldots, \hat{\alpha}_{[i_n,N]} < a_n)$$

$$= \prod_{i_k=1}^{n} \Pr(\hat{\alpha}_k < a_k | F_x(X_k) = \xi_k),$$

where $F_x(\cdot)$ is the marginal cumulative distribution function of X_i.

The result shows that the large joint distribution of a finite subset of induced order statistics will be determined solely by the relative ranking ξ_k, where ξ_k is determined by the order statistics $X_{i.N}$. Given the above asymptotic result, it seems that the induced ordering will not affect the statistical inferences if the correlation between X_i and $\hat{\alpha}_i$ is relatively small. However, Lo and MacKinlay (1990) show that induced ordering (through grouping or sorting of $[X_i, \hat{\alpha}_i]'$ according to the ordering of X_i) will introduce bias in hypothesis testing with some finite sample statistics. Their claims can be shown in two separate scenarios: tests using individual securities and tests using (grouped) portfolios.

For the tests using individual securities, Lo and MacKinlay (1990) evaluate the bias of induced ordering by assuming the following setting. Let the bivariate vectors $[X_i, \hat{\alpha}_i]$, $i = 1, \ldots, N$, where $n \ll N$, be independently and identically distributed bivariate normal random vectors with mean $[\mu_x, \alpha]'$ and variance $\left[\sigma_x^2, \sigma_\alpha^2\right]'$ and the correlation between $X_i, \hat{\alpha}_i$ be denoted as ρ, where $\rho \in (-1, 1)$. If under a finite subset of n securities where the selection is without any prior use of data, the test statistic for the null hypothesis as $\alpha = 0$ will be shown as

$$\theta = \frac{1}{\hat{\sigma}_\alpha^2} \sum_{i=1}^{n} \hat{\alpha}_i^2 \stackrel{d}{\longrightarrow} \chi_n^2,$$

a central chi-square statistic with degree of freedom n, where $\hat{\sigma}_\alpha^2$ is a consistent estimator of σ_α^2.

Now, on the other hand, let the statistic θ be calculated from the induced order statistics $\hat{\alpha}_{[i_k,N]}$ where $k = 1, \ldots, n$, such that

$$\widetilde{\theta} = \frac{1}{\hat{\sigma}_\alpha^2} \sum_{i=1}^{n} \hat{\alpha}_{[i_k,N]}^2.$$

Lo and MacKinlay (1990) show the following proposition that the test statistic $\widetilde{\theta}$ will follow a noncentral chi-square distribution.

Proposition 2.1 (Lo and MacKinlay (1990)) *Under the null hypothesis as* $\alpha = 0$, *and the above assumed setting for* $[X_i, \hat{\alpha}_i]$, $i = 1, \ldots, N$, *where* $N \longrightarrow \infty$, *the induced order statistics* $\hat{\alpha}_{[i_k,N]}$, *where* $k = 1, \ldots, n$, *will converge in distribution to independent Gaussian random variables with mean* μ_k *and variance* σ_k^2 *such that*

$$\mu_k = \rho \left(\frac{\sigma_\alpha}{\sigma_x} \right) \left[F_x^{-1}(\xi_k) - \mu_k \right] = \rho \sigma_\alpha \Phi^{-1}(\xi_k),$$

$$\sigma_k^2 = \sigma_\alpha (1 - \rho^2),$$

which implies that

$$\widetilde{\theta} \xrightarrow{d} (1 - \rho^2) \chi_n^2(\lambda),$$

with noncentrality parameter

$$\lambda = \sum_{k=1}^{n} \left(\frac{\mu_k}{\sigma_k} \right)^2 = \frac{\rho^2}{1 - \rho^2} \sum_{k=1}^{n} \left[\Phi^{-1}(\xi_k) \right]^2,$$

where $\Phi(\cdot)$ *is the standard normal cumulative distribution function and the correlation between* $X_i, \hat{\alpha}_i$ *is denoted as* ρ, *where* $\rho \in (-1, 1)$.

In other words, the induced ordering will create a bias of statistics since the mean of induced ordered $\hat{\alpha}_i$ will have some nonzero means which, in turn, depend on the correlation ρ and the relative rank ξ_k. In addition, the test statistic $\widetilde{\theta}$ will have a noncentral chi-square distribution. By varying different choices of $\widetilde{\theta}$ (according to the order statistic ξ_k), Lo and MacKinlay (1990) show the sizes of the chi-square test and the R^2

of the cross-sectional regression of $\hat{\alpha}_i$ on X_i (which is the representative figure of ρ^2) under the null hypothesis as $\alpha_i = 0$ across all different finite sample sizes from 10 to 100. The bias is significant when the R^2 increases. This shows that if the grouping is applied to the individual securities, the induced ordering will cause a bias of hypothesis testing when using the sample statistics from the finite samples unless the characteristics are evenly distributed in relative rankings.

However, since most empirical verification for asset pricing models is performed on the grouping of securities into portfolios, Lo and MacKinlay (1990) extend the above work into the sorted portfolios. Let $n = n_o q$ such that the securities are formed into q portfolios with n_o securities in each portfolio. Under the null hypothesis as $\alpha = 0$, and supposing the portfolios are formed randomly, then the statistics will show up as

$$\phi_k = \frac{1}{n_o} \sum_{j=(k-1)n_o+1}^{kn_o} \hat{\alpha}_j \xrightarrow{d} N\left(0, \frac{\sigma_\alpha^2}{n_o}\right), \quad k = 1, 2, \ldots, q$$

$$\theta_p = \frac{n_o}{\hat{\sigma}_\alpha^2} \sum_{k=1}^{q} \phi_k^2 \xrightarrow{d} \chi_q^2$$

where ϕ_k is the estimated α of portfolio k, and θ_p is the aggregate test statistic for the q portfolios together. However, when the induced order statistics are applied to form the sample statistics, it is obvious that the induced orderings will cause the bias in statistical inferences.

Proposition 2.2 (Lo and MacKinlay (1990)) *Under the null hypothesis as* $\alpha = 0$, *and the above assumed setting for* $[X_i, \hat{\alpha}_i]$, $i = 1, \ldots, N$, *where* $N \longrightarrow \infty$, *the induced order statistics* $\hat{\alpha}_{[i_k, N]}$, *where* $k = 1, \ldots, n$, *and the correlation between* $X_i, \hat{\alpha}_i$ *be denoted as* ρ, *where* $\rho \in (-1, 1)$, *the above statistics for the grouped portfolios will converge in distribution as*

$$\tilde{\phi}_k = \frac{1}{n_o} \sum_{j=(k-1)n_o+1}^{kn_o} \hat{\alpha}_{[i_k, N]} \xrightarrow{d} N\left(\sum_{j=(k-1)n_o+1}^{kn_o} \frac{\mu_j}{n_o}, \frac{\sigma_\alpha^2(1-\rho^2)}{n_o} \right),$$

$$\tilde{\theta}_p = \frac{n_o}{\hat{\sigma}_\alpha^2} \sum_{k=1}^{q} \tilde{\phi}_k^2 \xrightarrow{d} (1-\rho^2)\chi_q^2(\lambda),$$

with the noncentrality parameter

$$\lambda = \frac{n_o \rho^2}{1-\rho^2} \sum_{k=1}^{q} \left(\frac{1}{n_o} \sum_{j=(k-1)n_o+1}^{kn_o} [\Phi^{-1}(\xi_j)] \right).$$

The findings are even more stunning when Lo and MacKinlay (1990) tabularize the sizes of the chi-square statistics for grouped portfolios. For a given number of portfolios formed, the bigger the number of securities included in each portfolio, the higher the sizes of the tests under a fixed R^2 (or a constant level of correlation between $X_i, \hat{\alpha}_i$). Similarly, for the same number of securities included in each portfolio, and for a given level of correlation between $X_i, \hat{\alpha}_i$, the sizes of tests increase when the number of portfolios increases.

Loosely speaking, if the grouping of portfolios introduced the induced order statistics when the characteristics applied for the grouping are correlated with the sample statistics, an increase of sample size in the portfolios or the number of portfolios will make the statistical inferences even worse. The results also point out that by applying grouping/sorting in portfolios with the intent to reduce the size effect in testing empirical asset pricing models may actually be counter-productive for the robustness of empirical results based on statistical inferences.

Caution in using sampled data must be applied when verifying the hypothesized asset pricing models, even though the financial data are conventionally considered as ample for empirical verification. Given this, it is necessary to consider that all hypothesized and existing asset pricing models are only approximations for the financial data because the verifications are valid up to the chosen samples collected. Confirmations on postulated hypotheses when using the selected data can only, at best, be treated as undone tasks in the research.

The following Sect. 2.2 introduces some recent developments in specification tests for asset pricing models. Rigorous studies are provided where different methods are considered in the approach to theoretical explanations of asset returns. Nevertheless, the findings of Lo and MacKinlay (1990) indicate that all empirical verifications of asset pricing models must cautiously examine the results and cannot simply ignore the impact of preselected sampling schemes especially when induced orderings with grouping or sorting are applied, according to the firm's characteristics.

2.2 Model Specification Tests and Their Asymptotics

Recent model specification tests in asset pricing models and their asymptotics and applicability can be found in the following literature on the stochastic discount factor and beta-pricing models. The merit of the stochastic discount factor is that it doesn't depend on the a priori specifications on return processes. In other words, it does not need to hypothesize the possible regularity (such as in linear factor models) for returns in advance. Instead, the study only requires economic reasoning from the inter-temporal optimality of an individual investor's investment decisions and the no-arbitrage opportunity assumption. In other words, the analysis only considers the necessary condition of pricing securities so that any possible discount rate (which is also a random variable) will set the price functions (of securities) equal to the discounted expected payoffs in equilibrium. Hence, it does not require the assumption that there exists a "true" model of return processes.

Various works have been added to the literature of the stochastic discount factor including the tests for misspecifications, the extensions on the Hansen-Jagannathan variance lower bound, and the model selection test when using the Hansen-Jagannathan distance. The following section surveys the developments and critiques of this methodology.

2.2.1 Stochastic Discount Factor

2.2.1.1 Lower Variance Bound Test

Hansen and Jagannathan (1991) consider the admissible region for the means and standard deviations of the inter-temporal marginal rate of substitution of consumers on security market data, based on the inter-temporal asset pricing theory. The asset pricing model starts with an environment of multiple consumers in the security markets where the preferences and information sets of these consumers are heterogeneous.

Without any specific asset pricing model presumed for the asset returns, Hansen and Jagannathan (1991) provide a variance lower bound for the stochastic discount factor, where the specification tests for asset pricing models is based on the difference from the variance bound such as in Burnside (1994). In other words, without the setting of return processes (such as approximate factor structure, for instance), the bound can be used for the model specification test (on asset pricing models) as to whether the models provide more variation than the variance bound in Hansen and Jagannathan (1991).

One of the major features in Hansen and Jagannathan's derivation is that it is based on the gross returns of assets, instead of excess returns. The analysis is developed from the space of the future payoffs of risky assets and the reasoning of the law of one price. Consequently, the setting assumes the finiteness of the (second-order) moments of these gross returns, whose expectations are well-defined. For instance, in Hansen and Jagannathan (1991), the second-order moment of future payoffs (or gross returns) is assumed to be finite. In addition, the covariance matrix of these payoffs is also assumed to be finite and nonsingular.

However, these gross returns in empirical studies (such as $R_t = \frac{(p_t+d_t)}{p_{t-1}} = \frac{p_t}{p_{t-1}} + \frac{d_t}{p_{t-1}}$ = total return plus dividend–price ratio where d_t, p_t and p_{t-1} are dividend and asset prices at date t and $t-1$, respectively) may be subject to persistent time-series memories. Particularly when the time-series dependence of the dividend–price ratio is considered, nonstationarity in the gross returns may be exhibited. For instance, Lawrenz (2013) finds that the dividend–price ratio contains persistent time-series memory. Similar findings are also provided in Goyal and Welch (2003) where the dividend–price ratio cannot reject the null hypothesis of the existence of a unit root in the time-series models. Hence, assessments on stochastic discount factors may be more robust if the methodology applies excess returns in the empirical verifications. The extension of stochastic discount factors into excess-return payoff space is straightforward according to Kan and Zhou (1999), for instance.

Notice that the nonstationarity which results from the temporal long dependence of dividend yields does not necessarily imply the dividend yields follow exactly some I(1) process with a unit root. The long dependence conditions can also be of more general formats such as fractional-difference time-series models or self-similar processes.

Caution, however, must be exercised especially in estimating moments over different time horizons for the possible nonstationarity of gross returns since the validity of variance bound in Hansen and Jagannathan (1991) depends on the homogeneity and finiteness of second-order moments. As a result, the conventional conditions for estimates of moments and the weak convergence (for instance, the central limit theorem of mixing dependent observations with normality) in stationary time series may not necessarily apply here since the second-order moments may grow with sample size if nonstationarity exists.

The summary of the setting in Hansen and Jagannathan (1991) can be stated as follows. Let the payoffs of a set of securities at time τ be denoted as x in the payoff space $\widetilde{P}$, and the initial date be denoted as $t = 0$. It is argued that, given the expected utility function (say) conditional on the information set I^j for any particular consumer j, and the usual utility maximization scheme for an optimal solution,

$$mu_o^j \pi_I(x) = E(mu_\tau^j x | I^j),$$

where $mu_o^j > 0$, which represents the marginal utility of consumer j at the initial time $t = 0$, and mu_τ^j is the marginal utility of consumer j at time τ, $\pi_I(x)$ is the asset price the consumer is willing to pay, conditional on the information I^j. Denoting $m^j = mu_\tau^j / mu_o^j$ as the inter-temporal marginal rate of substitution for consumer j, and following the law of iterated expectations, it can be shown that

$$\pi_I(x) = E(xm^j | I), \tag{2.2.1}$$

for all x in $\widetilde{P}$. Given the common information sets and complete markets, these marginal rates of substitution are identical across all consumers. Hence, it follows that $m = m^j$ for all j. Therefore, it is feasible to see that at time $t = 0$, and the n-dimensional vector $\mathbf{x}$ of asset payoffs at time τ, the pricing equation is equivalent to

$$\mathbf{q} = E(\mathbf{x}m | I), \tag{2.2.2}$$

where m is denoted as the stochastic discount factor, and $\mathbf{q}$ is also an n-dimensional vector of asset prices at time $t = 0$.

Assumption 1 $E|m|^2 < \infty$, $E|\mathbf{x}|^2 < \infty$, $E[\mathbf{x}\mathbf{x}']$ is nonsingular, and $E|q| < \infty$.[1]

From the above setting, and by the law of iterated expectation, it is easy to see that

$$E(\mathbf{q}) = E(\mathbf{x}m). \tag{2.2.3}$$

In addition, the condition that $m > 0$ will imply the absence of arbitrage opportunity. Specifically, it will guarantee that the non-negative payoffs $\mathbf{x}$ which are strictly positive with positive probability (conditioned on information set I) will always have positive prices. That is, the stochastic discount factor should be strictly positive. By defining $\pi(x) \equiv E[\pi_I(x)]$ as the expected value of the prices also implies that $\pi(x) = E(mx)$ accordingly.

It follows that if the asset prices are observed at time $t = 0$ where $E(\mathbf{q}) = \mathbf{P}$, then this is equivalent to showing that Eq. (2.2.3) is equivalent to

$$E(m\mathbf{R}) = l_n, \tag{2.2.4}$$

where $R = \frac{\mathbf{x}}{\mathbf{P}}$ as the vector of gross returns for the assets when the division is considered element-wise for the payoff vector $\mathbf{x}$, and l_n is an $n \times 1$ vector of ones. Accordingly, all asset pricing models are simply different formats proposed to explain the stochastic discount factor m. In addition, if excess returns are applied to all assets, this is equivalent to writing the above equation as

$$E(m\mathbf{r}) = \underline{0}_n, \tag{2.2.5}$$

where $\mathbf{r} = \mathbf{R} - R_f$ is the (vector of) excess return.

Based on the given setting, Hansen and Jagannathan (1991) develop the variance bound for stochastic discount factor m.

(1) If there is a risk-free payoff "one" with probability one in $\widetilde{P}$:

Let there be a stochastic discount factor that could be an affine transformation of the payoffs such that there is a random variable m^*, or equivalently a projection of any stochastic discount factor m onto the payoff space as $m^* = \mathbf{x}'\alpha_o$, and

$$E(\mathbf{x}\mathbf{x}'\alpha_o) = E(\mathbf{q}).$$

It is feasible to solve for $\alpha_o = (E\mathbf{x}\mathbf{x}')^{-1}E(\mathbf{q})$. Now that any other stochastic discount factor m satisfies the condition as in Eq. (2.2.1), there is a risk-free payoff so that $Em = \pi(1) = Em^*$ according to the condition in (2.2.1) and that $E[\mathbf{x}(m - m^*)] = \underline{0}_n$, which implies the distance between m and m^* is orthogonal to $\mathbf{x}$. Hence,

$$E[\mathbf{x}(m - \mathbf{x}'\alpha_o)] = \underline{0}_n.$$

This implies that $E[\mathbf{x}m] = E[\mathbf{x}\mathbf{x}']\,\alpha_o$, and

$$\begin{aligned}\alpha_o &= E\left[\mathbf{x}\mathbf{x}'\right]^{-1} E[\mathbf{x}m],\\ m^* &= E[\mathbf{x}m]'E\left[\mathbf{x}\mathbf{x}'\right]^{-1}\mathbf{x}\\ &= E(\mathbf{q})'E\left[\mathbf{x}\mathbf{x}'\right]^{-1}\mathbf{x}.\end{aligned}$$

Now that m^* is considered as the projection of m onto $\widetilde{P}$ since the above equations are similar to the regression of m onto the payoff space, it can be shown that

$$\sigma^2(m) = \sigma^2(m^*) + \sigma^2(m - m^*).$$

That is,

$$\sigma(m) \geq \sigma(m^*), \qquad Em = Em^* \tag{2.2.6}$$

Alternatively, for each individual security or portfolio, since $E(mR_i) = 1$, $i = 1, \ldots, n$, it is feasible to consider as Back (2010) did that

$$1 = \mathrm{Cov}(m, R_i) + E[m]E[R_i],$$

according to the definition of covariance. Since there is a risk-free asset, it follows that if R_f is denoted as the return of the risk-free asset and $Em = \pi(1)$, then $Em = \frac{1}{R_f}$. Substituting this into the above equation, it can be denoted as

$$E[R_i] - R_f = -R_f\mathrm{Cov}(m, R_i).$$

Given this, and letting the correlation coefficient of m with R_i be denoted as $\rho_{m,R}$, and since $\mathrm{Cov}(m, R_i) = \rho_{m,R_i}\sigma_m\sigma_{R_i}$, where σ_m, σ_{R_i} are the standard deviations of m and R_i, respectively, then

$$\rho_{m,R_i}\sigma_m = -\frac{E\left[R_i\right] - R_f}{R_f\sigma_{R_i}},$$

or equivalently,

$$\sigma_m = -\frac{E\left[R_i\right] - R_f}{R_f\sigma_{R_i}}\frac{1}{\rho_{m,R_i}}.$$

Since $-1 \leq \rho_{m,R} \leq 1$, it follows that

$$\sigma_m \geq \frac{|E[R_i] - R_f|}{R_f \sigma_{R_i}}.$$

Given that $Em = \frac{1}{R_f}$, the above equation can be shown as

$$\frac{\sigma_m}{Em} \geq \frac{|E[R_i] - R_f|}{\sigma_{R_i}}. \qquad (2.2.7)$$

Notice that in the above Eq. (2.2.4), the right-hand side of the inequality is the absolute value of the Sharpe ratio for the portfolio i with return R_i.

(2) If there is no riskless payoff "one" in the payoff space of risky assets $\widetilde{P}$:

Hansen and Jagannathan (1991) expand the payoff space $\widetilde{P}$ to P^a by augmenting $\mathbf{x}$ with a unit payoff to $\mathbf{x^a}$. Given that $E[\mathbf{xx}']$ is nonsingular, $E\left[\mathbf{x^a x^{a\prime}}\right]$ is also nonsingular. Denote ν as the expected price of a unit payoff. It is feasible to see that for a random variable m_ν in P^a, where $E[\mathbf{x}m_\nu] = E(\mathbf{q}), E(m_\nu) = \nu$, and based on the earlier result with the existence of a risk-free payoff in the payoff space, $\sigma(m) \geq \sigma(m_\nu)$. In particular, the moment conditions can be rewritten as

$$\begin{aligned} E[(\mathbf{x} - E\mathbf{x})(m_\nu - \nu)] &= E(\mathbf{q}) - \nu E\mathbf{x}, \\ &= E[\mathbf{x}m_\nu] - E(m_\nu)E\mathbf{x}, \\ &= \mathrm{Cov}(\mathbf{x}, m_\nu). \end{aligned}$$

Given this, if we consider that $m_\nu = (\mathbf{x} - E\mathbf{x})\beta_\nu + \nu$, it is feasible to have

$$\beta_\nu = \Sigma_X^{-1}(E(\mathbf{q}) - \nu E\mathbf{x}),$$

where $\Sigma_X = E\left[(\mathbf{x} - \mathbf{Ex})(\mathbf{x} - \mathbf{Ex})'\right]$ as the covariance matrix of $\mathbf{x}$. Hence, it follows that

$$\sigma(m_\nu) = \left[(E(\mathbf{q}) - \nu E\mathbf{x})' \Sigma_X^{-1} (E(\mathbf{q}) - \nu E\mathbf{x})\right]^{\frac{1}{2}}.$$

Equivalently, according to Back (2010), for any stochastic discount factor m and for each individual security or portfolio,

$$1 = \text{Cov}(m, R_i) + E[m]E[R_i].$$

Therefore, by the definition of the correlation coefficient,

$$\rho_{m,R_i} \times \sigma_m \times \sigma_{R_i} = 1 - E[m]E[R_i],$$

where the range of the correlation coefficient lies between −1 and 1. Hence,

$$\sigma_m \geq \frac{|E[m]E[R_i] - 1|}{\sigma_{R_i}}. \tag{2.2.8}$$

2.2.1.2 *Hansen-Jagannathan Variance Bound Tests for Asset Pricing Models*

Burnside (1994) considers the consumption-based asset pricing models when using variance bounds. The specification tests for the asset pricing models are considered under the generalized method of moments (GMM) and based on the variance bounds for inter-temporal marginal rates of substitution developed by Hansen and Jagannathan (1991). Specifically, the statistical tests are derived based on the distance to Hansen and Jagannathan's volatility bound of stochastic discount factors.

For instance, based on Hansen and Jagannathan (1991), the basic property of stochastic discount factor (denoted as m) is shown that $l_n = E[m\mathbf{R}]$, where $\mathbf{R}$ represents the (say) $n \times 1$ vector of gross returns among n assets, and l_n is an $n \times 1$ vector of ones. If the m is projected onto a space spanned by the vector of asset returns and constant 1 such that

$$m = m^* + u = \widetilde{\mathbf{R}}'\theta_o + u, \tag{2.2.9}$$

where $\widetilde{\mathbf{R}}' = [\underline{l}'_n, \mathbf{R}']$, and $E[\widetilde{\mathbf{R}}u] = \underline{0}_n$, then it can be shown that since $\theta_o = [E(\widetilde{\mathbf{R}}\widetilde{\mathbf{R}}')]^{-1}E(\widetilde{\mathbf{R}}m)$,

$$\theta_o = \mathbf{M}_R^{-1}\begin{pmatrix} Em \\ l_n \end{pmatrix}, \tag{2.2.10}$$

where $\mathbf{M}_R$ is the second-order moment matrix of gross returns $\mathbf{R}$ as $\mathbf{M}_R = E(\mathbf{R}\mathbf{R}')$, l_n is an n-by-1 vector of ones. Given the above equation, it follows that

$$\begin{aligned}\text{Var}(m) &\geq \theta_o' E[(\widetilde{\mathbf{R}} - E\widetilde{\mathbf{R}})(\widetilde{\mathbf{R}} - E\widetilde{\mathbf{R}})']\theta_o \\ &= (Em\ l_n')\mathbf{M}_R^{-1} E[(\widetilde{\mathbf{R}} - E\widetilde{\mathbf{R}})(\widetilde{\mathbf{R}} - E\widetilde{\mathbf{R}})']\mathbf{M}_R^{-1} \begin{pmatrix} Em \\ l_n \end{pmatrix} \\ &= (l_n - EmE\mathbf{R})'\Sigma_R^{-1}(l_n - EmE\mathbf{R}).\end{aligned} \tag{2.2.11}$$

Or equivalently, the bound can be expressed in standard deviation as

$$\sigma_m \geq \left[(l_n - EmE\mathbf{R})'\Sigma_R^{-1}(l_n - EmE\mathbf{R})\right]^{1/2} \tag{2.2.12}$$

where Σ_R is the variance-covariance matrix of $\mathbf{R}$.

The test for consumption-based asset pricing models is then to test whether the models' variance of m (under alternative specifications of m) will exceed the lower bound as shown above. Burnside (1994) derives four test statistics for this purpose. Specifically, the vertical distance to standard deviation bound can be used to derive the test statistics such that

$$\hat{q} = s_m - \left[(l_n - \overline{m}\overline{\mathbf{R}})'\mathbf{S}_R^{-1}(l_n - \overline{m}\overline{\mathbf{R}})\right]^{1/2}, \tag{2.2.13}$$

where $\overline{m} = \frac{1}{T}\sum_{t=1}^{T} m_t$, $s_m = \left[\frac{1}{T}\sum_{t=1}^{T}(m_t - \overline{m})^2\right]^{1/2}$, $\overline{\mathbf{R}} = \frac{1}{T}\sum_{t=1}^{T}\mathbf{R}_t$, $\mathbf{S}_R = \frac{1}{T}\sum_{t=1}^{T}(\mathbf{R}_t - \overline{\mathbf{R}})(\mathbf{R}_t - \overline{\mathbf{R}})'$.

Burnside (1994) applies the GMM to the following moment conditions such that for all i's, $i = 1, 2, \ldots, n$,

$$\begin{aligned} E[m_t - \alpha_1] &= 0 \qquad\qquad j = 1, \ldots, i, \\ E[(m_t - \alpha_1)^2 - \alpha_2] &= 0 \\ E[R_{it} - \alpha_{2+i}] &= 0 \\ E[(R_{it} - \alpha_{2+i})(R_{jt} - \alpha_{2+j}) - \alpha_{2+k+p}] &= 0, \quad p = \frac{1}{2}i(i-1) + j \end{aligned}$$

In brief, these moment conditions can be written into the general format as

$$E[f(x_t, \underline{\alpha})] = 0,$$

where $f(.)$ can be (say) the log-likelihood function of the data x_t and $\underline{\alpha}$, x_t may include $\mathbf{R}_t$ and other variables such as m_t, $\underline{\alpha}$ is a $(2 + n + \frac{1}{2}n(n + 1)) \times 1$ vector of moments such as $E[m]$, σ_m^2, $E[\mathbf{R}]$ and Σ_R. The asymptotic covariance matrix of $\sqrt{T}(\hat{\underline{\alpha}} - \underline{\alpha})$ is given as $V(\hat{\underline{\alpha}}) = (\mathbf{D}_o' S_o^{-1} \mathbf{D}_o)^{-1}$ where

$$\mathbf{D}_o = \sum_{i=-\infty}^{\infty} E[f(x_t, \underline{\alpha}_o) f(x_{t-i}, \underline{\alpha}_o)']$$

and $\mathbf{D}_o = E\partial f(x_t, \underline{\alpha}_o)/\partial \underline{\alpha}$.

Given the estimate of asymptotic standard deviation of $\sqrt{T}(\hat{q} - q)$ as $\hat{\sigma}_q$, it is feasible to have the test statistic as

$$Z_1 = \sqrt{T}\frac{\hat{q}}{\hat{\sigma}_q} \xrightarrow{d} N(0, 1), \tag{2.2.14}$$

under the null hypothesis as $H_o : q = 0$, when $T \to \infty$. The test is consistent in the sense that $Z_1 \longrightarrow \infty$ when $T \to \infty$, if $q > 0$.

Notice that the above test depends critically on the sample estimate $\mathbf{S}_R$ for variance-covariance matrix Σ_R for the vector of gross returns $\mathbf{R}$. Given that the gross returns may contain temporal long dependence, the estimate for their asymptotic variance-covariance matrix even when using the so-called "heteroskedasticity-and-autocorrelation-consistent" (as given in Newey and West (1987) and Andrews (1991)) may not provide consistency in estimating Σ_R. In other words, empirical applications may require further caution regarding the proper estimate (of Σ_R) to obtain the correct lower bound of s_m.

In addition, Burnside (1994) also refers to the Cochrane-Hansen vertical distance test. This test is based on the moment condition such that

$$\begin{aligned} E(m^2) &\geq \theta_o' E(\widetilde{\mathbf{R}\mathbf{R}'})\theta_o, \\ &= \left(Em \ l_n' \right) \mathbf{M}_R^{-1} \begin{pmatrix} Em \\ l_n \end{pmatrix}, \end{aligned} \tag{2.2.15}$$

following from the projection in Eq. (2.2.1) and hence it is clear to see that

$$\zeta = E(m^2) - \left(Em\ l_n'\right) \mathbf{M}_R^{-1} \begin{pmatrix} Em \\ l_n \end{pmatrix} \geq 0.$$

Denote the estimate for $\mathbf{M}_R$ as $\hat{\mathbf{M}}_R = \frac{1}{T}\sum_{t=1}^{T} \widetilde{\mathbf{R}}_t \widetilde{\mathbf{R}}_t'$, then the estimated lower variance bound will become

$$\left(\overline{m}\ l_n'\right) \hat{\mathbf{M}}_R^{-1} \begin{pmatrix} \overline{m} \\ l_n \end{pmatrix}.$$

Given that $\overline{m} = \frac{1}{T}\sum_{t=1}^{T} m_t$, $\hat{M}_m = \frac{1}{T}\sum_{t=1}^{T} m_t^2$, the vertical distance is then defined as

$$\hat{\zeta} = \hat{M}_m - \left(\overline{m}\ l_n'\right) \hat{\mathbf{M}}_R^{-1} \begin{pmatrix} \overline{m} \\ l_n \end{pmatrix}. \tag{2.2.16}$$

By computing the asymptotic standard deviation of $\sqrt{T}(\hat{\zeta} - \zeta)$, it is feasible to consider the test statistic

$$Z_2 = \sqrt{T}\frac{\hat{\zeta}}{\hat{\sigma}_{\zeta}}, \tag{2.2.17}$$

$Z_2 \xrightarrow{d} N(0, 1)$ under the null hypothesis that $\zeta = 0$. The test is also shown as consistent as $Z_2 \longrightarrow \infty$, if $\zeta > 0$.

Another test (based on the generalized method of moments) is to consider the optimal distance toward the population second-moment bound such as

$$E(m^2) = \left(Em\ l_n'\right) \mathbf{M}_R^{-1} \begin{pmatrix} Em \\ l_n \end{pmatrix}.$$

The test is based on the minimization (with respect to ν) of the quadratic form where

$$J_T(\nu) = \left(\overline{m} - \nu,\ \hat{M}_m - (\nu,\ l_n')\hat{\mathbf{M}}_R^{-1} \begin{pmatrix} \nu \\ l_n \end{pmatrix}\right)$$
$$\times W_T \begin{pmatrix} \overline{m} - \nu \\ \hat{M}_m - (\nu,\ l_n')\hat{\mathbf{M}}_R^{-1} \begin{pmatrix} \nu \\ l_n \end{pmatrix} \end{pmatrix},$$

where W_T is a suitable positive-definite symmetric matrix chosen for the estimator $\hat{\nu}$ with the smallest asymptotic standard error and the test statistic is given as

$$\begin{aligned} C_1 &= 0 && \text{if} \quad \hat{\zeta} \geq 0 \\ &= TJ_T(\nu) && \text{if} \quad \hat{\zeta} < 0. \end{aligned} \tag{2.2.18}$$

The test statistic C_1 under the null hypothesis as $H_o : \zeta = 0$ is distributed as a $\chi^2(1)$ with probability $\frac{1}{2}$.

Although all these tests when using the Hansen and Jagannathan (1991) variance bound are developed to see if some proposed asset pricing models hold, they are not entirely the possible metrics to compare the models which reject the above null hypothesis. In other words, if the sampled data indicate that there are (equivalently) several models (for the stochastic discount factor) that exceed the Hansen and Jagannathan (1991) variance bound, we need to determine which one is to be selected. The study of determining which model to select when using the variance bound of Hansen and Jagannathan (1991) is extended by Kan and Robotti (2009).

In addition, according to Back (2010), the projection of m to the returns space in Eq. (2.2.9) such as m^* is an affine transformation of returns (where $m^* = \widetilde{\mathbf{R}}'\theta_o$) if and only if the projection return is on the efficient frontier. Therefore, it becomes essential that any possible structure (with variables or factors, for instance) which determines the returns process may affect the lower variance bound of Hansen and Jagannathan (1991).

Furthermore, since the projection m^* is on the efficient frontier, any diversifiable risk should have been diversified away already by the definition of efficient portfolios. This leads to the idea that determination of nondiversifiable factors that explain the returns become crucial to form the statistics established in Burnside (1994) and others. Kan and Zhou (1999) for instance discuss the issue as the usual "beta-pricing" models where the specifications of returns become critical and may affect the power of the tests and estimates for risk premiums when using the Hansen and Jagannathan variance bound.

2.2.1.3 Cross-Sectional Regressions for Model Misspecification

Jagannathan and Wang (1998) studied the cross-sectional regressions and suggested the applications of firm characteristics for detecting model misspecification such as factors. As is well-known in the literature, if a given factor structure for the returns is correctly specified and the factors are observed, the additional firm characteristics added to the set of explanatory variables should have their coefficients equal to zero in the specification of risk premiums. Accordingly, the conventional test statistics for these additional variables of cross-sectional regressions should be insignificant statistically.

However, if the dimension of the factor structure is given where a factor is incorrectly introduced, the estimated factor premium will contain bias and the corresponding t-statistics for the coefficients of firm-specific characteristics will converge to infinity in probability. Notice that the analysis is not to determine how many factors are needed for the factor structure. Instead, the emphasis is on the applications of cross-sectional regressions, such as in Fama and MacBeth (1973), to identify the factor premiums and consider the misspecification errors when the incorrect factor(s) (or proxies for factors) are introduced to estimate factor premiums where the number of (correct) factors is given.

There are several features of Jagannathan and Wang (1998) that may differ from the conventional setting of multivariate regressions. First, the arguments discuss the possible misspecification due to incorrect choices of factors when the number of factors is predetermined to span the stochastic discount factor (and the return process in time-series regressions). Second, the setting is based on the cross-sectional regression for factor premiums across all assets of interest even though the factor loadings are estimated from time-series regressions on return processes.

In Chap. 4, a similar notion is assumed where the emphasis is on the cross-sectional properties of the factor-pricing models. However, the test statistics and asymptotic arguments in Chap. 4 are different from Jagannathan and Wang (1998) since no assumption for the "correct" specification of risk premiums is given. Thus, a model search scheme is introduced to pursue the specifications of empirical asset pricing models. In addition, since no prerequisite is assumed for the existence of a *true* factor structure for returns, the arguments can be extended into random fields where both *presumed* dynamic and static factor structures can be discussed.

Specifically, following the setting of Jagannathan and Wang (1998), let $\mathbf{R} = (R_1, R_2, \ldots, R_n)'$ be an $n \times 1$ vector of gross returns of n assets with a covariance matrix Σ_R. The stochastic discount factor m can be considered as a random variable such that $E[mR_i] = 1$, for each $i = 1, 2, \ldots, n$. Now let $y = (y_1, y_2, \ldots, y_k)'$ be a $k \times 1$ vector of (common) factors and let the stochastic discount factor be spanned by the factors y such that $m = \theta_o + \theta' y$, where θ_o is a constant and θ is a $k \times 1$ vector of constant parameters.

Since $E[mR_i] = 1$, it can be shown that for each individual security i,

$$E[R_i] = a_o + b'\beta_i, \qquad i = 1, 2, \ldots, n,$$
$$\beta_i = \Omega^{-1} E[(y - E[y])(R_i - E[R_i])], \tag{2.2.19}$$

where Ω is the variance-covariance matrix of y. It is also claimed by Jagannathan and Wang that the asset returns will satisfy the above equations if and only if there are constants θ_o and θ such that $E[(\theta_o + \theta' y) R_i] = 1$ for all i. Now suppose additional firm-specific variables and characteristics are included in the expected returns and since $\text{Cov}(m, R_i) + E(m)E[R_i] = E[mR_i] = E[(\theta_o + \theta' y) R_i] = 1$, this implies that

$$1 = \text{Cov}\left((\theta_o + \theta' y), R_i\right) + E(m)E[R_i].$$

That is,

$$\theta' \text{Cov}(y, R_i) + \left(\theta_o + \theta' E[y]\right) E[R_i] = 1.$$

Hence, it is feasible to rewrite the equation as

$$E[R_i] = \left(\theta_o + \theta' E(y)\right)^{-1} - \left(\theta_o + \theta' E[y]\right)^{-1} \theta' \text{Cov}(y, R_i).$$

Thus, the expected returns, after reparametrization, can be shown as

$$E[R_i] = a_o + b'\beta_i,$$

where $\beta_i = \Omega^{-1} E[(y - E[y])(R_i - E[R_i])] = \Omega^{-1} \text{Cov}(y, R_i)$ and Ω is the variance-covariance matrix of y. Now if additional firm-specific characteristics are added to the above equations, we are led to the following model for expected returns such as for each security i, $i = 1, \ldots, n$,

$$E[R_i] = a_o + a' z_i + b'\beta_i, \tag{2.2.20}$$

where z_i is an $L \times 1$ vector of firm-specific characteristics/variables.

It is easy to see that Eq. (2.2.20) assumes that the possible factor premiums are denoted in the vector b. And if the firm-specific characteristics are needed to "price" the expected returns, the premiums for the characteristics will be considered in vector a, where a_o is a constant that may resemble the risk-free rate or constant mimicking return for the risk premiums over all asset returns. Hence, if the assumption that m is spanned only by the factors y holds, the coefficients in a should all be zeros (at least, theoretically). By stacking up the above Eq. (2.2.20) across all assets into a matrix and vector format, it can be shown that

$$B = E\left[(\mathbf{R} - E[\mathbf{R}])\,(y - E[y])'\right]\Omega^{-1}. \tag{2.2.21}$$

By denoting $c = (a_o, a', b')'$ as the vector of factor premiums (under the correct specification), $Z = (z_1, \ldots, z_n)'$ and $X = (l_n, Z, B)$ as an $n \times (k+L+1)$ matrix (where l_n represents an $n \times 1$ vector of ones), the above system can be rewritten as

$$E[\mathbf{R}] = l_n a_o + Za + Bb = Xc. \tag{2.2.22}$$

Now consider the above equation as a regression, and assume the matrix $X'X$ is invertible,

$$c = (X'X)^{-1}X'E[\mathbf{R}]. \tag{2.2.23}$$

Let there be T samples of returns and factors, the estimates for moments and covariance matrices and can be found as

$$\begin{aligned} \hat{\Sigma}_R &= \frac{1}{T}\sum_{t=1}^{T}\left(\mathbf{R}_t - \overline{\mathbf{R}}\right)\left(\mathbf{R}_t - \overline{\mathbf{R}}\right)', \\ \hat{\Omega} &= \frac{1}{T}\sum_{t=1}^{T}\left(y_t - \overline{y}\right)\left(y_t - \overline{y}\right)', \end{aligned} \tag{2.2.24}$$

where $\overline{\mathbf{R}}$ and $\overline{y}$ are the time-series averages for vectors of return $\mathbf{R}_t$ and factors y_t. In addition, the consistent estimators of $E[R_i]$ and β_i can be obtained as

$$\begin{aligned} \overline{R}_i &= \frac{1}{T}\sum_{t=1}^{T} R_{it} \\ \hat{\beta}_i &= \hat{\Omega}^{-1}\sum_{t=1}^{T}\left(y_t - \overline{y}\right)\left(R_{it} - \overline{R}_i\right). \end{aligned} \tag{2.2.25}$$

where $\hat{\beta}_i$ is a $k \times 1$ vector of estimated factor loadings. Denote $\hat{\mathbf{B}}$ as $\hat{\mathbf{B}} = \left(\hat{\beta}_1, \hat{\beta}_2, \ldots, \hat{\beta}_n\right)'$ as a matrix of estimated factor loadings for all asset returns, and let $\hat{X} = \left(l_n, Z, \hat{B}\right)$, for each time t, the estimated factor premiums (in cross-sectional regressions) at time t can be shown to be

$$\hat{c}_t = (\hat{X}'\hat{X})^{-1}\hat{X}'\mathbf{R}_t, \tag{2.2.26}$$

where $\hat{c} = \frac{1}{T}\sum_{t=1}^{T}\hat{c}_t$ and the variance of $\sqrt{T}(\hat{c} - c)$ is estimated by

$$\hat{V} = \frac{1}{T}\sum_{t=1}^{T}(\hat{c}_t - \hat{c})(\hat{c}_t - \hat{c})'. \tag{2.2.27}$$

If the GLS estimator is applied in the same format, it is feasible to have a consistent estimator $\hat{Q}$ for the symmetric positive definite matrix Q,

$$\begin{aligned} \hat{c}_t &= (\hat{X}'\hat{Q}\hat{X})^{-1}\hat{X}'\hat{Q}\mathbf{R}_t \\ \hat{c} &= (\hat{X}'\hat{Q}\hat{X})^{-1}\hat{X}'\hat{Q}\overline{\mathbf{R}}, \end{aligned} \tag{2.2.28}$$

and hence the estimate of the variance of $\sqrt{T}(\hat{c} - c)$ will be considered to be

$$\hat{V} = (\hat{X}'\hat{Q}\hat{X})^{-1}\hat{X}'\hat{Q}\left[\frac{1}{T}\sum_{t=1}^{T}(\mathbf{R}_t - \overline{\mathbf{R}})(\mathbf{R}_t - \overline{\mathbf{R}})'\right]\hat{Q}\hat{X}(\hat{X}'\hat{Q}\hat{X})^{-1}. \tag{2.2.29}$$

Given the estimates $\hat{c}$, it is shown that since $\overline{\mathbf{R}} = \hat{X}c + (\overline{\mathbf{R}} - E[\mathbf{R}]) - (\hat{\mathbf{B}} - \mathbf{B})b$,

$$\begin{aligned} \sqrt{T}(\hat{c} - c) &= (\hat{X}'\hat{Q}\hat{X})^{-1}\hat{X}'\hat{Q}\sqrt{T}(\overline{\mathbf{R}} - E[\mathbf{R}]) \\ &\quad - (\hat{X}'\hat{Q}\hat{X})^{-1}\hat{X}'\hat{Q}\sqrt{T}(\hat{\mathbf{B}} - \mathbf{B})b, \end{aligned} \tag{2.2.30}$$

where it is easy to see if the central limit theorem is assumed, asymptotic normality can be obtained for $\sqrt{T}(\overline{\mathbf{R}} - E[\mathbf{R}])$ as $T \to \infty$.

Now at any time t, is based on the time series regression such that

$$\mathbf{R}_t = A + \mathbf{B}y_t + u_t, \tag{2.2.31}$$

where $A = E[\mathbf{R}_t] - \mathbf{B}E[y_t]$ and $u_t = \mathbf{R}_t - A + \mathbf{B}y_t$, $E[u_t] = \underline{0}$, $E[u_t y_t'] = 0$. In other words, if the null hypothesis for the expected returns follow Eq. (2.2.20), the above time series regression can be rewritten as

$$\mathbf{R}_t = E[\mathbf{R}_t] + \mathbf{B}(y_t - E[y_t]) + u_t.$$

Jagannathan and Wang (1998) include additional assumptions of weak convergence such that the vector

$$(T^{\frac{1}{2}}(\overline{\mathbf{R}} - E[\mathbf{R}])', T^{-\frac{1}{2}}(\text{vec}(Y'U))')$$

will (in the central limit theorem) converge weakly to a normal distribution with zero mean and a variance-covariance matrix such that

$$\begin{pmatrix} \Psi & \Gamma \\ \Gamma' & \Pi \end{pmatrix},$$

where $Y_t = y_t - \bar{y}$, $Y = (Y_1, \ldots, Y_T)'$ and $U = (u_1, \ldots, u_T)'$, vec(.) stands for the operator that stacks up all columns in a matrix to a vector. Accordingly, it is straightforward to see that $\hat{\mathbf{B}} - \mathbf{B} = U'Y(Y'Y)^{-1}$. With this additional assumption, the asymptotic distribution for the estimates of factor premiums under the null hypothesis of correct specification in the cross-sectional regression is shown with the following theorem.

Theorem on asymptotic distribution for factor premiums: Suppose the matrix X in Eq. (2.2.22) is of full rank, then the vector $\sqrt{T}(\hat{c} - c)$ will converge in distribution, as $T \to \infty$, to a normal distribution with a mean zero vector and a covariance matrix $S = V + W - G$, where

$$V = (X'QX)^{-1} X'Q\Psi QX (X'QX)^{-1},$$

$$W = (X'QX)^{-1} X'Q (I_n \otimes (\Omega^{-1}b))' \Pi (I_n \otimes (\Omega^{-1}b)) QX (X'QX)^{-1},$$

$$G = (X'QX)^{-1} X'Q \left[\Gamma (I_n \otimes (\Omega^{-1}b)) + (I_n \otimes (\Omega^{-1}b))' \Gamma'\right] QX (X'QX)^{-1}.$$

Although the results are complicated in matrix form, it is easy to see that the matrix V represents the covariance matrix of the factor premiums. These estimates (with GLS, for instance) will contain bias in their asymptotic covariance matrix even when the central limit theorem applies. Loosely speaking, the claim simply states that the factor premium (when correct specification in cross-sectional regression is applied) will converge to a normal distribution with a mean-zero vector and the covariance matrix shown above. In addition, with the assumption of conditional homoskedasticity, it can simplify the above results.

Assumption of conditional homoskedasticity: Suppose Xs has full rank. The residual in the time-series regression model as in Eq. (2.2.31) will, conditional on factor values, have a zero mean and constant covariance such that

$$E[\text{vec}(U)|\, Y] = 0_{nT}$$
$$E[\text{vec}(U)\text{vec}(U)'|\, Y] = \Delta \otimes I_T,$$

where Δ is an $n \times n$ constant symmetric positive definite matrix and I_T is a $T \times T$ identity matrix.

Theorem of asymptotic distribution of estimates for factor premiums under conditional homoskedasticity: Under the assumption of conditional homoskedasticity, $\sqrt{T}(\hat{c} - c)$ will converge, as $T \rightarrow \infty$, to a normal distribution with zero-mean vector and covariance matrix $S = V + \widetilde{W}$, where matrix V is the same as stated earlier and

$$\widetilde{W} = \left(b'\Omega^{-1}b\right)\left(X'QX\right)^{-1} X'Q\Delta QX \left(X'QX\right)^{-1}.$$

Hence, according to Jagannathan and Wang (1998), since the matrix $\widetilde{W}$ is positive definite, the Fama-MacBeth method (on cross-sectional regressions) will overstate the precision of the estimates, under the assumption of conditional homoskedasticity.

One major development of their research is the provision of statistical inferences for the misspecification bias on the estimator of factor premiums when an incorrect vector of factors is introduced into the model in Eq. (2.2.20), given that the number of factors is already determined. However, there are two major assumptions in their analysis: (1) all the firm-specific characteristics and their coefficients are not different when different vectors of factors are applied; (2) there exists a correct specification for the determinants or factors in both the stochastic discount factor and the return process, even though they may not be known.

Notice that the work of Jagannathan and Wang (1998) is not to detect the missing "essential" factor outside the current information set. Instead, the study is to investigate the possible bias in estimated factor premiums when different factor loadings are obtained from an incorrect inclusion of factors in the current information set. More extended work can be found in Chap. 5 in this book where model search procedures are devised to ensure that, in each stage of the model search, the inclusion of the proxies or variables is verified with its essentiality.

For instance, let the correct model for the expected returns be shown as

$$E[\mathbf{R}] = l_n a_o + Za + \widetilde{\mathbf{B}}b, \qquad \widetilde{\mathbf{B}} = E[(\mathbf{R} - E[\mathbf{R}])(\widetilde{y} - E[\widetilde{y}])]\widetilde{\Omega}^{-1}, \tag{2.2.32}$$

where $\widetilde{y}$ represents the vector of correct factors. On the other hand, the researcher may include the vector of incorrect factors denoted as y, where $y \neq \widetilde{y}$. That is, some of the factors in $\widetilde{y}$ and y are different, even though their dimensions are identical. The misspecified model will become

$$E[\mathbf{R}] = l_n a_o + Za + \mathbf{B}b, \quad \mathbf{B} = E[(\mathbf{R} - E[\mathbf{R}])(y - E[y])]\Omega^{-1}. \tag{2.2.33}$$

Now suppose the model in Eq. (2.2.32) is the correct one, yet the researcher applies Eq. (2.2.33) instead. The "betas" then are estimated from the time-series regressions of returns $\mathbf{R}_t$ on the y_t, not $\widetilde{y}_t$. In other words, the incorrect specification of factors also applies to the return process where incorrect factors are included, even though the numbers of factors are identical or assumed to be known. However, the confusion for the above setting is that even with different estimates for factor loadings (say $\widetilde{\mathbf{B}}$ matrix versus $\mathbf{B}$ matrix), the factor premiums remain the same as b for different sets of factor loadings and factors.

In fact, their work shows that if under the null hypothesis there exists a correct specification of factor premiums (based on the "true" set of factors), then the asymptotic bias for estimators of factor premiums is based on the misspecified factor loadings (under incorrect set of factors). That is, Eq. (2.2.22) holds and the researcher applies y_t, not $\widetilde{y}_t$. in the time series regression of Eq. (2.2.31). Notice that these arguments are based on the asymptotic analysis when $T \to \infty$. That is, given the number of asset returns, the time horizon is expanding sufficiently large and the number of cross-sectional observations is given.

Theorem of asymptotic bias in estimating factor premiums: If the matrix X in Eq. (2.2.22) is of full rank, then $X = (l_n, Z, B)$. Let Eq. (2.2.32) hold so that there exists a correct specification of factor structure in the return process and stochastic discount factor. If the betas are estimated from the misspecified time-series regression on Eq. (2.2.31) where the misspecified vector factors y_t, not $\widetilde{y}_t$ are applied, then the vector of estimated factor premiums $\hat{c}$ will converge to $c+(X'QX)^{-1}X'Q\left(\widetilde{\mathbf{B}}-\mathbf{B}\right)b$ in probability such that

$$\underset{T\to\infty}{\text{plim}}\,\hat{c} = c + \left(X'QX\right)^{-1}X'Q\left(\widetilde{\mathbf{B}}-\mathbf{B}\right)b. \tag{2.2.34}$$

In addition, Jagannathan and Wang (1998) show that the t-statistics of the factor premiums based on the factor loadings estimated from the misspecified factor will converge to infinity in probability. That is, suppose the correct specification for expected returns as Eq. (2.2.32) holds such that

$$E[\mathbf{R}] = a_o + b_1\widetilde{\beta}_1, \quad \widetilde{\beta}_1 \neq 0,$$

and assume that the observations and misspecified factor are independent and identically distributed (i.i.d.) with finite fourth moments. Let the misspecified factor be uncorrelated with all returns. The t-statistic $\hat{t}_{b1}$ for the factor premium, when calculated from the Fama-MacBeth two-pass regression method, will converge to infinity in probability such that $\lim_{T\to\infty} P[\hat{t}_{b1} > \delta] = 1$ for any $\delta > 0$, if and only if $b_1 \neq 0$.

2.2.1.4 *The Specifications in Return Processes: A Critique on Stochastic Discount Factor Methodology*

Kan and Zhou (1999) present a critique and point out that the stochastic discount factor methodology which ignores the specification of underlying processes of asset returns can become a potential problem. Although the theoretical provision of the stochastic discount factor does not require the fully specified models for asset returns, the accuracy of parameter estimates for the factor premium can be poor. Basically, Kan and Zhou (1999) show that if a factor structure holds for the returns process, the ignorance of the return process in stochastic discount factor methodology causes a loss of efficiency in the estimation of the factor premium even though the test statistic (under the methodology of generalized method of moments) may still end up with an identical asymptotic distribution as the beta-pricing models.

Specifically, the specification tests based on these estimates may suffer lower power against misspecified models. Kan and Zhou (1999) apply a simple one-factor model to demonstrate their claims. Specifically, let the excess returns follow the one-factor model as follows:

$$\mathbf{r}_t = \widetilde{\alpha} + \beta f_t + \epsilon_t, \tag{2.2.35}$$

where f_t is the one factor of systematic risk at time t, $\mathbf{r}_t$ is an $n \times 1$ vector of excess returns, $E[\epsilon_t | f_t, I_{t-1}] = \underline{\mathbf{0}}_{\mathbf{n}}$, I_{t-1} is the information set at time $t-1$, Var$(\epsilon_t) = \Sigma$. In addition, $\underline{\mathbf{0}}_{\mathbf{n}}$ is an $n \times 1$ vector of zeros, $\beta = \text{Cov}[\mathbf{r}_t, f_t | I_{t-1}] / \text{Var}[f_t | I_{t-1}]$ is an $n \times 1$ vector of factor loadings with respect to the common factor f_t, and $\widetilde{\alpha}$ is an $n \times 1$ vector of expected excess returns. For simplicity, f_t is assumed to follow a martingale difference sequence such that $E[f_t | I_{t-1}] = 0$.

Notice that since Var$(\epsilon_t) = \Sigma$, the setting does not assume unconditional heteroskedasticity even though the conditional one may prevail. The intercept $\widetilde{\alpha} = E[\mathbf{r}_t | I_{t-1}]$ is considered to be an expected excess return where the beta pricing model would suggest

$$\widetilde{\alpha} = \beta \lambda^*,$$

where λ^* is the factor premium for f_t.

Alternatively, when under the stochastic discount factor methodology with a stochastic discount factor m_t, it follows that

$$E[\mathbf{r}_t m_t] = \underline{\mathbf{0}}_n. \tag{2.2.36}$$

Assume that the stochastic discount factor m_t follows the specification that

$$m_t = \delta_o - \delta_1 f_t, \tag{2.2.37}$$

for some constant coefficients δ_o and δ_1. After normalization, it is easy to state that

$$E\left[\mathbf{r}_t \left(1 - f_t \lambda^*\right)\right] = \underline{\mathbf{0}}_n. \tag{2.2.38}$$

Given the above setting, Kan and Zhou (1999) then demonstrate that (1) the above condition can be overstated when the proxies are substituted for factors, (2) although the asymptotic test statistics for the factor premium under beta-pricing models and the stochastic discount factor may have the same asymptotic distribution with identical degrees of freedom, the test statistic under the stochastic discount factor methodology may suffer from a higher asymptotic variance.

Counter examples include the following. Kan and Zhou (1999) demonstrate two possible cases (with a one-factor model) where the above condition can be satisfied with cases such as a noisy factor or unsystematic factor.

(1) Noisy factor: Let the noisy factor be denoted as

$$g_t = \frac{f_t + \varrho_t}{\sqrt{1 + \sigma_\varrho^2}},$$

where ϱ_t is a pure measurement error with mean zero and finite variance σ_ϱ^2, and which is independent of f_t and ϵ_t. By specifying the noisy factor, it can be shown that $\lambda_g = \lambda^* \sqrt{1 + \sigma_\varrho^2}$, and hence the condition in Eq. (2.2.36) can still be satisfied as

$$\begin{aligned} E[\mathbf{r}_t(1 - g_t\lambda_g)] &= E\left[\mathbf{r}_t\left(1 - \frac{f_t}{\sqrt{1 + \sigma_\varrho^2}}\lambda_g\right)\right] - \frac{E[\mathbf{r}_t\varrho_t]\lambda_g}{\sqrt{1 + \sigma_\varrho^2}} \\ &= E\left[\mathbf{r}_t\left(1 - f_t\lambda^*\right)\right] = \underline{\mathbf{0}}_n. \end{aligned}$$

That is, even with a noisy factor that contains a measurement error, the condition of Eq. (2.2.36) will still be satisfied. The difficulty is not merely the identification problem since the factor premium for the noisy factor is now larger than that of the true factor, depending on σ_ϱ^2.

(2) Unsystematic factor: Let the unsystematic factor be defined as

$$h_t = \frac{\beta \Sigma^{-1} \epsilon_t}{\sqrt{\beta' \Sigma^{-1} \beta}},$$

h_t is a linear combination of ϵ_t. Accordingly, the parameter λ_h will be denoted as

$$\lambda_h = \lambda^* \sqrt{\beta' \Sigma^{-1} \beta}$$

and hence,

$$\begin{aligned} E\left[\mathbf{r}_t\left(1 - h_t\lambda_h\right)\right] &= E[\mathbf{r}_t] - \frac{E[\epsilon_t\epsilon_t']\Sigma^{-1}\beta}{\sqrt{\beta'\Sigma^{-1}\beta}} \\ &= \widetilde{\alpha} - \beta\lambda^* \\ &= \underline{\mathbf{0}}_n. \end{aligned}$$

In other words, when the unsystematic factor is substituted into the necessary condition for the stochastic discount factor, it will still satisfy the condition. Specifically, there is no way to distinguish whether the factor is either noisy or unsystematic from the said condition.

Asymptotic Test Statistics

Test Statistic Based on Beta-Pricing Models

According to the setting and whether the GMM is applied to the simple beta pricing model, the moment conditions can be set as

$$\begin{aligned} E\left[\epsilon_t\right] &= E\left[\mathbf{r}_t - \widetilde{\alpha} - \beta f_t\right] = E\left[\mathbf{r}_t - \beta\lambda^* - \beta f_t\right] = \underline{\mathbf{0}}_{\mathbf{n}}, \\ E\left[\epsilon_t f_t\right] &= E\left[(\mathbf{r}_t - \widetilde{\alpha} - \beta f_t) f_t\right] = E\left[\left(\mathbf{r}_t - \beta\lambda^* - \beta f_t\right) f_t\right] = \underline{\mathbf{0}}_{\mathbf{n}}. \end{aligned}$$

Define the sample moments as

$$g_{1T}(\lambda^*, \beta) = \frac{1}{T}\sum_{t=1}^{T}\left[\mathbf{z}_t \otimes \left(\mathbf{r}_t - \beta\lambda^* - \beta f_t\right)\right],$$

where $\otimes$ represents the Kronecker products and $\mathbf{z}_t = [\mathbf{1}, f_t]'$. Assuming f_t and ϵ_t are jointly stationary and ergodic with finite fourth moments then, under the true parameters,

$$\sqrt{T} g_{1T}(\lambda^*, \beta) \xrightarrow{d} N(\underline{\mathbf{0}}_{\mathbf{2n}}, \mathbf{S}_1),$$

where $\mathbf{S}_1$ is an $2n \times 2n$ positive definite constant matrix. In using the GMM methodology, the estimates $\hat{\lambda}^*$ for λ^* and that of β can be obtained from the solution to the minimization problem such as

$$\min_{\lambda^*, \beta} g_{1T}(\lambda^*, \beta)' \mathbf{W}_{1T} g_{1T}(\lambda^*, \beta),$$

where $\mathbf{W}_{1T}$ is an $2n \times 2n$ positive definite matrix with limit $\mathbf{W}$ as positive definite and nonstochastic. The usual approach is to select the consistent estimate for $\mathbf{S}_1^{-1}$. Likewise, the usual test statistic for the null hypothesis as the constraint $\widetilde{\alpha} = \beta\lambda^*$ is denoted as

$$J_1 = Tg_{1T}(\hat{\lambda}^*, \beta^*)'\mathbf{W}_{1T}g_{1T}(\hat{\lambda}^*, \beta^*) \sim \chi^2_{n-1}, \tag{2.2.39}$$

where χ^2_{n-1} is a chi-squared distribution with degree $n-1$, $\mathbf{W}_{1T}$ is some consistent estimate of the optimal weighting matrix.

Test Statistic Under a Stochastic Discount Factor

Now applying the necessary condition of a stochastic discount factor such that $E\left[\mathbf{r}_t\left(1 - f_t\lambda^*\right)\right] = \underline{\mathbf{0}}_n$ and define $\mathbf{u}_t = \mathbf{r}_t\left(1 - f_t\lambda^*\right)$, $\mathbf{g}_{2T} = \frac{1}{T}\sum_{t=1}^{T}\mathbf{u}_t$. Let the central limit theorem hold for $\mathbf{g}_{2T}$ such that

$$\sqrt{T}\mathbf{g}_{2T} \xrightarrow{d} N(\underline{\mathbf{0}}_n, \mathbf{S}_2)$$

for some positive definite matrix $\mathbf{S}_2$. The parameter λ^* can be estimated from the equation such as

$$\hat{\lambda} = \text{argmin}_{\lambda}\mathbf{g}'_{2T}(\lambda^*)\mathbf{W}_{2T}\mathbf{g}_{2T}(\lambda^*),$$

where $\mathbf{W}_{2T}$ is a consistent estimate for $\mathbf{S}_2^{-1}$. Likewise, the GMM estimate for the stochastic discount factor is

$$\hat{\lambda} = \left(\mathbf{D}'_{2T}\mathbf{W}_{2T}\mathbf{D}_{2T}\right)^{-1}\left(\mathbf{D}'_{2T}\mathbf{W}_{2T}\bar{\mathbf{r}}_T\right),$$

where $\mathbf{D}_{2T} = \frac{1}{T}\sum_{t=1}^{T}\mathbf{r}_t f_t$, $\bar{\mathbf{r}}_t = \frac{1}{T}\sum_{t=1}^{T}\mathbf{r}_t$. And hence, the test statistics under the stochastic discount factor becomes

$$J_2 = T\mathbf{g}'_{2T}(\hat{\lambda})\mathbf{W}_{2T}\mathbf{g}_{2T}(\hat{\lambda}) \xrightarrow{d} \chi^2_{n-1}.$$

Thus, if the return process is correctly specified, the test statistics under the beta-pricing model and stochastic discount factor methodology will end up with the same asymptotic distribution. However, the test statistic $\hat{\lambda}$ in a stochastic discount factor may end up with higher asymptotic variance than $\hat{\lambda}^*$ of the beta-pricing model. That is, Avar($\hat{\lambda}$) > Avar($\hat{\lambda}^*$), where

Avar(·) represents the asymptotic variance of the statistic for the factor premium.

Notice that the arguments of Kan and Zhou (1999) are based on a simplified one-factor model for the return process. That is, their work is developed under the assumption that the one-factor model is a correct specification for the return process. In other words, no concern is given to the model misspecifications of return process and/or the stochastic discount factor. In addition, Kan and Zhou (1999) consider the factor premium under the beta-pricing model and the stochastic discount factor to be identical, even though the test statistics when using GMM have different conditions to satisfy.

2.2.1.5 *The Arguments with Reparametrization and Asymptotic Equivalence*

Jagannathan and Wang (2002), in response to the claim of Kan and Zhou (1999), state that the stochastic discount factor methodology is as efficient as the classical beta-pricing models. They show that the claim of Kan and Zhou (1999) suffers from: (1) the risk premiums in these two methods are not identical; (2) by assuming the factor can be standardized as mean zero and unit variance is equivalent to state that the factor's mean and variance are known. Specifically, Jagannathan and Wang (2002) consider the comparison of these two methods as the following.

(1) Beta-pricing models: Let the return process be specified as in Eq. (2.2.32) where excess returns are of interest. Let μ and σ^2 be the mean and variance of the factor f_t. Notice that the mean of the factor is not especially denoted by zero. The beta-pricing model shows that

$$E[\mathbf{r}_t] = \beta\lambda^*, \tag{2.2.40}$$

where λ is the factor premium, and $\beta = \frac{\text{Cov}(\mathbf{r}_t, f_t)}{\sigma^2}$. Hence, given the beta-pricing model where $\widetilde{\alpha} = (\lambda^* - \mu)\beta$, the return process in Eq. (2.2.32) can be rewritten as

$$\mathbf{r}_t = (\lambda^* - \mu + f_t)\beta + \epsilon_t. \tag{2.2.41}$$

Applying the GMM, the conditions for the above Eq. (2.2.38) can be shown as

$$\begin{aligned} E[\mathbf{r}_t - (\lambda^* - \mu + f_t)\beta] &= \underline{\mathbf{0}}_n \\ E[(\mathbf{r}_t - (\lambda^* - \mu + f_t)\beta)f_t] &= \underline{\mathbf{0}}_n \\ E[f_t - \mu] &= 0 \\ E[(f_t - \mu)^2 - \sigma^2] &= 0. \end{aligned}$$

Notice that the above conditions set the error term of (2.2.38) to be mean zero and orthogonal to the factor. These conditions are then estimated with the sample moments where the central limit theorem is applied.

(2) Stochastic discount factor: By substituting $\beta = \frac{\mathrm{Cov}(\mathbf{r}_t, f_t)}{\sigma^2}$ into the equation as $E[\mathbf{r}_t] = \beta\lambda^*$, it is feasible to see that

$$E[\mathbf{r}_t] - \lambda^* \frac{\mathrm{Cov}(\mathbf{r}_t, f_t)}{\sigma^2} = \underline{\mathbf{0}}_n.$$

Since $\mathrm{Cov}(\mathbf{r}_t, f_t) = E[\mathbf{r}_t f_t] - E[\mathbf{r}_t]\mu$, this implies that

$$\left(1 + \frac{\mu\lambda^*}{\sigma^2}\right) E[\mathbf{r}_t] - \left(\frac{\lambda^*}{\sigma^2}\right) E[\mathbf{r}_t f_t] = \underline{\mathbf{0}}_n.$$

Rearranging the equation, it can be shown that

$$E\left[\mathbf{r}_t \left(1 - \frac{\lambda^*}{\sigma^2 + \mu\lambda^*}\right) f^t\right] = \underline{\mathbf{0}}_n.$$

Given that the stochastic discount factor methodology shows that

$$E[\mathbf{r}_t m_t] = \underline{\mathbf{0}}_n, \tag{2.2.42}$$

where $m_t = 1 - \lambda f$, the above equation will provide that

$$\lambda = \frac{\lambda^*}{\sigma^2 + \mu\lambda^*}. \tag{2.2.43}$$

Based on this result, it can be shown that the factor risk premium for stochastic discount factor λ is not identical to the factor premium λ^* under the beta-pricing model. Furthermore, it is shown that the stochastic discount factor under the linear one-factor model of excess returns and the GMM moment restriction is given as

$$E[\mathbf{r}_t(1 - \lambda f_t)] = \underline{\mathbf{0}}_n. \tag{2.2.44}$$

With the reparameterization of factor premiums, Jagannathan and Wang (2002) show that the asymptotic variance of the statistic for the factor premium is identical. That is, given the beta representation such as Eq. (2.2.40) and the SDF as Eq. (2.2.42), $\text{Avar}(\hat{\lambda}) = \text{Avar}(\hat{\lambda}^*)$.

2.2.1.6 Stochastic Discount Factor Bounds with Conditioning Information
Given the setting in Hansen and Jagannathan (1991), the stochastic discount factor m with minimum variance for expectation $E(m)$ can be denoted as in Eq. (2.2.11) where

$$m = E(m) + [l_n - E(m)\mu]'\Sigma_R^{-1}(\mathbf{R} - \mu)$$

and the variance of m is

$$\sigma_m^2 = [l_n - E(m)\mu]'\Sigma_R^{-1}[l_n - E(m)\mu],$$

where $E[\mathbf{R}] = \mu$, and Σ_R is the covariance matrix of $\mathbf{R}$, where $\mathbf{R}$ is an $n \times 1$ vector of the gross returns of assets. However, Ferson and Siegel (2003) show that the variance bound of Hansen and Jagannathan (1991) may incur finite-sample biases, which may reject asset-pricing models too often. The finding is based on the variance bound with the conditional setting in Gallant et al. (1990) and the portfolios derived in Ferson and Siegel (2001).

Ferson and Siegel (2003) consider the variance bound when a lagged information set is applied. The stochastic discount factor under the conditional setting is shown as

$$E(m_t\mathbf{R}_t|Z_{t-1}) = l_n, \tag{2.2.45}$$

where l_n represents a vector of ones, $\mathbf{R}_t$ is an $n \times 1$ vector of gross returns. Given Eq. (2.2.41), it is easy to see that

$$E(m_t\mathbf{R}_t - l_n|Z_{t-1}) = \underline{\mathbf{0}}_n. \tag{2.2.46}$$

This condition is equivalent to

$$E(m_t\mathbf{R}_t - l_n)f(Z_{t-1}) = \underline{\mathbf{0}}_n, \tag{2.2.47}$$

for all bounded measurable scalar functions $f(.)$ as if the unconditional expectation exists.

Hence, if $\mathbf{R}_t f(Z_{t-1})$ is considered as the payoff for dynamic trading strategies with the prices represented by $l_n f(Z_{t-1})$, then the stochastic discount factor m_t (with the conditional information) should also apply to the dynamic strategies. In addition, it is straightforward to see that, the larger the set of strategies is applied, the smaller the set of m that can satisfy the condition and hence with a tighter bounds. If $f(.)$ is chosen to be the set of all portfolio weight functions, the above Eq. (2.2.43) will become

$$E[(m_t\mathbf{R}_t - l_n)'\omega(Z_{t-1})] = 0, \tag{2.2.48}$$

for all n-vector valued functions $\omega(Z_{t-1})$, with $\omega'(Z_{t-1})l_n = 1$.

Under the conditioning setting, Ferson and Siegel (2001) provide the variance bound for the efficient portfolio. Let Z represent the conditioning information where the time subscript is suppressed for simplicity, and let $\omega = \omega(Z) = (\omega_1(Z), \omega_2(Z), \ldots, \omega_n(Z))'$ be the weights of assets in the portfolio, where $\omega'(Z)l_n = 1$, and $\mathbf{R}_p = \omega'(Z)\mathbf{R}$ is the gross return of the portfolio. Then, the unconditional mean μ_p and variance σ_p^2 of the portfolio can be expressed as

$$\begin{aligned}
\mu_p &= E[\omega'(Z)\mu(Z)], \\
\sigma_p^2 &= E\left\{\omega'(Z)\left[\mu(Z)\mu(Z)' + \Sigma_\epsilon(Z)\right]\omega(Z)\right\} - \mu_p^2,
\end{aligned}$$

where $\mu(Z) = E[\mathbf{R}|Z]$ is the conditional mean and $\Sigma_\epsilon(Z)$ is the conditional covariance matrix of n asset returns based on the information Z, respectively. Now define the following constants as

$$\alpha_1 = E\left(\frac{1}{l_n'\Lambda l_n}\right)$$

$$\alpha_2 = E\left(\frac{l_n'\Lambda\mu(Z)}{l_n'\Lambda l_n}\right)$$

$$\alpha_3 = E\left[\mu'(Z)\left(\Lambda - \frac{\Lambda l_n l_n'\Lambda}{l_n'\Lambda l_n}\right)\mu(Z)\right],$$

where $\Lambda = \Lambda(Z) = [E(\mathbf{RR}'|Z)]^{-1} = [\mu(Z)\mu(Z)' + \Sigma_\epsilon(Z)]^{-1}$.

Proposition of the efficient portfolio (UE) bound: Given the above setting, the optimal weights of the portfolio that has the minimum unconditional variance with unconditional mean as μ_p are

$$\omega'(Z) = \frac{l_n'\Lambda}{l_n'\Lambda l_n} + \frac{\mu_p - \alpha_2}{\alpha_3}\mu(Z)'\left(\Lambda - \frac{\Lambda l_n l_n'\Lambda}{l_n'\Lambda l_n}\right). \tag{2.2.49}$$

Hence, the variance of the portfolio defined in Eq. (2.2.45) is

$$\sigma_p^2 = \left(\alpha_1 + \frac{\alpha_2}{\alpha_3}\right) - \frac{2\alpha_2}{\alpha_3}\mu_p + \frac{1-\alpha_3}{\alpha_3}\mu_p^2. \tag{2.2.50}$$

Notice that what Ferson and Siegel (2001) have shown is the unconditional variance of the optimal portfolio given the specifications of the conditional mean and variance of the returns. Hence, the specifications of the conditional mean $\mu(Z)$ and conditional variance $\Sigma_\epsilon(Z)$ are critical for portfolio efficiency. On the other hand, Ferson and Siegel (2003) also enlist the variance bound developed by Gallant et al. (1990) where the conditional mean of the stochastic discount factor m is explicitly shown and the following conditional efficient set of constants are given such that

$$\alpha(Z) = l_n'\Sigma_\epsilon^{-1}(Z)l_n$$

$$\beta(Z) = l_n'\Sigma_\epsilon^{-1}(Z)\mu(Z)$$

$$\gamma(Z) = \mu'(Z)\Sigma_\epsilon^{-1}(Z)\mu(Z)$$

Proposition of Optimal H-J Bound (Gallant et al. 1990): The stochastic discount factor m with the minimum variance for its expectation as $E[m]$ that satisfies $E(m\mathbf{R}|Z) = l_n$,[2] is given as

$$m = \zeta(Z) + [l_n - \zeta(Z)\mu(Z)]'\Sigma_\epsilon^{-1}(Z)[\mathbf{R} - \mu(Z)], \tag{2.2.51}$$

where $\zeta(Z) = E[m|Z]$ is the conditional mean of m given conditional information Z and is defined as

$$\zeta(Z) = \frac{\beta(Z)}{1+\gamma(Z)} + \frac{1}{1+\gamma(Z)}\left\{\frac{E(m) - E\left(\frac{\beta(Z)}{1+\gamma(Z)}\right)}{E\left(\frac{1}{1+\gamma(Z)}\right)}\right\}$$

and the unconditional variance of m is shown as

$$\widetilde{\sigma}_m^2 = \frac{\left[E(m) - E\left(\frac{\beta(Z)}{1+\gamma(Z)}\right)\right]^2}{E\left(\frac{1}{1+\gamma(Z)}\right)} + E[\alpha(Z)] - E\left[\frac{\beta^2(Z)}{1+\gamma(Z)}\right] - [E(m)]^2. \tag{2.2.52}$$

However, even with the adjustments for the variance bounds for the stochastic discount factor with conditional information, these bounds are still subject to bias when finite-sample time-series observations are applied. Ferson and Siegel (2003) correct the bias in estimating the variance bound when sampled observations are applied. For instance, let T independent observations of asset return vector $\mathbf{R}$ be collected and let $\hat{\mu}$, S denote the sample mean and sample covariance matrix for the return respectively. The maximum likelihood estimate of the variance bound (such as in Hansen and Jagannathan) can be denoted as

$$\hat{\sigma}_m^2 = [l_n - E(m)\hat{\mu}]'S^{-1}[l_n - E(m)\hat{\mu}].$$

Assuming normality, the above quadratic form will result in a noncentral chi-squared distribution. Given this, Ferson and Siegel (2003) derive the mean of $\hat{\sigma}_m^2$ and the unbiased estimate for the variance (of the stochastic discount factor) such that

$$E(\hat{\sigma}_m^2) = \frac{n}{T-n-2}[E(m)]^2 + \frac{T}{T-n-2}\sigma_m^2 \tag{2.2.53}$$

and the unbiased estimator of the variance is given as

$$\hat{\sigma}^2_{m,\text{adjusted}} = \left(1 - \frac{n+2}{T}\right)\hat{\sigma}^2_m - \frac{n}{T}[E(m)]^2, \tag{2.2.54}$$

where $E(\hat{\sigma}^2_{m,\text{adjusted}}) = \sigma^2_m$.

Based on the above result, Ferson and Siegel (2003) extend the result to the bias correction in both σ^2_p and $\widetilde{\sigma}^2_m$. When T independent time-series observations of return vector $\mathbf{R}$ are sampled, and if the asset returns are jointly normal, conditional on information Z where the maximum likelihood estimates for $E[\mathbf{R}|Z]$ and $\Sigma_\epsilon(Z)$ are applied to estimate σ^2_m, the biased-corrected estimator for the variance bound is

$$\hat{\sigma}^2_{m,\text{adjusted}} = \left(\frac{T-n-2}{T}\right)\hat{\sigma}^2_{\mathbf{m}*} - \frac{n}{T}[E(m)]^2 + \frac{2}{T}\text{var}[E(m|Z)], \tag{2.2.55}$$

where $\hat{\sigma}^2_{\mathbf{m}*}$ represents the variance bound as σ^2_p or $\widetilde{\sigma}^2_m$.

Hence, the variance bound of the stochastic discount factor when conditional information is applied requires (1) correct specification of the conditional mean and conditional variance for the stochastic discount factor, and (2) additional adjustments to correct for bias even when the maximum likelihood estimation is applied with independent time-series observations. The results lead to further discussions on the model specification and the selection of conditional expectations of stochastic discount factors. In other words, inclusion of different conditioning variables may alternate the above variance bound. In addition, specification of the stochastic discount factor conditional on the available information (whether it is sufficient or not) will also determine the variance bound. Optimality in choices of state variables or factors for the stochastic discount factor is crucial for the variance bounds and, hence, on the pricing kernel of securities. The following two sections discuss the possible linear models (with factors or state variables) that may be applied to estimate and infer the stochastic discount factors.

2.2.1.7 *A New Variance Bound on the Stochastic Discount Factor (Based on State Variables)*

Kan and Zhou (2006) extend the framework of Hansen and Jagannathan (1991) to consider the possible tighter variance bound for the stochastic discount factor. Instead of projecting the stochastic discount factor onto the (gross) return space as in Eq. (2.2.5), they propose projecting the factor onto a vector of state variables, where $m = m(x)$, and x is a vector of state variables. Based on the pricing kernel, the stochastic discount factor m_{t+1} is defined as

$$E[\mathbf{R}_{t+1} m_{t+1} | I_t] = l_n,$$

where l_n is an n-vector of ones, $\mathbf{R}_{t+1}$ is the gross returns on N assets at time $t + 1$, and I_t is the information set available at time t. By suppressing the time index and applying the unconditional form of the equality above (after applying the iterated law of expectations), it is shown that

$$E[\mathbf{R}m] = l_n.$$

It is known that the m^* of a minimum-variance portfolio (with linear combinations of asset returns) can be considered as the projection of the stochastic discount factor onto the space spanned by the assets' gross returns. It also serves as a stochastic discount factor such that

$$m^* = \mu_m + (l_n - \mu_m \mu)' \Sigma_R^{-1} (\mathbf{R} - \mu) \tag{2.2.56}$$

where $\mu_m = E[m]$ is the mean of m, and μ and Σ_R are the mean vector and covariance matrix of asset (gross) returns $\mathbf{R}$. Kan and Zhou (2006) propose that the projection of the stochastic discount factor onto the $k \times 1$ vector of state variables is given as

$$m^* = \alpha + \beta' \mathbf{x} + \epsilon^*, \tag{2.2.57}$$

where $E[\epsilon^*] = 0$, and $\mathrm{Cov}(\epsilon^*, x) = 0$. The setting stipulates that the minimum-variance stochastic discount factor m_o can be explained by some state variables $\mathbf{x}$. Hence, the lower bound for the stochastic discount factor can be made more precise or tighter. Kan and Zhou (2006) argue that when $\mu_m = E[m(\mathbf{x})]$, the variance bound of the stochastic discount factor can be shown as

$$\mathrm{Var}(m(\mathbf{x})) \geq \frac{1}{\rho^2_{\mathbf{x},m^*}} \mathrm{Var}(m^*), \tag{2.2.58}$$

where $\rho^2_{\mathbf{x},m^*}$ is the multiple correlation coefficient between $\mathbf{x}$ and m^*, and the equality holds if and only if $m(x) = \alpha + \beta' \mathbf{x}$.

More intuitively, Kan and Zhou (2006) elaborate the variance lower bound of Hansen and Jagannathan (1991) by projecting the minimum-variance portfolio's stochastic discount factor m^* onto a set of state variables. Since the correlation coefficient between $-1 \leq \rho_{\mathbf{x},m^*} \leq 1$, the lower bound in Eq. (2.2.51) is higher than that of Hansen and Jagannathan (1991). Although the analysis is more extended than the results of Hansen and Jagannathan (1991), the difficulty still lies in the identification of m^*. Given that m^* is not entirely observable (at least, empirically), the identification of state variables $\mathbf{x}$ still requires specification tests.

One question remains unanswered: if one identifies a set of state variables (or proxies) that may result in a higher correlation coefficient $\rho^2_{\mathbf{x},m^*}$ (which reduces the variance lower bound as above), will this be a better set of variables for asset pricing models? How can one compare several candidate models when they all reduce the variance lower bound? Furthermore, since the regression of m^* onto state variables x may not necessarily be linear, Kan and Zhou (2006) extend the above claim that includes the nonlinear regression as $m^* = f(\mathbf{x}) + \epsilon_o$ such that

$$\mathrm{Var}(m(\mathbf{x})) \geq \frac{1}{\rho^2_{f(\mathbf{x}),m^*}} \mathrm{Var}(m^*), \tag{2.2.59}$$

where $\rho_{f(\mathbf{x}),m^*}$ is the multiple correlation coefficient between $f(\mathbf{x})$ and m^*.

The derived bound of Kan and Zhou (2006) may then be applied to a consideration of the model diagnostic for a given set of state variables x and asset pricing models. However, the difficulty is that the selection or determination of the set of state variables remains an open question. For instance, in Kan and Zhou (2006), the comparison of bounds when using Fama-French factors are shown. Yet, the results are demonstrations of tighter variance bound when the state variables have already been chosen as those in Fama and French (1993). Another difficulty is that the above unconditional variance bound does not take into account the fact that asset returns (and hence the stochastic discount factor) may be subject to time-changing variance or heteroskedasticity. In addition, even in the nonlinear format of m^*, the variance bound relies on the stable figure of multiple correlation coefficient $\rho_{f(\mathbf{x}),m^*}$.

On the other hand, it is not feasible to observe the moments of the stochastic discount factors and their correlation coefficients with the factors. Hence, estimation of these parameters is crucial to identify the correct specification of stochastic discount factors. Furthermore, if proxies for factors are proposed, it is necessary to consider the model choices on these proxies for the stochastic discount factor.

In addition, since the stochastic discount factor m^* represents what is subject to the (global) minimum variance portfolio, this shows that the m^* is on the efficient frontier, accordingly. Given this, the proxies/variables that are still correlated with m^* can also be considered as nondiversifiable because anything diversifiable should be diversified away with the portfolios that lie on the efficient frontier. In other words, the derivation of Kan and Zhou (2006) simply points out the possible approach in identifying the essentiality of factors that should be included in the empirical asset pricing models.

2.2.1.8 Model Selection (for Factors) of the Stochastic Discount Factor

Kan and Robotti (2009) consider the model comparison of stochastic discount factors based on the Hansen-Jagannathan distance (denoted H-J distance henceforth) defined in the following. Specifically, let m be a proposed stochastic discount factor[3] and as denoted earlier let $\mathbf{R}$ be a vector of gross returns on n portfolios. By the necessary condition of the stochastic discount factor, the pricing error e, where $e = E[\mathbf{R}m] - l_n$, should be equal to $\mathbf{0}_n$ if the stochastic discount factor m correctly prices the n securities or portfolios. If the stochastic discount factor m is a misspecified model, this pricing error will likely become nonzero. Specifically, let the stochastic discount factor m be denoted as $m = m(\lambda)$, where λ are some unknown parameters. The pricing error will then become

$$e(\lambda) = E[\mathbf{R}m(\lambda)] - l_n \neq \underline{\mathbf{0}}_n,$$

if the $m(\lambda)$ is a misspecified model. Based on this setting, the H-J distance is denoted as

$$\delta = \left[e(\lambda)'\mathbf{M}_R^{-1}e(\lambda)\right]^{1/2}$$

where $\mathbf{M}_R = E[\mathbf{R}\mathbf{R}']$ is the second moment matrix of $\mathbf{R}$. Hence, given that the models can possibly be misspecified, the rationality of model choices lies in the H-J distance defined as

$$\delta = \left[\min_{\lambda}\ e(\lambda)'\mathbf{M}_R^{-1}e(\lambda)\right]^{1/2}.$$

Now suppose under the linear asset pricing models that the stochastic discount factor $m(\lambda) = \lambda_o + \lambda_1' f = \lambda' x$, where $x = [1, f']'$ and $\lambda = [\lambda_o, \lambda_1']'$, where $m(\lambda)$ is a linear function of k systematic factors denoted in the $k \times 1$ vector f, and λ is a $(k+1) \times 1$ vector of parameters for factors. Specifically, when denoting $Y = [f', \mathbf{R}']'$, the mean and covariance matrix of Y can be given as

$$\mu = E[Y] = \begin{bmatrix} \mu_1 \\ \mu_2 \end{bmatrix},$$

$$V = \mathrm{Var}(Y) = \begin{bmatrix} V_{11} & V_{12} \\ V_{21} & V_{22} \end{bmatrix}.$$

Hence, the pricing errors of n assets can be written as

$$e(\lambda) = E[\mathbf{R}m(\lambda)] - l_n = E[\mathbf{R}x'\lambda] - l_n = D\lambda - l_n, \tag{2.2.60}$$

where $D = E[\mathbf{R}x'] = [\mu_2, V_{21} + \mu_2\mu_1']$ is an $n \times (k+1)$ matrix since λ is nonstochastic. Assuming that V_{21} is of full column rank, the squared H-J distance is then given as

$$\begin{aligned} \delta^2 &= \min_{\lambda} (D\lambda - l_n)' V_{22}^{-1} (D\lambda - l_n) \\ &= l_n' V_{22}^{-1} l_n - l_n' V_{22}^{-1} D \left(D' V_{22}^{-1} D\right)^{-1} D' V_{22}^{-1} l_n. \end{aligned}$$

The unique λ that minimizes the H-J distance can be given as

$$\lambda_{\mathrm{HJ}} = \left(D' V_{22}^{-1} D\right)^{-1} \left(D' V_{22}^{-1} l_n\right). \tag{2.2.61}$$

In the following, Kan and Robotti (2009) consider the asymptotic properties and distribution (when time-series horizon $T \to \infty$) of the λ_{HJ} (factor loadings for the stochastic discount factor) that minimizes the H-J distance of a particular model (both correctly and incorrectly specified) as the test statistics for model specification tests. Since all these moment matrices are not observable, the sample H-J distance is applied instead. That is, let $Y_t = [f_t', \mathbf{R}_t']'$ where f_t is a vector of proposed factors or proxies at time t, and $\mathbf{R}_t$ is an $n \times 1$ vector of gross returns of n assets at time t. Denote the sample moments of Y_t as follows:

$$\widehat{\mu} = \begin{bmatrix} \widehat{\mu}_1 \\ \widehat{\mu}_2 \end{bmatrix},$$

$$\widehat{V} = \begin{bmatrix} \widehat{V}_{11} & \widehat{V}_{12} \\ \widehat{V}_{21} & \widehat{V}_{22} \end{bmatrix} = \frac{1}{T}\sum_{t=1}^{T}(Y_t - \widehat{\mu})(Y_t - \widehat{\mu})',$$

and hence, the sample squared H-J distance and sample parameters for the stochastic discount factor are then defined as

$$\begin{aligned} \widehat{\delta}^2 &= l_n'\widehat{V}_{22}^{-1}l_n - l_n'\widehat{V}_{22}^{-1}\widehat{D}\left(\widehat{D}'\widehat{V}_{22}^{-1}\widehat{D}\right)^{-1}\widehat{D}'\widehat{V}_{22}^{-1}l_n, \\ \widehat{\lambda} &= \left(\widehat{D}'\widehat{V}_{22}^{-1}\widehat{D}\right)^{-1}\left(\widehat{D}'\widehat{V}_{22}^{-1}l_n\right), \end{aligned} \tag{2.2.62}$$

where $\widehat{D} = [\widehat{\mu}_2, \widehat{V}_{21} + \widehat{\mu}_2\widehat{\mu}_1']$. Under the hypothesis of correct specification, $\delta = 0$, Jagannathan and Wang (1996) show that

$$T\widehat{\delta}^2 \xrightarrow{d} \sum_{i=1}^{n-k-1} \xi_i x_i, \tag{2.2.63}$$

where x_i's are independent chi-squared (denoted as χ^2) random variables where the weights ξ_i's are equal to the nonzero eigenvalues of the matrix as

$$S^{\frac{1}{2}}V_{22}^{-1}S^{\frac{1}{2}} - S^{\frac{1}{2}}V_{22}^{-1}D\left(D'V_{22}^{-1}D\right)^{-1}D'V_{22}^{-1}S^{\frac{1}{2}},$$

and S is the asymptotic variance matrix of

$$\frac{1}{\sqrt{T}}\sum_{t=1}^{T}\left(\mathbf{R}_t x_t'\lambda - l_n\right).$$

In other words, the asymptotic distribution of the sample squared H-J distance under the null hypothesis of correct specification (for the stochastic discount factor) will converge to a weighted sum of chi-squared distributed random variables. However, since the genuine specification of the stochastic discount factor is unknown, Kan and Robotti (2009) consider the model selection of the factor where the emphasis of study is on the derivation of $\hat{\lambda}$, particularly under potentially misspecified models.

Proposition of the asymptotic distribution of estimated factor loadings in the stochastic discount factor: under a potentially misspecified model (for the stochastic discount factor), as $T \rightarrow \infty$,

$$\sqrt{T}\left(\hat{\lambda} - \lambda\right) \xrightarrow{d} N\left(\underline{0}_{k+1}, V(\hat{\lambda})\right), \tag{2.2.64}$$

where $\underline{0}_{k+1}$ is a $(k+1) \times 1$ vector of zeros, and $V(\hat{\lambda}) = \sum_{j=-\infty}^{\infty} E[h_t h_{t+j}']$, with

$$h_t = -HD'V_{22}^{-1}\mathbf{R}_t m_t + H\left[D'V_{22}^{-1}(\mathbf{R}_t - \mu_2) - x_t\right]\mathbf{u}_t + \lambda, \tag{2.2.65}$$

where $H = \left(D'V_{22}^{-1}D\right)^{-1}$ and $\mathbf{u}_t = e'V_{22}^{-1}\mathbf{R}_t$, and e stands for the pricing error in Eq. (2.2.60). In addition, if the model is correctly specified, $e = \underline{0}_n$, and $\mathbf{u}_t = 0$, and h_t can be simplified as

$$h_t = -HD'V_{22}^{-1}\mathbf{R}_t m_t + \lambda.$$

The difficulty of the above proposition is due to the estimation of asymptotic variance $V(\hat{\lambda})$, particularly through the standard error h_t. However, Kan and Robotti (2009) are able to develop the model selection test based on the above derivation of H-J distance when using the sample observations. The concept is to consider the test of equality of the H-J distance between two models.

Model selection for stochastic discount factors: consider two competing models for the stochastic discount factor such that $x_1 = [1, f_1', f_2']'$ and $x_2 = [1, f_1', f_3']'$. Hence, there are sets of factors as $\{f_i\}_{i=1,2,3}$ and of the dimensions as $K_i \times 1$, $i = 1, 2, 3$, respectively. Two competing models are considered such that $m_1 = \eta' x_1$, and the other is $m_2 = \lambda' x_2$. Following the above proposition, and letting $D_1 = E[\mathbf{R}x_1']$ and $D_2 = E[\mathbf{R}x_2']$ where D_1 and D_2 are assumed to have full column rank, the parameters that minimize the H-J distance for each model are given as

$$\begin{aligned} \eta &= \left(D_1'V_{22}^{-1}D_1\right)^{-1} D_1'V_{22}^{-1}l_n, \\ \lambda &= \left(D_2'V_{22}^{-1}D_2\right)^{-1} D_2'V_{22}^{-1}l_n. \end{aligned} \tag{2.2.66}$$

Hence, the pricing errors and squared H-J distance of the two models are denoted as

$$e_i = \left(D_i' V_{22}^{-1} D_i\right)^{-1} D_i' V_{22}^{-1} l_n - l_n, \qquad i = 1, 2,$$
$$\delta_i^2 = l_n' V_{22}^{-1} l_n - l_n' V_{22}^{-1} D_i \left(D_i' V_{22}^{-1} D_i\right)^{-1} D_i' V_{22}^{-1} l_n. \tag{2.2.67}$$

Based on the above setting, it is easy to see that if $K_1 = 0$, the two models will not have any common factor. When $K_2 = 0$, the second model nests the first one. When $K_3 = 0$, the first model nests the second one. If both $K_2 > 0$ and $K_3 > 0$, the two models share some common factor f_1 and they are not nested. The test statistics then can be formed with both the nested and non-nested models.

(1) Nested model: let $K_2 = 0$ so that model 2 nests model 1. In other words, model 2's factor f_3 has no impact on the specification of the stochastic discount factor. Based on this case, Kan and Robotti (2009) provide the following lemma and proposition.

Lemma for the squared H-J distance under *nested* models: $\delta_1^2 = \delta_2^2$ if and only if $\lambda_2 = \underline{0}_{K_3}$, where λ_2 is a vector of the last K_3 elements of λ, where λ is a vector of factor loadings for the stochastic discount factor in model 2.

Given this result, it is easy to see that under the null hypothesis $H_o : \lambda_2 = \underline{0}_{K_3}$, and to suppose that $\widehat{V}(\hat{\lambda}_2)$ is a consistent estimator of the asymptotic variance of $\sqrt{T}(\hat{\lambda}_2 - \lambda_2)$,

$$T\hat{\lambda}_2 \left(\widehat{V}(\hat{\lambda}_2)\right)^{-1} \hat{\lambda}_2 \xrightarrow{d} \chi^2_{K_3},$$

as $T \to \infty$.

Notice that although the above statistics are intuitive enough to understand, the test requires the estimation of $\widehat{V}(\hat{\lambda}_2)$ which (in the current scheme) is under the misspecified models since neither model 1 nor model 2 is a correct model for the stochastic discount factor. This in turns needs to apply the estimator in Eq. (2.2.65). Alternatively, Kan and Robotti (2009) also develop the asymptotic distribution for the difference of the H-J distance in the two models as $\hat{\delta}_1^2 - \hat{\delta}_2^2$ under the null hypothesis as $\delta_1^2 = \delta_2^2$. The idea is to consider the difference of the squared H-J distance for these two models when $\lambda_2 = \underline{0}_{K_3}$, where the factor f_3 in model 2 is not influential on the specification of the stochastic discount factor.

Proposition of the asymptotic distribution of the difference in the squared H-J distance: partition the matrix $H_2 = \left(D_2' V_{22}^{-1} D_2\right)^{-1}$ as

$$H_2 = \begin{bmatrix} H_{2,11} & H_{2,12} \\ H_{2,21} & H_{2,22} \end{bmatrix},$$

where $H_{2,22}$ is a $K_3 \times K_3$ matrix. Under the null hypothesis as $H_o : \delta_1^2 = \delta_2^2$

$$T\left(\hat{\delta}_1^2 - \hat{\delta}_2^2\right) \xrightarrow{d} \sum_{i=1}^{K_3} \xi_i x_i, \tag{2.2.68}$$

where $\{x_i\}_{i=1,\ldots,K_3}$ are independent chi-squared (denoted as χ^2) random variables, and $\{\xi_i\}_{i=1,\ldots,K_3}$ are the eigenvalues of the matrix $H_{2,22}^{-1} V(\hat{\lambda}_2)$, with $V(\hat{\lambda}_2)$ being the asymptotic variance of $\sqrt{T}(\hat{\lambda}_2 - \lambda_2)$.

In empirical applications, since the hypothesis does not assume the models are correctly specified, a robust version of $V(\hat{\lambda}_2)$ should be used to test the null hypothesis. In addition, the sample statistics such as $\hat{\xi}_i$ is substituted for ξ_i, where $\hat{\xi}_i$'s are the eigenvalues of $\hat{H}_{2,22}^{-1} \hat{V}(\hat{\lambda}_2)$, $\hat{H}_{2,22}$ and $\hat{V}(\hat{\lambda}_2)$, are consistent estimators of $H_{2,22}$ and $V(\hat{\lambda}_2)$, respectively.

(2) Non-nested models: notice that when non-nested models are considered, the hypothesis as $\delta_1^2 = \delta_2^2$ can occur in cases such as (1) $m_1 = m_2$, or (2) $m_1 \neq m_2$, and $e_1' V_{22}^{-1} e_1 = e_2' V_{22}^{-1} e_2$. In the first case, since $m_1 = m_2$, this implies that $e_1 = e_2$ and $\delta_1^2 = \delta_2^2$. In the second case, even though $m_1 \neq m_2$ (and hence $e_1 \neq e_2$), the squared H-J distances are identical as $\delta_1^2 = \delta_2^2$. Hence, Kan and Robotti (2009) consider the following conditions. Partition the factor loading (for stochastic discount factors) for different models as $\eta = [\eta_1', \eta_2']'$, $\lambda = [\lambda_1', \lambda_2']'$, where η_1, λ_1 are the first $K_1 + 1$ elements of η and λ, respectively. Therefore, for the non-nested models, the following conditions hold when $m_1 = m_2$.

Conditions for the equality of two stochastic discount factors (for non-nested models under misspecification): for non-nested models, $m_1 = m_2$ if and only if $\eta_2 = \underline{0}_{K_2}$ and $\lambda_2 = \underline{0}_{K_3}$.

Given the null hypothesis H_o : $\eta_2 = \underline{0}_{K_2}, \lambda_2 = \underline{0}_{K_3}$, let $\psi = [\eta_2', \lambda_2']'$ and $\hat{\psi} = [\hat{\eta}_2', \hat{\lambda}_2']'$, then the asymptotic distribution of $\hat{\psi}$ under potentially misspecified models is given as

$$\sqrt{T}(\hat{\psi} - \psi) \xrightarrow{d} N\left(0_{K_2+K_3}, V(\hat{\psi})\right), \tag{2.2.69}$$

where $V(\hat{\psi}) = \sum_{j=-\infty}^{\infty} E[\widetilde{h}_t \widetilde{h}_{t+j}']$, and

$$\widetilde{h}_t = \begin{bmatrix} \widetilde{h}_{1t} \\ \widetilde{h}_{2t} \end{bmatrix} = \begin{bmatrix} -H_{1b}D_1'V_{22}^{-1}\mathbf{R}_t m_{1t} + H_{1b}[D_1'V_{22}^{-1}(\mathbf{R}_t - \mu_2) - x_{1t}]u_{1t} + \eta_2 \\ -H_{2b}D_2'V_{22}^{-1}\mathbf{R}_t m_{2t} + H_{2b}[D_2'V_{22}^{-1}(\mathbf{R}_t - \mu_2) - x_{2t}]u_{2t} + \lambda_2 \end{bmatrix}$$

where $u_{1t} = e_1'V_{22}^{-1}\mathbf{R}_t$, and $u_{2t} = e_2'V_{22}^{-1}\mathbf{R}_t$, H_{1b} is the last K_2 rows of matrix $\left(D_1'V_{22}^{-1}D_1\right)^{-1}$, and H_{2b} is the last K_3 rows of matrix $\left(D_2'V_{22}^{-1}D_2\right)^{-1}$. Thus, under the null hypothesis as $\psi = \underline{0}_{K_2+K_3}$ as a $(K_2 + K_3) \times 1$ vector of zeros, and if $\hat{V}(\hat{\psi})$ is a consistent estimator of $V(\hat{\psi})$,

$$T\hat{\psi}'\hat{V}(\hat{\psi})^{-1}\hat{\psi} \xrightarrow{d} \chi^2_{K_2+K_3}. \tag{2.2.70}$$

However, this statistic requires a consistent estimator of the matrix $V(\hat{\psi})$. More difficulties include the fact that these test statistics are not nuisance-parameter-free since $\psi = [\eta_2', \lambda_2']'$ and $\hat{\psi} = [\hat{\eta}_2', \hat{\lambda}_2']'$ may also depend on the estimates of coefficients in the other components/factors of the models unless all the included factors are orthogonal to each other. The following proposition also requires the same condition, which makes the empirical applications of the test statistics relatively complicated. Besides, the purpose is to identify which model (between two candidate models) is better for the stochastic discount factor when they both are misspecified. Yet, in empirical applications, the model selection can be of more complicated orders or sequences for any plausible alternatives. The setting in Chaps. 4 and 5 of this book is to derive easier statistics where sequential model selection can be implemented.

Proposition for the difference of the squared H-J distances for non-nested models under misspecification: let $H_1 = \left(D_1'V_{22}^{-1}D_1\right)^{-1}$ and

$H_2 = \left(D_2' V_{22}^{-1} D_2\right)^{-1}$, and partition these matrices as

$$H_1 = \begin{bmatrix} H_{1,11} & H_{1,12} \\ H_{1,21} & H_{1,22} \end{bmatrix}, \quad H_2 = \begin{bmatrix} H_{2,11} & H_{2,12} \\ H_{2,21} & H_{2,22} \end{bmatrix},$$

where $H_{1,11}$ and $H_{2,11}$ are both $(K_1 + 1) \times (K_1 + 1)$ matrices. Under the null hypothesis as $H_o : m_1 = m_2$, the difference of the squared H-J distances

$$T\left(\hat{\delta}_1^2 - \hat{\delta}_2^2\right) \xrightarrow{d} \sum_{i=1}^{K_2+K_3} \xi_i x_i, \tag{2.2.71}$$

where $\{x_i\}_{i=1,\ldots,K_2+K_3}$ are independent χ^2 random variables, and the ξ_i's are the eigenvalues of

$$\begin{bmatrix} -H_{1,22}^{-1} & 0_{K_2 \times K_3} \\ 0_{K_3 \times K_2} & H_{2,22}^{-1} \end{bmatrix} V(\hat{\psi}). \tag{2.2.72}$$

It can be found that these test statistics all depend on the estimates of moment matrices such as V_{22} and $V(\hat{\psi})$, for instance. Besides, the setting of the null hypothesis is to consider two non-nested models that are equivalent to each other where the noncommon factors in both models are to be deleted. Another important issue is that the test of the difference of the squared H-J distances does not consider a possible sequential approach to selecting the optimal model.

2.2.2 Modification of Beta-Pricing Regression Models

In this section, the recent development and empirical research of beta-pricing models (including the time-varying coefficients framework) will be surveyed to consider further potential difficulties and improvements.

2.2.2.1 Issues of Market Indices, Nonlinearity, and Seasonal Anomalies

For the issues such as the selection of market indices to represent market portfolio, the nonlinearity problem, and anomalies related to firm size or January seasonality, Tinic and West (1986) provide the tests for the two-parameter capital asset pricing model according to extended sample sizes. Initially, as devised by Fama and MacBeth (1973), the two-pass regressions are well-known in the finance literature for verification of the

CAPM in the risk premium of a market portfolio. Based on the "betas" originally estimated from the first-pass time-series regressions of return series, Fama and MacBeth estimate the coefficients of the monthly cross-sectional regressions over 20 portfolios from January 1935 to June 1968 denoted as

$$\tilde{\mathbf{R}}_{pt} = \tilde{\gamma}_{ot} + \tilde{\gamma}_{1t}\beta_{pt-1} + \tilde{\gamma}_{2t}\beta^2_{pt-1} + \tilde{\gamma}_{3t}S(e_{pt-1}) + \tilde{u}_{pt}, \tag{2.2.73}$$

where $\tilde{\mathbf{R}}_{pt}$ is the return on the portfolio p in month t (measured in percentage per month), β_{pt-1} is the average of the estimated β coefficients of the stocks in the pth portfolio at the beginning of the month for which the return is calculated, β^2_{pt-1} is the squared β_{pt-1} coefficient, and $S(e_{pt-1})$ is the average of the estimated unsystematic risk e_{pt-1} of the securities in portfolio p at the beginning of the month t, where $\tilde{u}_{pt}$ is a random error term. The reason that Fama and MacBeth apply the estimated β coefficients or various portfolios is to avoid the "errors-in-variables" problem. They form 20 portfolios on the basis of ranked values of betas for individual stocks. In addition, since the betas may be subject to time-varying mean reversion over different time periods, they are recomputed for each individual stock in the subsequent time periods. Thus, the betas are estimated with a "rolling" method over the time-series observations. Then, they apply a third nonoverlapping subperiod to obtain the monthly returns on portfolios and to estimate the cross-sectional regressions shown as Eq. (2.2.73). Hence, a time series of estimates for $\tilde{\gamma}_{1t}$, $\tilde{\gamma}_{2t}$ and $\tilde{\gamma}_{3t}$ is constructed.

As stated, the coefficients $E(\tilde{\gamma}_{2t})$ and $E(\tilde{\gamma}_{3t})$ should both be zero and $E(\tilde{\gamma}_{1t})$ should be positive from the theoretical perspective of CAPM. While the estimated coefficients of $\tilde{\gamma}_{2t}$ and $\tilde{\gamma}_{3t}$ fluctuate over different subperiods, Fama and MacBeth (1973) found that the values of $\tilde{\gamma}_{2t}$ and $\tilde{\gamma}_{3t}$ are not significantly different from zero for the entire period, where $\tilde{\gamma}_{1t}$ across all months is positive and significant.

For the seasonality issue, Tinic and West (1986) also consider the second-pass regressions on the seasonal dummies denoted as binary variables from February to December for the year such as

$$\bar{\gamma}_{jt} = \beta_1 + \sum_{i=2}^{12} \beta_i D_i + \bar{e}_{jt},$$

where $\bar{\gamma}_{jt}$ is the average factor premiums estimated from Eq. (2.2.73), $j = 0, \ldots, 3$.

Tinic and West (1986) expand the time horizon of stock returns (and hence portfolios) from January 1935 to December 1982. They apply the same two-pass regression method as in Fama and MacBeth (1973). In particular, they examine the average of estimated coefficients in the month of January and in the remaining months of the year, and their movements over all the months for different subperiods. For the above Eq. (2.2.73), Tinic and West apply two weighted indices to examine the possible impacts from different choices of representatives of the market portfolio. Their findings indicate that the seasonality such as the month of January has a nonignorable impact on the risk premiums across all subperiods they sampled. In order to consider the possible claim on the cause of the January effect being due to a small-firm effect, the study also includes the sizes of firms as an additional explanatory variable for Eq. (2.2.73). These nonstationary seasonals are also present even when different market indices are applied. In addition, the coefficients for nonlinearity and residual variance $\tilde{\gamma}_{2t}$, and $\tilde{\gamma}_{3t}$ are also significant, respectively. However, the findings are based on the conventional t-statistics. The econometric analysis such as that given by Shanken (1992) shows that the conventional two-pass regressions are subject to the errors-in-variable problems where the estimated coefficients could be of less asymptotic variance and hence the test statistics can be overvalued and become statistically significant too often. On the other hand, the heteroskedasticity (conditional or unconditional) in the data and its impact on the statistics of estimated coefficients is not considered.

2.2.2.2 *Time-Varying Coefficients in CAPM*

An example of the CAPM with time-varying covariances can be found in Bollerslev et al. (1988). In particular, their work develops a multivariate GARCH for the conditional variance of each asset return with respect to a market portfolio. Hence, the betas in the CAPM will be time-varying and forecastable.

The CAPM with time-varying covariances (Bollerslev et al. 1988): let $\mathbf{r}_t$ represent the vector of excess returns in the market during period t and let μ_t and $\mathbf{H}_t$ be the conditional mean vector and conditional variance matrix of these excess returns given the information available at time $t-1$. Let $\mathbf{w}_{t-1}$ be the vector of value weights at the end of the previous period and hence the market excess return is defined as $r_{m_t} = \mathbf{r}_t'\mathbf{w}_{t-1}$. Thus, the vector of covariances (of these excess returns) with the market is given as $\mathbf{H}_t\mathbf{w}_{t-1}$ so that the CAPM will be expressed as

$$\mu_t = \delta \mathbf{H}_t \mathbf{w}_{t-1},$$

where δ is a scalar which can be an aggregate measure of relative risk aversion in equilibrium. Notice that the conditional variance of the market excess return is shown as $\sigma^2_{m_t} = \mathbf{w}'_{t-1}\mathbf{H}_t\mathbf{w}_{t-1}$, where the conditional mean is $\mu_{m_t} = \mathbf{w}'_{t-1}\mu_t$ and $\mu_{m_t} = \delta\,\sigma^2_{m_t}$. Denoting $\beta_t = \mathbf{H}_t\mathbf{w}_{t-1}/\sigma^2_{m_t}$ gives the "beta" expression of the CAPM such that

$$\mu_t = \beta_t\,\mu_{m_t}$$

Bollerslev et al. (1988) introduce the multivariate GARCH in mean model for the above setting. Explicitly, for $\mathbf{r}_t$ as an $n \times 1$ vector of excess returns, the conditional mean and conditional variance equations can be expressed as

$$\begin{aligned} \mathbf{r}_t &= \mathbf{b} + \delta \mathbf{H}_t \mathbf{w}_{t-1} + \mathbf{e}_t, \\ \text{vech}(\mathbf{H}_t) &= \mathbf{C} + \sum_{i=1}^{q} \mathbf{A}_i \text{vech}(\mathbf{e}_t\mathbf{e}_t') + \sum_{j=1}^{p} \mathbf{B}_j \text{vech}(\mathbf{H}_{t-j}), \qquad (2.2.74) \\ \mathbf{e}_t|\psi_{t-1} &\sim N(0, \mathbf{H}_t), \end{aligned}$$

where vech(·) represents the column stacking operator of the lower portion of a symmetric matrix, $\mathbf{b}$ is an $n \times 1$ vector of constants, $\mathbf{e}_t$ is an $n \times 1$ vector of innovations, $\mathbf{C}$ is a $\frac{1}{2}(n(n+1)) \times 1$ vector, and $\mathbf{A}_i$, $i = 1, \ldots, q$, and $\mathbf{B}_j$, $j = 1, \ldots, p$ are $\frac{1}{2}(n(n+1)) \times \frac{1}{2}(n(n+1))$ matrices. The conditional log likelihood function for the above system of equations can be shown as

$$L_t(\Theta) = -\frac{n}{2}\log(2\pi) - \frac{1}{2}\log|\mathbf{H}_t(\Theta)| - \frac{1}{2}\mathbf{e}_t'(\Theta)'\mathbf{H}_t^{-1}(\Theta)\mathbf{e}_t(\Theta),$$

where $\Theta' = \left(\mathbf{b}', \delta, \mathbf{C}', \text{vec}(\mathbf{A}_1)', \ldots, \text{vec}(\mathbf{A}_q)', \text{vec}(\mathbf{B}_1)', \ldots, \text{vec}(\mathbf{B}_p)'\right)$ is an $m \times 1$ vector of parameters. And hence, given the time series observations at $t = 1, \ldots, T$, the log likelihood function can be written as

$$L(\Theta) = \sum_{t=1}^{T} L_t(\Theta).$$

Since the number of parameters in the above general form of multivariate GARCH is relatively large, Bollerslev et al. (1988) simplify the setting by assuming that $p = q = 1$, and imposing the diagonality on the matrices $\mathbf{A}_1$ and $\mathbf{B}_1$. Thus, the simplified multivariate GARCH in the mean model becomes

$$\begin{aligned} \mathbf{r}_{it} &= \mathbf{b}_i + \delta \sum_j \mathbf{w}_{jt} \widetilde{h}_{ijt} + \epsilon_{it}, \\ \widetilde{h}_{ijt} &= \gamma_{ij} + \alpha_{ij}\epsilon_{it-1}\epsilon_{jt-1} + \beta_{ij}\widetilde{h}_{ijt-1}, \quad i,j = 1, \dots, n, \\ \mathbf{e}_t | \psi_{t-1} &\sim N(0, \mathbf{H}_t), \end{aligned} \tag{2.2.75}$$

The return series included in their empirical studies for $\mathbf{r}_t$ is constructed of six-month Treasury bills, 20-year Treasury bonds, and stocks. Hence, the setting in Eq. (2.2.73) or (2.2.74) is a trivariate system. The data are quarterly percentage returns from the first quarter of 1959 to the second quarter of 1984, as a total of 102 observations. The three-month Treasury bill rate is chosen as a representative risk-free rate. Two return series are collected for applications of the above setting, one is the Standard and Poor's 500 index series, and the other is the New York Stock Exchange value-weighted equity returns.

The empirical findings show that (1) although theoretical models suggest that no intercepts are needed, the estimated coefficients in the conditional mean equation show that these intercepts are still important for risk premiums, especially as they are negative in sign; (2) the "beta"s are time-varying and forecastable; (3) the conditional variance and covariances are time-varying and significant for determining risk premiums; (4) the conditional covariance matrix of the asset returns is strongly autoregressive; (5) risk premiums are better represented by covariances with the implied market than by their own variances; (6) information in addition to past innovations of asset returns such as lagged excess holding yields and innovations in consumption can be explanatory variables for the risk premiums and asset returns.

However, although the findings confirm the conjecture that the time-varying moments of these asset returns are important in determining the risk premiums of asset returns, the approximations for the time-varying variances and covariances are based on ad hoc models for both the time-series dynamics and inclusion of essential variables in model specifications (especially for the conditional covariances). As the authors admit that

GARCH specification does not arise directly from any economic theory, the fact is that multivariate GARCH is (an extension) of the traditional autoregressive moving-average time-series analogue, which is aimed at constructing the parsimonious approximation to the heteroskedasticity of economic time series. Furthermore, the study is based on the CAPM and under the assumption that correct (dynamic) specification for asset returns is granted. More explicitly, the specification of the so-called conditional mean equation assumes that the conditional CAPM holds where all essential variables are correctly observed and identified.

2.2.2.3 Further Discussions on the Estimation of Beta-Pricing Models

Shanken (1992) provides additional research on the econometric view of the two-pass regression methods for multifactor models, especially on the "errors-in-variables" problem. Again, the analysis is based on the correct specification of the factor structure of asset returns, where the factor-portfolio returns (in addition to the common factors) are also included. As such, no discussions of model search or model selection prior to the verifications on risk premiums are considered. Therefore, the verification of the essentiality of factors depends critically on the statistical significance of factor premiums per se. In other words, the study considers that under the correct specification of factor structure, the asymptotic properties and distributions for the statistics of generalized two-pass regressions can be obtained when the time-series horizon $T \to \infty$, especially under the assumption of the correct specification of factor premiums (in terms of "betas"). In addition, the study also provides asymptotic analysis for the second-pass regressions when the number of cross-sectional observations $n \to \infty$.

As denoted in Tinic and West (1986), the inclusions of different variables (such as seasonality, nonlinearity, and different market index returns) may cause the results of empirical research to vary. Even though the findings of Tinic and West (1986) are subject to concerns of econometric issues, the choices of variables or model selection over the presumed variables or factors/proxies should be considered in advance, as a common practice of exploratory data analysis. The emphasis of empirical asset pricing models should be on identifying the essential variables for asset returns, prior to the studies in verifying the factor premiums. The setting of Shanken's studies is denoted as

$$
\begin{aligned}
E[\mathbf{R}] &= [l_n, B]\Gamma \\
\mathbf{R}_t &= a + BF_t + \underline{\epsilon}_t, t = 1, \ldots, T
\end{aligned}
\tag{2.2.76}
$$

where l_n is an $n \times 1$ vector of ones, F_t is a $k \times 1$ vector of factors, F_{1t} is a $k_1 \times 1$ vector of general factors, and F_{2t} is a $k_2 \times 1$ vector of factors that are portfolio returns, where $k = k_1 + k_2$, $\underline{\epsilon}_t$ is an $n \times 1$ vector of idiosyncratic risk and factor loadings are nonstochastic such that

$$B_{n\times k} = [B_1,\ B_2],$$
$$F_t = (F'_{1t},\ F'_{2t})',$$

and Γ is a $(k+1) \times 1$ vector of factor premiums such as

$$\Gamma = (\gamma_0,\ \gamma'_1,\ \gamma'_2)',$$

which implies that the multifactor asset pricing model holds where the risk premiums of asset returns are of a linear function with factor risk premiums versus the associated betas.

Now if the factor portfolios also satisfy the linear risk-return relation such that the factor portfolio returns

$$\gamma_2 = E(F_2) - \gamma_0 l_{k_2}, \tag{2.2.77}$$

take the average of Eq. (2.2.76) over time and hence

$$\overline{R} = a + B_1\overline{F}_1 + B_2\overline{F}_2 + \overline{\epsilon},$$

and considering that $E[\mathbf{R}] = a + B_1E(F_1) + B_2E(F_2)$ so that $a = \underline{E}[\mathbf{R}] - B_1E(F_1) - B_2E(F_2)$, then substituting a into the above equation of $\overline{R}$, and applying the equality that $E[\mathbf{R}] = \gamma_0 + B_1\gamma_1 + B_2\gamma_2$, it is feasible to have

$$\overline{\mathbf{R}} = [l_n,\ B]\overline{\Gamma} + \overline{\epsilon}, \tag{2.2.78}$$

where

$$\overline{\Gamma} = (\gamma_0,\ \overline{\gamma}'_1,\ \overline{\gamma}'_2)',$$
$$\overline{\gamma}_1 = \gamma_1 + \overline{F}_1 - E(F_1),$$
$$\overline{\gamma}_2 = \gamma_2 + \overline{F}_2 - E(F_2) = \overline{F}_2 - \gamma_0 l_{k_2},$$

which implies that, given the correct specifications of factor structure and factor premiums and following the weak law of large numbers when $T \to \infty$, these parameters $\overline{\gamma}_1$ and $\overline{\gamma}_2$ will converge to γ_1 and γ_2 since the mean deviations such as $\overline{F}_1 - E(F_1)$ and $\overline{F}_2 - E(F_2)$ will converge to $o_p(1)$.

Shanken generalizes the two-pass regression approach of Fama and MacBeth (1973) and Black et al. (1972) to estimate the betas. In particular, Fama and MacBeth apply a series of cross-sectional regressions based on the "rolling" betas (of subperiods), while Black, Jensen, and Scholes use a single cross-sectional regression on the betas estimated from the entire time series of the given data. Based on Eqs. (2.2.76) and (2.2.77), it is feasible to write the system of equations as

$$\begin{aligned} E[\mathbf{R}] - B_2 E(F_2) &= E[\mathbf{R}] - B_2(\gamma_2 + \gamma_1 l_{k_2}) \\ &= (\gamma_0 + B_1\gamma_1 + B_2\gamma_2) - B_2(\gamma_2 + \gamma_1 l_{k_2}) \\ &= \gamma_0(l_n - B_2 l_{k_2}) + B_1\gamma_1 \\ &= X\Gamma_{01}, \end{aligned} \tag{2.2.79}$$

where X is an $n \times (k_1 + 1)$ matrix such that

$$X = [l_n - B_2 l_{k_2},\ B_1],$$

and Γ_{01} is a $k_1 \times 1$ vector of factor premiums, and

$$\Gamma_{01} = (\gamma_0,\ \gamma_1')'.$$

The typical two-pass regression method (to estimate Γ_{01}) is to replace the B_1 and B_2 with their estimates as $\hat{B}_1$ and $\hat{B}_2$ (from time-series regressions), respectively, and then regress $\overline{\mathbf{R}} - \hat{B}_2\overline{F}_2$ on the above matrix X to obtain the estimate for Γ_{01}. The estimate for γ_2 can be obtained as $\overline{F}_2 - \hat{\gamma}_0 l_{k_2}$ from cross-sectional regression. Instead of the ordinary least squares, the weighted least squares or generalized least squares can be applied to the second-pass regression such that

$$\hat{\Gamma}_{01} = \hat{A}[\overline{\mathbf{R}} - \hat{B}_2\overline{F}_2], \tag{2.2.80}$$

where $\hat{A}\hat{X} = I_{k_1+1}$ for some random $(k_1 + 1) \times n$ matrix $\hat{A}$, especially when $\hat{A} = \left(\hat{X}'\hat{X}\right)^{-1} \hat{X}'$ for the ordinary least squares, and $\hat{A} = \left(\hat{X}'\hat{\Sigma}^{-1}\hat{X}\right)^{-1} \hat{X}'\hat{\Sigma}^{-1}$ if generalized least squares is applied. The weighted least squares is applied when the off-diagonal elements of $\hat{\Sigma}$ are set to zeros.

A major contribution of Shanken's study is on the asymptotic arguments for consistency in estimates (and their asymptotic covariance matrix) of generalized two-pass regressions. In addition, based on the results, the adjusted method for errors-in-variable issues is provided. Claims for consistency in estimates of cross-sectional regressions when the number of assets is large are provided also. To show these results, additional assumptions are imposed. The first assumption is on the time-series properties of idiosyncratic risk where the conditional mean of idiosyncratic risk is an $n \times 1$ vector of zeros, and the conditional covariance matrix (based on the factors) is not time-varying, or so-called conditional homoskedasticity.

However, given the many empirical findings in the financial data, it is unlikely that the idiosyncratic risk is even conditionally homoskedastic. For example, the work of Bollerslev et al. (1988) has already shown that time-varying conditional moments prevail in the financial time series. The issue of conditional heteroskedasticity will have significant impact on the asymptotic properties of the two-pass regressions. The second assumption is for the properties of stochastic process $\{F_t\}_{t=1,\ldots,T}$. Yet, no memory conditions of the stochastic process are considered. In particular, the following lemma assumes that the factor process can possibly be jointly normally distributed and independent over time.

Assumption (ID) for idiosyncratic risk: the vector ϵ_t is i.i.d. distributed over time, and in addition,

$$E(\epsilon_t | F) = \underline{\mathbf{0}}_n$$

and

$$\mathrm{Var}(\epsilon_t | F) = \Sigma$$

where Σ is the conditional covariance matrix of ϵ_t with rank n.

Assumption (FF) for the stochastic process $\{F_t\}_{t=1,\ldots,T}$: the $k \times 1$ vector of factors $\{F_t\}_{t=1,\ldots,T}$ is generated by a stationary process such that the first and second sample moments converge in probability to the finite true moments as $T \to \infty$. $\overline{F}_t$ is asymptotically normally distributed.

Lemma for $\sqrt{T}$-consistency of estimators for factor loadings in generalized two-pass procedures: let B_v (and $\hat{B}_v$) be an $nk\times 1$ vector obtained by the vectorization of the matrix B (and $\hat{B}$) which transposes the rows of B (and $\hat{B}$) and stacking up these $k \times 1$ vector across all n assets. Let H be denoted as the random $(n + nk + k) \times 1$ vector as $\left[\overline{\epsilon}', \ (\hat{B}_v - B_v)', \ (\overline{F} - E(F))'\right]'$ and let g be a $k \times 1$ vector of constants. Then, given the above assumptions (ID) and (FF),

(1) $\hat{B}$, $\overline{\epsilon}$, $\overline{F}$ are uncorrelated unconditionally and conditional on F. If ϵ_t is jointly normally distributed conditional on F, then $\hat{B}$, $\overline{\epsilon}$, and $\hat{\Sigma}$ are independently conditional on F, where $\overline{\epsilon}$ and $\hat{\Sigma}$ are independent of $\overline{F}$. If F_t is jointly normally distributed independently over time, then $\hat{B}$ and $\overline{F}$ are also independent.
(2) $\sqrt{T}H$ converges in distribution to a normal distribution with mean zero and a black diagonal covariance matrix with blocks as $\left(\Sigma, \ \Sigma \otimes \Sigma_F^{-1}, \ \Sigma_F\right)$, as $T \to \infty$.
(3) $\sqrt{T}\left(\hat{B} - B\right)g$ converges in distribution to a normal distribution with mean zero and covariance matrix as $\left(g'\Sigma_F^{-1}g\right)\Sigma$, when $T \to \infty$.

Notice that the above lemma establishes the root-T convergence for the first-pass regression of the two-pass procedures under the assumptions such as (1) the number of factors k is correctly identified and included in the model(s); (2) all factors (including the factor portfolios) are identified or known, where correct specification of factor premiums is given; and (3) the idiosyncratic risk (where conditional homoskedasticity is assumed) does not contain any omitted systematic factor. In other words, there's no discussion on the possible omitted factors in the presumed asset pricing models. In addition, the asymptotic arguments assume that the number of asset returns n is finite, and the time-series horizon $T \to \infty$.[4]

Following the above lemma, and denoting the vector $\Gamma_{12} = (\gamma_1', \gamma_2')'$, Shanken provides the asymptotic arguments on the second-pass estimators. In particular, the bias of asymptotic covariance matrix (denoted as c in the following theorem) due to the errors-in-variables (EIV) issue is shown in the asymptotic arguments. Notice that since

$$\overline{\mathbf{R}} - B_2\overline{F}_2 = X\overline{\Gamma}_{01} + \overline{\epsilon},$$

and denoting $\hat{X} = [l_n - \hat{B}_2 l_{k_2}, \hat{B}_1]$, it can be shown that

$$\overline{\mathbf{R}} - \hat{B}_2 \overline{F}_2 = \hat{X}\overline{\Gamma}_{01} + [\overline{\epsilon} - U\overline{\Gamma}_{12}],$$

where $U = \hat{B} - B$, $\overline{\Gamma}_{01} = [\gamma_0, \overline{\gamma}_1]$, and $\overline{\Gamma}_{12} = [\overline{\gamma}_1', \overline{\gamma}_2']'$, and $\overline{\gamma}_1$ and $\overline{\gamma}_2$ are defined in Eq. (2.2.78). It is apparent that the second part of the above equation contains the measurement errors of betas. By applying the central limit theorem (as $T \to \infty$) on $\overline{\epsilon} - U\overline{\Gamma}_{12}$, it is feasible to obtain the following convergence in distribution for statistics of factor premiums.

Theorem for the asymptotic distribution of the second-pass estimators (ordinary least squares (OLS), generalized least squares (GLS), or weighted least squares (WLS)) of factor premiums: let $\hat{\Gamma}_{01} = \hat{A}\left[\overline{\mathbf{R}} - \hat{B}_2\overline{F}_2\right]$ with $\hat{A}\hat{X} = I_{k_1+1}$ and $\underset{T\to\infty}{\text{plim}}\hat{A} = A$. Let $\hat{\gamma}_2 = \hat{F}_2 - \hat{\gamma}_0 l_{k_2}$. Given the above assumptions (ID) and (FF), it can be shown that as $T \to \infty$,

(1) $\hat{\Gamma}$ is a T-consistent estimator for factor premium Γ.

(2) $\sqrt{T}\left(\hat{\Gamma} - \overline{\Gamma}\right)$ converges in distribution to a normal distribution with mean zero and a $(k+1) \times (k+1)$ covariance matrix as $(1 + \mathbf{c}^\star)\,\Omega$ where $\mathbf{c}^\star = \Gamma_{12}'\Sigma_F^{-1}\Gamma_{12}$, and the upper left block of Ω (as a $(k_1+1)\times(k_1+1)$ matrix) equals $A\Sigma A'$. And let ν be the first column of this block and ν_o be the first element of ν. The lower right block of Ω (as $k_2 \times k_2$ matrix) equals $\nu_o l_{k_2} l_{k_2}'$ and the upper right block is a $(k_1+1) \times k_2$ matrix with each column equal to $-\nu$.

(3) $\sqrt{T}\left(\hat{\Gamma} - \Gamma\right)$ converges in distribution, as $T \to \infty$, to a normal distribution with mean zero and $(k+1)\times(k+1)$ covariance matrix $(1 + \mathbf{c}^\star)\Omega + \Sigma_F^*$, where Σ_F^* is the bordered version of Σ_F where the top row and left column are zeros, with Σ_F as in the lower right block such that

$$\Sigma_F^* = \begin{bmatrix} 0 & 0 \\ 0 & \Sigma_F \end{bmatrix}.$$

Accordingly, $\mathbf{c}^\star$ is the asymptotic adjustment for the EIV issue, and the $\mathbf{c}^\star\Omega$ is the EIV component of variance. In other words, the conventional two-pass regressions which under-estimate the asymptotic variance may make the test statistics overvalued and hence reject the null hypotheses too often.

In addition, the above theorem is based on the asymptotic arguments as $T \to \infty$. Notice that the result of (2) is for the weak convergence of $\hat{\Gamma} - \overline{\Gamma}$, not $\hat{\Gamma} - \Gamma$.

Subsequently, Shanken (1992) shows that the traditional time-series approach in estimating the factor premiums which ignores the possible EIV problem will not accurately provide the estimates for factor-related variation. The traditional time-series approach for factor premiums is to perform cross-sectional regressions of $\mathbf{R}_t - \hat{B}_2 F_{2t}$ on $\hat{X}$ each period, where $\hat{X} = [l_n - \hat{B}_2 l_{k_2}, \hat{B}_1]$. And hence the procedure generates a time series of estimates for Γ_{01}. Taking the mean of these estimates will produce the cross-sectional regression estimate $\hat{\Gamma}_{01}$ for factor premiums. Shanken (1992) shows that an adjustment method is needed for the correct assessment of the asymptotic covariance matrix of estimated factor premiums.

Theorem of the asymptotic covariance matrix of factor premiums with the traditional time-series approach: let $\hat{\Gamma}_{01t} = \hat{A}[\mathbf{R}_t - \hat{B}_2 F_{2t}]$, $t = 1, \ldots, T$, where $\hat{A}\hat{X} = I_{k_1+1}$, and let $\underset{T\to\infty}{\text{plim}} \hat{A} = A$. Let $\hat{\gamma}_{2t} = F_{2t} - \hat{\gamma}_{0t} l_{k_2}$. Then, given the above assumptions on idiosyncratic risk and stochastic process $\{F_t\}_{t=1,\ldots,T}$, the sample covariance matrix $\hat{W}$ of the $\hat{\Gamma}_t$ series converge in probability to $W \equiv \Omega + \Sigma_F^*$ as $T \to \infty$. And hence a T-consistent estimator for the asymptotic covariance matrix is given as

$$(1 + \hat{c}) \left[\hat{W} - \hat{\Sigma}_F^* \right] + \hat{\Sigma}_F^*,$$

where $\hat{c} = \hat{\Gamma}_{12}' \hat{\Sigma}_F^{*-1} \hat{\Gamma}_{12}$, and $\hat{\Sigma}_F^*$ is an autocorrelation-consistent estimator of Σ_F^*. In other words, the correction for the understated asymptotic covariance matrix for factor premiums can be obtained by using the sample statistics and sample covariance matrix.

For additional analyses, Shanken (1992) also provides the n-consistent estimator for $\overline{\Gamma}$ in Eq. (2.2.78) as $n \to \infty$, while time-series horizon T is fixed. In short, the analysis provides the consistency in the cross-sectional estimators for the (average) factor premiums when the number of cross-sectional asset returns grows large. The results are based on the following lemma.

Lemma for expectations (conditional on F) of the regressor matrix in second-pass regression: given the above assumption (ID), it is feasible to show that

$$E\left(\hat{X}'\hat{X}\right) = X'X + qM'\hat{\Sigma}_F^{-1}M,$$

and

$$E\left[\hat{X}'\left(\overline{\mathbf{R}} - \hat{B}_2\overline{F}_2\right)\right] = \left(X'X\right)\overline{\Gamma}_{01} - qM'\hat{\Sigma}_F^{-1}\overline{F}_2^*,$$

where

$$q \equiv \mathrm{tr}(\Sigma)/(T-1),$$

$\overline{F}_2^*$ is a $k \times 1$ vector of k_1 zeros followed by $\overline{F}_2$, M is a $k \times (k_1 + 1)$ matrix with $-l_{k_2}$ in the lower left corner, l_{k_1} is in the upper right corner with zeroes elsewhere, and $\mathrm{tr}(\Sigma)$ represents the trace of the matrix Σ. Given this lemma, it is shown that the n-consistent estimator for factor premiums $\overline{\Gamma}_{01}$ is available when $n \to \infty$.

Theorem for the cross-sectional n-consistent estimator for factor premiums: provided with the assumption (ID), and supposing that there exists sufficiently weak cross-sectional dependence between residual disturbances, then

$$\left[\hat{X}'\hat{X} - \hat{q}M'\hat{\Sigma}_F^{-1}M\right]^{-1}\left[\hat{X}'\left(\overline{\mathbf{R}} - \hat{B}_2\overline{F}_2\right) + \hat{q}M'\hat{\Sigma}_F^{-1}\overline{F}_2^*\right]$$

is a consistent estimator for $\overline{\Gamma}_{01}$, where $\hat{q} = \mathrm{tr}(\hat{\Sigma})/(T-1)$.

From the above analyses, it is easy to see that these arguments are based on correct specifications of factor structure and factor premiums. For instance, the weak cross-sectional dependence is assumed on the residual disturbances (of cross-sectional regressions) in the above theorem. In other words, there is no missing systematic pricing factor in the factor structure (and hence on the projections for factor premiums) that may cause significant pricing errors. All the verifications on factor premiums, henceforth, are to see if the factors or proxies are properly priced in statistical inferences. That is, whether the factor premiums explain the expected returns for the assets cross-sectionally or not.

The logics seems somewhat tautological to each other. Presumably, if one assumes that a factor structure is already correct a priori, it is strange that one still has to ask to see if these factors (with the betas) are properly pricing the expected returns and risk premiums of assets accordingly. The question may become confusing and complicated when the empirical tests for factor premiums (in the second-pass regressions of cross-sectional asset returns) actually show statistical insignificance for some presumed/identified factors. Is this pricing error due to incorrect specification of factor structure or measurement errors? Is it due to the sampling errors (such as data snooping) when the data are collected? Or, is it due to the incorrect specification of factor premiums which may be subject to (say) theoretical flaws such as misspecified functional form?

The issue is, if one knows the factor structure presumed is correct already, these factors will be priced (at least) theoretically. Theoretical asset pricing models associate these parameters of interest (on time-series or cross-sectional regressions) with additional restrictions. Unfortunately, it is a luxury for the empirical researcher to know in advance whether the factor structure is indeed correctly specified or not.

Further extensions on the tests for empirical asset pricing models can be found in Lewellen et al. (2010) where proxies are considered in these models. With the factor structure assumed where correct specification of risk premiums is prescribed, it is likely that if the proxies are correlated with the returns only through the common variation of the (true) factors where the proxies are only slightly correlated with the factors, the proxies may perfectly explain the cross-section of expected returns. Hence, the empirical studies that apply the R^2 for verifications of asset pricing models could be overstating things. Notice that the arguments are based on the assumption that there exists a factor structure which explains the expected returns. Hence, there is no missing systematic factor in the discussions. For instance, let $\mathbf{R}$ be an $n \times 1$ vector of excess returns for n assets. And let F be a $k \times 1$ vector of k factors of the following factor structure which perfectly explains expected returns such that

$$\mathbf{R} = BF + e,$$

with an $n \times k$ matrix of factor loadings $B = \text{Cov}(\mathbf{R}, F)\text{Var}(F)^{-1}$, and the expected returns μ_R of these assets are expressed as

$$\mu_R = B\mu_k,$$

where μ_k represents the factor premiums. In addition, let P represent the $k \times 1$ vector of proxies for factors. Suppose the model with proxies is applied to explain asset returns so that the factor loadings C for these proxies are shown as $C = \text{Cov}(R, P)\text{Var}(P)^{-1}$, and the cross-sectional regression (for expected returns) is shown as

$$\mu_R = zl + C\lambda + \nu,$$

where λ represents the vector of regression slopes (or so-called factor premiums). The coefficient z should be close to zero and λ will be nonzero according to theory. The pricing error ν should be negligible as a random noise.

Lewellen et al. (2010) shows that if F and P have the same number of factors where Cov(F, P) is nonsingular, then P will perfectly explain the cross-section of expected returns. It is easy to see that $C = \text{Cov}(R, P)\text{Var}(P)^{-1} = B\text{Cov}(F, P)\text{Var}(P)^{-1}$. Define the matrix $Q = \text{Cov}(F, P)\text{Var}(P)^{-1}$, which shows that $C = BQ$. Hence, $\mu_R = C\lambda$, where $\lambda = Q^{-1}\mu_F$. In other words, even if the factors F and proxies P are only slightly related where $\text{Cov}(F, P) \neq 0$, the factor loadings of these proxies (and their associated factor premiums) will form a good model for explaining the expected returns of assets.

In short, if both the factor structure and expected returns (or risk premiums) of these assets when based on the "betas" are correctly specified, even though the proxies applied for factors are not strongly related to the "true" factors, the theoretical second-pass regressions for cross-sectional expected returns when using the betas of these proxies will have a relatively high R^2, if the proxies are orthogonal to the idiosyncratic risk in the factor structure of asset returns. In other words, when the factor structure in asset returns is correctly identified, using any proxies (for factors) that are only barely relevant to the "true" factors may still be a good model for risk premiums in the usual sense where R^2 is relatively high, if these proxies are orthogonal to the idiosyncratic risk in asset returns.

Although the emphasis of Lewellen et al. (2010) is to consider that the high R^2 in cross-sectional (second-pass) regression is not a good hurdle for certifying a good model, it suffices to show that the traditional search for empirical asset pricing models which starts with the a priori assumption of a correct factor structure is not necessarily flawless. These claims of empirical evidence provided are all based on the assumption (and the correctness) of the factor structure in asset returns. Accordingly, model specification tests for asset returns and factor premiums also rely on the validity of these assumed factor structures. Hence, identification of the existence of a factor structure in asset returns or proper approximations on the asset returns with robust reduction of dimensionality should precede the statistical verification on theoretical works of so-called factor premiums and risk premiums of asset returns.

2.3 Recent Development of Tests for the Number of Factors

Earlier studies in approximate factor structure of asset returns can be found in the literature, such as Connor and Korajczyk (1993). The derived statistical inferences are useful to identify the factor structure by using the cross-sectional arguments of the mean square of the (presumed) idiosyncratic risk. Other studies such as Onatski (2009, 2010) extend the analysis to include the dynamic factor structure where time-series dependence is also considered in the structure.

However, as denoted in many empirical studies, the paradigm in testing the number of factors, although well-suited to the rigors of asymptotic arguments, the lack of economic interpretation, or empirical practicality nonetheless is the main shortcoming of this tread of analyses in asset pricing models. More specifically, the approach to identify the factor structure should focus more on the direction in model searching where testing additional proxies for the determinants of asset returns is of meaningful interest. In other words, instead of merely considering the factor structure as a genuine data generating mechanism and the testing for the number of factors, these analyses should pave the way toward deciding whether certain (economic) variables are needed to explain the asset returns or not. After all, the emphasis from empirical asset pricing models is to identify a plausible mechanism that would help to explain and track the asset returns.

2.3.1 Connor and Korajczyk's Test

Connor and Korajczyk's test is based on the assessment of a significant decrease of the cross-sectional mean square of idiosyncratic risk if an additional factor is introduced. That is, if the correct number of factors is k, then increasing the number of factors to $k + 1$ will not show some significant decrease of the cross-sectional mean square of idiosyncratic risk. Their setting can be shown as follows:

$$\begin{aligned} r_t &= \underline{\alpha} + Bf_t + \epsilon_t, \\ E[\epsilon_t | f_t] &= \underline{0}, \end{aligned} \tag{2.3.1}$$

where r_t is an $n \times 1$ vector of n rates of return at time t, $\underline{\alpha}$ is an $n \times 1$ vector of intercepts, B is an $n \times k$ matrix of factor loadings, f_t is a $k \times 1$ vector of presumed factors, and ϵ_t is an $n \times 1$ vector of n idiosyncratic risk that can be cross-sectionally correlated at time t.

In addition, $\lim_{n \longrightarrow \infty} \frac{1}{n} B'B = \Xi$, Ξ is nonsingular, $E\left[\epsilon_t \epsilon_t'\right] = V_n$, $\lim_{n \longrightarrow \infty} \frac{1}{n} ||V_n|| \leq \gamma < \infty$, where V_n matrix is not necessary a diagonal matrix, and $||.||$ is the matrix norm that is based on the largest eigienvalue of the matrix.[5]

For the cross-sectional dependence of idiosyncratic risk $\{\epsilon_{it}\}_{i=1,2,\ldots,\infty}$, Connor and Korajczyk assume an α mixing condition such that for $\alpha(m) = \sup_n \alpha\left(\mathscr{F}^n_{-\infty}, \mathscr{F}^{\infty}_{n+m}\right)$, where $\alpha\left(\mathscr{F}^n_{-\infty}, \mathscr{F}^{\infty}_{n+m}\right) = \sup_{\left\{G \in \mathscr{F}^n_{-\infty}, H \in \mathscr{F}^{\infty}_{n+m}\right\}} |P(G \cap H) - P(G)P(H)|$, where $\mathscr{F}^n_{-\infty}$, and $\mathscr{F}^{\infty}_{n+m}$ represent the σ-fields of idiosyncratic risk generated by $(\epsilon_{-\infty,t}, \ldots, \epsilon_{n,t})$ and $(\epsilon_{n+m,t}, \ldots, \epsilon_{\infty,t})$ respectively and that are separated by m cross-sectional idiosyncratic risk,[6]

$$\alpha(m) = O(m^{-\lambda}), \tag{2.3.2}$$

where $\lambda > 2$, under the assumption that k is the number of factors for Eq. (2.3.1).

Notice that the strong mixing condition here concerns contemporaneous cross-sectional dependence only. Their setting actually assumes inter-temporally independent and identically distributed idiosyncratic risk over different time horizons when comparing the mean squares (over all other dates) of idiosyncratic risk on k-presumed factors versus $(k+1)$-factor setting.

In other words, their setting allows cross-sectional dependence when satisfying the strong mixing condition on any date to establish the conditions of approximate factor structure. However, the possible dependence over time-series observations is not considered. Nor is the heteroskedasticity (conditional or unconditional) considered in the setting.

Accordingly, with the assumed mixing conditions for cross-sectional dependence of idiosyncratic risk, Connor and Korajczyk show that (1) if the moment condition such as

$$E[|\epsilon_{it}|^{2(1+\delta)}]_{i=1,2,\ldots,\infty} < \infty,$$

for all i and for some $\delta > \frac{2}{\lambda - 2}$, then the eigenvalues of V_n are bounded when $n \longrightarrow \infty$.

In other words, the structure as in (2.3.1) will satisfy the conditions of approximate factor structure as if the correct number of factors is equal to k. (2) The weak law of large numbers will hold for the asymptotic variance σ_ϵ such that $\frac{1}{n}\epsilon_t'\epsilon_t \xrightarrow{p} \sigma_\epsilon < \infty$, where $\sigma_\epsilon = \lim_{n\longrightarrow\infty} E[\frac{1}{n}\epsilon_t'\epsilon_t]$.

Now suppose there is a possible pseudo-factor f_t^* in the system of equations (2.3.1), then the equations will be rewritten as

$$r_t = \underline{\alpha} + Bf_t + \beta^* f_t^* + \epsilon_t^*, \tag{2.3.3}$$

where β^* is the $n \times 1$ vector of nonstochastic factor loadings of the pseudo-factor f_t^*. If the pseudo-factor f_t^* is not really essential, it is easy to see that

$$\begin{aligned} \operatorname*{plim}_{n\to\infty}\frac{1}{n}\epsilon_t'\epsilon_t &= f_t^{*2}\lim_{n\to\infty}\frac{1}{n}\beta^{*\prime}\beta^* + \operatorname*{plim}_{n\to\infty}\frac{1}{n}\epsilon_t^{*\prime}\epsilon_t^*, \\ &= \operatorname*{plim}_{n\to\infty}\frac{1}{n}\epsilon_t^{*\prime}\epsilon_t^*. \end{aligned} \tag{2.3.4}$$

That is, the pseudo-factor has no additional explanatory power when the number of security returns increases. Then, with $t = 1, 2, \ldots, T$ time-series observations, Connor and Korajczyk consider the inter-temporal statistic

$$\Delta_s^n = \left(\frac{1}{n}\epsilon_{2s-1}'\epsilon_{2s-1}\right) - \left(\frac{1}{n}\epsilon_{2s}^{*\prime}\epsilon_{2s}^*\right), s = 1, 2, \ldots, \frac{T}{2} \tag{2.3.5}$$

That is, the inter-temporal difference between the mean square of idiosyncratic risk with k factors and that of idiosyncratic risk under a $(k+1)$-factor structure.[7]

Notice that Conor and Korajczyk apply the inter-temporal difference on Δ_s^n since the contemporaneous difference $\left(\frac{1}{n}\epsilon_t'\epsilon_t\right) - \left(\frac{1}{n}\epsilon_t^{*\prime}\epsilon_t^*\right) = f_t^{*2}\frac{1}{n}\beta^{*\prime}\beta^*$ will be equal to zero almost uniformly for all t's under the null hypothesis when the k-factor structure is the correct specification.

In addition, the contemporaneous statistic will have a degenerated distribution under the null hypothesis if contemporaneous difference is applied since it is always equal to zero under the null. Thus, from Eq. (2.3.4)

$$\frac{1}{n}\epsilon_{2s-1}'\epsilon_{2s-1} = f_{2s-1}^{*2}\frac{1}{n}\beta^{*\prime}\beta^* + \frac{1}{n}\epsilon_{2s-1}^{*\prime}\epsilon_{2s-1}^* \tag{2.3.6}$$

Under the independent and identically distributed assumption of (say) ϵ_{is} and $\epsilon_{j\tau}$ where $s \neq \tau$ for all $(i,j)_{i,j=1,2,\ldots,n}$, it is easy to see that under the null hypothesis $E[\Delta_s^n | f_{2s-1}^{*2}] = f_{2s-1}^{*2} \left(\frac{1}{n}\beta^{*\prime}\beta^*\right)$ will converge to zero when $n \rightarrow \infty$ if the additional pseudo-factor is not essential over all security returns, while the statistic Δ_s^n will not have a degenerated distribution (asymptotically). On the other hand, if the alternative hypothesis holds, the statistic Δ_s^n will be positive since it will contain a term $f_{2s-1}^{*2} \left(\frac{1}{n}\beta^{*\prime}\beta^*\right) > 0$ when $n \rightarrow \infty$.

Hence, given the strong mixing condition assumed, the statistic $(n^{-1/2}\epsilon_t'\epsilon_t - \sigma_\epsilon)$ will converge in distribution to a normal distribution such that (for all t's) $(n^{-1/2}\epsilon_t'\epsilon_t - \sigma_\epsilon) \xrightarrow{d} N(0, \psi)$ as $n \rightarrow \infty$, where

$$\psi^{a,n} \xrightarrow{p} \psi$$

$$\psi^{a,n} = \text{var}\left(n^{-\frac{1}{2}} \sum_{i=a+1}^{a+n} \epsilon_{it}^2\right)$$

uniformly for all a's, and $0 < \psi < \infty$.[8] It is straightforward to see that

$$\begin{aligned}
\Delta_s^n &= f_{2s-1}^{*2} \frac{1}{n}\beta^{*\prime}\beta^* + \frac{1}{n}\epsilon_{2s-1}^{*\prime}\epsilon_{2s-1}^* - \frac{1}{n}\epsilon_{2s}^{*\prime}\epsilon_{2s}^* \\
&= f_{2s-1}^{*2} \frac{1}{n}\beta^{*\prime}\beta^* + \left(\frac{1}{n}\epsilon_{2s-1}^{*\prime}\epsilon_{2s-1}^* - \sigma_\epsilon\right) - \left(\frac{1}{n}\epsilon_{2s}^{*\prime}\epsilon_{2s}^* - \sigma_\epsilon\right).
\end{aligned}$$

Hence, the statistic Δ_s^n will have its mean equal to zero under the null hypothesis when the correct specification is a k-factor structure where the pseudo-factor is not essential.

Given the convergence in distribution for $(n^{-1/2}\epsilon_t'\epsilon_t - \sigma_\epsilon) \xrightarrow{d} N(0, \psi)$ as $n \rightarrow \infty$, it can be shown that the asymptotic distribution of $n^{-1/2}\Delta_s^n$ will be $N(0, 2\psi)$ since there are two independent $(n^{-1/2}\epsilon_t'\epsilon_t - \sigma_\epsilon)$ components in the statistic. Therefore, the stacked-up vector (across all $\frac{T}{2}$ independent and identically distributed time-series observations) of $\left\{\Delta_s^n\right\}_{s=1,2,\ldots,\frac{T}{2}}$ (denoted as Δ^n) will converge in distribution to a multivariate normal distribution such that

$$\sqrt{n}\Delta^n \xrightarrow{d} N(\underline{0}, 2\psi I) \tag{2.3.7}$$

where I is a $\frac{T}{2} \times \frac{T}{2}$ identity matrix.

In applications, however, it is necessary to estimate the parameter ψ. Given the cross-sectional dependence of $\{\epsilon_{it}\}_{i=1,2,\dots,n}$, the conventional standard deviation is not applicable. Hence, Connor and Korajczyk provide the time-series estimates:

$$\overline{\Delta^n} = \frac{2}{T}\sum_{s=1}^{\frac{T}{2}} \hat{\Delta}_s^n,$$
$$2\widehat{\psi^n} = \frac{\sum_{s=1}^{T/2}\left(\hat{\Delta}_s^n - \overline{\Delta^n}\right)^2}{\left(\frac{T}{2}-1\right)}, \tag{2.3.8}$$

and the statistic $\overline{\Delta^n}\left(2\widehat{\psi^n}\right)^{-1/2}$ will follow the Student t-distribution with $\frac{T}{2}$ degree of freedom.

Notes

1. Since $\mathbf{x}$ is an n-dimensional vector, the moment condition is applied to each element of the vector. The same assumption holds for the price vector $\mathbf{q}$ as well.
2. The time subscript is suppressed for simplicity of expression.
3. The time sub-index is suppressed for simplicity.
4. Later work in Shanken and Zhou (2007) relaxes the assumption of correct specification of factor premiums by introducing a residual or pricing error in the expected returns. However, the analysis is still based on the correct identification of factor structure.
5. In fact, this setting is identical to Chamberlain and Rothschild (1983) and Ingersoll (1984) in approximate factor structure.
6. Notice that the notation "$-\infty$" does not necessarily mean there are negative infinite observations. It only depicts the possible initial observations of cross-sectional idiosyncratic risk that are distant from the present collections.
7. Implicitly, their work assumes that the $\frac{T}{2}$ is an integer already so that the inter-temporal differences are always feasible.
8. This condition is to ensure that asymptotic variance of the cumulative sum of these squared idiosyncratic risks exists and is finite under the null hypothesis.

References

Aldous, D. 1989. *Probability Approximation via the Poisson Clumping Heuristic.* New York: Springer.

Andrews, D.W.K. 1991. Heteroskedasticity and Autocorrelation Consistent Covariance Matrix Estimation. *Econometrica* 59: 817–858.

Back, K. 2010. *Asset Pricing and Portfolio Choice Theory.* Oxford: Oxford University Press.

Black, F., M.C. Jensen, and M. Scholes. 1972. The Capital Asset Pricing Model: Some Empirical Tests. In *Studies in the Theory of Capital Markets*, 79–121. New York: Praeger.

Bollerslev, T., R. Engle, and J. Wooldridge. 1988. A Capital Asset Pricing Model with Time-Varying Covariances. *Journal of Political Economy* 96: 116–131.

Burnside, C. 1994. Hansen-Jagannathan Bound as Classical Tests of Asset-Pricing Models. *Journal of Business and Economic Statistics* 12: 57–79.

Chamberlain, G., and M. Rothschild. 1983. Arbitrage, Factor Structure, and Mean-Variance Analysis on Large Asset Markets. *Econometrica* 51: 1281–1304.

Connor, G., and R. Korajczyk. 1993. A Test for the Number of Factors in an Approximate Factor Model. *Journal of Finance* 48: 1263–1291.

Fama, E.F., and K.R. French. 1993. Common Risk Factors in the Returns on Stocks and Bonds. *Journal of Financial Economics* 25: 23–49.

Fama, E.F., and J.D. MacBeth. 1973. Risk, Return and Equilibrium: Empirical Tests. *Journal of Political Economy* 81: 607–636.

Ferson, W.E., and A.F. Siegel. 2001. The Efficient Use of Conditional Information in Portfolios. *Journal of Finance* 56: 967–982.

Ferson, W.E., and A.F. Siegel. 2003. Stochastic Discount Factor Bounds with Conditioning Information. *Review of Financial Studies* 16: 567–595.

Gallant, A.R., L.P. Hansen, and G. Tauchen. 1990. Using Conditional Moments of Asset Payoffs to Infer the Volatility of Intertemporal Marginal Rate of Substitution. *Journal of Econometrics* 45: 141–179.

Goyal, A., and I. Welch. 2003. Predicting the Equity Premium with Dividend Ratios. *Management Science* 49: 639–654.

Hansen, L.P., and R. Jagannathan. 1991. Implications of Security Market Data for Models of Dynamic Economies. *Journal of Political Economy* 99: 225–262.

Ingersoll, J. 1984. Some Results in the Theory of Arbitrage Pricing. *Journal of Finance* 39: 1021–1039.

Jagannathan, R., and Z. Wang. 1996. The Conditional CAPM and the Cross-Section of Expected Returns. *Journal of Finance* 51: 3–53.

Jagannathan, R., and Z. Wang. 1998. An Asymptotic Theory for Estimating Beta-Pricing Models using Cross-Sectional Regression. *Journal of Finance* 53: 1285–1309.

Jagannathan, R., and Z. Wang. 2002. Empirical Evaluation of Asset-Pricing Models: A Comparison of the SDF and Beta Methods. *Journal of Finance* 57: 2337–2367.
Kan, R., and C. Robotti. 2009. Model Comparison Using Hansen-Jagnnathan Distance. *Review of Financial Studies* 22: 3449–3490.
Kan, R., and G. Zhou. 1999. A Critique of the Stochastic Discount Factor Methodology. *Journal of Finance* 54: 1221–1248.
Kan, R., and G. Zhou. 2006. A New Variance Bound on the Stochastic Discount Factor. *Journal of Business* 79: 941–961.
Lawrenz, J. 2013. Time-Series Properties of the Dividend-Price Ratio with Social Dynamics. *Applied Economics* 45: 569–579.
Lewellen, J., S. Nagel, and J. Shanken. 2010. A Skeptical Appraisal of Asset Pricing Tests. *Journal of Financial Economics* 96: 175–194.
Lo, A.W., and A.C. MacKinlay. 1990. Data Snooping Biases in Tests of Financial Asset Pricing Models. *Review of Financial Studies* 3: 431–467.
Newey, W.K., and K.D. West. 1987. A Simple Positive Semi-Definite Heteroskedasticity and Autocorrelation Consistent Covariance Matrix. *Econometrica* 55: 703–708.
Onatski, A. 2009. Testing Hypotheses About the Number of Factors in Large Factor Models. *Econometrica* 77: 1447–1479.
Onatski, A. 2010. Determining the Number of Factors from Empirical Distribution of Eigenvalues. *The Review of Economics and Statistics* 92: 1004–1016.
Shanken, J. 1992. On the Estimation of Beta-Pricing Models. *Review of Financial Studies* 5: 1–33.
Shanken, J., and G. Zhou. 2007. Estimating and Testing Beta Pricing Models: Alternative Methods and Their Performance in Simulations. *Journal of Financial Economics* 84: 40–86.
Tinic, S.M., and R.R. West. 1986. Risk, Return and Equilibrium: A Revisit. *Journal of Political Economy* 94: 126–147.
Yang, S.S. 1977. General Distribution Theory of the Concomitants of Order Statistics. *Annals of Statistics* 5: 996–1002.

CHAPTER 3

Statistical Inferences with Model Selection Criteria

Deficiency in the empirical applications of asset pricing models leads research toward some model selection criteria to justify the search. Unfortunately, with criteria that either emphasize the forecastability of models or impose a penalty for the increase of dimensionality (or complexity), the search for empirical asset pricing models tends to ignore the necessary role of the identified variables or factors to portrait the systematic and intrinsic commonality for all asset returns. That is to say, the coherence or strength of this systematic and intrinsic commonality in asset returns should be emphasized—in addition to the dimensionality and complexity. (Asymptotic) non-diversifiability, for instance, is an obvious requirement. In addition, almost all of this field of research into model selection of asset returns assumes that there exists a "true" (or correct) factor-pricing model in the data generating mechanism. Although robustness in asymptotic arguments are all provided in these studies, little discussion is provided for the soundness of such an assumption.

Applications of model selection criteria such as Akaike Information Criterion, Bayesian Information Criterion, stochastic complexity, and data description length with application of penalty functions over the number of necessary variables are provided in the econometric/finance literature. However, the emphasis (which should be claimed pervasively) is that these model selection approaches can only identify tentative approximations for asset returns. Specifically, many empirical studies that apply or develop schemes of model search are subject to the limitation of the time period

J.-L. Jeng, *Empirical Asset Pricing Models*,
https://doi.org/10.1007/978-3-319-74192-5_3

selected or the data stream chosen. Justification of asset pricing models requires further caution regarding their role in explainability or tractability. This chapter will cover the discussion on these issues.

3.1 Current Model Selection Criteria and Their Applications in Empirical Asset Pricing Models

According to Lehmann (1990), a statistical model for the issue of interest can be classified into two categories: the empirical model and the explanatory model. The empirical model basically is used as a guide for deciding which may base on the forecasts on what to expect from future observations, while the explanatory model searches for the basic mechanism to achieve understanding. When applying Lehmann's (1990) view on model searching, differences in the purpose of the models will facilitate different schemes for the validation of asset-pricing models in finance.

For empirical finance, obtaining the best-fitted model(s) with various statistical methods is the goal. However, to obtain an explanatory model, ideally the model identification will need to incur detailed information as to where the model should contain elaboration that provides the fittedness not only for some particular phenomena of interest but for the essentiality that may prevail in the related circumstances. For an essential empirical asset pricing model identified or proposed, it should be clear that the model needs to overcome certain challenges on the forecastability (in real time) of the model. Yet, it is equally important that the model should offer some plausibility as to the security returns that may provide a reasonable understanding and exposition according to the well-suited economic/finance theories or to logic explanation.[1]

From that perspective, it is not difficult to see that hasty applications of model selection criteria (or tests) in various asset pricing models for empirical data merely facilitate the preliminary model search for the goal of empirical models. In other words, such kinds of models can perhaps provide a viewpoint for the current data stream or time horizon, but they may fail to represent the essential explanation of the fundamentals for the market's determination of expected rates of return. Although this is not wrong (for anyone) when identifying some tractable models of asset returns in the search for possible predictability versus profitability in investing portfolios, it is not a happy situation to observe the highly sophisticated knowledge on finance literature resulting in the abandonment of logic and no improvement on the challenge.[2]

In addition, as in many practices of model selection for empirical asset pricing models, the conclusion is usually nonrobust for various reasons regardless of whether the purpose is to obtain predictability or explainability. For instance, as pointed out in Hansen (2005), the model (or models) selected should be considered merely as an approximation for the underlying unknown data generating mechanism. The evaluation of these models must refer to their purpose (as discussed in Lehmann 1990) where model uncertainty should be taken into account. Usually, when model selection is considered, the consistency in the selection scheme needs to show that the method(s) will approach the correct data generating mechanism as the sample size increases. In fact, this approach of proving consistency usually assumes the correct model is within the set of models to choose from. For empirical asset pricing models (of security returns), this is really a luxury because the vision of the underlying data generating mechanism for financial data is (at best) only a very fuzzy picture. Although Hansen also emphasizes the inclusion of a semiparametric vision for the discussion of model selection, these concerns over selection in econometric methods meet precisely the requirements in choosing the empirical asset pricing models for security returns, of which the underlying data generating mechanism is evolving over time.

A more conservative screening of the systematic properties of these to-be-identified variables (or proxies) is required for any hypothesized or empirical models on security returns. In other words, the model search for proxies of factors or characteristic variables in empirical asset pricing models needs to verify whether the coherence of the proposed variables is strong enough to preserve the systematic influence among all assets of concern. In other words, one is able to identify some variables of interest that influence asset returns among the various data sets. However, to explain the systematic components of asset returns, these presumed factors must demonstrate that their impacts are pervasive enough to prevail in cross-sectional studies. And, more importantly, the models so far devised in the selection methods can only be a tentative approximation for security returns based on the current stage of available information.

Forecastability in time series is certainly essential for empirical asset pricing models. However, forecastability for these models is only meaningful when the identification of the presumed factors is shown as cross-sectionally persistent among all asset returns where this persistence arises from theoretical interpretation (or as a consequence) based on financial/economic reasoning.

Model selection in empirical asset pricing models is not simply to devise some model selection criteria that include time-series forecastability or a penalty for network complexity or dimensionality. Instead, justification of the essentiality of presumed variables should verify this cross-sectional persistence/unanimity of the variables (or factors) among all asset returns through the development of model selection criteria or specification tests in the model search. In other words, model selection criteria that are simply based on (time-series) forecastability or complexity of models may not suffice to verify the model search for empirical asset pricing models.

The following discussions concern the newly developed model selection criteria that are deliberately focused on the determination of a number of factors in the factor structure model. Specifically, these settings all assume that there exists a factor structure for the variables of interest (in asset pricing models). In other words, the existence of a factor structure is already given so that development for determining the number of factors and statistical inference for the factor structure models can be provided.

3.1.1 *Bai and Ng (2002) Determining the Number of Factors in Approximate Factor Models*

Bai and Ng (2002) assume a general factor structure such as

$$Y_{it} = \lambda_i' F_t^o + e_{it}, \tag{3.1.1}$$

for $i = 1, 2, \ldots, n$ and $t = 1, 2, \ldots, T$, where Y_{it} is the (i, t)-th observation of the dependent variable, and the $r \times 1$ vector of common factors is denoted as F_t with the $r \times 1$ vector of factor loadings as λ_i as the possible impacts on the i-th dependent variable; e_{it} is the idiosyncratic risk. In more compact matrix form, the i-th cross-sectional observation $i = 1, 2, \ldots, n$ can be denoted as

$$\underline{Y}_i = F^o_{(T \times r)} \lambda_i^o + \underline{e}_i, \tag{3.1.2}$$

where $\underline{Y}_i$ is a $T \times 1$ vector of time-series observations for the i-th cross-sectional observation, F^o is a $T \times r$ matrix of common factors, and λ_i^o is a $r \times 1$ vector of factor loadings and $\underline{e}_i$ is a $T \times 1$ vector of time-series observations for the i-th idiosyncratic risk. In a more compact form of display, the entire system can be written in panel-time-series form as

$$Y_{(T\times n)} = F^{o}_{(T\times r)}\Lambda^{o\prime}_{(r\times n)} + e_{(T\times n)}. \tag{3.1.3}$$

Define tr(A) as the trace of the matrix A, and the matrix norm $||A|| =$ [tr($A'A$)]. Bai and Ng (2002) provide a set of asymptotic conditions for which the factor structure may entail consistency in the model selection criteria.

(a) For the factors, the setting assumes that there is no redundancy of factors such that

$$E||F^o_t||^4 < \infty, \quad T^{-1}\sum_{t=1}^{T} F^o_t F^{o\prime}_t \underset{T\to\infty}{\longrightarrow} \Sigma_f$$

and Σ_f is some positive definite matrix.

(b) For the factor loadings, the setting provides a sufficient condition for the systematic components of approximate factor structure such as

$$||\lambda_i|| \le \bar{\lambda} < \infty, \; ||(\Lambda^{o\prime}\Lambda^{o}/n) - D|| \underset{n\to\infty}{\longrightarrow} 0 \quad ,$$

for some $r \times r$ positive-definite matrix D.[3]

Bai and Ng (2002) introduce some additional assumptions for the time-series and cross-sectional dependence conditions including the weak dependence between factors and idiosyncratic risk for the system.

(c) For the factors and the idiosyncratic risk, there exists a positive constant $M < \infty$, such that for all n, T,

1. $E[e_{it}] = 0$, $E|e_{it}|^8 \le M^4$;
2. $E[e'_s e_t/n] = E(\frac{1}{n}\sum_{i=1}^{n} e_{is}e_{it}) = \gamma_n(s,t)$, $|\gamma(s,s)| \le M$, for all s, and $\frac{1}{T}\sum_{s=1}^{T}\sum_{t=1}^{T}|\gamma(s,t)| \le M$;
3. $E[e_{it}e_{jt}] = \tau_{ij,t}$ with $|\tau_{ij,t}| \le |\tau_{ij}|$ for some τ_{ij} and for all t, where $\frac{1}{n}\sum_{i=1}^{n}\sum_{j=1}^{n}|\tau_{ij}| \le M^5$;
4. $E[e_{is}e_{jt}] = \tau_{ij,ts}$ and $\frac{1}{nT}\sum_{i=1}^{n}\sum_{j=1}^{n}\sum_{t=1}^{T}\sum_{s=1}^{T}|\tau_{ij,ts}| \le M$;
5. For every (t,s), $E|n^{-\frac{1}{2}}\sum_{i=1}^{n}[e_{is}e_{it} - E(e_{is}e_{it})]|^4 \le M$.

(d) For the weak dependence between factors and idiosyncratic risk[6]:

$$E\left(\frac{1}{n}\sum_{i=1}^{n}\parallel\frac{1}{\sqrt{T}}\sum_{t=1}^{T}F_t^o e_{it}\parallel^2\right)\leq M.$$

The reason why Bai and Ng (2002) derive all these conditions for determining the number of factors is that these factors are to be estimated from the data. They are not directly observable. In essence, Bai and Ng (2002) apply the asymptotic principal components for the estimates on the approximate factor structure. By starting with an arbitrary number k of factors, $k < \min(n, T)$, the estimates for both λ^k and F_t^k are obtained by solving the following constrained optimization problem:

$$V(k) = \min_{\Lambda, F^k}(nT)^{-1}\sum_{i=1}^{n}\sum_{t=1}^{T}\left(Y_{it} - \lambda_i^k F_t^k\right)^2 \tag{3.1.4}$$

subject to either $\frac{1}{n}\Lambda^{k\prime}\Lambda^k = I_k$ or $\frac{1}{T}F^{k\prime}F^k = I_k$. The estimation for the factor matrix can be done by concentrating on Λ first, which will reduce the above optimization to maximizing $\mathrm{tr}\,(F'(XX')F)$.

Notice that the asymptotic principal component analysis is almost identical to the standard principal component analysis except that the sample size of the cross-sectional observations will expand asymptotically. However, the solutions to the above optimization problem is not unique. Bai and Ng (2002) provide two possible sets of solutions. The first one is to concentrate the Λ^k out and use normalization such as $\frac{1}{T}F^{k\prime}F^k = I_k$. The factor matrix is denoted as $\widetilde{F^k}$, which is the $\sqrt{T}$ times the eigenvectors corresponding to the k largest eigenvalues of the $T\times T$ matrix YY'. Another set of solutions is $(\overline{F^k}, \overline{\Lambda^k})$, where $\overline{\Lambda^k}$ is constructed as $\sqrt{n}$ times the eigenvectors corresponding to the k largest eigenvalues of the $n\times n$ matrix $Y'Y$ and the normalization as $\frac{1}{n}\overline{\Lambda^k}'\overline{\Lambda^k} = I_k$.

Now define $\widehat{F^k} = \overline{F^k}(\overline{F^k}'\overline{F^k}/T)^{\frac{1}{2}}$ as a rescaled factor matrix. Bai and Ng (2002) show the following convergence condition such that for any fixed

$k \geq 1$, there exists a $(r \times k)$ matrix H_k with $\text{rank}(H_k) = \min(k.r)$, and $C_{nT} = \min(\sqrt{n}, \sqrt{T})$,

$$C_{nT}^2 \left(\frac{1}{T} \sum_{t=1}^{T} \| \widehat{F}_t^k - H_k' F_t^o \|^2 \right) = O_p(1). \tag{3.1.5}$$

More specifically, the above equation actually states that the multiplication of C_{nT}^2 (which implies the smaller of the cross-sectional sample size or time-series horizon may grow sufficiently large) with the time average of the squared difference between the estimated factors and the factor space spanned by the true factors will be finite. In other words, as $n, T \to \infty$, this implies that the time average of the squared deviation of the estimate factors and those in the true factor space will vanish. In terms of the estimated factors, the number of factors is determined by the criterion

$$\text{PC}(k) = V(k, \widehat{F}^k) + kg(n, T), \tag{3.1.6}$$

where $V(k, \widehat{F}^k) = \min_{\Lambda} \frac{1}{nT} \sum_{i=1}^{n} \sum_{t=1}^{T} \left(Y_{it} - \lambda_i^{k'} \widehat{F}_t^k \right)^2$ and $g(n, T)$ is the penalty function for consistently estimating the number of factor r. The work of Bai and Ng (2002) is based on the assumption that there exists a bounded integer $k\max$ such that $r \leq k\max$.

Bai and Ng (2002) provide a theorem that shows the consistency concerns estimating the number of true factors with the above criterion in Eq. (3.1.6) such that if the above conditions (a)–(d) hold and that the k factors are estimated with principal components, then let $\hat{k} = \text{argmin}_{0 \leq k \leq k\max} \text{PC}(k)$. It follows that

$$\lim_{n,T \to \infty} \text{Prob}[\hat{k} = r] = 1, \tag{3.1.7}$$

if (i) $g(n, T) \to 0$ and (ii) $C_{nT}^2 g(n, T) \to \infty$ as n, $T \to \infty$, where $C_{nT} = \min(\sqrt{n}, \sqrt{T})$ and there's no particular restriction on the growth rates for the dimensions of cross-sections and time series. They also provide another alternative criterion:

$$\text{IC}(k) = \ln(V(k, \widehat{F}^k)) + kg(n, T), \tag{3.1.8}$$

which will also provide a consistent estimate for r. More specifically, Bai and Ng (2002) offer additional specifications of the penalty function $g(n, T)$:

$$\begin{aligned}
\mathrm{PC}(k) &= V(k, \widehat{F^k}) + k\hat{\sigma}^2 \left(\frac{n+T}{nT}\right) \ln\left(\frac{nT}{n+T}\right); \\
\mathrm{PC}(k) &= V(k, \widehat{F^k}) + k\hat{\sigma}^2 \left(\frac{n+T}{nT}\right) \ln C_{nT}^2; \\
\mathrm{PC}(k) &= V(k, \widehat{F^k}) + k\hat{\sigma}^2 \left(\frac{\ln C_{nT}^2}{C_{nT}^2}\right),
\end{aligned} \tag{3.1.9}$$

where $V(k, \widehat{F^k}) = n^{-1} \sum_{i=1}^{n} \hat{\sigma}_i^2$, and $\hat{\sigma}_i^2 = \hat{e}_i' \hat{e}_i / T$. Since the estimate $\hat{\sigma}_i^2$ depends on the number of factors undertaken, it may be seen that the penalty functions in the criteria of Eq. (3.1.9) will also depend on the assumed $k\max$. Hence, the determination of the number of factors when using the criteria in Eq. (3.1.9) will similarly depend on $k\max$. As indicated in Ahn and Horenstein (2013), the estimators need to be sensitive to the choice of $k\max$.

3.1.2 Bai's (2003) Inferential Theory for Factor Models

The work in Bai and Ng (2002) is to develop the criteria for determining the number of factors when (asymptotic) principal component analysis is applied. Although consistency is obtained for determining the necessary number of factors when a "true" factor structure is assumed, no asymptotic distribution for the estimators is provided. Bai (2003) extends the earlier work to discuss the asymptotic properties such as convergence rates and limiting distributions for the estimated factors, factor loadings, and common components (from principal component estimators) in factor models. Given the above assumptions from (a) to (d) in Bai and Ng (2002), and the number of factor r is known, Bai (2003) adds the following additional weak dependence conditions (of Assumption (c)) in Sect. 3.1.1 to the set of assumptions:

(e) There exists an $M < \infty$ such that for all n and T, and for every $t \leq T$ and every $i \leq n$,

$$1. \sum_{s=1}^{T} |\gamma_n(s,t)| \leq M.$$

$$2. \sum_{k=1}^{n} |\tau_{ki}| \leq M.$$

(f) Moments and central limit theorem: there exists an $M < \infty$ such that for all n and T,

(1) for each t, where F^o is denoted for the "true" factors,

$$E \parallel \frac{1}{\sqrt{nT}} \sum_{t=1}^{T} \sum_{k=1}^{n} F_s^o \left[e_{ks}e_{kt} - E\left(e_{ks}e_{kt}\right)\right] \parallel^2 \leq M,$$

(2) the $r \times r$ matrix satisfies

$$E \parallel \frac{1}{\sqrt{nT}} \sum_{t=1}^{T} \sum_{k=1}^{n} F_s^o \lambda_k^{o\prime} e_{kt} \parallel^2 \leq M,$$

(3) for each t, as $n \rightarrow \infty$,

$$\frac{1}{\sqrt{n}} \sum_{i=1}^{n} \lambda_i^o e_{it} \xrightarrow{d} N(0, \Gamma_t),$$

where $\Gamma_t = \lim_{n\to\infty} \frac{1}{n} \sum_{i=1}^{n} \sum_{j=1}^{n} \lambda_i^o \lambda_j^{o\prime} E\left(e_{it}e_{jt}\right)$,

(4) for each i, as $T \rightarrow \infty$,

$$\frac{1}{\sqrt{T}} \sum_{t=1}^{T} F_t^o e_{it} \xrightarrow{d} N(0, \Phi_i),$$

where $\Phi_i = \text{plim}_{T\to\infty} \left(\frac{1}{T}\right) \sum_{s=1}^{T} \sum_{t=1}^{T} E\left[F_t^o F_s^{o\prime} e_{is} e_{it}\right]$.

(g) The eigenvalues of the $r \times r$ matrix $(\Sigma_\Lambda \cdot \Sigma_F)$ are distinct.

Proposition 1 (Bai 2003) *Under the Assumptions (a)–(d) and (g), denote $\tilde{F}$ as the (principal component) estimator matrix for F^o from Eq. (3.1.4),*

$$plim_{T,n\to\infty}\frac{\tilde{F}F^o}{T}=Q,$$

where the matrix Q is invertible and $Q=V^{\frac{1}{2}}\Upsilon'\Sigma_{\Lambda}^{\frac{1}{2}}$, $V=diag\left(\upsilon_1,\upsilon_2,\ldots,\upsilon_r\right)$, $\upsilon_1>\upsilon_2>\cdots>\upsilon_r>0$ are the eigenvalues of $\Sigma_{\Lambda}^{\frac{1}{2}}\Sigma_F\Sigma_{\Lambda}^{\frac{1}{2}}$ and Υ is the corresponding eigenvector matrix such that $\Upsilon'\Upsilon=I_r$.

Given that the factor matrix and factor loadings are not identifiable, for the principal component estimator $\tilde{F}$, there exists an invertible matrix H such that $\tilde{F}$ is an estimator of F^oH and the estimated factor loading $\tilde{\Lambda}$ is an estimator of $\Lambda^o\left(H'\right)^{-1}$, where $\tilde{F}\tilde{\Lambda}'$ is an estimator of the common components $F^o\Lambda^{o\prime}$. In the following, Bai (2003) provides the asymptotic normality of the estimators of factors and factor loadings when both n and T become sufficiently large. The convergence rates are also provided. The convergence rates for the estimated factors and factor loadings are $\min\left(\sqrt{n},T\right)$ and $\min\left(\sqrt{T},n\right)$, respectively.

Theorem 1 (Bai 2003) *Limiting distribution of estimated factors: given the Assumptions (a)–(g), as n, $T\to\infty$,*

(i) if $\frac{\sqrt{n}}{T}\to 0$, then for each t,

$$\sqrt{n}\left(\tilde{F}_t-H'F_t^o\right)=V_{nT}^{-1}\left(\frac{\tilde{F}'F^o}{T}\right)\frac{1}{\sqrt{n}}\sum_{i=1}^{n}\lambda_i^o e_{it}+o_p(1)$$
$$\xrightarrow{d}N\left(0,\ V^{-1}Q\Gamma_tQ'V^{-1}\right),$$

where V_{nT} is a diagonal matrix consisting of the first r eigenvalues of $\left(\frac{1}{nT}\right)XX'$ in decreasing order, V and Q are from Proposition 1 and Γ_t is from Assumption (f) (3).

(ii) If $\liminf\frac{\sqrt{n}}{T}\geq\tau>0$, then

$$T\left(\tilde{F}_t-H'F_t^o\right)=O_p(1).$$

Theorem 2 (Bai 2003) *Limiting distribution of estimate factor loadings: given that Assumptions (a)–(g) and Proposition 1, let n, T* $\to \infty$,

(i) *if* $\frac{\sqrt{T}}{n} \to 0$, *then for each i,*

$$\sqrt{T}\left(\tilde{\lambda}_i - H^{-1}\lambda_i^o\right) = V_{nT}^{-1}\left(\frac{\tilde{F}F^o}{T}\right)\left(\frac{\Lambda^{o\prime}\Lambda^o}{n}\right)\frac{1}{\sqrt{T}}\sum_{t=1}^{T} F_t^o e_{it} + o_p(1)$$
$$\xrightarrow{d} N\left(0, \left(Q'\right)^{-1}\Phi_i Q^{-1}\right),$$

where V_{nT} *is as defined in Theorem 1,* Φ_i *is from Assumption (f) (4).*

(ii) *if* $\liminf \frac{\sqrt{T}}{n} \geq \tau > 0$, *then*

$$n\left(\tilde{\lambda}_i - H^{-1}\lambda_i^o\right) = O_p(1).$$

Theorem 3 (Bai 2003) *Limited distribution of estimated common components: denote* $C_{it}^o = F_t^{o\prime}\lambda_i^o$ *and* $\tilde{C}_{it} = \tilde{F}_t'\tilde{\lambda}_{it}$. *Under the Assumptions (a)–(f) and n, T* $\to \infty$, *then for each i and t,*

$$\left(\frac{1}{n}V_{it} + \frac{1}{T}W_{it}\right)^{-\frac{1}{2}}\left(\tilde{C}_{it} - C_{it}^o\right) \xrightarrow{d} N(0, 1),$$

where $V_{it} = \lambda_i^{o\prime}\Sigma_\Lambda^{-1}\Gamma_t\Sigma_\Lambda^{-1}\lambda_i^o$, $W_{it} = F_t^{o\prime}\Sigma_F^{-1}\Phi_i\Sigma_F^{-1}F_t^o$, *the matrices* Σ_Λ, Γ_t, Σ_F, *and* Φ_i *are all defined in Assumptions (a)–(f). The matrices* V_{it} *and* W_{it} *can be replaced with their consistent estimators.*

Notice that these results are based on the assumption that there exists a "true" factor structure. In addition, the asymptotic convergence is for the principal component estimators for the true factors, their factor loadings, and common components. The convergence is obtained under the condition that both the cross-sectional number of asset returns *n* and the time-series observations *T* can grow sufficiently large.

3.1.3 *Ouysse's (2006) Variable Selection*

Ouysse (2006), in following the framework of Bai and Ng (2002), develops a different approach to variable selection in large panel data. By assuming the known orderings of the potential candidate factors needed to enter the system first, the issue (as is the case with many discussions of factor pricing in security returns in the finance literature) is reduced to determining the number of factors (or dimension needed) for the approximate factor structure.[7] In doing so, the BIC criterion is provided to determine the dimension of the factor structure.

The major difference between Bai and Ng (2002) and Ouysse (2006) is that, in the former, the factors are unobservable and estimated with asymptotic principal component analysis. In Ouysse (2006), the discussions are on the potential candidate factors where only the true set of factors is unknown. The assumptions are: (1) the size of these true sets of factors does not depend of n or T, (2) these true sets of factors lie inside of the set of potential candidate factors, (3) the ordering of factors is known.

However, in the original approximate factor structure, these (so-called) factors are unobservable a priori. Instead, the orderings of factors in Ouysse (2006) may refer to the orderings of "reference variables" as proxies for factors defined in Reisman (1988, 1992). In that case, the orderings may become an essential issue for variable selection because the sequence of reference variables introduced to the system may influence the model selection.

The approach then is extended to consider the orderings of the observable factors to the system. In that case, the issue becomes the identification of both the dimension of factor structure with optimal ordering of the factors and, more importantly, on variable selection. Hence, to identify an optimal ordering of possible explanatory variables (or observable factors), the partial R^2 rule is applied first, and then the Bayesian information criterion to estimate the coefficients and model consistently. Similar to the previous tests for the number of factors in asset returns, Ouysse (2006) assumes that there exists a "true" approximate factor structure for dependent variables in the large panel of both cross-sectional and time-series observations.

The two-step approach can be applied to the approximate factor structure where the idiosyncratic risk is subject to limited cross-sectional and serial dependence. Since the framework assumes the factors are observable, Ouysse (2006) extends the analysis for the approximate factor structure to consider both the number of (observable) factors needed for dimension reduction and the model selection through choices of variables. Basically, the search for factor(s) starts with a partial R^2 criterion to sort the order of regressors and then an information criterion is applied to determine the optimal number of factors.

Specifically, Ouysse (2006) shows that given an approximate factor structure such that for each asset return i, $i = 1, 2, \ldots, n$,

$$Y_i = X^o \lambda_i^o + \epsilon_i, \tag{3.1.10}$$

where Y_i is a $T \times 1$ vector of asset returns, X^o is a $T \times r$ matrix of factors, λ_i^o is a $r \times 1$ vector of factor loadings, r is the correct number of factors under the approximate factor structure, and ϵ_i is a $T \times 1$ vector of the idiosyncratic risk. Or, in time index $t, t = 1, 2, \ldots, T$,

$$y_t' = x_t^{o\prime} \Lambda^o + \epsilon_t' \tag{3.1.11}$$

where y_t is an $n \times 1$ vector of dependent variables, Λ^o is a $r \times n$ matrix of factor loadings across n assets, ϵ_t is an $n \times 1$ vector of idiosyncratic risk.

The model criterion for the correct number of factors is shown as

$$\min_{k=0,1,\ldots K} EC(k)_{R\overline{\Lambda}=0} = \frac{1}{n}\mathrm{tr}(\widehat{\Sigma}_k) + kg(n, T), \tag{3.1.12}$$

where $\widehat{\Sigma}_k = \frac{1}{T}\sum_{t=1}^{T}(y_t - \hat{\Lambda}^{(k)}x_t^{(k)})'(y_t - \hat{\Lambda}^{(k)}x_t^{(k)})$ is the sample covariance matrix (for idiosyncratic risk) under k-factor representation and hence $\frac{1}{n}\mathrm{tr}(\widehat{\Sigma}_k) = \frac{1}{nT}\sum_{i=1}^{n}\sum_{t=1}^{T}(Y_{it} - \hat{\lambda}_i^{(k)\prime}x_t^{(k)})^2$. In addition, $g(n, T)$ is the penalty function that specifies the penalty for over-fittedness with an excessive number of factors and omission of essential ones, and K is the upper bound of the possible number of factors. Notice that the index of elements in X^o is not necessary $\{1, \ldots, r\}$. Instead the set can be the index $\mathbf{J} = \{j_1, \ldots, J_r\} \subseteq \{1, \ldots, K\}$.

The null hypothesis is given that $R\overline{\Lambda} = \left[0_{(K-k)\times k}, I_{(K-k)}\right] = 0$, where $\overline{\Lambda}$ is the factor loading matrix when all K factors are fitted to the model. In other words, the null hypothesis states that the last $K-k$ columns of factor loadings are equal to zero. Ouysse (2006) shows that given the assumptions similar to Bai and Ng (2002) and Bai (2003), the consistency in estimating the correct number of factors can be achieved with the objective function in Eq. (3.1.3).

Theorem 3.1.3.a (Ouysse 2006) *Given the above approximate factor structure in Eq. (3.1.1) or (3.1.2), and the model selection criterion (3.1.3), if the ordering of factors is known and the penalty function* $g(n,T)$ *satisfies the conditions such that (1)* $\lim_{n,T\to\infty} g(n,T) = 0$, *and (2)* $\lim_{n,T\to\infty} Tg(n,T) = +\infty$, *then under the assumptions of approximate factor structure, the estimated number of factors* $\hat{r}$ *will converge almost surely to* r, *where* $\hat{r} = \underset{k=0,1,\ldots,K}{\operatorname{argmin}} EC(k)$.

Nevertheless, the result in Theorem 3.1.3 depends on the orderings of factors to be selected for the model. Ouysse (2006) then applies a modified version of the stage-wise regression or projection pursuit regression to consider the order of factors. The procedures are: (1) identify the most highly correlated factor for the response variable (such as excess returns of assets) in the ordinary least-squares regressions, and denote it as the first factor. Then, obtain the residuals of the regressions (of asset returns) on this identified first factor. (2) Perform the regressions of these residuals on the second possible factor (of those which remain) which is most correlated with the residuals from (1). (3) Continue the above procedures until all possible K-factors are ordered or until the r-th order statistic is found. Consider the i-th cross-section for asset return i as

$$Y_i = \sum_{j\in \mathbf{J}} X_j^o \lambda_{i,j} + \epsilon_i,$$

where $Y_i = [y_{1i}, y_{2i}, \ldots, y_{Ti}]'$ as a $T \times 1$ vector of asset returns, $X^o = \left[X_{j_1}, \ldots, X_{j_r}\right]$ is the r-subset of true common factors. The sum of squared residuals from regression on factor X_j (at the first stage) is denoted by $\text{SSE}_j^1 = Y'M_jY$, where $M_j = I_T - X_j(X_j'X_j)^{-1}X_j'$ and $e_j = M_jY$. The first factor $\tilde{X}_1$ is chosen such that $\tilde{X}_1$ minimizes the SSE_j^1, $j = 1, \ldots, K$.

For the later stages, let $\ell \geq 2$ denote the stage, define $\mathbf{M}^\ell = \Pi_{j=1}^{\ell-1}\tilde{M}_{\ell-j}$, where $\tilde{M}_h = I_T - \tilde{X}_h(\tilde{X}_h'\tilde{X}_h)^{-1}\tilde{X}_h$, $\tilde{X}_h$ represents the optimal factor chosen in the previous stage h, and let $\text{SSE}_j^\ell = \mathbf{M}^{\ell\prime}M_j\mathbf{M}^\ell$ be the sum of squared residuals at step ℓ. The optimal factor for step ℓ is chosen as the factor that minimizes the sum of squared residuals among all left-over factors. Define $\hat{\phi}$ as the random variable representing the number of correct factors in the sequence of selecting the factors. Ouysse (2006) provides the following theorem as

Theorem 3.1.3.b (Ouysse 2006) *Under the assumptions given, there exists an optimal ordering of* $\tilde{X}_1, \ldots, \tilde{X}_K$, *where each* $\tilde{X}_j$ *represents the optimal factor that minimizes the sum of squared residuals among all the left-over factors* $j \neq 1, \ldots, h$ *where* h *represents the previous steps of optimal factors found. If* $\hat{\phi}$ *is the estimated number of correct factors in the sequence* $\{\tilde{X}_1, \ldots, \tilde{X}_K\}$, *then* $\hat{\phi} \xrightarrow{a.s.} r$.

A similar search for optimal set(s) of proxies in the presumed factor structure of asset returns is shown in Chap. 5 of this book. Differing from Ouysse (2006), a specification test based on the non-diversifiability of factors is performed in each stage of model expansion. Hence, instead of using the two-step procedures of Ouysse (2006) to identify the factors, the procedures of model search in Chap. 5 approximate the return processes (of assets of interest) with a presumed factor structure where no knowledge of factor structure is assumed or the sets of "true" factors are unknown and may not be included in the set of candidate factors or proxies. In contrast, the work in Ouysse (2006) assumes that there is a true factor structure in the asset returns. In addition, the factors are observable and the "true" set of factors is a (proper) subset of the set of all known factors.

3.1.4 Ahn and Horenstein (2013) Eigenvalue Ratio Test

The work of Ahn and Horenstein (2013) considers a setting similar to that of Bai and Ng (2002), where the model is assumed to be

$$Y_{(T\times n)} = F_{(T\times r)}\Lambda^{o\prime}_{(r\times n)} + e_{(T\times n)},$$

where $F = (f_1, \ldots, f_T)$ is the $T \times r$ matrix of factors, $\Lambda^{o}_{(r\times n)} = (\lambda^o_1, \lambda^o_2, \ldots, \lambda^o_n)'$ is the matrix of factor loadings. Let the matrix norm defined as $||A|| = [\mathrm{tr}(A'A)]$, and let c_1 and c_2 be two generic positive constants. For any real number z, $[z]$ represents the integer part of z. Let $\psi_k(A)$ denote the k-th largest eigenvalue of a positive semidefinite matrix A, and hence define

$$\tilde{\mu}_{nT,k} \equiv \psi_k[YY'/(nT)] = \psi_k[Y'Y/(nT)].$$

In addition, let $m = \min(n, T)$, $M = \max(n, T)$.

They propose two alternative "eigenvalue ratio" (ER) and "grow ratio" (GR) estimators for the number of factors. These estimators are easier to compute. For example, the ER estimator is obtained by maximizing the ratio of two adjacent eigenvalues in descending order. The assumptions of factor structure are given as follows.

Assumption 1 (i) Let $\mu_{nT,k} = \psi_k[(\Lambda^{o\prime}\Lambda^o/n)(F'F/T)]$ for $k = 1, \ldots, r$. And for each $k = 1, \ldots, r$, $\text{plim}_{m\to\infty}\mu_{nT} = \mu_k$, and $0 < \mu_k < \infty$. (ii) r is finite.

Assumption 2 (i) $E||f_t||^4 < c_1$ and $||\lambda_i^o|| < c_1$ for all i and t. (ii) $E(||n^{-\frac{1}{2}}\sum_i \epsilon_{it}\lambda_i^o||^2) < c_1$ for all t. (iii) $E(n^{-1}\sum_i ||T^{-\frac{1}{2}}\sum_t \epsilon_{it}f_t||^2) = E[(nT)^{-1}||e'F||^2 < c_1$.

Assumption 3 (i) $0 < y \equiv \lim_{m\to\infty} m/M \leq 1$. (ii) $e = R_T^{\frac{1}{2}}UG_n^{\frac{1}{2}}$, where $U' = [u_{it}]_{n\times T}$, $R_T^{\frac{1}{2}}$ and $G_n^{\frac{1}{2}}$ are the symmetric square roots of $T \times T$ and $n \times n$ positive semidefinite matrices R_T and G_n, respectively. (iii) The u_{it} are independent and identically distributed random variables with uniformly bounded moments up to the fourth order. (iv) $\psi_1(R_T) < c_1$ and $\psi_1(G_n) < c_1$, uniformly in T and n, respectively.

Assumption 4 (i) $\psi_T(R_T) > c_2$ for all T. (ii) Let $y^* = \lim_{m\to\infty} m/M = \min(y, 1)$. Then, there exists a real number $d^* \in (1 - y^*, 1]$ such that $\psi_{[d^*n]}(G_n) > c_2$ for all n.

Assumptions 1–3 are similar to the work of Bai and Ng (2002), and Assumption 3 (ii) introduces additional restrictions on the covariance structure of the errors, which allows both autocorrelation and cross-sectional correlation in the errors. Notice that the assumptions already consider that the setting of specification for factor structure is correct in advance.

Assumption 4 is to control both the cross-sectional correlations and inter-temporal dependence among the (idiosyncratic) errors. Assumption 4 (i) assumes that none of the idiosyncratic errors and their linear functions can be perfectly predicted by their past values. Assumption 4 (ii) assumes that for an asymptotically non-negligible number of the eigenvalues of G_n are bounded below by a positive number.

The criteria defined by Ahn and Horenstein (2013) are:

(1) ER-

$$\mathrm{ER}(k) \equiv \frac{\tilde{\mu}_{nT,k}}{\tilde{\mu}_{nT,k+1}}, \quad k = 1, 2, \ldots, k\max,$$

(2) GR-

$$\begin{aligned}\mathrm{GR}(k) &\equiv \frac{\ln[V(k-1) - V(k)]}{\ln[V(k)/V(k+1)]} \\ &= \frac{\ln(1 + \tilde{\mu}^*_{nT,k})}{\ln(1 + \tilde{\mu}^*_{nT,k+1})}, \qquad k = 1, 2, \ldots, k\max,\end{aligned}$$

where $V(k) = \sum_{j=k+1}^{m} \tilde{\mu}_{nT,j}$ and $\tilde{\mu}^*_{nT,k} = \mu_{nT,k}/V(k)$. The estimators for the number of factor r are given as

$$\tilde{k}_{\mathrm{ER}} = \max_{1 \le k \le k\max} \mathrm{ER}(k); \qquad \tilde{k}_{\mathrm{GR}} = \max_{1 \le k \le k\max} \mathrm{GR}(k).$$

Given the estimators, Ahn and Horenstein (2013) provide asymptotic arguments for the consistency in estimating the number of factors for the factor structure assumed. Similar to the earlier studies, the arguments are based on the existence of a true factor structure. In addition, the setting does not discuss possible structural change (of factor structure) over the time horizons when $T \to \infty$.

A theorem for the almost-certain consistency of estimators in the number of factors (Ahn and Horenstein 2013) is as follows. Suppose the Assumptions 1–4 hold with $r \ge 1$. Then, there exists $d^c \in (0, 1]$ such that

$$\lim_{m\to\infty}\Pr(\tilde{k}_{\mathrm{ER}} = r) = \lim_{m\to\infty}\Pr(\tilde{k}_{\mathrm{GR}} = r) = 1,$$

for any $k\max \in (r, [d^c m] - r - 1]$.[8]

3.2 Essentiality of Factors

With the current volume of asset pricing models devised in the finance literature, it is easy to locate the abundant discussions of factor pricing (and those for the determination of the number of factors) in the academic journals. Some provide evidence for the extension of asset pricing models with additional factors including liquidity (such as Keene and Peterson 2007) or even locations of the firms (Tuzel and Zhang 2017) where local risk and local factors are also taken into account. Although interesting, the inclusion of any proposed factor or proxy needs to pass the minimal justification of its essential role which is not merely limited to the statistical inferences with the significance of (say) conventional t-(or F-) test statistics (or p-values) for the variables of interest.

Striving for ways to explain the asset returns is indeed a formidable task. All possible improvements count. However, the real issue is that the (proxies for) factors or candidate variables in the empirical asset pricing models should be critical enough to uphold their essential explanatory role across various time horizons and/or all asset returns cross-sectionally. This argument should also hold for the time-varying coefficient/expectation models on asset returns. Regardless of the abundant coverage of model selection in the statistical/econometric literature, the conventional setting of model selection typically applies the assumption of the existence of a "true" factor structure (whether the number of factors is known or not) for the data generating mechanism. However interesting this is, the setting of a well-behaved (factor) structure in asset returns is enunciated for the follow-ups with empirical evidence.

For instance, in Reisman (1992), the approximate multi-beta representation when using the "reference variables" for factors may hold if there exists an approximate factor structure in asset returns. In essence, the existence of a factor structure (which no one actually knows) is critical for the claim to hold. Unfortunately, this prior knowledge of the existence of a factor structure is usually a presumption (for many studies in finance) where statistical inferences are simply drawn to concur with the tautological results: "when there is a factor structure, there is a statistical approximation with something similar (for the factor structure)". Notice that the original statistical analyses such as principal component analysis and factor analysis are mainly for the purpose of reducing the dimensionality. For instance, principal component analysis is for considering what the orthogonal (linear) transformation will be for the data (sequentially) to explain the highest variation of the data parsimoniously. Extension with asymptotic principal component analysis for the increasing cross-sectional sample size (and time horizon) does not necessarily confirm (or refute) the existence of a factor structure in empirical asset pricing models of asset returns. To the best extent for analyses, they are only approximations.

While expanding empirical asset pricing models with new findings is inspiring, any modeler should be aware that almost all empirical models for asset returns are (to the best extent) only plausible approximations to the data. Demanding questions for these models relate to (1) the theoretical work required to increase logical support and (2) further advancements of statistical inferences to confirm the essentiality of additional variables. And this is not simply a variable-selection issue. For analyses in empirical asset pricing models, the search for possible models should focus on the minimal set of properties for candidate variables that are considered essential and impeccable for explainability, provided that the prior knowledge of any model is only presumptuous. Unless the modeler only intends to find some temporal models for asset returns that would possibly fit the tentative regularity (or incident) that the data may show, the specification tests for empirical asset pricing models should be more intricate so as to deal with the utmost requirement for rigor and parsimony, and not merely for fittedness or predictability.

Intuitively, these so-called proxies for factors or explanatory variables should satisfy several necessary conditions. Namely, the identified variables should constitute the empirical evidence and/or results of possible efficiency in almost all pervasive portfolio constructions already devised.[9] It is hard to imagine that the essential variables for the (equilibrium) asset pricing models that identify the benchmark returns of risky assets still contain some features which incur difficulties in efficiency—unless it is intrinsic to the system or regime. If so, then the immediate and necessary work is to identify the causes and reasons for such inefficiency in the capital market. Apparently, the essential issue of interest is to identify the evidence and cause of such inefficiency prior to any attempt to explain the regularity of asset returns.

Following from the discussions on the stochastic discount factor (SDF), the derivation of the variance lower bound in Hansen and Jagannathan (1991) is based on the projection of the SDF onto the space spanned by the gross returns (or payoffs) of all assets. The projected component m_o (as denoted in Chap. 2 Sect. 2.2) is treated as an SDF for the minimum-variance portfolio per se regardless of the specifications for the SDF m in any possible asset pricing model. Given this, it is straightforward to consider the efficiency in the introduction of empirical asset pricing models.

On the other hand, it is not difficult to consider the possibility that the multi-factor asset pricing models can be applied to explain the SDF. For instance, as shown in Campbell (2000), it is denoted that

$$m_t = a_t + \sum_{j=1}^{k} b_{jt} f_{jt},$$

where $\{f_{jt}\}_{j=1,2,...k,}$ is the set of possible factors for SDF specification in a linear multifactor specification and m_t is the SDF at time t. This in turns results in the multi-beta representation of risk premiums for asset returns accordingly.

Notice that the derivation of SDF is based on (1) the optimality condition of the representative agent in allocations of current consumption and portfolio construction, and (2) the rationality of the law of one price (and/or the implication of no arbitrage opportunity). The capital market equilibrium is formed according to the efficiency in the portfolio construction and market mechanism. It is then difficult to imagine that something that ought to be diversifiable still remains as the determinant for the benchmark returns.

Therefore, if the empirical asset pricing models are to be devised, this rudimentary condition of efficiency should be satisfied. In fact, according to Ferson and Jagannathan (1996), the SDF representation is equivalent to the multi-beta model. Since SDF incurs optimality conditions in the utility maximization of a representative agent, a similar efficiency condition should apply to the multi-beta models where possible factor pricing is considered. More explicitly, it was shown in Ferson and Jagannathan (1996) that the SDF m_{t+1} (with conditional information set I_t, and gross return R_{t+1}) which is defined as

$$E[m_{t+1}R_{t+1} - 1|I_t] = 0, \quad (3.2.13)$$

where I_t is the information set up to time t and the multi-beta model given as

$$E[R_{t+1}] = \lambda_{ot} + \sum_{j=1}^{k} \beta_{ijt}\lambda_{jt}, \quad (3.2.14)$$

are equivalent. More specifically, the SDF m_{t+1} can be expressed as

$$m_{t+1} = c_{ot} + \sum_{j=1}^{k} c_{jt} f_{jt+1}, \tag{3.2.15}$$

with the coefficients as

$$c_{ot} = \frac{1 + \sum_{j=1}^{k} \{\lambda_{jt} E_t[f_{jt+1}]/\mathrm{Var}_t(f_{jt+1})\}}{\lambda_{ot}} \tag{3.2.16}$$

$$c_{jt} = -\frac{\lambda_{jt}}{\lambda_{ot} \mathrm{Var}_t(f_{jt+1})}, \tag{3.2.17}$$

$E_t(.)$ and $\mathrm{Var}_t(.)$ stand for the conditional expectation and conditional variance, respectively. Namely, identification of essential factors for the empirical asset pricing models (for instance, in so-called multi-beta representation) should already incorporate the optimality in the diversification and efficiency of portfolio constructions when reasoning from the setting of the SDF.

Likewise, evidence of certain possible variables of interest in explaining asset returns must be taken into account cautiously. If shown, one should carefully investigate why these variables are essential for the asset returns. Are these evidence of deficiency in optimality or market anomalies? Why wouldn't investors take advantage of these anomalies and profit from them? If they were to take advantage (possibly everyone in the market), why would these anomalies still prevail? Or is it that such anomalies are frictions (from data sources and statistics) that everyone would already be aware of and which are common knowledge for every investor? Practices and the search for empirical asset pricing models are not just about creating something new. Confirmation through statistical inferences on certain variables of interest for these models is only a beginning for further enhancement. The bona fide task is to devise continuing ways that would provide a truth-finding scheme which leads to a better understanding and a better search.

Notes

1. In terms of Lehmann (1990), he noted that "the explanation must provide a detailed fit not only for the particular phenomenon at hand but must also fit appropriately in to the existing scientific fabric or related phenomena in which it is to become embedded."
2. Elton (1999) shows that the emphasis in studies on asset pricing models should focus on the specification of the expected rates of return, not on the realized rates of return. For instance, the realized rate of return may contain some information surprises where the latter affect the rates of return. The question is whether these information surprises should be priced into the expected rates of return or not in any plausible asset pricing model. This incurs additional caution when statistical procedures or inferences on asset pricing models are to be developed.
3. In fact, these conditions are to ensure that the factors are essential. Given that Bai and Ng (2002) devise the criterion of determining the number of essential factors in the system where approximate factor structure exists, the analysis covers more extended issues than those in asset pricing models. A more extended condition is provided in Chap. 4 of this book to generalize the idea to non-diversifiability of factor structure where no correct number of factors is presumed at the outset of the model search.
4. In other words, this condition precludes those random processes that don't have finite higher-order moments.
5. Specifically, these conditions assume that the idiosyncratic risk does not have any cross-sectional/temporal long dependence already. Specifically, the conditions already assume that there exists an approximate factor structure with the correct number of factors.
6. In fact, this condition will ensure that the estimators, which are as simple as ordinary least squares, will be able to obtain consistent estimates for the factor loadings.
7. In other words, the sequence or ordering of these explanatory variables (to be considered as factors) is already predetermined.
8. Ahn and Horenstein also consider the case when $r = 0$ in the additional corollary. However, since the interest of study is to identify the correct number of factors of asset returns, the extended claim is not covered here, accordingly.
9. This efficiency is not the statistical efficiency for the estimators in statistical inferences.

References

Ahn, S.C., and A.R. Horenstein. 2013. Eigenvalue Ratio Test for the Number of Factors. *Econometrica* 81: 1203–1227.

Bai, J. 2003. Inferential Theory for Factor Models of Large Dimensions. *Econometrica* 71: 135–171.

Bai, J., and S. Ng. 2002. Determining the Numbers of Factors in Approximate Factor Models. *Econometrica* 70: 191–221.

Campbell, J. 2000. Asset Pricing at the Millennium. *Journal of Finance* 55: 1515–1567.

Elton, E.J. 1999. Presidential Address: Expected Return, Realized Return, and Asset Pricing Tests. *Journal of Finance* 54: 1199–1220.

Ferson, W.E., and R. Jagannathan. 1996. Econometric Evaluation of Asset Pricing Models, Research Report 206, Federal Reserve Bank of Minneapolis.

Hansen, B. 2005. Challenges for Econometric Model Selection. *Econometric Theory* 21: 60–68.

Hansen, L.P., and R. Jagannathan. 1991. Implications of Security Market Data for Models of Dynamic Economies. *Journal of Political Economy* 99: 225–262.

Keene, M.A., and D.R. Peterson. 2007. The Importance of Liquidity as a Factor in Asset Pricing. *Journal of Financial Research* 30: 91–109.

Lehmann, E.L. 1990. Model Specification: The Views of Fisher and Neyman, and Later Developments. *Statistical Science* 5: 160–168.

Ouysse, R. 2006. Consistent Variable Selection in Large Panels when Factors are Observable. *Journal of Multivariate Analysis* 97: 946–984.

Reisman, H. 1988. A General Approach to the Arbitrage Pricing Theory. *Econometrica* 56: 473–476.

Reisman, H. 1992. Reference Variables, Factor Structure, and the Approximate Multibeta Representation. *Journal of Finance* 47: 1303–1314.

Tuzel, S., and M.B. Zhang. 2017. Local Risk, Local Factors, and Asset Prices. *Journal of Finance* 72: 325–370.

PART II

The Alternative Methodology

CHAPTER 4

Finding Essential Variables in Empirical Asset Pricing Models

The author develops the alternative methodology in (1) cross-sectional properties of presumed (economic) factors/proxies that are considered essential for asset returns asymptotically, and (2) test statistics that can be applied to test these cross-sectional properties for empirical asset pricing models. Many model specification tests for these models have emphasized the statistical inferences on time-series properties of estimators and test statistics.

However, the emphasis on any empirical asset pricing models of asset returns should be on how well these presumed (or identified) variables have helped explain the cross-sectional association or commonality of all asset returns. In particular, studies ought not to be specification tests that confirm (or refute) the inclusion of these variables merely through the conventional test statistics under certain significance levels.

Notice that, differing from statistical inferences or the science of decision making, the focus on empirical asset pricing models is not only to devise methods for inferring the regularity or any other time-series properties (such as the change of betas, heteroskedasticity, or serial dependence) that the security returns may possess, or to identify which proxy or variable can predict better. Instead, what is important is to consider (1) whether the variables may help to explain the security returns (from the perspectives of finance or economic reasoning) and (2) whether these variables help to identify the essential commonality or feature that the security returns may share.

J.-L. Jeng, *Empirical Asset Pricing Models*,
https://doi.org/10.1007/978-3-319-74192-5_4

In other words, the inferences for empirical asset pricing models should provide cross-sectional identification of these presumed determinants in explaining asset returns versus verification of time-series properties for forecasting—if meaningful interpretation is expected. Certainly, the identification of cross-sectional association for these determinants may not necessarily improve time-series forecasts to a much greater magnitude. However, the trade-off is whether we want to pursue a search for some meaningful and applicable asset pricing models or simply to find some tracking mechanisms per se.

For instance, for systematic components of asset returns it is usual to assume that these components are non-diversifiable. Loosely speaking, this means that these components can't be diversified away with any well-diversified (linear) cross-sectional combination of these asset returns asymptotically.

As concluded in Grinblatt and Titman (1985), this kind of systematic commonality (of non-diversifiable factors) should not be hidden even with repackaging securities asymptotically. This claim leads to inquiring as to whether these presumed (or identified) economic variables (and their innovations that are claimed as proxies for factors) really assume the role of explaining the systematic commonality among all the asset returns. That is, the exhibition of systematic commonality of these variables should prevail among all assets.

In fact, this systematic commonality should provide some asymptotic conditions which test statistics for (economic) factors in empirical asset pricing models will contain. For instance, for the property of non-diversifiability of systematic factors, it is straightforward to show that the cross-sectional memory condition(s) of these factors should be persistent enough to justify their roles. In addition, given the definition of non-diversifiability and its extent, the convergence rate for the (weighted) cross-sectional sum of these factors may also be applied to test for the intensity of the identified factors in explaining the pricing kernel of asset returns.

In empirical studies, it is not surprising that one may occasionally identify some (economic) variables that help to forecast the asset returns in certain time periods. However, it is also imperative to see that these variables actually share the (asymptotic) properties that explain the cross-sectional commonality among the asset returns. Unfortunately, only a few of them in the contemporaneous empirical research contribute to the explanation of essentiality among asset returns in theory or in different time horizons.

Hence, development for the required (cross-sectional) properties for statistical inferences should be considered as fundamental in the search for tractability of empirical asset pricing models. In a sense, this is similar to the idea of the stochastic discount factor of Hansen and Jagannathan (1991) where all asset pricing models should satisfy the lower bound of unconditional variance—regardless of the possible data structures or genuine underlying processes for asset returns. However, in this chapter an alternative step is suggested that emphasizes the non-diversifiability of any proxy variables which would resemble the intrinsic features of a pricing kernel of asset returns.

Differing from the conventional approach in asset pricing models (which mainly assume that there is a "true" model for security returns), the following analysis starts from the initiative of model searching. In other words, the approach is not to assume or derive a ubiquitous model specification where the stock returns are applied to consider/confirm the model's fittedness through empirical data over selected time periods. Instead, the approach is to devise some statistical tests that will provide possible directions to facilitate the explanations for stock returns and hence lead to a scheme for model searching.

4.1 The Presumed Factor-Pricing Model

To derive the test, there are a few prerequisites. Definition D1 describes a Hilbert space of (real) squared-integrable random variables defined on the probability space. The excess returns of assets forms a subset of this Hilbert space. Assumption A1 shows the conditions of factors or prespecified reference variables applied as factors. The assumption allows different choice sets of instrumental or reference variables applied to specify the risk premium. These choice sets may be evolving over time or be different sample sizes. In particular, the reference variables may be generated by the innovations from the multivariate time-series models of prespecified economic variables in a conditional expectation approach.

Assumption A2 is to describe the presumed multifactor model of the asset returns. Assumption A3 shows the possible missing factor and idiosyncratic risk in the excess return after projecting on the presumed explanatory variables. Assumption A4 provides a condition for diversification of the genuine noises in pricing models.

Definition D1 Let $\mathscr{H} = L^2(\Omega, \mathscr{F}, P)$ be a Hilbert space of squared-integrable real-valued random variables (with respect to probability measure P on a complete probability space $(\Omega, \mathscr{F}, P)$, where $\mathscr{H}$ is endowed with L^2-norm$\|\|$ such that $\|x\| = (\int |x|^2 dx)^{1/2}$ for $x \in \mathscr{H}$. Let the inner product of $\mathscr{H}$ be denoted as $\langle x, y \rangle = E[xy]$ for all $x, y \in \mathscr{H}$. Let $\{r_{it}\}_{i=1,2,...,n,t=1,2,...T,}$ represent a sequence of all excess returns of assets contained in $\mathscr{H}$.

Assumption A1 Let $f_t = (f_{1t}, f_{2t}, \ldots, f_{pt})'$ be a vector of p presumed proxies for factors in the information set $I_t, p \geq 1$, and $E|f_{jt}| = 0$, where $E|f_{jt}|^2 = \sigma_{jt}^2$ (defined in $\mathscr{H}$) at time t for the presumed multifactor pricing model, f_{jt} is the j-th proxy for factor at time t, for all $j = 1, 2, \ldots, p$, $t = 1, 2, \ldots, T$. In addition, the information set I_t may also contain the other known explanatory variables $\{\widetilde{x_{st}}\}_{s=1,2,...,u}$, $u \geq 1$ for specification of asset returns, where $\{\widetilde{x_{st}}\}_{s=1,2,...,u}$, $u \geq 1$ can only consist of constants.

Assumption A2 Let the excess return r_{it} of each asset i at time t be projected on the ***presumed*** factor structure (at the k-th stage of model search, $k \geq 1$) as

$$r_{it} = E\left[r_{it}|I_t\right] + \epsilon_{it} = \mu_i + \sum_{s=1}^{q} b_{is}\widetilde{x_{st}} + \sum_{j=1}^{k} \beta_{ij} f_t^{(j)} + \epsilon_{it}, \tag{4.1.1}$$

where $i = 1, 2, \ldots n$, as randomly assigned subindices for asset returns, and $t = 1, 2, \ldots T$, where $n, T \to \infty, E\left[\epsilon_{it}|I_t\right] = 0$, and I_t represents the information filtration (including lagged dependent variables, economic variables, and the proxies for factors) up to time t, $1 \leq k \leq p, \mu_i + \sum_{s=1}^{q} b_{is}\widetilde{x_{st}} + \sum_{j=1}^{k} \beta_{ij} f_t^{(j)}$ stands for the conditional expected excess return $E\left[r_{it}|I_t\right]$, where μ_i is the constant term and the prespecified common variables for all asset returns are $\{\widetilde{x_{st}}\}_{s=1,2...,q}$, $0 \leq q \leq u$.

Specifically, the model in Eq. (4.1.1) is only a presumed approximation for the explanation of excess returns. Since the model is considered at the k-th stage of the model search, this implies that the essentiality (such as non-diversifiability) of the already included variables is verified a priori. In particular, the already included explanatory variable in Eq. (4.1.1) can only contain a constant term μ_i (that is, when $q = 0$) as the initial stage of the model search (where all the other variables $\{\widetilde{x_{st}}\}_{s=1,2,\ldots,q}$, can be suppressed). For instance, at the initial stage of the model search and letting the search follow the forward selection approach, the presumed factor structure may be expressed as

$$r_{it} = \mu_i + \beta_{ij}f_t^{(j)} + \epsilon_{it},$$

where no other explanatory variables (such as firm-specific characteristics or economic variables) are included. In this case, two tasks are needed. The first task is to identify which factor in $\left\{f_t^{(j)}\right\}_{j=1,\ldots,p}$ is essential (as non-diversifiable or systematic) to be included in the model, and the second one is to see if the presumed idiosyncratic risk still contains any omitted non-diversifiable factor(s).

The conventional approach in empirical asset pricing models usually begins with hypothesizing and identifying the statistically significant variable(s) first (using t-tests, generalized method of moments (GMM), or other robust methods, for instance) on the time-series regressions of asset returns and then proceeding to consider the estimations and tests for the factor premiums. The essentiality issue is then examined by considering the statistical significance of these estimated factor premiums, where most of the earlier studies were devoted to conquering the errors-in-variables issues, measurement errors or nonstationarity in distribution (such as conditional/unconditional heteroskedasticity). Even in the stochastic discount factor methodology, where model selection over the factors (or state variables) is discussed, few model search schemes are devised. Most studies simply include all possible explanatory variables (from the presupposed standards or hypotheses) in feasible data sets and consider the statistical inferences of these variables of interest.

Since stock market data are sensitive toward the status of the economy, it is not difficult to identify variables that are statistically significant when relating them to the asset returns. More explicitly, the statistical significance of the parameters or coefficients of the included variables (or proxies for factors) throughout these statistics does not necessarily justify essentiality. If the identification of essential factors is not correct in a model specification of return processes, the inferences for factor premiums when based on the incorrectly identified betas (or risk) are usually ambiguous.

Instead, the approach of empirical asset pricing models should begin with the proper identification of explanatory variables (with model searching) first. Confirmation of the specification of factor premiums can only be possible once the "essential" variables are already identified. As a matter of fact, due to the evolving nature of the financial markets, the approach of model searching should be a continuing forum in finding the pricing kernels of asset returns.

Hence, the setting here is for the allowance of the expansion of dimensionality when the forward selection procedure is pursued. In other words, if the idiosyncratic risk identifies that there is a possible omitted non-diversifiable factor, the model search should proceed to discover what proxy (or proxies) is needed to expand the model. This search-oriented approach is discussed in Chap. 5 of this book.

The preselected factor $\left\{f_t^{(j)}\right\}_{j=1,\ldots,k} \subseteq (f_{1t}, f_{2t}, \ldots, f_{pt})'$ is a subset of known proxies for factors, and $\left\{f_t^{(j)}\right\}_{j=1,\ldots,k}$ does not have to follow the identical order of a designated sequence for proxies in $f_t = (f_{1t}, f_{2t}, \ldots, f_{pt})'$, ϵ_{it} stands for the projection error (or so-called "presumed" idiosyncratic risk) for asset i at time t with the assumed multifactor pricing model, $\{\beta_{ij}\}_{i=1,2,\ldots,n}^{j=1,2,\ldots,k}$ are the stochastic factor loadings (independent of) the presumed factors/proxies f_t.[1]

Notice that the setting in Eq. (4.1.1) may include the possible conditional asset pricing models when the information set is reduced to the set I_{t-1} of past information. In that case, the parameters may also be denoted as time-varying where both the coefficients of common (economic) variables and factor loadings of presumed included factors are of a time-changing nature. Therefore, the estimation for these parameters can apply the recursive (or rolling) approach over different time periods.

In addition, the included proxies for factors may be the innovations of the prespecified common variables where the number of factors (k) is identical to the number of included common variables (s) where $f_t^{(j)} = \widetilde{x}_{jt} - E[\widetilde{x}_{jt} | \{\widetilde{x}_{st-1}\}_{s=1,2,\ldots,u}]$. It is also easy to consider that the conventional asset pricing models (including the arbitrage pricing theory and multifactor models) are to impose (parametric) restrictions on these variables and factors. Nevertheless, the current setting does not assume any particular asset pricing model holds true. Nor does it assume that there is an approximate factor structure of asset returns. The setting is only to assume that the excess returns for securities are projected onto an information set (possibly subjective) in a linear setting where no "true" model of asset pricing is actually given for the data generating mechanism.

Criticisms of the determination of factors are given in many sources where (given that the factors are unobservable) the dimensionality of factors can always be alternated. For instance, Cochrane (2001) shows that multi-beta or multifactor representation can always be alternated into a single-beta representation[2] and hence the discussion of the number of factors is not a meaningful one. However, it is still essential to consider the question from the perspective of the empiricist when considering the model search with different sets of proxies applied to determine the best possible approximation. Regardless of whether there is (truly) a factor structure or not, it is necessary to discuss the selection of variables (or proxies) for the underlying asset returns so that a tractable approximation (for the data generating mechanism) can be obtained. In other words, to determine the inclusion and relevancy of explanatory variables is still vital.

Given this, the test for factor structure should focus on the minimal set of restrictions that (at least) fulfills the requirement of empirical asset pricing models. In short, if some factor structures are essential (for the purpose of tractability and reduction of dimensionality), this pattern of commonality should prevail across all asset returns. Thus, instead of emphasizing the arguments of the existence of a factor structure, determining the essentiality of certain arguments for the model of interest is perhaps a more critical task for empirical asset pricing models.

Henceforth, the following assumptions and definitions provide a condition such as non-diversifiability as a minimal requirement for the inclusion(s) of certain proxies of factors. The non-diversifiability is only to depict the essentiality for the models of interest. The following Assumption A3 can be applied to any possible factor (or proxy for factor) when one considers some possibilities for the expansion of the dimensions of the model.

Assumption A3 Let the projection error or idiosyncratic risk (if it contains a hidden factor) be expressed as a linear model such that $\epsilon_{it} = \eta_{it} + \nu_{it} = \beta_i^h f_{ht} + \nu_{it}$, where f_{ht} represents a stationary stochastic hidden factor with a nondegenerated distribution, $E[f_{ht}] = 0$, $f_{ht} \in \mathscr{H}$, such that f_{ht} is orthogonal to all selected proxies or factors $\left\{f_t^{(j)}\right\}_{j=1,\ldots,k}$, and f_{ht} is cross-sectionally stationary for all assets and inter-temporally independent over time.

β_i^h represents the real-valued stochastic unobservable factor loading for asset i on the hidden factor f_{ht} and assuming that $E[\beta_i^h] = 0$ for all

$i = 1, 2, \ldots n$.[3] ν_{it} is a mean-zero (diversifiable) random noise with finite moments and independent of $\{\eta_{it}\}_{i=1,2,\ldots,n,t=1,2,\ldots,T}$ at any time t such that $E[\nu_{it}\eta_{it}] = 0$, where $E[\epsilon_{it}|f_t] = 0$, $E|\nu_{it}|^2 < \infty$ for all $i = 1, 2, \ldots n$. In addition, let $\sup_i E|\beta_i^h|^2 < \infty, i = 1, 2, \ldots n$, such that $\{\beta_i^h\}_{i=1,2,\ldots} \in B$, where $B \subseteq L^2$ is a proper factor-loading subspace of L^2-space, and L^2-space contains all sequences $\{x_i\}_{i=1,2,\ldots}$, such that $E|x_i|^2 < \infty$.[4]

Notice that Assumption A2 does not claim that the model expressed in Eq. (4.1.1) is a correct specification. Instead, it is only a presumed (multi-)factor pricing model that may approximate to the data generating mechanism. In fact, if one needs to verify the one-factor asset pricing model for risk premiums as the theory (such as unconditional capital asset pricing model (denoted as CAPM heretofore)) proclaims, it is easy to see that it would require an additional restriction such as

$$\mu_i = E[r_{it}] = \beta_i \lambda_{ft},$$

where λ_{ft} stands for the factor premium for f_t. Or, if conditional expectation (with lagged information set I_{t-1}) is of interest, it can be shown that

$$\mu_i = E[r_{it}|I_{t-1}] = \beta_i \tilde{\lambda}_{ft-1},$$

where $\tilde{\lambda}_{ft-1}$ represents the conditional factor premium associated with the included factor in the asset pricing model. Specifically, these verifications when using the above restrictions are related to Fama and MacBeth's second-pass cross-sectional regressions. Likewise, based on Eq. (4.1.1), the second-pass regressions will verify the factor premiums such that $\mu_i = 0, b_{is} = \beta_{ij}$ where $s = j, q = k$, and $\widetilde{x_s} = \varphi(f_j)$ provided that $\varphi(f_j)$ is the factor premium of factor f_j for all asset returns $i = 1, 2, \ldots n$. This is the so-called "beta-pricing" model of asset returns, which incurs additional restrictions on the parameters of the model in Eq. (4.1.1). Yet, it is crucial that the betas should be correctly identified before the second-pass regression method can be applied.

A critical issue is to identify the necessary factor(s) as the initial stage of the model search in empirical asset pricing models, before any further statistical procedure to examine the verification of theoretical models such as the determination of factor premiums. The emphasis then is on the minimal sets of properties which these models (of proxies or explanatory variables as pricing factors) need to satisfy. Thus, the attempt to verify the additional restrictions on these asset pricing models can only proceed after these prerequisites have already been identified. In fact, if the "beta-pricing" models hold so that the constant term can be expressed as

$$\mu_i = \sum_{j=1}^{k} \beta_{ij}\varphi(f_{jt}),$$

where $\{f_{jt}\}_{j=1,\ldots,k}$ are the non-diversifiable factors, and $\varphi(\cdot)$ is the factor premium on factors, substituting this expression into Eq. (4.1.1) will result in

$$\begin{aligned} r_{it} &= \mu_i + \sum_{s=1}^{q} b_{is}\widetilde{x_{st}} + \sum_{j=1}^{k} \beta_{ij} f_t^{(j)} + \epsilon_{it}, \\ &= \sum_{s=1}^{q} b_{is}\widetilde{x_{st}} + \sum_{j=1}^{k} \beta_{ij}(f_t^{(j)} + \varphi(f_{jt})) + \epsilon_{it}. \\ &= \sum_{s=1}^{q} b_{is}\widetilde{x_{st}} + \sum_{j=1}^{k} \beta_{ij}\overline{f_t^{(j)}} + \epsilon_{it}. \end{aligned}$$

Hence, the arguments in the following Theorem 4.1 still hold on the verification of cross-sectional long dependence when the factors or hidden omitted factor are non-diversifiable (due to the factor loadings $\{\beta_{ij}\}_{i=1,\ldots,n}$ and the essentiality of $\{b_{is}\}_{i=1,\ldots,n}$.

In brief, verification should first focus on the "essentiality" of the (proxies for) factors in the model specification prior to the hypothesis tests for the specifications in risk premiums (for instance, as $\mu_i = \beta_i\lambda_f$ where λ_f represents the factor premium) that finance theories suggest. Specifically, model specifications and verifications of factor premiums in asset pricing models should incur additional restrictions on the parameters of interest. Claims for factor premiums which require additional restrictions on the coefficients of asset pricing models should only be considered after the identification of essential factors (or proxies) for asset returns in empirical studies. The so-called two-pass regression method or the other robust procedures (such as the maximum likelihood estimation) for the search for verification of risk premiums (or factor premiums) can only be pursued after the identification of essential factors. Although concerns over the errors-in-variables problem (in betas) may prevail in almost all empirical asset pricing models, the sequential orthogonalization which can reduce the interdependence among residuals, proxies for factors, and returns may assist the empirical model search.

More precisely, for development of empirical asset pricing models, we should start with the most primitive conditions as the "essentiality" of the pricing kernel and consider elaborations afterward. Otherwise, the building approach of the model will not only incur the errors-in-variables problem but be self-fulfilling as one may develop theoretical models and hypotheses which, in turn, mold the data (through statistics or otherwise) to confirm the expected answers. For example, conventional beta-pricing models may suffer from the possible data snooping problem and difficulties in determining the number of factors and so offer explicit interpretations for factors. On the other hand, the development of the stochastic discount factor may also encounter model specification errors where the necessary conditions of the factor are not detected.

Given this, the following setting aims to develop a possible model search scheme for the exploratory data analysis in empirical asset pricing models, with some minimum sets of restrictions, where no assumption concerning the return process or the necessary condition for the stochastic discount factor is imposed on the search. Additional verification for theoretical concerns can be pursued afterward, when these basic conditions have been satisfied. In addition, as mentioned earlier, the empirical asset pricing models may continuously entail economic/financial foundations and/or theoretical thoughts to facilitate further enhancement based on an evolving data generating mechanism when a new data stream becomes available. The reason for this is that all models are only approximations.

Earlier studies such as Ross (1976), Chamberlain and Rothschild (1983), Connor and Korajczyk (1993), Bai and Ng (2002) and many other extended studies all assume that there exists an underlying data generating mechanism for the approximate factor structure of the security returns. However, Assumption A2 considers that the security returns are projected onto a presumed linear structure given the currently available information (for empiricists). No a priori information of factor structure is granted. More specifically, since the interest of study is on the identification of possible non-diversifiable factors with possible diagnostic tests, it is assumed that the set of common prespecified variables $\{\widetilde{x_{st}}\}_{s=1,2,\ldots,q}$, $0 \leq q \leq u$ has already been chosen or is merely an intercept.

For the purposes of model searching, the step-wise stages for the factor(s) are assumed to start initially from the lower-dimensional setting with the subsequent addition of (proxies for) factors when needed. In other words, the setting entails the model search for any potential non-diversifiable factor(s) left in the error terms from the presumed asset pricing models.[5]

Given the concerns regarding over-fittedness and the purposeful exaggeration of empirical evidence in asset pricing models (on either explainability or predictability), the model search ought to be cautiously parsimonious. For this reason, the setting here assumes the initial stage of the model search is from the lower-dimensional setting and expands to the higher-dimensional ones when theories and data show this. Therefore, the specification test developed later on considers the detection of possible omitted non-diversifiable factors after the presumed projection of asset returns onto the known explanatory variables of the current stage of the model search. In other words, since the setting considers the model search, the diagnostic test can be applied to detect the need to expand the dimensions of the model.

The setting of factors (or proxies of factors) in Assumption A1 and A2 includes the framework in Campbell (1996) and Petkova (2006) where innovations from the vector autoregression (VAR) of certain (economic) variables are used to approximate the factors. In other words, the so-called factors can be generated (through their time-series models) from the other known variables which may be considered as plausible explanatory variables for asset returns.

In addition, Assumption A3 imposes an asymptotic condition for the absolute factor loading(s) on the hidden factor. This is to ensure that, as the size of the portfolio expands, the factor loadings won't explode—provided that the excess returns are in the Hilbert space $\mathscr{H}$. To apply the ideas of diversification, a few definitions of the feasible weights in the factor pricing models are introduced in the following.

Assumption A4 is to formulate the diversification in an infinite dimensional opportunity set for a sequence of feasible weights applied to each asset. The tail condition is given to prevent the diversifying weight from collapsing too soon. The definition of the diversification functional is provided in D2. The notation $n, T \to \infty$ represents the number of assets n; time T will grow sufficiently large. In addition, the setting, although allowing cross-sectional/inter-temporal dependence for the idiosyncratic risk in Eq. (4.1.1), does not assume any specific a priori dependence condition (such as mixing conditions).

The following Assumption A4 considers the possible weight sequences which diversification is based on. Notice that, for simplicity, the time index is suppressed for convenience of exposition. The weights are allowed to be time-varying also. Since the definition of diversifiability is considered as the cross-sectional dimension expands, the same concept can be applied to any time frame as it expands.

Assumption A4 Let W be a compact subspace of ℓ_2 space endowed with the ℓ_2 norm that for any $y = (y_1, y_2, \ldots) \in \ell_2, \sum_{i=1}^{\infty} y_i^2 < \infty$, where W consists of all real bounded sequences of nondegenerated deterministic feasible weights $\underline{\omega}$, such that $\underline{\omega} \equiv \{\omega_i\}_{i=1,2,\ldots} \in \ell_2$ and $\underline{\omega} \notin \ell_2^o$, where ℓ_2^o contains sequences $\{\omega_i\}_{i=1,2,\ldots}$ with finitely many nonzero weights. In particular, for all $\underline{\omega} \in W$, and for arbitrarily small $\epsilon > 0$, $\epsilon \in R$, there exists some $\gamma > 0$ (which may be distinctive for different $\underline{\omega}$'s) such that

$$\liminf_{\substack{n\to\infty \\ \sum_{i=1}^{n} \omega_i^2 < \infty}} \{|\omega_i|\}_{i=1,2,\ldots,n} L(n) n^{\gamma} = \sup_{\substack{n\to\infty \\ \sum_{i=1}^{n} \omega_i^2 < \infty}} \{\inf_{m \leq n} (|\omega_i|)_{i=1,2,\ldots,m}\} L(m) m^{\gamma} \geq \epsilon, \tag{4.1.2}$$

where $L(j)$ is a slowly varying function of j such that $\lim_{j\to\infty} \frac{L(\lambda j)}{L(j)} = 1$, for $\lambda > 0$, $\lambda \in R$. Let the factor loadings of a hidden factor be given as $\beta_H = (\beta_1^h, \beta_2^h, \ldots, \beta_n^h, \ldots)'$, $\beta_H \in B$,[6] where $B \subseteq L^2$ is a proper factor-loading subspace endowed with L^2-norm where $\sup_{i=1,2,\ldots,\infty} E|\beta_i^h|^2 < \infty$.

In the following, Assumption A5 provides the objective functional for the diversification problem in the infinite dimensional setting. Furthermore, Definition D5 considers well-diversified portfolios such that the weighted sums of the diversifiable random noises converge to zero. The notation $\sum_{i=1}^{\infty} \omega_i^2$ is denoted as $\lim_{n\to\infty} \sum_{i=1}^{n} \omega_i^2$, and $\sum_{i=1}^{\infty} \omega_i = \lim_{n\to\infty} \sum_{i=1}^{n} \omega_i = 1$.

Assumption A5 There exists a W-continuous diversification functional $f(\underline{\omega}, \beta_H) : W \otimes B \to R$, defined as $f(\underline{\omega}, \beta_H) = E\left(\sum_{i=1}^{\infty} \omega_i \beta_i^h f_{ht}\right)^2$ for any given β_H in B at any time t, where the non-null solution for portfolio optimization as $\inf_{\omega \in W^\star} f(\underline{\omega}, \beta_H)$ exists, in which $W^\star$ is a closed non-null subset of W, for $\underline{\omega} \in W^\star$, such that $\limsup_{n\to\infty}[n(\varpi_n^2)] = 0$, where $\varpi_n = \sup(|\omega_1|, |\omega_2|, \ldots, |\omega_n|)$, $\sum_{i=1}^{\infty} \omega_i = 1$, $\sum_{i=1}^{\infty} \omega_i^2 < \infty$.

Definition D2 A portfolio with weight $\underline{\omega}, \underline{\omega} \equiv \{\omega_i\}_{i=1,2,\ldots} \in W^\star$ in the diversification problem as $\inf_{\omega \in W^\star} f(\underline{\omega}, \beta_H)$ is denoted as well-diversified if the weighted sum for idiosyncratic random noises converges such that $\sum_{i=1}^{\infty} \omega_i \nu_i \xrightarrow{L_2} 0$, for some $\underline{\omega} \in W^\star$ and as $n \to \infty$, where $\xrightarrow{L_2}$ stands for convergence at the second-order moment.

Given Definition D2 and Assumption A5, and similar to Chamberlain (1983), it is straightforward to verify that $\sum_{i=1}^{\infty} \omega_i^2 = \lim_{n\to\infty} \sum_{i=1}^{n} \omega_i^2 = 0$ for all well-diversified portfolios in $W^\star$ where idiosyncratic risk is diversified away. That is, the sum of infinite series of $\{\omega_i^2\}_{i=1,2,\ldots}$ in $W^\star$ should be nil for all well diversified portfolios. For instance, if $\omega_i = \frac{1}{n}$, and n is the number of assets, then $\lim_{n\to\infty} \sum_{i=1}^{n} \omega_i^2 = \lim_{n\to\infty} \frac{n}{n^2} = 0 = \sum_{i=1}^{\infty} \omega_i^2$. However, this does not imply that all weights $\{\omega_i\}_{i=1,2,\ldots}$ are all identically equal to zeros for all $i = 1, 2, \ldots$. Notice that the well-diversified portfolios are defined on that infinite-dimensional optimization problem. And hence, the efficiency is defined on the asymptotic arguments and not for the finite-dimensional optimality in portfolio construction.

Therefore, the idea of diversifiable/non-diversifiable factor focuses on the opportunity set of the infinite dimensional optimization in diversification with as many assets as possible. Notice that the diversification functional provided in Assumption A5 does not assume that it is homoskedastic over time. In addition, since the definition is given for cross-sectional diversification for any time t, the functional is applicable to the diversification over time period as $t \in [0, \ldots, T]$ as well, as long as the time subindex is applied to denote the optimization over different time spans.

For the non-diversifiable factor, its hidden factor loadings shouldn't be eliminated by any possible sequences of weights of the well-diversified portfolios in $W^\star$ as $n \to \infty$. Otherwise, there would exist a possibility that certain sequences of weights of some well-diversified portfolios in $W^\star$ would eliminate that risk entirely.

In contrast, if the factor is diversifiable, then its factor loadings should be eliminated by ***all*** possible sequences of weights in the ***well-diversified portfolios*** if these portfolios are called well-diversified. This is straightforward since $\epsilon_{it} = \eta_{it} + \nu_{it} = \beta_i^h f_{ht} + \nu_{it}$; and if f_{ht} is diversifiable, then the entire ϵ_{it} can be denoted as a diversifiable idiosyncratic risk as $\nu_{it}^{\star}$. This implies that any well-diversified portfolio should diversify it away to enable establishment of portfolio efficiency. Otherwise, there is a contradiction of the idea of portfolio efficiency of the so-called well-diversified portfolios. Therefore, the notion of diversifiability in essence should only refer to the opportunity set of weights in all well-diversified portfolios, not all possible weights in their entirety for all portfolios.

Definition D3 The hidden factor f_{ht} with the stochastic factor loadings $\beta_H = \left(\beta_1^h, \beta_2^h, \ldots, \beta_n^h, \ldots\right)' \in B$ where $B \subseteq L^2$ is denoted as W^*-diversifiable if and only if $\inf_{\omega \in W^\star} f(\underline{\omega}, \beta_H) = 0$ for all well-diversified portfolios $\underline{\omega}$, $\underline{\omega} \equiv \{\omega_i\}_{i=1,2,\ldots} \in W^\star$. On the other hand, the hidden factor f_{ht} is non-diversifiable in $W^\star$ if and only if $\inf_{\omega \in W^\star} f(\underline{\omega}, \beta_H) \neq 0$ for all well-diversified portfolios in $W^\star$.

Although the current setting is to devise the diagnostic specification test (for idiosyncratic risk), the setting in Definition D3 should apply to all possibly included variables for the empirical asset pricing models since the non-diversifiability of the (proxies) for factors is essential to verify the necessity of inclusion. More explicitly, the results of the following Theorem 4.1 should hold for all factor loadings (and the coefficients of explanatory variables) such as $\{b_{is}\}_{s=1,\ldots,q}$ and $\left\{\beta_{ij}\right\}_{j=1,\ldots,k}$ in the already included variables in the current stage of model search where the above Definition D3 can also be applied to all factors (or proxies for factors) needed for the pricing kernel of asset returns. Hence, this condition should be satisfied for the already included factors and explanatory variables for the pricing kernel.

In Jeng and Tobing (2012), a similar framework is also established with developed two panel CUSUM-(cumulative sum) based tests. The study emphasizes the model search approach when applying the tests to the empirical data. The present study differs from the previous one by focusing on the development of the intensity of non-diversifiability which provides the conditions for discussion on the Hurst exponent of the (cross-sectional) memory conditions of the idiosyncratic risks. The intensity of non-diversifiability in Sect. 4.4 emphasizes the convergence condition of the partial sums of the (cumulative sum) CUSUMs of idiosyncratic risks—although incidentally it can be shown that if this intensity of non-diversifiability is set to zero, these partial sums will simply conform with (the cross-sectional version of) Kwiatkowski-Phillips-Schmidt-Shin (KPSS) (1992) test statistics at each date. Hence, the emphasis in this chapter is to establish an analysis for the estimation in intensity of the non-diversifiability of (hidden) factor(s) in diagnostic tests.

Theorem 4.1 *Given the above setting and arbitrarily selected orders of cross-sectional index i, if for any time t,* $t \leq T, T \rightarrow \infty$, *there exists a non-diversifiable stationary hidden factor in idiosyncratic risk* $\epsilon_{it} = \eta_{it} + \nu_{it} = \beta_i^h f_{ht} + \nu_{it}$. *Let the distance function between the indices of asset returns (denoted as l and i respectively) be defined as* $m = |l - i|$ *for l,* $i = 1, 2, \ldots n, \ldots$, *and let the cross-sectional covariance function be* $\rho_{it}^{\epsilon}(m) = E\left[\epsilon_{it}\epsilon_{(i+m),t}\right] = \sigma_{ht}^2 E\left[\beta_i^h \beta_j^h\right], j = i + m$, *under the assumption that* $E(\beta_i^h) = 0$, *for all* $i = 1, 2, \ldots n, \ldots$, *then* $\{\epsilon_{it}\}_{i=1,2,\ldots}$ *is a cross-sectional perturbed long dependent series for any given time t, such that* $\sum_{m=0}^{\infty} |\rho_{it}^{\epsilon}(m)| = \infty$ *for idiosyncratic risk* $\{\epsilon_{it}\}_{i=1,2,\ldots}$ *as the number of asset returns n grows. On the other hand, if* $E(\beta_H) \neq \underline{0}_n$, *where n in the number of asset returns, and* $n \rightarrow \infty$, *this will imply that the row (or column) norm of the second-order moment matrix* $E[\beta_H \beta_H']$ *will grow with the number of cross-sectional observations n, where* $\beta_H = \left(\beta_1^h, \beta_2^h, \ldots \beta_n^h\right)'$.

Conversely, if $\{\beta_i^h\}_{i=1,2,\ldots}$ is of cross-sectional long dependence such that the variance of the sum of factor loadings is denoted as $\text{Var}\left(\sum_{i=1}^n \beta_i^h\right) = E|\sum_{i=1}^n \beta_i^h|^2 = n^{2H}L(n) \rightarrow \infty$, as $n \rightarrow \infty$, $\frac{1}{2} < H < 1$, where $E[\beta_i^h] = 0$, for $i = 1, \ldots, n$ and $L(n)$ is a slowly varying function at infinity, then the hidden factor is non-diversifiable in $\mathscr{W}^{\star}$.[7]

Lemma 4.1.a *Given the Definitions D1–D3, there exists a local optimum for the constrained minimization problem in D3.*

Proof of Lemma 4.1.a It is straightforward to verify that the functional $|\varphi(\underline{\omega}, \beta_H)|$ is weakly lower and semicontinuous such that for every sequence $\underline{\omega} \equiv \{\omega_i\}_{i=1,2,\ldots,}$ that converge weakly to some $\overline{\omega} \in \mathscr{W}^{\star}$, where $\liminf_{n\rightarrow\infty} |\varphi(\underline{\omega}, \beta_H) \geq |\varphi(\overline{\omega}, \beta_H)|$. Since the constrained set is closed such that every sequence in $\mathscr{W}^{\star}$ contains a weakly convergent subsequence with a limit belonging to $\mathscr{W}^{\star}$, $\mathscr{W}^{\star}$ is also weakly sequentially compact. Hence, by Theorem 2.3 in Jahn (2007), there exists a local minimal solution for the constrained optimization problem.

Proof of Theorem 4.1 Given the model and Lemma 4.1.a, where $\{\beta_i^h\}_{i=1,2,\ldots}$ are covariance-stationary, and for sufficiently large M and N, it can be shown that for any well-diversified portfolio with n number of assets

$$\begin{aligned}
\sigma_{pt}^2 &= \sum_{i=1}^{n}\left(\omega_i^2 E\left[\beta_i^{h^2}\right]\right)\sigma_{ht}^2 + 2\sum_{i=1,}^{n}\sum_{i\neq j,j=1}^{n}\omega_i\omega_j E(\beta_i^h\beta_j^h)\sigma_{ht}^2 + o_p(1),\\
&\leq \sum_{i=1}^{n}\left(\omega_i^2 E\left[\beta_i^{h^2}\right]\right)\sigma_{ht}^2 + 2\sum_{i=1,}^{n}\sum_{i\neq j,j=1}^{n}|\omega_i||\omega_j||E(\beta_i^h\beta_j^h)|\sigma_{ht}^2,\\
&\leq M\sigma_{ht}^2\sum_{i=1}^{n}\omega_i^2 + 2\sum_{i=1,}^{n}\sum_{i\neq j,j=1}^{n}|\omega_i||\omega_j||E(\beta_i^h\beta_j^h)|\sigma_{ht}^2,\\
&\leq M\sigma_{ht}^2\sum_{i=1}^{n}\omega_i^2 + 2\overline{\omega}_{n(o)}^2\sum_{j=1}^{n}(n-j)\,|E(\beta_i^h\beta_j^h)|\sigma_{ht}^2,\\
&\approx o(1) + 2\overline{\omega}_{n(o)}^2\sum_{j=1}^{n}(n-j)\,|E(\beta_i^h\beta_j^h)|\sigma_{ht}^2,\\
&\leq o(1) + 2n\overline{\omega}_{n(o)}^2\sum_{j=1}^{n}|E(\beta_i^h\beta_j^h)|\sigma_{ht}^2,\\
&\leq o(1) + 2(\limsup_{n\to\infty}[n\overline{\omega}_{n(o)}^2])\sum_{j=1}^{n}|E(\beta_i^h\beta_j^h)|\sigma_{ht}^2
\end{aligned}$$

If the hidden factor is non-diversifiable, it is conceivable to have $\lim_{n\to\infty}\sigma_p^2 > 0$. However, since $\limsup_{n\to\infty}[n\overline{\omega}_{n(o)}^2] = o(1)$, if $\lim_{n\to\infty}\sum_{k=1}^{n}|E(\beta_i^h\beta_j^h)| < \infty$, this will imply from the above inequality that $\sigma_p^2 = o(1)$ also. This will violate the assumption that the hidden factor is non-diversifiable. Hence, $\lim_{n\to\infty}\sum_{j=1}^{n}|E(\beta_i^h\beta_j^h)|$ cannot be finite if the hidden factor is non-diversifiable.

In fact, $\lim_{n\to\infty}\sum_{j=1}^{n}|E(\beta_i^h\beta_j^h)|$ must grow at a rate (at least) as great as n to ensure the above inequality. Therefore, $\lim_{n\to\infty}\sum_{j=1}^{n}|E(\beta_i^h\beta_j^h)| \to \infty$. In other words, if $\{\beta_i^h\}_{i=1,2,\ldots}$ are covariance-stationary and non-diversifiable, the idiosyncratic risks of the presumed factor structure will have some cross-sectional long memories.

Conversely, if idiosyncratic risks are of cross-sectional long memory, they are $\mathscr{W}^\star$-non-diversifiable. Suppose this is not the case; then let them be $\mathscr{W}^\star$-diversifiable instead. Since the definition of diversifiable factor(s) refers to all well-diversified weights in $\mathscr{W}^\star$, it follows that $\lim_{n\to\infty} E|\sum_{i=1}^n \omega_i\beta_i^h|^2 = 0$ for all well-diversified portfolios in $\mathscr{W}^\star$.

Choose a well-diversified portfolio $\underline{\omega} \in \mathscr{W}^\star$ with all positive weights for included assets, where $0 < a(n) \leq \omega_i$ for all $i = 1, 2, \ldots n, \ldots$ and let $\lim_{n\to\infty} a(n) = 0$ such that $a(n) \approx o(1)$. Then, for any n, given that $\{\epsilon_{it}\}_{i=1,2\ldots}$ are of cross-sectional long memory, we have

$$
\begin{aligned}
E|\sum_{i=1}^n \omega_i\beta_i^h|^2 &\geq a(n)^2 E|\sum_{i=1}^n \beta_i^h|^2 \\
&\geq a(n)^2 n^{2H} L(n)^2 \\
&\approx o(n^o)O(n^{2H}) \approx o(n^{2H}).
\end{aligned}
$$

That is to say, the lower bound of the variance of weighted hidden factor loadings does not converge to zero unless it was multiplied by n^{-2H}. This violates $\lim_{n\to\infty} E|\sum_{i=1}^n \omega_i\beta_i^h|^2 = 0$. Hence, the hidden factor with assumed cross-sectional long memory should be non-diversifiable in $\mathscr{W}^\star$. Given the above results, if $E(\beta_H) \neq \underline{0}_n$, for $i = 1, 2, \ldots n, \ldots$, then the sum of each column (or row) of the matrix $E[\beta_H\beta_H']$ will grow with the number of cross-sectional observations. Hence, the matrix norm will also grow with the number of asset returns included. The extreme case when $\{\beta_i^h\}_{i=1,\ldots n}$ are non-stochastic also follows when $E[\beta_H\beta_H']$ is replaced by $\beta_H\beta_H'$.

Corollary 4.2 *Given the result in Theorem 4.1, if the hidden factor in the idiosyncratic risks* $\{\epsilon_{it}\}_{i=1,2,\ldots}$ *is diversifiable, then for all well-diversified portfolios* $\underline{\omega} \in \mathscr{W}^\star$, $\lim_{n\to\infty} \sum_{i=1}^n \omega_i\beta_i^h \xrightarrow{p} 0$. *In particular, if the factor loadings for the hidden factor are nonstochastic, the idiosyncratic risk* $\{\epsilon_{it}\}_{i=1,2,\ldots}$ *will be of cross-sectional short memory such that* $\sum_{j=1}^\infty \rho_{it}^\epsilon(j) < \infty$.

Proof Since convergence in moments implies convergence in probability, it is straightforward to see that with a diversifiable hidden factor, the weighted sums of the factor loadings of this hidden factor will converge to zero in probability. Besides, $\lim_{n\to\infty} \sum_{j=1}^{n} |E(\beta_i^h \beta_j^h)| \to \infty$ will become $\lim_{n\to\infty} \sum_{j=1}^{n} |\beta_i^h \beta_j^h| \to \infty$ when the factor loadings of the hidden factor are nonstochastic. By the definition of cross-sectional long memory in Theorem 4.1, it is easy to show that the idiosyncratic risks will be of cross-sectional long memory.

Notice however that the concept of long dependence (or long memory) of stochastic processes does not necessarily imply that there exists a unit-root representation in a time-series setting (such as the autoregressive format). Instead, it only implies that the absolute sum of the covariance functions over (cross-sections or time horizons) will not converge. These covariance functions could be insignificant individually. Yet, their absolute sums will not converge asymptotically.

The typical unit-root representation is only a special case under such a concept. Notice that even in the short-memory random fields, the asymptotic variance of the partial sum across the two-dimensional lattice may also grow with the cardinality of the dimensions or its area. Instead, Theorem 4.1 only states that if there is a hidden non-diversifiable factor in the (presumed) idiosyncratic risk, the "cross-sectional" memory of the risk will be persistent at any particular time t. Thus, the sum of cross-sectional covariances for presumed idiosyncratic risk (for a particular asset i) will approach infinity asymptotically. This property should be satisfied at all stages of the model search for empirical asset pricing models. In other words, the already included variables and (proxies for) factors should entail this property at every stage of the model search. Detailed descriptions for the model search procedures are discussed in Chap. 5 of this book.

More importantly, the cross-sectional long dependence of these factors may introduce different asymptotic properties where the asymptotic distribution of conventional statistics may not necessarily follow traditional weak convergence, such as the central limit theorem. In other words, the conventional test statistics (based say on generalized method of moments (GMM) or maximum likelihood estimation) that ignore the possible cross-sectional long dependence, may fail to have the proper power for the tests, especially when the asymptotic arguments are based on the number of cross-sectional observations of asset returns growing sufficiently large. Likewise, empirical studies based on these test statistics may be ambiguous. For instance, when long dependence is present, the partial sum of these random variables of long dependence may require different schemes of normalization. Hence the statistics of interest may not converge in distribution to the conventional standard normal random variable.

In addition, the cross-sectional long dependence due to the hidden non-diversifiable factor exhibits itself regardless of the orderings of the selected securities of interest. Likewise, if the securities are selected randomly across all assets (without prespecified grouping or sorting), this cross-sectional long dependence will prevail if there is a hidden non-diversifiable factor in the presumed idiosyncratic risk at each stage of the model search. Given that traditional tests on empirical asset pricing models are usually based on selected samples or ranked (or sized) portfolios, the results in Theorem 4.1 can be applied to the random samples of security returns without using preselected (or constructed) portfolios. Although there have been attempts to use sorting or grouping portfolios to undermine the errors-in-variables issues for betas, these regrouping methods are possibly subject to data snooping problems. A more positive alternative instead is to devise some plausible test statistics which are robust even under the errors-in-variables problems per se and which do not require inferences based on preselected (or constructed) samples. As such, a more useful approach is to start with the exploratory data analysis which identifies the essential systematic variables/proxies for the asset returns prior to the assessments of factor premiums to verify (or refute) the theoretical models. In particular, verification of the essential role of these variables should confirm their functionality as non-diversifiable for any efficient portfolio.

More specifically, the conditions in Theorem 4.1 and Corollary 4.2 are for the asymptotic sum of cross-sectional covariances in the presumed idiosyncratic risk. The analyses do not state that the asymptotic variance of the partial sums of all excess returns will become finite across all cross-sectional and time-series observations when there is no hidden non-diversifiable factor. In addition, the order of the cross-sectional index can be randomly determined or selected with some arbitrary orders; additionally, it does not depend on the firm's characteristics in sorting or grouping which may induce a data snooping problem since the result doesn't depend on the grouping schemes in forming portfolio returns to test the cross-sectional dependence. Besides, the claim of Theorem 4.1 holds for a sufficiently large number of individual stock returns where Shanken (1992) and Gagliardini et al. (2016) have shown the consistency in estimators of the factor loadings.

Therefore, the conclusion of Theorem 4.1 is that the "presumed" idiosyncratic risk in the current stage of the model search of empirical asset pricing models will show some cross-sectional long dependence if there exists an omitted non-diversifiable factor contained in the risk. The concern with the possible selection bias is discussed in the following Corollary 4.3.

4.1.1 Selection Bias of Empirical Studies with Stock Returns

An essential issue for specification tests on empirical asset pricing models is the possible selection bias or survivorship bias when the individual stock returns data collected are only from the firms that survived over the time periods. In that case, given Eq. (4.1.1) for the asset returns and Assumption A3, the fitted model of the preselected data (under the assumed sample selection rules such as $\widetilde{\xi}(\epsilon_{it}) > 0$) may contain the selection bias such that (by assuming the included variables are independent of the selection rule)

$$\begin{aligned}
r_{it} &= E\left[r_{it}|\widetilde{\xi}(\epsilon_{it}) > 0\right] + E\left[\epsilon_{it}|\widetilde{\xi}(\epsilon_{it}) > 0\right] + \ddot{v}_{it}, \\
&= \mu_i + \sum_{s=1}^{q} b_{is}\widetilde{x_{st}} + \sum_{j=1}^{k} \beta_{ij} f_t^{(j)} + E\left[\beta_i^h f_{ht} + v_{it}|\widetilde{\xi}(\epsilon_{it}) > 0\right] + \ddot{v}_{it}, \\
&= \mu_i + \sum_{s=1}^{q} b_{is}\widetilde{x_{st}} + \sum_{j=1}^{k} \beta_{ij} f_t^{(j)} + \widetilde{\epsilon}_{it}, \\
&= \left(\mu_i + E\left[\beta_i^h f_{ht} + v_{it}|\widetilde{\xi}(\epsilon_{it}) > 0\right]\right) + \sum_{s=1}^{q} b_{is}\widetilde{x_{st}} + \sum_{j=1}^{k} \beta_{ij} f_t^{(j)} + \ddot{v}_{it},
\end{aligned} \tag{4.1.3}$$

where $\widetilde{\xi}(\epsilon_{it}) > 0$ is the data selection rule that determines the selected samples and, if the selection bias is not specified explicitly for estimation, the error term shows as $\widetilde{\epsilon}_{it} = \widetilde{\psi}_{it} + \ddot{v}_{it}, \widetilde{\psi}_{it} = E\left[\epsilon_{it}|\widetilde{\xi}(\epsilon_{it}) > 0\right]$. Similarly, Eq. (4.1.3) can also be modified to the panel data framework with an (endogenous) unspecified individual effect such as $\mu_i^{\star} = \mu_i + E\left[\beta_i^h f_{ht} + v_{it}|\widetilde{\xi}(\epsilon_{it}) > 0\right]$.

Although various empirical studies attempt to reduce the possible selection bias (or possibly measurement errors) by regrouping the asset returns by using certain properties (or characteristics) of the firms or otherwise, the formation of portfolios may not necessarily reduce the bias with the further introduction of subjectivity. In fact, the regrouping procedure may, instead, introduce the data snooping problem. Nevertheless, it is easy to see that if the selection bias and the idiosyncratic risk $\{\ddot{\upsilon}_{it}\}_{i=1,2,...}$ are weakly dependent for any time index t, and under the assumption that the selection bias (which is the conditional expectation of idiosyncratic risk under the selection rule) is Fréchet differentiable, it is feasible to show that the proclaimed cross-sectional long dependence for the perturbed idiosyncratic risk will still hold if there is a hidden non-diversifiable factor in the idiosyncratic risk. In other words, the results in Theorem 4.1 still hold for individual stock returns even though there is a possible selection bias due to survivorship.

In other words, even with the possible selection bias for the asset returns, the validity of the cross-sectional long dependence of these asset returns still holds, if there is an omitted non-diversifiable factor in the presumed idiosyncratic risk. Hence, in empirical verification of hidden non-diversifiable factor(s), there is no need to repack the asset returns into different portfolios for possible selection bias. For simplicity, the selection rule $\widetilde{\xi}(\epsilon_{it}) > 0$ is assumed to be continuously differentiable from now on.[8]

Definition D6 A functional T that maps from an open subset D of $\mathscr{H}$ to $\mathscr{H}$ is Fréchet differentiable at $\theta \in D$, when the following limit exists where

$$\lim_{||h||\to 0} \frac{||T(\theta + h) - T(\theta) - T'(\theta)h||}{||h||} = 0,$$

where $T'(.)$ is the (first) variation of the functional T.

Corollary 4.3 *Given the same setting as in Theorem 4.1, at any time t, and with the selection bias continuously Fréchet differentiable on D, D is an open subset of $\mathscr{H}$ where $\mathscr{H} = L^2(\Omega, \mathscr{F}, P)$ is a Hilbert space of squared-integrable real-valued random variables (with respect to probability measure P on a complete probability space $(\Omega, \mathscr{F}, P)$), then if the hidden factor is non-diversifiable, the error terms in Eq. (4.1.3) (denoted as $\{\widetilde{\epsilon}_{it}\}_{i=1,2...,n}$) will contain cross-sectional long dependence even with possible selection bias where $\widetilde{\epsilon}_{it} = \widetilde{\psi}_{it} + \ddot{\upsilon}_{it} = E\left[\epsilon_{it} | \widetilde{\xi}(\epsilon_{it}) > 0\right] + \ddot{\upsilon}_{it}$ under the data selection rule $\widetilde{\xi}(\epsilon_{it}) > 0$.*

Proof Notice that the conditional expectation from $\mathscr{H}$ to $\mathscr{H}$ is a continuous linear functional on Hilbert space $\mathscr{H}$ with L^2-norm. Hence, it is feasible to consider that there exists a finite positive number $\Lambda > 0, \Lambda < \infty$, such that

$$\left|E\left[\epsilon_{it}|\widetilde{\xi}(\epsilon_{it}) > 0\right]\right| \leq \Lambda||\epsilon_{it}|| \leq \Lambda||\beta_i^h f_{ht} + \nu_{it}|| * ||\widetilde{\xi}(\epsilon_{it})|| < \infty.$$

Hence, the selection bias $\widetilde{\psi}_{it}$ is also bounded. Given that the selection bias is continuously Fréchet differentiable, it is feasible to see that for all $x \in D$, and for all $\ddot{x} = x + \alpha h, 0 \leq \alpha \leq 1$,

$$||\widetilde{\psi}_{it}(\ddot{x}) - \widetilde{\psi}_{it}(x)|| \leq ||h|| \sup_{0<\alpha<1} ||\widetilde{\psi}'_{it}(\ddot{x})||,$$

where $\widetilde{\psi}'_{it}(\ddot{x})$ is the Fréchet derivative of $\widetilde{\psi}_{it}(x)$ at x and $||\widetilde{\psi}'_{it}(\ddot{x})|| > 0$. Since the norm defined in $\mathscr{H}$ is the L^2-norm, and assuming that $\sup_{0<\alpha<1} ||\widetilde{\psi}'_{it}(\ddot{x})|| < \Lambda$, it is easy to see that when $||h|| \to 0$, the $\widetilde{\psi}_{it}(\ddot{x})$ converges to $\widetilde{\psi}_{it}(x)$ in L^2-norm. In other words, the convergence (in the second-order moments) of selection bias is also well defined in the space $\mathscr{H}$. In addition,

$$\begin{aligned}\widetilde{\psi}_{it}(\epsilon_{it}) &= E\left[\epsilon_{it}|\widetilde{\xi}(\epsilon_{it}) > 0\right]\\ &= E\left[\beta_i^h f_{ht} + \ddot{\nu}_{it}|\widetilde{\xi}(\epsilon_{it}) > 0\right].\end{aligned}$$

Since the selection bias is defined as a linear mapping that maps $\{\epsilon_{it}\}_{i=1,2,\ldots,n}^{t=1,2,\ldots,T}$ in $\mathscr{H}$ to $\mathscr{H}$ with the same L^2-norm, it is feasible to consider the selection bias with a Taylor series expansion endowed with Fréchet derivatives and with a chain rule for differentiation such that the selection bias can be expanded (around an arbitrary $\theta \in \mathscr{H}$, $||\theta|| \to 0$) as

$$\widetilde{\psi}_{it}(\epsilon_{it} + \theta) \approx \widetilde{\psi}_{it}(\theta) + \widetilde{\psi}'_{it}(\theta)\widetilde{\xi}'(\theta)\left((\beta_i^h f_{ht} + \ddot{\nu}_{it}) - \theta\right) + R_m,$$

where R_m is the remainder term of the expansion.

Given that the Fréchet differential of selection bias is finite, and letting $\widetilde{\psi}_{it}(\theta) \to 0$ as $||\theta|| \to 0$ for simplicity, it is easy to see that the selection bias can be approximated by the linear combinations of $\beta_i^h f_{ht} + \ddot{\nu}_{it}$ such that for any given time t, $\mathring{\varphi}_{it}(\theta) \neq 0, \mathring{\varphi}_{it}(\theta) < \infty$,

$$\begin{aligned}\widetilde{\psi}_{it}(\epsilon_{it}) &\approx \widetilde{\psi}'_{it}(\theta)(\widetilde{\xi}'(\theta))\left((\beta_i^h f_{ht} + \ddot{v}_{it}) - \theta\right) + R_m,\\ &\approx \mathring{\varphi}_{it}(\theta)\left((\beta_i^h f_{ht} + \ddot{v}_{it})\right) + \widetilde{R}_m,\end{aligned}$$

where $\widetilde{R}_m = R_m - \widetilde{\psi}'_{it}(\widetilde{\xi}'(\theta))\theta$ as a remainder term. Hence, the same cross-sectional memory conditions for $\{\epsilon_{it}\}_{i=1,2,\ldots,n}^{t=1,2,\ldots,T}$ will also be present in the selection bias $\widetilde{\psi}_{it}(\epsilon_{it})$ given that $\mathring{\varphi}_{it}(\theta) = \widetilde{\psi}'_{it}(\theta)(\widetilde{\xi}'(\theta)), \mathring{\varphi}_{it}(\theta) < \infty$, and $\mathring{\varphi}_{it}(\theta) \neq 0$. Hence, at any time t and for any arbitrary asset return indexed by i, there is a hidden non-diversifiable factor in the presumed idiosyncratic risk,

$$\lim_{n\to\infty} |\mathring{\varphi}_{it}(\theta)| \sum_{j=1}^{n} |E(\beta_i^h \beta_j^h)| \longrightarrow \infty.$$

Likewise, if the hidden factor is non-diversifiable, which leads to Theorem 4.1 that entails cross-sectional long dependence among $\{\epsilon_{it}\}_{i=1,2,\ldots,n}^{t=1,2,\ldots,T}$ at any time t, the conditional expectation $\widetilde{\psi}_{it}(\epsilon_{it})$ that is identified as selection bias will also have the cross-sectional long dependence. Therefore, at any time t, the error term $\{\widetilde{\epsilon}_{it}\}_{i=1,2\ldots,n}$ still contains cross-sectional long dependence when there is a hidden non-diversifiable in the idiosyncratic risk even if the selection bias is not explicitly specified. Although the selection bias is limited to Fréchet differentials in the above arguments, it can be shown that, given the appropriate conditions, the selection bias will still present cross-sectional long dependence if the model concurrently applied omits a non-diversifiable factor.

4.1.2 *Comparison with Stochastic Discount Factor Methodology*

Notice that if following the stochastic discount factor methodology and if the stochastic discount factor m_t can be spanned by systematic factors such that $m_t = \lambda_o + \lambda_1' f_t$ with no missing non-diversifiable factor regardless of the data processes of $\mathbf{r}_t$, the necessary condition for the stochastic discount factor m will show that

$$E[\mathbf{r}_t m_t] = E[\mathbf{r}_t(\lambda_o + \lambda_1' f_t)] = \underline{\mathbf{0}}_n, \tag{4.1.4}$$

where $\mathbf{r}_t$ is an $n \times 1$ vector of excess returns, and $\underline{\mathbf{0}}_n$ is an $n \times 1$ vector of zeros, respectively.

However, as suggested by Kan and Zhou (1999) the stochastic discount factor methodology (although rigorous in theory) tends to dismiss the specifications for the return processes. If, for instance, the process of $\mathbf{r}_t$ follows the Assumption A2 where $\mathbf{r}_t$ is projected on the given information such that $r_{it} = \mu_i + \sum_{s=1}^{q} b_{is}\widetilde{x_{st}} + \sum_{j=1}^{k} \beta_{ij}f_t^{(j)} + \epsilon_{it}$ for each excess return i, $i = 1, \ldots, n$ and when the drifts $\underline{\mu} = (\mu_1, \ldots, \mu_n)'$ are non-stochastic, then Eq. (4.1.3) should give

$$E\left[\left(\underline{\mu} + B\widetilde{X}_t + \underline{\beta}f_t + \underline{\epsilon}_t\right)\left(\lambda_o + \lambda_1' f_t\right)\right] = \underline{\mathbf{0}}_n \tag{4.1.5}$$

where $\widetilde{X}_t = \left(\widetilde{x_{1t}}, \ldots, \widetilde{x_{qt}}\right)'$,$f_t = \left(f_t^{(1)}, \ldots, f_t^{(k)}\right)'$, and $B = \left(a_1, \ldots, a_q\right)$ is an $n \times q$ matrix, and $\underline{\beta}$ is an $n \times k$ matrix of factor loadings on the presumed proxies for factors.

Now suppose that both the specifications of m_t and r_t fail to include a non-diversifiable hidden factor f_{ht} so that the "presumed" idiosyncratic risk $\epsilon_{it} = \beta_i^h f_{ht} + \nu_{it}$, where f_{ht} is orthogonal to all the other factors/proxies already included. In addition, let the *correct* specification of the stochastic discount factor be given as $\tilde{m}_t = \lambda_o + \lambda_1' f_t + \lambda_2 f_{ht}$, where $\lambda_2 \neq 0$ is a non-stochastic parameter. The hidden non-diversifiable factor is included in the "correctly specified" stochastic discount factor since it is also a pricing-kernel determinant.

Suppose that the current misspecified model is denoted as $m_t = \lambda_o + \lambda_1' f_t$, it is easy to see that under the correct specifications, the necessary condition of the stochastic discount factor should give

$$\begin{aligned}
E[\mathbf{r}_t\tilde{m}_t] &= E[\mathbf{r}_t(\lambda_o + \lambda_1' f_t + \lambda_2 f_{ht})] \\
&= E\left[\left(\underline{\mu} + B\widetilde{X}_t + \underline{\beta}f_t + \beta_H f_{ht} + \nu_{it}\right)\left(\lambda_o + \lambda_1' f_t + \lambda_2 f_{ht}\right)\right] \\
&= E\left[\left(\underline{\mu} + B\widetilde{X}_t + \underline{\beta}f_t + \nu_{it}\right)\left(\lambda_o + \lambda_1' f_t\right)\right] + E\left[\beta_H \lambda_2 f_{ht}^2\right] \\
&= E\left[\left(\underline{\mu} + B\widetilde{X}_t + \underline{\beta}f_t + \nu_{it}\right)\left(\lambda_o + \lambda_1' f_t\right)\right] + \lambda_2 E[\beta_H] E[f_{ht}^2] \\
&= E[\mathbf{r}_t m_t] + \lambda_2 E[\beta_H] E[f_{ht}^2] \\
&= \underline{\mathbf{0}}_n,
\end{aligned} \tag{4.1.6}$$

since $E[f_t f_{ht}] = \underline{\mathbf{0}}_k$ is a $k \times 1$ vector of zeros.

In other words, the pricing error e_t (as an $n \times 1$ vector) in using the misspecified model of the stochastic factor can be written as

$$\begin{aligned} e_t &= \underline{\mathbf{0}}_n - E\left[\left(\underline{\mu} + B\widetilde{X}_t + \underline{\beta} f_t + \nu_{it}\right)\left(\lambda_o + \lambda_1' f_t\right)\right] \\ &= \underline{\mathbf{0}}_n - E[\mathbf{r}_t m_t] \\ &= -\lambda_2 E[\beta_H] E[f_{ht}^2]. \end{aligned}$$

Notice that the same pricing error can also be written in terms of specification errors such that since $\underline{\epsilon}_t = \beta_H f_{ht} + \underline{\nu}_t$,

$$\begin{aligned} e_t &= E[\mathbf{r}_t(m_t - \tilde{m}_t)] \\ &= E\left[\left(\underline{\mu} + B\widetilde{X}_t + \underline{\beta} f_t + \beta_H f_{ht} + \nu_{it}\right)(-\lambda_2 f_{ht})\right] \\ &= E\left[\left(E[\mathbf{r}_t | I_t] + \underline{\epsilon}_t\right)(-\lambda_2 f_{ht})\right] \\ &= -\lambda_2 E[\beta_H] E[f_{ht}^2], \end{aligned}$$

according to Assumption A2 and that $E[\mathbf{r}_t | I_t]$ is orthogonal to f_{ht}.

However, if $E[\beta_H] = \underline{\mathbf{0}}_n$,[9] and if one applies the misspecified model for return processes that omits the hidden non-diversifiable factor f_{ht} when considering the necessary condition for stochastic discount factors spanned by presumed factors, will end up with a pricing error $-\lambda_2 E[\beta_H] E[f_{ht}^2] = \underline{\mathbf{0}}_{\mathbf{n}}$. In that case, the claim of using cross-sectional regressions in identifying specification errors of omitted factor(s) (in both return process and the stochastic discount factor) of Jagannathan and Wang (1998) may not hold because the pricing errors will be equal to zero almost surely.

That is, the pricing error is always equal to an $n \times 1$ vector of zeros for Eq. (4.1.5) even though there is a missing non-diversifiable factor in the return process—unless $E[\beta_H] \neq \underline{\mathbf{0}}_{\mathbf{n}}$ or β_H is non-stochastic and $\beta_H \neq \underline{\mathbf{0}}_n$.[10] In addition, when $E[\beta_H] \neq \underline{\mathbf{0}}$ or β_H is non-stochastic and $\beta_H \neq \underline{\mathbf{0}}_n$, and the pricing error $-\lambda_2 E[\beta_H] E[f_{ht}^2]$ is non-null, identification of the "essentiality" or "non-diversifiability" of the missing factor is still required because the omitted factor may not be needed for the pricing kernel of asset returns. Therefore, simply investigating the pricing error alone will not necessarily detect the need for the additional factor.

That is to say, if the empirical asset pricing models omit an essential non-diversifiable factor (with stochastic factor loadings of mean zero) in the return process, and if one assumes the stochastic discount factor m_t is well-specified under the preselected factors without including the additional factor, the pricing errors may possibly fail to detect the error simply by using Eq. (4.1.4) as the necessary condition for any stochastic discount factor. In other words, even if the return processes are specified and the stochastic discount factor is modeled accordingly, the application of stochastic discount factor methodology may not detect an omitted non-diversifiable factor (with zero-mean random factor loadings) in the return processes. Nevertheless, the results of Theorem 4.1 hold true either of the expected factor loadings such as $E[\beta_H] = \underline{\mathbf{0}}_n$ or $E[\beta_H] \neq \underline{\mathbf{0}}_n$ of the hidden non-diversifiable factor with random factor loadings.

For instance, if the second-order moment for the specification errors in the stochastic discount factor is considered, it can be shown that either $E[\underline{\beta}^h] = \underline{\mathbf{0}}_n$ or $E[\underline{\beta}^h] \neq \underline{\mathbf{0}}_n$, and that the product matrix of $\mathbf{r}_t(m_t - \tilde{m}_t)$ will show that

$$\begin{aligned} E\left[(\mathbf{r}_t(m_t - \tilde{m}_t))\,(\mathbf{r}_t(m_t - \tilde{m}_t))'\right] &= E\left[\lambda_2^2\left(\underline{\epsilon}_t f_{ht}\right)\left(\underline{\epsilon}_t f_{ht}\right)'\right] \\ &= E\left[\lambda_2^2 f_{ht}^2\left(\underline{\epsilon}_t \underline{\epsilon}_t'\right)\right] \\ &= \lambda_2^2 E\left[f_{ht}^2\left(\beta_H \beta_H' f_{ht}^2\right)\right] + o_p(1) \\ &= \lambda_2^2 E\left[f_{ht}^4\right] E\left[\beta_H \beta_H'\right] + o_p(1), \end{aligned} \tag{4.1.7}$$

provided that $E\left[f_{ht}^4\right] < \infty$.

By considering the second-order moment of the specification errors in the stochastic discount factor as in Eq. (4.1.6), an additional condition for pricing errors can be developed and reduced to the checking of the norms of the matrix $E\left[\beta_H\beta_H'\right]$ of random factor loadings when $E[\beta_H] = \underline{\mathbf{0}}_n$ or $E[\beta_H] \neq \underline{\mathbf{0}}_n$. Likewise, it can be shown that the norms of the matrix $E\left[\beta_H\beta_H'\right]$ depends on the cross-sectional memory of β_H as discussed in Theorem 4.1. For instance, the column norm $\tau(\cdot)$ of the matrix $E\left[\beta_H\beta_H'\right]$ can be defined as

$$\tau\left(E\left[\beta_H\beta_H'\right]\right) = \max_{1\le j\le n} \sum_{i=1}^{n} |E\left(\beta_i^h \beta_j^h\right)|,$$

which in turn depends on the cross-sectional memory condition of the presumed idiosyncratic risk as shown in Theorem 4.1. In other words, the checking for specification errors in both the return process and the stochastic discount factor can be combined together by using the conclusion of Theorem 4.1.

On the other hand, let the number of essential factors be known, where the factor loadings are non-stochastic. Also let $\widetilde{y}$ be the vector of correct non-diversifiable factors and y be the vector of misspecified factors, respectively, where some elements in $\widetilde{y}$ and y are different, as in Jagannathan and Wang (1998). If the incorrect factors included in y are diversifiable, applying the theorem of Jagannathan and Wang (1998) in Eq. (2.2.34) will show that the variance of the estimation bias $(X'QX)^{-1} X'Q \left(\widetilde{\mathbf{B}} - \mathbf{B}\right) b$ will grow with the number of cross-sectional observations. This is because the matrix $\widetilde{\mathbf{B}} - \mathbf{B}$ can be shown as

$$\widetilde{\mathbf{B}} - \mathbf{B} = \begin{bmatrix} \underline{\widetilde{\beta}} - \underline{\beta} \\ \underline{0}_p \end{bmatrix},$$

where $\underline{\widetilde{\beta}}$ and $\underline{\beta}$ are both $(k - p) \times 1$ vectors of factor loadings where $\underline{\beta}$ represents the factor loadings of misspecified factors included in y, and p is the number of identical factors included in $\widetilde{y}$ and y and k are the number of factors predetermined. If the incorrect factors included in y are all diversifiable, and if the spectral norm (or Frobenius norm) is applied to the matrix $\widetilde{\mathbf{B}} - \mathbf{B}$, the norm of this matrix will grow with the number of cross-sectional observations n since $\tau(\widetilde{\mathbf{B}} - \mathbf{B}) \geq \tau(\widetilde{\mathbf{B}}) - \tau(\mathbf{B})$, and $\tau(\widetilde{\mathbf{B}})$ grows with n while $\tau(\mathbf{B})$ is finite. In other words, the results in Theorem 4.1 include the specification errors stated in Jagannathan and Wang (1998).

Loosely speaking, the conditions in Eq. (4.1.3) or (4.1.4) can only be treated as the "first-order" condition for the pricing kernel of asset returns, either from the perspective of beta-pricing models or from the stochastic discount factor methodology. However, the condition in Eq. (4.1.3) or (4.1.4) may fail to detect model misspecification in (say) either the returns processes or the stochastic discount factor. Although both the arguments of the stochastic discount factor and those of Kan and Zhou (1999) are well-established, the claim of Kan and Zhou (1999) is developed under the assumption of a "*known*" or "*true*" one-factor model. Yet, in empirical studies, the correct identification of the factor premium is only feasible when the factor(s) (and the number of factor(s)) is obtained.

It seems that the factor(s) included in the return process and stochastic discount factor must be essential for the pricing kernel of the assets. If so, these "presumed" factors should be non-diversifiable with all efficient portfolios. Therefore, if both m_t and $\tilde{m}_t$ are nested models, it is easy to see that if the omitted factor is "essential" and "non-diversifiable", the "second-order" condition of pricing errors in Eq. (4.1.6) will provide the direction for diagnostic tests in the model search.

4.2 Statistical Diagnostic Tests with Applications of Theorem 4.1

Earlier empirical work in Jeng and Liu (2012) applies the claim from Theorem 4.1 to test whether there is any additional hidden non-diversifiable factor in the forecast errors of the Fama-French three-factor model of stock returns.[11] It is shown that there is no such non-diversifiable factor in the forecast errors of the Fama-French three-factor model even though much empirical research indicates that there are additional (economic) variables needed for the explanation of security returns. Notice that the conventional findings of additional variables are based on the usual test statistics (such as t-tests or robust generalized method of moments (GMM) tests) which only show that these variables are significantly related to stock returns statistically. However, these results do not confirm these identified variables are essential in pricing the returns since many economic variables are somewhat related to stock returns statistically.

In particular, the model search with the cross-sectional extended rescaled-variance test is performed with the backward elimination method. The reduction of the dimension of the model is considered when the extended cross-sectional rescaled-variance test of the forecast errors (of the model at the current stage of search) fails to reject the null hypothesis of a cross-sectional short memory at each stage of the search. In other words, even if the test is considered as diagnostic, it can be applied as a tool for model selection. On the other hand, an alternative method with forward selection is described in Chap. 5 of this book where the forward selection algorithm is introduced for the possible expansion of the model. Specifically, similar tests can be developed so that they can be applied as an equivalence rule and elimination rule for model confidence, as in Hansen et al. (2011).

For the specification test in the model search, the framework of the rescaled-variance test of Giraitis et al. (2003) is modified for the finite forecast horizon T to test the cross-sectional memory condition of idiosyncratic risks in multifactor pricing models by assuming that $E(\beta_H) = \underline{0}_n$. The test statistics converge asymptotically to the T-sample Watson's test statistic on a unit circle where the asymptotic distribution is shown in Maag (1966). For the framework of analysis, it is assumed that the time horizon is fixed. That is, the time horizon T for performing the test is finite while the numbers of cross-sectional observations can be extended asymptotically as $n \to \infty$. Hence, the asymptotic arguments for the test statistics are established given that the cross-sectional number of securities included can expand as large as is needed. This assumption is well made in hypothesis tests of empirical asset pricing models since the number of traded securities in the market is enormous.

For the derivation of the cross-sectional extended rescaled-variance test, a few definitions and assumptions are needed to establish the prerequisites. Definition D4 defines the self-similar processes where the Hurst exponent is applied. Definition D5 defines a diffusion process denoted as fractional Brownian motion which may be long dependent or otherwise, depending on the Hurst exponent. Assumption A6 states the invariance principle for partial sums of idiosyncratic risks converging in distribution to a long-memory fractional Brownian motion, when the idiosyncratic risks have a hidden non-diversifiable factor. Conversely, an invariance principle for the partial sums of idiosyncratic risks with a mixing short-memory condition is given in Assumption A7.

Definition D4 A random process $X(\tau)$ is called "self-similar" if and only if

$$X(\lambda\tau) \overset{d}{\equiv} \lambda^H X(\tau), \tag{4.2.1}$$

for $\lambda > 0$, $\tau \in R$, $\tau \geq 0$, where $H \geq 0$, is the Hurst exponent and the notation $\overset{d}{\equiv}$ stands for the equivalence of distributions. In addition, without loss of generality, we set the initial condition $X(0) = 0$ (almost certainly). According to Embrechts and Maejima (2002), for any self-similar process, $H = 0$ if and only if $X(\tau) = X(0)$, $\forall\tau \geq 0$ (almost certainly). If $H = 1$, this implies that all autocorrelations of $X(\tau)$ are equal to one.

Definition D5 Let $0 < H \leq 1$, be a zero-mean Gaussian process $\{B_H(\tau), \tau > 0\}$, called "fractional Brownian motion", if

$$E\left[B_H(\tau) B_H(s)\right] = \frac{1}{2}\left\{\tau^{2H} + s^{2H} - |\tau - s|^{2H}\right\} E\left[B_H(1)\right]^2. \tag{4.2.2}$$

In particular, when $\frac{1}{2} < H < 1$, the process will have long dependence. When $H = \frac{1}{2}$, $\{B_H(\tau), \tau > 0\}$ will become the usual Brownian motion with independent identically distributed increments. If $0 < H < \frac{1}{2}$, the process is called "antipersistent" with the sum of the auto-covariances being finite.

Assumption A6 Given Theorem 1.1, let $\{\epsilon_{it}\}_{i=1,2,\ldots}$, if it contains a cross-sectional long memory, be covariance-stationary with cross-sectional covariances $\rho_{it}^{\epsilon}(j) = j^{-\alpha} L(j), \alpha = 2-2H, \frac{1}{2} < H < 1$, for all $i = 1, 2, \ldots, n$, $n \to \infty$, while $\{\epsilon_{it}\}_{i=1,2,\ldots}$ are inter-temporal independent for any date t, $t = 1, 2, \ldots, T$. Denote the partial sum of $\{\epsilon_{it}\}_{i=1,2,\ldots}$ as $\ddot{S}_{nt} = \sum_{i=1}^{n} \epsilon_{it}$, $\ddot{\sigma}_t^2 = \mathrm{Var}(\ddot{S}_{nt}) \approx n^{2H} L^2(n), L(n)$ is a slowly varying function of n such that $\lim_{n \to \infty} \frac{L(\lambda n)}{L(n)} = 1$ for all $\lambda > 0$. Then, for any date t, $t = 1, 2, \ldots, T$, the weighted cross-sectional partial sum of $\{\epsilon_{it}\}_{i=1,2,\ldots}$ will converge in distribution as

$$\frac{1}{\sqrt{\mathrm{Var}\left(\ddot{S}_{nt}\right)}} \sum_{i=1}^{[n\tau]} \epsilon_{it} \xrightarrow{d} B_{H_t}(\tau), \tag{4.2.3}$$

where $0 < \tau \leq 1$, $\frac{1}{2} < H < 1$, $[n\tau]$ is the largest integer less than or equal to $n\tau$, $B_{H_t}(\tau)$ and is a fractional Brownian motion at date t with Hurst exponent H.

Assumption A7 Let the idiosyncratic risks $\{\epsilon_{it}\}_{i=1,2,\ldots}$ for date t, $t = 1, 2, \ldots, T$, be inter-temporal independent while containing only cross-sectional short memory as $\widetilde{\sigma}_t^2 = \sum_{j=0}^{\infty} \rho_{it}^{\epsilon}(j) < \infty$, and $\{\epsilon_{it}\}_{i=1,2,\ldots}$ satisfies the mixing conditions such that the mixing coefficient $\alpha(j) \to 0$ as $j \to \infty$, where the mixing coefficient is defined as

$$\alpha(j) = \sup_{A \in F_{-\infty}^{0}, B \in F_j^{\infty}} |P(A \cap B) - P(A) P(B)|,$$

where F_l^{l+m} represents the σ-field generated by $\{\epsilon_{lt}, \epsilon_{l+1,t}, \ldots \epsilon_{l+m,t}\}$, the cross-sectional partial sums of $\{\epsilon_{it}\}_{i=1,2,\ldots}$ will follow the invariance principle such that as $n \to \infty$

$$\frac{1}{\sqrt{n}\widetilde{\sigma}_t} \sum_{i=1}^{[n\tau]} \epsilon_{it} \xrightarrow{d} B_t(\tau), \tag{4.2.4}$$

where $[n\tau]$ is the largest integer less than or equal to $n\tau$, $B_t(\tau)$ is a Brownian motion, for $0 < \tau \leq 1$, and $B_t(0) = 0$.

The rescaled-variance statistic of Giraitis et al. (2003) is henceforth extended to a cross-sectional test with a finite T-sample time horizon. Notice that Assumption A6 can be extended to include the (cross-sectional) heteroskedasticity in $\{\epsilon_{it}\}_{i=1,2,\ldots}$, so that the following $V_{n,T}$ statistic still converges to the same functional of the Brownian bridge even though $\{\epsilon_{it}\}_{i=1,2,\ldots}$ is not covariance-stationary. The conditions still hold under the nonstationary case as indicated by Giraitis et al. (2003).

Theorem 4.4 *Given Definitions D4, D5, and Assumption A7, for any time t, $t = 1, 2, \ldots, T$, $T \geq 2$, T is the finite time horizon for hypothesis testing, where* $\sup\limits_h \sum_{r,s=-n}^{n} |\kappa_t(h, r, s)| < \infty$,

$$\begin{aligned}\kappa_t(h, r, s) =& E\left[(\epsilon_{it} - \mu_\epsilon)(\epsilon_{i+h,t} - \mu_\epsilon)(\epsilon_{i+r,t} - \mu_\epsilon)(\epsilon_{i+s,t} - \mu_\epsilon)\right] \\ &- \left(\rho_{it}^\epsilon(h)\,\rho_{it}^\epsilon(r-s) + \rho_{it}^\epsilon(r)\,\rho_{it}^\epsilon(h-s) + \rho_{it}^\epsilon(s)\,\rho_{it}^\epsilon(h-r)\right)\end{aligned} \tag{4.2.5}$$

is the fourth-order cumulant of cross-sectional covariance stationary $\{\epsilon_{it}\}_{i=1,2,\ldots}$ at time t. Then, if $\{\epsilon_{it}\}_{i=1,2,\ldots}$ are of cross-sectional short memory, the T-sample cross-sectional extended rescaled-variance test statistic when denoted as

$$\begin{aligned}V_{n,T} =& \frac{1}{T}\left\{\sum_{t=1}^{T}\left(\frac{1}{\hat{s}_{nt}^2 n^2}\right)\sum_{m=1}^{n}\left(\sum_{i=1}^{m}(\epsilon_{it} - \overline{\epsilon}_{nt})\right)^2\right. \\ &\left. - \frac{1}{nT}\left(\sum_{t=1}^{T}\left(\frac{1}{\hat{s}_{nt} n}\right)\sum_{m=1}^{n}\sum_{i=1}^{m}(\epsilon_{it} - \overline{\epsilon}_{nt})\right)^2\right\},\end{aligned} \tag{4.2.6}$$

will converge to a functional of the Brownian bridge such that

$$V_{n,T} \xrightarrow{d} \frac{1}{T}\sum_{t=1}^{T}\int_{o}^{1}\left(\widetilde{B}_t(\tau)\right)^2 d\tau - \left(\overline{\int_{o}^{1}\widetilde{B}_t(\tau)\,d\tau}\right)^2, \tag{4.2.7}$$

as $n \to \infty$, *where* $\overline{\int_o^1 \widetilde{B}_t(\tau)\,d\tau} = \frac{1}{T}\sum_{t=1}^{T}\left(\int_o^1 \widetilde{B}_t(\tau)d\tau\right), 0 < \tau \leq 1$, $\{\widetilde{B}_1(\tau), \widetilde{B}_2(\tau), \ldots, \widetilde{B}_T(\tau)\}$ *are* T *independent Brownian bridges,* $B_t^o(\tau) = B(\tau) - \tau B(1), \overline{\epsilon}_{nt} = \frac{1}{n}\sum_{i=1}^{n}\epsilon_{it}$, *is the cross-sectional average of* $\{\epsilon_{it}\}_{i=1,2,\ldots,n,\ldots}$, *the error terms from the presumed asset pricing models for a given date* t, $t = 1, 2, \ldots, T$. *The estimator for long-run variance* $\widetilde{\sigma}_t^2$ *is denoted as* $\hat{s}_{nt}^2 = \frac{1}{n}\sum_{i=1}^{n}(\epsilon_{it} - \overline{\epsilon}_{nt})^2 + 2\sum_{j=1}^{q}\overline{\omega}_j(q)\hat{\gamma}_{jt}, \overline{\omega}_j(q) = 1 - \frac{j}{q+1}$ *are the Bartlett weights where* $q \to \infty$, $\frac{q}{n} \to 0$ *as* $n \to \infty$. *The sample cross-sectional covariances for a given date* t *are defined as* $\hat{\gamma}_{jt} = \frac{1}{n}\sum_{i=1}^{n-j}(\epsilon_{it} - \overline{\epsilon}_{nt})(\epsilon_{i+j,t} - \overline{\epsilon}_{nt}), 0 \leq j < n$.

Conversely, if $\{\epsilon_{it}\}_{i=1,2,\ldots,n,\ldots}$, are subject to cross-sectional long memory due to a possibly hidden non-diversifiable factor, let the slowly varying function in Assumption A6 be denoted by $L(n) = C_o$ for simplicity, and let $\sup_h \sum_{r,s=-n}^{n} |\kappa_t(h,r,s)| = O(n^{2H-1})$ then

$$\left(\frac{q}{n}\right)^{2H-1} V_{n,T} \xrightarrow{d} \left(\frac{1}{T}\right)\sum_{t=1}^{T}\int_{o}^{1}\left(\widetilde{B}_{H_t}(\tau)\right)^2 d\tau - \left(\overline{\int_{o}^{1}\widetilde{B}_{H_t}(\tau)\,d\tau}\right)^2, \tag{4.2.8}$$

where $\widetilde{B}_H$ is a fractional Brownian bridge with Hurst exponent H, and the test is consistent in that $V_{n,T} \longrightarrow \infty$ as $n \to \infty$ when $\{\epsilon_{it}\}_{i=1,2,\ldots,}$ is of cross-sectional long memory.

Proof For each time t, since the test statistics depend crucially on the estimates of the long-run cross-sectional variance (regardless that the underlying process is self-similar to $\frac{1}{2} < H < 1$ or is a fractional-difference model as $0 < d < \frac{1}{2}$) and the hidden factor is stationary, it is easy to set d in the assumptions of Giraitis et al. (2003) as $d = H - \frac{1}{2}$ without loss of generality. Since the estimate $\widehat{s}_{nt}^2 = \frac{1}{n}\sum_{i=1}^{n}(\epsilon_{it} - \overline{\epsilon}_{nt})^2 + 2\sum_{j=1}^{q}\varpi_j(q)\hat{\gamma}_{jt}$ is a consistent estimate for the long-run cross-sectional variance $\widetilde{\sigma}_t^2$ as $n \to \infty$, and given the memory condition $\{\epsilon_{it}\}_{i=1,2...}$ in Assumption A6, and by the continuous mapping theorem,

$$V_{nT} = \frac{1}{T}\left\{\sum_{t=1}^{T}\left(\frac{1}{\hat{s}_{nt}^2 n^2}\right)\sum_{m=1}^{n}\left(\sum_{i=1}^{m}(\epsilon_{it}-\overline{\epsilon}_{nt})\right)^2 - \frac{1}{nT}\left(\sum_{t=1}^{T}\left(\frac{1}{\hat{s}_{nt}n}\right)\sum_{m=1}^{n}\sum_{i=1}^{m}(\epsilon_{it}-\overline{\epsilon}_{nt})\right)^2\right\},$$

will converge to a functional of the Brownian bridge such that

$$V_{n,T} \xrightarrow{d} \frac{1}{T}\sum_{t=1}^{T}\int_{o}^{1}\left(\widetilde{B}_t(\tau)\right)^2 d\tau - \left(\int_{o}^{1}\widetilde{B}_t(\tau)\,d\tau\right)^2.$$

In addition, if there is a non-diversifiable hidden factor in the idiosyncratic risk such that the latter contains long memory as in Assumption A5, and letting $L(n) = C_o$ for simplicity, and assuming the cumulant condition that $\sup_h \sum_{r,s=-n}^{n} |\kappa_t(h,r,s)| = O(n^{2H-1})$, it can be shown that for each time t, $q^{2H-1}\hat{s}_{nt}^2 \xrightarrow{p} \ddot{\sigma}_t^2$, where $\ddot{\sigma}_t^2$ is the long-run cross-sectional variance of $\{\epsilon_{it}\}_{i=1,2...}$ when they have cross-sectional long memory. Hence,

$$\left(\frac{q}{n}\right)^{2H-1} V_{nT} \xrightarrow{d} \left(\frac{1}{T}\right)\sum_{t=1}^{T}\int_{o}^{1}\left(\widetilde{B}_{H_t}(\tau)\right)^2 d\tau - \left(\int_{o}^{1}\widetilde{B}_{H_t}(\tau)\,d\tau\right)^2,$$

where $\widetilde{B}_{H_t}$ is a fractional Brownian bridge at date t with Hurst exponent H, $\frac{1}{2} < H < 1$. Since the rescaled variance is positive, $\frac{q}{n} \to 0$ as $n \to \infty$, and $2H-1 > 0$, $V_{nT} \to \infty$ when $n \to \infty$, hence the test is consistent.

Notice that the asymptotic distribution of $V_{n,T}$ (denoted as $F(V_{n,T} \leq \delta)$) is shown by Maag (1966); for $T \geq 2, F(V_{n,T} \leq \delta) = \phi_{T-1}$, for $T = 1$, $F(V_{n,T} \leq \delta) = \phi_1$, where the function ϕ_T is defined as $\phi_T = \frac{2}{(2\delta)^{T/2}\sqrt{\pi}}\sum_{r=0}^{\infty}(-1)^r\binom{-T}{r}\exp\left\{\frac{-(2r+T)^2}{8\delta}\right\}H_{T-1}\left(\frac{2r+T}{2\sqrt{2\delta}}\right)$, $H_{T-1}(z)$ is the Hermite polynomial of order $T-1$ for argument z. Hence, hypothesis testing can be performed with this denoted distribution.

In addition, when $T = 1$, the above statistic will reduce to the original rescaled-variance test of Giraitis et al. (2003), where under the null hypothesis of short memory, the distribution function will be reduced to $F(x) = 1 + 2\sum_{i=1}^{\infty}(-1)^i \exp\left(-2i^2\pi x\right)$.

Since the asymptotic distribution is nonconventional, we reject the null hypothesis of short memory when the p-value of $V_{n,T}$ is relatively small compared to the significance level. This test statistic converges to the same functional as Maag's (1966) statistic in hypothesis testing for the identical cumulative distribution function of the T groups of data.

However, the above result is based on the idiosyncratic risk $\{\epsilon_{it}\}_{i=1,2,\ldots,}$ and the test is only on the memory conditions of $\{\epsilon_{it}\}_{i=1,2,\ldots,}$. In the empirical studies, we can only observe either residuals or (out-of-sample) forecast errors from the fitted asset pricing models. Hence, we need to obtain the consistency of the sample statistics for any given (out-of-sample) forecast errors with cross-sectional observations $i = 1, 2, \ldots, n$.

Notice that the consistency for parameter estimates has been established for misspecified econometric models in many studies such as White (2001). In addition, as long as the hidden factor (diversifiable or not) is orthogonal to the known factors included, the consistency for parameter estimates in linear regression can be easily established.

Furthermore, for empirical applications, our interest should be on whether the idiosyncratic risks $\{\epsilon_{it}\}_{i=1,2,\ldots,}$ are diversifiable or not. Hence, the test statistic can even be simplified under the null hypothesis that there is no non-diversifiable factor in the idiosyncratic risks. Given the null hypothesis and the weak law of large numbers, we have $\ddot{\epsilon}_{nt} = \overline{\epsilon}_{nt} + o_p(1)$, where $\ddot{\epsilon}_{nt} = \frac{1}{n}\sum_{i=1}^{n}\hat{\epsilon}_{it} = \frac{1}{n}\sum_{i=1}^{n}\epsilon_{it} + o_p(1) \xrightarrow{p} 0$, as $n \to \infty$, since an equally weighted portfolio is also a well-diversified portfolio as defined. Hence, as n is sufficiently large, it can be shown that

$$\frac{1}{\widetilde{s_{nt}^2} n^2}\sum_{m=1}^{n}\left(\sum_{i=1}^{m}\left(\hat{\epsilon}_{it} - \ddot{\epsilon}_{nt}\right)\right)^2 \cong \frac{1}{\widetilde{s_{nt}^2} n^2}\sum_{m=1}^{n}\left(\sum_{i=1}^{m}\hat{\epsilon}_{it}\right)^2 + o_p(1).$$

Therefore, the cross-sectional extended rescaled-variance test using residuals or forecast errors under the null will be modified as

$$\hat{V}_{n,T} = \frac{1}{T}\left\{\sum_{t=1}^{T}\left(\frac{1}{\widetilde{s_{nt}^2} n^2}\right)\sum_{m=1}^{n}\left(\sum_{i=1}^{m}\hat{\epsilon}_{it}\right)^2 - \frac{1}{nT}\left(\sum_{t=1}^{T}\left(\frac{1}{\widetilde{s_{nt}} n}\right)\sum_{m=1}^{n}\sum_{i=1}^{m}\hat{\epsilon}_{it}\right)^2\right\}, \tag{4.2.9}$$

and given that $B(0) = 0$ as stated in Assumption A7, it is also valid to apply the same asymptotic distribution of $V_{n,T}$—since $B(0) = B(1) = 0$ in this special case—provided that a Brownian bridge is a tied-down Brownian motion $B(\tau), 0 \leq \tau \leq 1$, where $B(0) = B(1)$.

In other words, this is the special case of the $\hat{V}_{n,T}$ statistic with the $\ddot{\epsilon}_{nt} = \overline{\epsilon}_{nt} + o_p(1) = \frac{1}{n}\sum_{i=1}^{n}\epsilon_{it} + o_p(1) \overset{p}{\longrightarrow} 0$, as $n \to \infty$, under the null hypothesis that there is no hidden non-diversifiable factor in idiosyncratic risks. The following theorem is to show that the cross-sectional extended rescaled-variance test for cross-sectional memory can be performed by using the residuals/forecast errors from the presumed asset pricing model(s) under the null hypothesis and that the test is consistent also.

Theorem 4.5 *Given that* $\{\hat{\epsilon}_{it}\}_{i=1,2,\ldots,}$ *for any time t in the finite time horizon T are the forecast errors for the presumed asset-pricing model(s) where the parameters of the presumed asset pricing model(s)* $\{\beta_{ij}\}_{i=1,2,\ldots,j=1,2,\ldots,p}$ *are consistently estimated for the known factors included, and* $\{\epsilon_{it}\}_{i=1,2,\ldots,}$ *are of cross-sectional short memory as in Assumption A6, and under the null hypothesis that there is no hidden non-diversifiable factor in* $\{\epsilon_{it}\}_{i=1,2,\ldots,}$*, then when* $n \to \infty$*, the forecast error based on the rescaled-variance test for cross-sectional memory is shown as*

$$\hat{V}_{n,T} = \frac{1}{T}\left\{\sum_{t=1}^{T}\left(\frac{1}{\widetilde{s}_{nt}^{2}n^{2}}\right)\sum_{m=1}^{n}\left(\sum_{i=1}^{m}\hat{\epsilon}_{it}\right)^{2} - \frac{1}{nT}\left(\sum_{t=1}^{T}\left(\frac{1}{\widetilde{s}_{nt}n}\right)\sum_{m=1}^{n}\sum_{i=1}^{m}\hat{\epsilon}_{it}\right)^{2}\right\}, \tag{4.2.10}$$

where

$$\hat{V}_{n,T} \longrightarrow \frac{1}{T}\sum_{t=1}^{T}\int_{o}^{1}\left(\widetilde{B}_t(\tau)\right)^2 d\tau - \left(\int_{o}^{1}\widetilde{B}_t(\tau)\,d\tau\right)^2, \tag{4.2.11}$$

and $\widetilde{s}_{nt}^{2}$ *is the estimate for long run variance* $\widetilde{\sigma}_{t}^{2}$ *using the forecast errors* $\{\hat{\epsilon}_{it}\}_{i=1,2,\ldots}$ *from the presumed asset pricing model(s) when setting* $\ddot{\epsilon}_{nt} = \frac{1}{n}\sum_{i=1}^{n}\hat{\epsilon}_{it} = \overline{\epsilon}_{nt} + o_p(1) = 0$.

Proof Denote the fitted asset pricing model (at any time t as we suppress the time index for simplicity) as

$$R_n = \widetilde{Bf} + \underline{\epsilon},$$

where $R_n = (r_1, r_2, \dots r_n)'$ is a n-by-one vector of excess returns in n assets, B is a n-by-p matrix of factor loadings such that $\{\beta_{ij}\}_{i=1,\dots,n}^{j=1,\dots,p}$ represents the elements on i-th row and j-th column of B matrix, $\widetilde{f} = \left(1, f_1, f_2, \dots f_p\right)' = (1, f')'$ is the $(p+1)$-by-one vector of known factors in the presumed model, $\underline{\epsilon} = (\epsilon_1, \epsilon_2, \dots, \epsilon_n)'$ is a n-by-one vector of idiosyncratic risks, and $\underline{\hat{\epsilon}} = (\hat{\epsilon}_1, \hat{\epsilon}_2, \dots, \hat{\epsilon}_n)'$ is a n-by-one vector of forecast errors conditional on the factors included in the model.

Given Theorem 4.4, it is sufficient to show that the $\widetilde{s}_{nt}^2$ is also a consistent estimator for $\widetilde{\sigma}_t^2$. Let $\overline{\epsilon}_n = \frac{1}{n}\sum_{i=1}^n \epsilon_i$, and $\ddot{\epsilon}_n = \frac{1}{n}\sum_{i=1}^n \hat{\epsilon}_i$, respectively. Also let $e_m = (1, 1, \dots, 0, 0, \dots, 0)'$ be a n-by-one vector of m elements of ones and $n - m$ elements of zeros, $m = 1, 2, \dots, n$. Then, letting $\hat{B}$ be the matrix of consistently estimated factor loadings, it can be shown with simple linear algebra that $\underline{\hat{\epsilon}} - e_n\ddot{\epsilon}_n = (\underline{\epsilon} - e_n\overline{\epsilon}_n) - \left(I_n - \frac{1}{n}e_ne_n'\right)\left(\hat{B} - B\right)\widetilde{f}$, and that the cumulative sums are $m = 1, 2, \dots, n$,

$$
\begin{aligned}
\sum_{i=1}^{m} (\hat{\epsilon}_i - \ddot{\epsilon}_n) &= e_m'\left[(\underline{\epsilon} - e_n\overline{\epsilon}_n) - M_n\left(\hat{B} - B\right)\widetilde{f}\right] \\
&= \sum_{i=1}^{m} (\epsilon_i - \overline{\epsilon}_n) - e_m'M_n\left(\hat{B} - B\right)\widetilde{f},
\end{aligned}
$$

where $M_n = I_n - \frac{1}{n}e_ne_n'$ and I_n is an n-by-n identity matrix. Since $\hat{B} - B \to o_p(1)$ when estimated consistently, $M_n \to I_n$ as $n \to \infty$, it is easy to see that $\sum_{i=1}^m (\epsilon_i - \overline{\epsilon}_n) = \sum_{i=1}^m (\hat{\epsilon}_i - \ddot{\epsilon}_n) + o_p(1)$. Since $\gamma(j) = \frac{1}{n}\sum_{i=1}^{n-j} (\epsilon_i - \overline{\epsilon}_n)\left(\epsilon_{i+j} - \overline{\epsilon}_n\right)$, let the selection matrices be denoted as $A_j = \left[I_{n-j}, O_{(n-j),j}\right], B_j = \left[O_{(n-j),j}, I_{n-j}\right]$, where $O_{(n-j),j}$ is an $(n-j)$-by-j matrix of zeros. We now have

$$
\begin{aligned}
\ddot{\gamma}(j) &= \frac{1}{n}\left[\left(A_j\left(\underline{\hat{\epsilon}} - e_n\ddot{\epsilon}_n\right)\right)'\left(B_j\left(\underline{\hat{\epsilon}} - e_n\ddot{\epsilon}_n\right)\right)\right] \\
&= \frac{1}{n}\left[\left(\underline{\hat{\epsilon}} - e_n\ddot{\epsilon}_n\right)' A_j'B_j\left(\underline{\hat{\epsilon}} - e_n\ddot{\epsilon}_n\right)\right] \\
&= \frac{1}{n}\left[\left(\underline{\hat{\epsilon}} - e_n\ddot{\epsilon}_n\right)' N_n(j)\left(\underline{\hat{\epsilon}} - e_n\ddot{\epsilon}_n\right)\right],
\end{aligned}
$$

where $N_n(j)$ is an n-by-n matrix. Hence, as $n \to \infty$,

$$\begin{aligned}
\ddot{\gamma}(j) &= \frac{1}{n}\left[\left((\underline{\epsilon} - e_n\overline{\epsilon}_n) - M_n\left(\hat{B}-B\right)\widetilde{f}\right)' N_n(j)\left((\underline{\epsilon} - e_n\overline{\epsilon}_n) - M_n\left(\hat{B}-B\right)\widetilde{f}\right)\right] \\
&= \hat{\gamma}(j) - \frac{2}{n}\left(\hat{\underline{\epsilon}} - e_n\ddot{\epsilon}_n\right)' N_n(j) M_n\left(\hat{B}-B\right)\widetilde{f} \\
&\quad + \frac{1}{n}\left[\widetilde{f}'\left(\hat{B}-B\right)' M_n N_n(j) M_n\left(\hat{B}-B\right)\widetilde{f}\right] \\
&= \hat{\gamma}(j) - o_p(1) + \frac{1}{n}\mathrm{tr}\left[\left(\hat{B}-B\right)' M_n N_n(j) M_n\left(\hat{B}-B\right)\widetilde{f}\widetilde{f}'\right] \\
&= \hat{\gamma}(j) - o_p(1) + \frac{1}{n}\mathrm{Vec}\left[\left(\hat{B}-B\right)' M_n N_n(j) M_n\left(\hat{B}-B\right)\right]' \mathrm{Vec}\left(\widetilde{f}\widetilde{f}'\right) \\
&= \hat{\gamma}(j) - o_p(1) + \mathrm{Vec}\left[\left(\hat{B}-B\right)' M_n N_n(j) M_n\left(\hat{B}-B\right)\right]' \mathrm{Vec}\left(\frac{1}{n}\widetilde{f}\widetilde{f}'\right) \\
&= \hat{\gamma}(j) - o_p(1),
\end{aligned}$$

provided that $\hat{B} - B \to o_p(1)$ and $\frac{1}{n}\widetilde{f}\widetilde{f}' \xrightarrow{p} \Sigma_f$, where Σ_f is a positive-definite matrix. Thus, given the consistency of $\ddot{\gamma}(j)$ and $\hat{\gamma}(j)$ in estimating the cross-sectional covariances under the null hypothesis of cross-sectional short memory in $\{\epsilon_{it}\}_{i=1,2,\ldots}$, the estimate $\widetilde{s}_{nt}^2$ for long-run cross-sectional variance $\widetilde{\sigma}_t^2$ is also consistent since $\widetilde{s}_{nt}^2 - \widetilde{s}_{nt}^2 = o_p(1)$. The case when $\overline{\epsilon}_n = \ddot{\epsilon}_n = o_p(1)$ only simplifies the notation where the terms $e_n\overline{\epsilon}_n$ or $e_n\ddot{\epsilon}_n$ drop out of the above matrix equations. The logic still follows.

In addition, since under the null hypothesis the idiosyncratic risks are diversifiable when there is no non-diversifiable hidden factor, we have $\overline{\epsilon}_n \equiv \ddot{\epsilon}_n \equiv o_p(1)$, uniformly for all n's sufficiently large. Therefore, the modified nondemeaned extended rescaled-variance test in Eq. (4.2.10) is equivalent to the $V_{n,T}$ statistics where the cumulative sums for the $\overline{\epsilon}_n$ term such as $\sum_{i=1}^{m} \frac{1}{\sqrt{n}\sigma_t}\overline{\epsilon}_{nt}$ are set to zero uniformly for all m's, $m = 1, 2, \ldots, n, \ldots,$ under the null hypothesis.

However, since $\frac{1}{\sqrt{n}\sigma_t}\sum_{i=1}^{[n\tau]}\epsilon_{it} \xrightarrow{d} B_t(\tau)$, $\sum_{i=1}^{m}\frac{1}{\sqrt{n}\sigma_t}\overline{\epsilon}_{nt} = \frac{m}{n}\frac{1}{\sqrt{n}\sigma_t}\sum_{i=1}^{n}$

$\epsilon_{it} \xrightarrow{d} \tau\ B_t(1) = 0$, for all τ's, where $0 < \tau \leq 1$. In other words, we have $B_t(0) = B_t(1) = 0$, accordingly. Given the definition of a

Brownian bridge, this is to state that $\frac{1}{\sqrt{n}\sigma_t}\sum_{i=1}^{[n\tau]}\epsilon_{it}\xrightarrow{d}B_t(\tau)$, is actually a convergence toward a Brownian bridge under the null. Hence, the modified nondemeaned extended rescaled-variance test $\hat{V}_{n,T}$ statistic in Eq. (4.2.10) is equivalent to the original $V_{n,T}$ or $\hat{V}_{n,T}$ test under the null.

4.2.1 *Empirical Applications with Backward Elimination in the Model Search*

To consider the model search, the applications consider the Fama and French (1993) model as the starting point. The search begins with studying the forecast errors of the model(s) that contain any particular unobservable non-diversifiable factor when using the result of Theorem 4.1. Specifically, the diagnostic tests start when the presumed idiosyncratic risks in the Fama and French (1993) model contain a hidden non-diversifiable factor or not. In other words, the model search starts with the model that is considered the most comprehensive one within the current information set.[12]

The empirical work in Jeng and Liu (2012) collect the excess returns from 1391 randomly selected firms with different capitalizations and from different industries, including agricultural products, chemical products, finance, transportation, consumer goods, retail, and entertainment.[13] These excess returns are obtained from the firms in CRSP that have continuous monthly data in our sample period from January 1987 to December 2006. If there is a hidden non-diversifiable factor in idiosyncratic risks from the Fama and French (1993) model, the finding of persistent cross-sectional memory in these idiosyncratic risks may provide the empirical evidence to verify the claim for its existence.

For the possibility of survivorship bias in the Center for Research in Security Prices (CRSP) data source, Li and Xu (2002) argue that such bias is unlikely to be significant for US stock returns. In addition, Barber and Lyon (1997) also show that the selection bias does not significantly affect the estimated factor premiums in the equity returns of the Fama and French (1993) model.

In addition, as was shown earlier, the selection bias (of the presumed idiosyncratic risk) will still contain the portrait of cross-sectional long dependence under suitable conditions even if the bias is left as unspecified. In particular, given that the results in Theorem 4.1 are not influenced by the orderings of excess returns and for the avoidance of the data snooping problem, no grouping or sorting is performed on these excess returns.

Specifically, the data are collected from individual securities from Center for Research in Security Prices CRSP data while no characteristics of these firms are considered for sorting/grouping the excess returns of these securities.

For the model search of empirical asset pricing models, the explanatory variables for the regressions are selected as in the Fama and French (1993) model, as the model of interest at the initial stage. Similar to the procedures in backward elimination of model selection, the model search will consider whether some parsimonious models with a lower number of explanatory variables will suffice. To consider the possibility of reducing dimensionality, the same diagnostic tests are also performed on the forecast errors from the Capital Asset Pricing Model (denoted as CAPM) for the second stage of the model search where no other variables, except the market index premium, are included.

Furthermore, to avoid the possible doubts arising from the concerns of selectivity using continuously existing firms, and following the argument of Li and Mayer (2007) that correction of dynamic selection bias does not improve the accuracy of forecasts of the model, the forecast errors from the fitted model are applied for the tests. More specifically, the out-of-sample forecast errors of both the Fama and French (1993) model and Capital Asset Pricing Model are applied to test the null hypothesis that the hidden factor is diversifiable in the presumed idiosyncratic risks.

Based on the tables and asymptotic cumulative distribution function provided by Maag's (1966), the 24 months out-of-sample forecast errors are collected (that is, $T = 24$) for the test period in verifying the cross-sectional memory of idiosyncratic risks. The forecast errors for all these excess returns are obtained with the parameters estimated in the previous months of the in-sample period from January 1987 to December 2004, which are conditional on the updated explanatory variables in the asset pricing models applied here.

The test period is from January 2005 to December 2006. The test statistics for different forecast horizons are calculated from $T = 1$ to $T = 24$ using the asymptotic cumulative distribution functions from Maag (1966). Notice that when $T = 2$, the test statistic actually conforms with Watson's (1961) two-sample test where its asymptotic distribution is identical to the statistic in Giraitis et al. (2003). Hence, the asymptotic distributions applied to $T = 2$ and $T = 1$ are identical according to the asymptotic arguments in Maag (1966) and Watson (1961) as far as the two-sample tests are of concern, with an empirical application of Maag's (1966) tests as shown in Brown (1994).

The cross-sectional extended rescaled-variance $\hat{V}_{n,T}$ tests (with finite time horizons of forecasts) are performed under the null hypothesis that the hidden factor is diversifiable. The p-values of the statistics are calculated from the asymptotic cumulative distribution function provided by Maag (1966). Since the distribution function is not conventional, and that Maag's (1966) tabulation of critical values is limited to the case when the maximum forecast horizon is $T = 5$, the $\hat{V}_{n,T}$ statistics are considered as rejecting the null (when using the p-values) when the p-values are relatively smaller than the given 5% or 1% significance levels.

Table 4.1 presents the $\hat{V}_{n,T}$ test statistics and the corresponding p-values for testing the cross-sectional memory of idiosyncratic risks in the Fama and French (1993) model. These test statistics are provided with different selections of q, which are denoted as the lags for possible cross-sectional short-run memory in estimating long run variances of idiosyncratic risk under the null. For simplicity of exposition, we only report cases when $q = 5, 10, 15$, respectively.

For alternative models, the same diagnostic tests are performed on the forecast errors from alternative models such as the CAPM and the over-simplified case when excess returns are regressed only with a constant term.

The test statistics of alternative models are shown in Tables 4.2 and 4.3, respectively. All test statistics from these two alternative models reported in Tables 4.2 and 4.3 show that their p-values are all well below the 1% confidence level. These statistics reject the null hypothesis that there is no hidden non-diversifiable factor in the idiosyncratic risks of the fitted model and suggest that there is a persistent cross-sectional memory in the risks. In other words, these results imply that there is at least one hidden non-diversifiable factor in the idiosyncratic risks for both the CAPM and the over-simplified model within the sample window, and that these two models are incomplete and in need of additional factor(s) to explain asset returns.

In particular, it is noticeable that the $\hat{V}_{n,T}$ statistics from these two alternative models are much greater than those in the Fama and French (1993) model reported in Table 4.1. For instance, the test statistics for idiosyncratic risks from CAPM models are much greater than those in the Fama and French (1993) model across the forecast horizon. In particular, when the forecast horizon expands to $T \geq 4$, the test statistics increase sharply relative to the previous months and all these p-values from CAPM

Table 4.1 T-sample rescaled-variance tests on forecast errors of the Fama and French (1993) model

T	$q = 5$	$q = 10$	$q = 15$
1	$0.175^{(0.063)}$	$0.181^{(0.056)}$	$0.178^{(0.059)}$
2	$0.213^{(0.221)}$	$0.221^{(0.197)}$	$0.217^{(0.208)}$
3	$0.219^{(0.575)}$	$0.226^{(0.542)}$	$0.222^{(0.559)}$
4	$0.192^{(0.947)}$	$0.196^{(0.940)}$	$0.193^{(0.945)}$
5	$0.200^{(0.994)}$	$0.203^{(0.993)}$	$0.199^{(0.953)}$
6	$0.717^{(0.062)}$	$0.636^{(0.143)}$	$0.602^{(0.199)}$
7	$0.694^{(0.199)}$	$0.622^{(0.352)}$	$0.591^{(0.433)}$
8	$0.824^{(0.143)}$	$0.753^{(0.258)}$	$0.723^{(0.314)}$
9	$1.004^{(0.067)}$	$0.917^{(0.156)}$	$0.879^{(0.203)}$
10	$1.042^{(0.111)}$	$0.952^{(0.230)}$	$0.913^{(0.295)}$
11	$1.004^{(0.285)}$	$0.918^{(0.462)}$	$0.880^{(0.549)}$
12	$1.207^{(0.182)}$	$1.122^{(0.253)}$	$1.086^{(0.306)}$
13	$1.123^{(0.458)}$	$1.044^{(0.550)}$	$1.010^{(0.623)}$
14	$1.431^{(0.097)}$	$1.333^{(0.192)}$	$1.282^{(0.262)}$
15	$1.357^{(0.280)}$	$1.265^{(0.440)}$	$1.218^{(0.533)}$
16	$1.538^{(0.163)}$	$1.436^{(0.293)}$	$1.384^{(0.378)}$
17	$1.710^{(0.096)}$	$1.601^{(0.191)}$	$1.543^{(0.264)}$
18	$1.913^{(0.043)}$	$1.789^{(0.103)}$	$1.718^{(0.162)}$
19	$2.243^{(0.006)}$	$2.054^{(0.030)}$	$1.953^{(0.063)}$
20	$2.141^{(0.032)}$	$1.961^{(0.111)}$	$1.865^{(0.194)}$
21	$2.060^{(0.105)}$	$1.885^{(0.272)}$	$1.793^{(0.404)}$
22	$1.986^{(0.255)}$	$1.819^{(0.498)}$	$1.730^{(0.642)}$
23	$1.912^{(0.482)}$	$1.751^{(0.733)}$	$1.666^{(0.841)}$
24	$1.903^{(0.626)}$	$1.741^{(0.844)}$	$1.655^{(0.919)}$

Notes: The time index T stands for each month in the forecast horizon. For instance, $T = 1$ stands for January 2005, $T = 2$ stands for February 2005, and so on. The table reports the test statistic with corresponding p-values denoted in parentheses. If the p-value is less than the significance levels such as 5% or 1%, the null hypothesis that there is no non-diversifiable hidden factor is rejected

models are far less than 1% when using the asymptotic distribution function provided by Maag (1966).

On the other hand, the $\hat{V}_{n,T}$ statistics for the CAPM in Table 4.2 are well below those for the over-simplified model in Table 4.3, indicating that the CAPM does possess a certain level of explanatory power for asset returns,

Table 4.2 T-sample rescaled-variance test on forecast errors from the CAPM

T	$q = 5$	$q = 10$	$q = 15$
1	$0.283^{(0.008)}$	$0.292^{(0.006)}$	$0.288^{(0.007)}$
2	$0.580^{(0.007)}$	$0.577^{(0.007)}$	$0.581^{(0.008)}$
3	1.353*	1.197*	1.132*
4	4.241*	3.192*	2.776*
5	6.157*	5.094*	4.629*
6	7.668*	6.383*	5.834*
7	7.996*	6.805*	6.316*
8	7.316*	6.277*	5.854*
9	6.780*	5.862*	5.477*
10	7.285*	6.207*	5.763*
11	6.670*	5.683*	5.277*
12	6.322*	5.395*	5.014*
13	7.503*	6.425*	5.953*
14	7.033*	6.025*	5.581*
15	7.274*	6.269*	5.828*
16	6.900*	5.966*	5.558*
17	7.328*	6.327*	5.883*
18	7.171*	6.217*	5.789*
19	7.646*	6.562*	6.081*
20	7.323*	6.298*	5.846*
21	7.174*	6.202*	5.768*
22	7.121*	6.166*	5.738*
23	6.886*	5.964*	5.551*
24	6.626*	5.740*	5.324*

Notes: Only the p-values of the first two months on the forecast horizon are presented in parentheses. Other p-values are replaced with an asterisk since they are much lower than 0.1%. The null hypothesis that there is no hidden non-diversifiable factor is rejected for all levels of T and q since all p-values are below the 1% significance level

and that the so-called systematic risk (or the beta) in CAPM proves to be a contributing factor for asset returns.

The findings from the Fama and French (1993) model in Table 4.1, however, are quite different. Out of the 72 $\hat{V}_{n,T}$ statistics in the sample window, only three (namely, the ones for $q = 5, T = 18$; $q = 5, T = 20$; and $q = 10, T = 19$) are significant at the 5% level and only one (for $q = 5$,

Table 4.3 T-sample rescaled-variance tests on forecast errors when excess returns are regressed on a constant

T	$q = 5$	$q = 10$	$q = 15$
1	7.743*	5.773*	4.924*
2	8.912*	6.514*	5.488*
3	23.424*	16.985*	14.472*
4	25.959*	18.326*	15.484*
5	24.348*	17.407*	14.751*
6	20.823*	14.959*	12.716*
7	20.436*	14.621*	12.427*
8	23.315*	17.108*	14.719*
9	22.281*	16.506*	14.268*
10	26.299*	18.956*	16.224*
11	25.187*	18.308*	15.742*
12	23.392*	17.055*	14.689*
13	23.745*	17.267*	14.842*
14	22.408*	16.337*	14.053*
15	22.720*	16.757*	14.492*
16	21.322*	15.731*	13.609*
17	22.582*	16.339*	14.043*
18	21.976*	15.986*	13.765*
19	21.978*	15.974*	13.749*
20	21.181*	15.426*	13.295*
21	20.209*	14.716*	12.682*
22	21.388*	15.572*	13.411*
23	21.026*	15.371*	13.259*
24	20.185*	14.758*	12.731*

Notes: All p-values are replaced by an asterisk as they are much lower than 0.1%, and therefore the null hypothesis that there is no hidden non-diversifiable factor is rejected for all levels of T and q

$T = 19$) is significant at the 1% level. As the number of lags q increases from 5 to 10 or from 10 to 15, even these become statistically insignificant.

Thus, the null hypothesis that there is no hidden non-diversifiable factor cannot be rejected for the Fama and French (1993) model within the sample window. In other words, convincing evidence is lacking that the forecast errors from the Fama and French (1993) model may contain a hidden non-diversifiable factor. Although the finding here may be subject to the time horizon chosen, where a time-varying nature may present itself, the attempts to expand the Fama and French (1993) model should pay additional attention to the verification of essentiality in these proclaimed explanatory variables.

Intuitively speaking, if the idiosyncratic risks of a fitted asset pricing model do indeed contain a hidden non-diversifiable factor, more supporting statistics for the need for non-diversifiable factor(s) should result when more months are included, especially when forecasting is applied. In other words, as T increases, the statistics should show more supporting evidence for the alternative hypothesis.

Specifically, since this test is a one-sided test, more significant test statistics should appear when T expands, indicating that there is a higher likelihood that the tests may reject the null. However, the results from Table 4.1 do not support this. Although when $T = 1$ where the $\hat{V}_{n,T}$ test statistics of the Fama and French (1993) model coincide with Watson's statistics and the p-values for these test statistics are slightly greater than 5%, the p-values of the vast majority of these test statistics in Table 4.1 are not significantly lower when T expands.

More specifically, given the cumulative distribution provided by Maag (1966), the p-values increase sharply from 0.063 in January 2005 (when $T = 1$) to 0.994 in May 2005 (when $T = 5$). This indicates a decreasing likelihood for the idiosyncratic risk of the Fama and French (1993) model identifying a non-diversifiable hidden factor, probably due to increasing stock market volatility and information flow during this period of time.

This result, nevertheless, shows that higher market volatility and noisy intermarket information flows may not give rise to a non-diversifiable factor. However, after June 2006 and up until August 2006, some p-values of $\hat{V}_{n,T}$ statistics do drop to a level that is lower than 5% when $q = 5$. This may indicate there is a possibility that an additional hidden factor is needed as the tests may show. However, when q expands, the p-values increase again even for the same month.

The test statistics in Table 4.1 overall do not support the persistence of cross-sectional memory across different forecast horizons, offering little evidence that an additional non-diversifiable factor is needed for the Fama and French (1993) model. In contrast, all the p-values for $\hat{V}_{n,T}$ test statistics (across all different q's) of CAPM models in Table 4.2 and those of the over-simplified model in Table 4.3 are far lower than the 1% level from the start of the forecast horizon, indicating the existence of non-diversifiable factors and the need to include additional variables for the CAPM and the over-simplified model.

In summary, for the Fama and French (1993) model, the diagnostic test statistics in general do not reject the null hypothesis that there is no hidden non-diversifiable factor and show that the idiosyncratic risks do not have persistent cross-sectional memory. Therefore, convincing evidence is lacking for the existence of a hidden non-diversifiable factor in the idiosyncratic risks from the model. In contrast, the idiosyncratic risks from the CAPM and the over-simplified model reject the null hypothesis, suggesting that there may be a need for additional variables to explain the hidden non-diversifiable factor(s). And hence, the model search at this stage is not reducible to dimensionality.

Notice that the result does not say there is no other variable that can be applied to explain the asset returns, at least, in the short run. Instead, the result only states that there is no additional non-diversifiable factor in the idiosyncratic risk of the Fama and French (1993) model. The study mainly points out that any additional explanatory variable added to the (Fama and French 1993) model may still present some explanatory power for the asset returns in the short-term scale to confirm the proclaimed hypotheses in empirical asset pricing models. However, there is no indication from the cross-sectional extended rescaled-variance test that the idiosyncratic risk from the Fama and French (1993) model still contains the non-diversifiable factor(s) which require additional proxies to price them in the asset returns.

In other words, additional variables added to the Fama and French (1993) model can only be considered as proxies for explanation in temporal variations of asset returns. Nevertheless, they are not essential for the identification of pricing kernels of asset returns in (say) capital market equilibrium. And hence, model expansion after this stage may incur the risk of introducing additional short-term explanatory variables where the model may become overfitted.

On the other hand, if the model search is performed as if reduced dimensionality was preferred, the same test statistics applied to the CAPM show that the forecast errors of the latter do indicate that there is an omitted non-diversifiable factor in the presumed idiosyncratic risk. Thus, backward elimination does not end up with a better model since the smaller model does not perform (at least as) equally well.

Furthermore, the tests performed are based on the forecast errors of the presumed models. If additional non-diversifiable factors are present in the idiosyncratic risk of the models applied, the cross-sectional strong memory should be detected accordingly since the forecast errors would contain the information for model misspecification/deficiency due to the omitted critical factors. The above empirical results may however indicate that many alternative models when extending the findings of the Fama and French (1993) model could possibly suffer from the criticism of data snooping with planned (or intended) results, if no further confirmatory discovery or theoretical rigor is provided.

From the results in Theorem 4.1, we can see that if there is a hidden non-diversifiable factor in the idiosyncratic risk, a persistent cross-sectional dependence will appear on the presumed idiosyncratic risk from the fitted models. This result provides a property for empirical asset pricing models in diagnostic/specification tests on the model search for factor(s).

In other words, when the expansion of dimensions is of concern, this necessary property of non-diversifiability (for factors) can be applied to guide the directions. In particular, the property of cross-sectional long dependence developed as a necessary condition for essentiality can also be applied as specification tests and a model search on the common explanatory variables $\{\widetilde{x_{st}}\}_{s=1,2,\ldots,q}$. Specifically, the cross-sectional long dependence is a necessary condition for any possible non-diversifiable factor in the empirical asset pricing models. It is not a sufficient condition.

Notice that since the indexing of excess returns is not of any particular ordering or sorting, the above result holds for the situation where different sequences of orderings are applied for excess returns across all selected assets (or portfolios). That is, if there is a missing non-diversifiable factor in the error terms of the presumed asset pricing models, any repackaging of asset returns can't eliminate the impact from this hidden non-diversifiable factor.

Therefore, the above claim should also be extended to the task of identifying some possible non-diversifiable factors (or proxies). As such, these proxies must show cross-sectional long dependence among the asset returns to certify the findings—if the interest of the studies is to identify the ultimate determinants for empirical asset pricing models. In other words, the conventional specification tests (such as the Lagrange multiplier (LM) test or others) that show the statistical significance of parameters in the presumed asset pricing models are not sufficient to justify the essential role of the variables (or proxies for factors)—even though they may involve robust statistics with (conditional) heteroskedasticity or mixing conditions.

The model search for empirical asset pricing models is not merely to identify the variables that are (statistically) significant as explanatory or predictive determinants. Instead, one can easily expand the empirical models to include as many variables so as to explain the asset returns if over-fittedness of data snooping is not of concern. As for finance, the number of factors in asset pricing models can range from one to more than 10 (as denoted in Onatski (2009)). However, the real issue is not on how to expand the models to fit certain objectives in applications or otherwise. Instead, the focus should be on what the essentially fundamental explanatory variables are, and how they are distinguished from the other non-fundamental variables.

Specification tests for the empirical asset pricing models to identify essential variables should incorporate this non-diversifiability property in the model search. Searching for other variables without cross-sectional long dependence for extended model specification or forecasting is still worth studying. Ensuing studies may consider improvements of temporal forecasts or corporate finance issues, for instance, and would be additional chapters for the *finale* of empirical asset pricing models.

In other words, the claim of cross-sectional long dependence provides an alternative statistical test to identify the hidden factor without using the conventional (or extended) tests which are based on the eigenvalues of the variance–covariance matrix. In particular, specification of empirical asset pricing models is not merely to identify possible factors that may explain security returns. Instead, the formidable task is to depict the necessary and non-diversifiable factors that constitute the systematic components of security returns.

It is also interesting to see that this cross-sectional strong dependence may lead to discussion of the Hurst exponent in some stochastic processes that provide an alternative test for hidden non-diversifiable factor(s). With the additional framework (in Sect. 4.4 of this chapter) for the summability of the cumulative sums (CUSUM) of idiosyncratic risk or presumed error terms for any stage of the model search for empirical asset pricing models, these summability conditions (which are directly related to the non-diversifiability of hidden factors) can be shown to relate to the Hurst exponent in (say) the fractional Brownian motion, where the range of the Hurst exponent will determine the (cross-sectional) memory conditions. In brief, the statistical inference for the Hurst exponent will provide the findings as to whether there is an omitted non-diversifiable factor/determinant or not.

4.3 Discussion on Earlier Studies and Reasons for a Sequential Model Search

Independently, Chudik et al. (2011) also develop some conditions for cross-sectional weak and strong dependence in panel data, especially in the linear factor models. Although similar, their analysis does not formally show that the existence of cross-sectional long dependence is possibly the necessary consequence of hidden non-diversifiable factor in the linear factor structure of asset returns. For the model specification in empirical asset pricing models, finding the minimal set of properties of factors (or proxies of factors) is fundamentally required to establish the sequence of the model search.

More explicitly, the definition of their cross-sectional weak and strong dependence in panel data is based on the stronger properties of conditional moments.[14] For instance, when, under the definition of cross-sectional weak dependence in Chudik et al. (2011), the identification of cross-sectional dependence is shown for any weight sequence subject to a uniform convergence rate (or so-called granuality condition) at any time t

$$||\underline{\omega_{nt}}|| = O(n^{-\frac{1}{2}}),$$

$$\frac{\omega_{n,jt}}{||\underline{\omega_{nt}}||} = O(n^{-\frac{1}{2}}),$$

for any $j \in n$, $n \in \mathbb{N}$, where $||.||$ is the sup norm of the sequence of non-stochastic weights denoted by a weight vector $\omega_{nt} = (\omega_{n,1t}, \omega_{n,2t}, \ldots, \omega_{n,nt})$, t is the time index, n stands for the number of cross-sectional items (or assets) included, and the cross-sectional weak dependence (conditional on information set I_{t-1}) is defined as for stochastic process $\{z_{it}\}_{i=1,2,\ldots,n}^{t=1,2,\ldots T}$ at time t when

$$\lim_{n\to\infty} \mathrm{Var}(\omega_t' z_t | I_{t-1}) = 0.$$

For the cross-sectional strong dependence, Chudik et al. (2011) state that there exists a sequence of weight vectors ω_t such that for a constant K independent of n, and n sufficiently large,

$$\mathrm{Var}(\omega_t' z_t | I_{t-1}) \geq K > 0.$$

Since the definition of cross-sectional weak dependence is based on the conditional information I_{t-1}, if the asset returns satisfy the dependence as in Chudik et al. (2011), and if the weight sequences satisfy the definition of well-diversified portfolios where the above limit exists, the conditional variance, as the cross-sectional sample expands, will show that the underlying stochastic process may show a similar cross-sectional short memory as given in Corollary 4.2. However, the converse is not necessarily true. In particular, the condition for cross-sectional strong dependence may allow unboundedness for the upper bound of the conditional variance of the weighted sums.

In addition, according to the above definition of a cross-sectional strong dependence, the condition as $\mathrm{Var}(\omega_t' z_t | I_{t-1}) \geq K > 0$ does not guarantee that the unconditional variance such as $\mathrm{Var}(\omega_t' z_t)$ will not vanish as the sequence of weight vectors expands because it depends on the information set I_{t-1} (and the associated variables in the information set). For instance, the conditional expectation of $E[\epsilon_t | I_{t-1}] = x_{t-1} \neq 0$ for some variables x_{t-1} in information set I_{t-1} does not guarantee that $E[\epsilon_t] \neq 0$—since it is possible that $E[x_{t-1}] = 0$ if the means of $x_t's$ are equal to zero uniformly for all $t's$.

For the purpose of portfolio diversification, the claim of the existence of such weight vectors (or linear combinations) for asset returns to provide the nondegenerated conditional variance does not entail the implication of hidden non-diversifiable factors. In fact, the factor(s) can be non-diversifiable only if *all* weight vectors (or sequences) of ***well-diversified portfolios*** fail to reduce the variance.

In other words, the cross-sectional weak dependence (in conditional variance) as defined in Chudik et al. (2011) is a sufficient condition, not a necessary one, for cross-sectional diversifiability. Specifically, the definition of diversifiable versus non-diversifiable factor (or risk) with Definitions D2 and D3 may encompass that of Chudik et al. (2011) under the weight sequences of well-diversified portfolios. Likewise, verification of cross-sectional (conditional) dependence conditions may not provide the finding of a hidden non-diversifiable factor given that the diversifiability is defined on the set of efficient portfolios. It is not defined over the randomly chosen weights that simply satisfy the "granuality" conditions.

Caution is needed, however, when ascertaining whether cross-sectional long dependence is only a verification of the necessary condition for a non-diversifiable hidden factor in empirical asset pricing models. Although the conditions of cross-sectional (conditional) dependence in Chudik et al.

(2011) may influence the properties of statistical inferences in panel data, it is not necessarily a legitimate condition for verifying the existence of diversifiable/non-diversifiable factors in asset pricing models.

On the other hand, the existence of cross-sectional long dependence (in the known factors or idiosyncratic risk) helps to improve model searching in empirical asset pricing models since it provides an alternative to identify the necessary variables (or proxies) for model specification. Using this property as a minimum set of requirements in model searching, it is feasible to consider test statistics that may enhance the model specification for asset returns.

4.3.1 Other Findings and Comparisons

Let the hidden factor loadings for all asset returns be nonstochastic for simplicity, and let the hidden factor have a constant variance $E\left[f_{ht}^2\right] = \sigma_h^2$ from now on. In Bai's (2003) assumption of factor loadings, the Frobenius norm of the factor loading matrix is shown as $||\frac{\Lambda_o'\Lambda_o}{n} - \Sigma_n|| \to 0$ when $n \to \infty$, for some $r{\times}r$ positive definite matrix Σ_n, where Λ_o is an $n{\times}r$ matrix of factor loadings for n asset returns of r factors. This implies that the factor loading matrix $\frac{\Lambda_o'\Lambda_o}{n}$ converges to a positive definite matrix coordinate-wise when $n \to \infty$.

Accordingly, if the number of hidden non-diversifiable factors is equal to one, the convergence of the Frobenius norm for factor loadings shows $|\frac{\sum_{j=1}^n \beta_j^{h2}}{n} - \tilde{\sigma}^2| \to 0$, for $\tilde{\sigma}^2 > 0$ as $n \to \infty$. This, in turn, shows that $\sum_{j=1}^n \beta_j^{h2}$ grows at the same rate as n and $\sum_{j=1}^n \beta_j^{h2} \to \infty$ when $n \to \infty$. Since $\left(\sum_{j=1}^n |\beta_j^h|\right) \geq \left(\sum_{j=1}^n \beta_j^{h2}\right)^{\frac{1}{2}}$ for all $n \in N$, where N is the set of all positive integers, and $\ell_1 \subset \ell_2$ where the space of the squared-summable real sequences encompasses the space of the absolute-summable sequences of real numbers, implies $\lim_{n\to\infty} \sum_{j=1}^n |\beta_j^h| \to \infty$.

Pick an arbitrary asset and denote its factor loading as β_o^h, where $\beta_o^h \neq 0$. It can be shown that $\lim_{n\to\infty} \sum_{j=1}^n |\beta_o^h||\beta_j^h| = \sum_{j=1}^\infty |\beta_o^h\beta_j^h| \to \infty$. Applying the definition of covariance in Theorem 4.1, and denoting $\rho_{ot}^\epsilon(j) = E\left[\epsilon_{ot}\epsilon_{jt}\right] = \beta_o^h\beta_j^h\sigma_h^2$, we can see that Bai's (2003) assumption of factor loadings will lead to the cross-sectional long memory such that $\sum_{j=1}^\infty |\rho_{ot}^\epsilon(j)| = \sigma_h^2 \sum_{j=1}^\infty |\beta_o^h\beta_j^h| \to \infty$. Notice that our condition for non-diversifiable factor loadings $\sum_{j=1}^{n} \beta_j^{h^2} \rightarrow \infty$ is more general than Bai's assumption since we do not assume its growth rate is $O(1)$.

The present study also encompasses the test provided by Connor and Korajczyk (1993) when the factor loadings are nonstochastic. Their argument is that if k is the correct number of factors needed, then there should be no significant decrease in the cross-sectional mean square of the idiosyncratic risk when moving from k to $k+1$ factors. From Assumptions A2 and A3, we may express the cross-sectional mean squares of $\{\epsilon_{it}\}_{i=1,2,\ldots,}$ as

$$\operatorname*{plim}_{n\rightarrow\infty} \frac{1}{n} \sum_{i=1}^{n} \epsilon_{it}^2 = f_{ht}^2 \lim_{n\rightarrow\infty} \frac{1}{n} \sum_{i=1}^{n} \beta_i^{h^2} + \operatorname*{plim}_{n\rightarrow\infty} \frac{1}{n} \sum_{i=1}^{n} \nu_{it}^2. \tag{4.3.1}$$

If an additional factor is needed, according Connor and Korajczyk (1993), the limit of the partial sums of the squared factor loadings of the additional hidden factor (denoted as $\lim_{n\rightarrow\infty} \sum_{i=1}^{n} \beta_i^{h^2}$) will approach infinity with a faster rate than n, the sample size. In other words, the factor loadings are not in the ℓ_2 space. Hence, it is not in the ℓ_1 space either, since $\ell_1 \subset \ell_2$. That is to say, $\lim_{n\rightarrow\infty} \sum_{i=1}^{n} |\beta_i^h| \rightarrow \infty$. Pick an arbitrary asset and denote its factor loading as $\beta_o^h \neq 0$. $\lim_{n\rightarrow\infty} \sigma_h^2 \sum_{j=1}^{n} |\beta_o^h||\beta_j^h| = \lim_{n\rightarrow\infty} \sigma_h^2 \sum_{j=1}^{n} |\beta_o^h \beta_j^h| = \sigma_h^2 |\beta_o^h| \lim_{n\rightarrow\infty} |\beta_j^h| \rightarrow \infty$. This shows that the cross-sectional idiosyncratic risk will have long dependence accordingly.

On the other hand, if $\lim_{n\rightarrow\infty} \sum_{i=1}^{n} \beta_i^{h^2} < \infty$, or when $\lim_{n\rightarrow\infty} \sum_{i=1}^{n} \beta_i^{h^2}$ approach infinity with a slower rate than n, both cases will imply that $\lim_{n\rightarrow\infty} \frac{1}{n} \sum_{i=1}^{n} \beta_i^{h^2} \rightarrow 0$, and the test of Connor and Korajczyk (1993) will indicate that there is no need for additional factor(s). However, the convergence as $\lim_{n\rightarrow\infty} \frac{1}{n} \sum_{i=1}^{n} \beta_i^{h^2} \rightarrow 0$ may not necessarily imply that $\lim_{n\rightarrow\infty} \sum_{i=1}^{n} |\beta_i^h| < \infty$, since $\ell_1 \subseteq \ell_2$, the real sequences in ℓ_2 space may not also lie in ℓ_1 space. In that case, for some $\{\beta_i^h\}_{i=1,2,\ldots}$ where $\lim_{n\rightarrow\infty} \sum_{i=1}^{n} |\beta_i^h| \rightarrow \infty$, the partial sums of the absolute factor loadings may grow with a faster rate than n. Thus, $\lim_{n\rightarrow\infty} \frac{1}{n} \sum_{i=1}^{n} |\beta_i^h| \nrightarrow 0$, even though $\lim_{n\rightarrow\infty} \frac{1}{n} \sum_{i=1}^{n} \beta_i^{h^2} \rightarrow 0$ in Eq. (4.1.4). Hence, their test may tend to accept the null hypothesis that no additional factor is needed and so will fail to identify some essential non-diversifiable hidden factors.

Another difficulty of the test for the number of factors in Connor and Korajczyk (1993) is that the test is based on the difference of the mean-square errors of the idiosyncratic risk between k and $k+1$ hypothesized factors. Given a finite sample of real-time observations, the difference between these sums of squared errors when the additional factor is assumed is almost always finite or trivial before multiplication by the sample size n—even though they show that the test statistic will approximate to the normal distribution when the number of security returns grows asymptotically.

In addition, let us assume some asset-pricing models of a single known systematic factor f_t and a hidden factor f_{ht} in the framework of Goyal and Santa-Clara (2003) with nonstochastic factor loadings. Let the hidden factor f_{ht}, the idiosyncratic noise, and the known systematic factors all be mutually orthogonal, where the average stock volatility without serial dependence may be expressed as

$$\frac{1}{n}\sum_{i=1}^{n} r_{it}^2 = \frac{1}{n}\sum_{i=1}^{n} \mu_i^2 + \frac{1}{n}\sum_{i=1}^{n} \beta_i^2 f_t^2 + \left(\frac{1}{n}\sum_{i=1}^{n} \beta_i^{h^2}\right) f_{ht}^2 + \frac{1}{n}\sum_{i=1}^{n} v_{it}^2. \tag{4.3.2}$$

And let the equally weighted stock excess returns be expressed as

$$r_{\text{ewd}} = \overline{\mu} + \frac{1}{n}\sum_{i=1}^{n} \beta_i f_t + \frac{1}{n}\sum_{i=1}^{n} \beta_i^h f_{ht} + o_p(1). \tag{4.3.3}$$

Suppose the hidden factor is non-diversifiable so that $\frac{1}{n}\sum_{i=1}^{n} \beta_i^h$ will not converge to zero as $n \to \infty$. Assuming its limit exists such that $\lim_{n\to\infty} \frac{1}{n}\sum_{i=1}^{n} |\beta_i^h| \geq \lim_{n\to\infty} |\frac{1}{n}\sum_{i=1}^{n} \beta_i^h| > \delta > 0$. Thus, the partial sums $\sum_{i=1}^{\infty} |\beta_i^h| \to \infty$, accordingly. This implies that the sequence $\{\beta_i^h\}_{i=1,2\ldots}$ cannot be in the ℓ_1 space. However, this setting does not necessarily imply that $\lim_{n\to\infty} \sum_{i=1}^{n} \beta_i^{h^2} \to \infty$ since the real sequences that are not in the ℓ_1 space may still be in the ℓ_2 space—provided that some absolute nonsummable real sequences may still be squared-summable.

Specifically, it is possible that for some $\{\beta_i^h\}_{i=1,2,\ldots}$, the term $\lim_{n\to\infty} \frac{1}{n}\sum_{i=1}^{n} \beta_i^{h^2} \to 0$ and vanishes from Eq. (4.3.2) as $n \to \infty$. In other words, the average stock volatility in Eq. (4.3.2) may actually fail to pick up the hidden non-diversifiable factor even though it is apparent in the equally weighted portfolio's rate of return in Eq. (4.3.3).

On the other hand, let us extend the over-simplified framework in Eq. (4.3.3) to the weighted market excess returns, where the excess returns of the included assets are not necessarily equally weighted with $\frac{1}{n}$, and obtain the so-called aggregate market volatility as $E\left[r_{mt} - E\left(r_{mt}\right)\right]^2 = \left(\sum_{i=1}^{n} \omega_i \beta_i\right)^2 \sigma_t^2 + \left(\sum_{i=1}^{n} \omega_i \beta_i^h\right)^2 \sigma_{ht}^2$, where σ_t^2 and σ_{ht}^2 are the variances for the known systematic factor and the hidden factor, respectively.

Assuming that the weighted sums of the factor loadings for the known systematic factor are shown as $\sum_{i=1}^{n} \omega_i \beta_i = \theta_n$, where $\lim_{n\to\infty} \theta_n = \theta \neq 0$ since the systematic factor f_t is non-diversifiable. Let $\sigma_{ht}^2 = \sigma_h^2$, for simplicity. It is easy to find that

$$\sigma_{mt}^2 = E\left[r_{mt} - E\left(r_{mt}\right)\right]^2 = \theta_n^2 \sigma_t^2 + \left(\sum_{i=1}^{n} \omega_i \beta_i^h\right)^2 \sigma_h^2. \tag{4.3.4}$$

Suppose, as assumed in Ang et al. (2006), there exists a volatility measure based on Chicago Board Option Exchange's VIX index $\hat{\sigma}_{mt}$ for σ_{mt} such that

$$\hat{\sigma}_{mt}^2 = \sigma_{mt}^2 + o_p(1),$$

$$\sigma_t^2 = \sigma_{t-1}^2 + \pi_t,$$

$$\pi_t = \tau f_{ht}. \tag{4.3.5}$$

It can be shown that even if the hidden factor is diversifiable as $\lim_{n\to\infty} \sum_{i=1}^{n} \omega_i \beta_i^h \to 0$,

$$r_{it} = \mu_i + \beta_i f_t + \frac{\beta_i^h}{\tau} \pi_t + v_{it} = \mu_i + \beta_i f_t + \frac{\beta_i^h}{\tau \theta_n^2} \Delta\hat{\sigma}_{mt} + v_{it}, \tag{4.3.6}$$

where $\Delta\hat{\sigma}_{mt} = \hat{\sigma}_{mt}^2 - \hat{\sigma}_{mt-1}^2$. This shows that innovation of the proxy for aggregate market volatility may become an explanatory variable for asset i's excess return even though $\lim_{n\to\infty} \sum_{i=1}^{n} \omega_i \beta_i^h \to 0$. Therefore, although the innovation of market aggregate volatility may be related to the assets' excess return, it does not necessarily imply valid identification for some hidden non-diversifiable factor(s).

Hence, studies on asset pricing models may not be limited only to identifications of the relevant instrumental variables or the reduction of dimensionality such as principal component analysis or statistical factor analysis. In essence, the studies on the factor structure of asset returns should include discussions on whether the identified factors are entirely non-diversifiable or not. In other words, having cross-sectional memories (possibly due to a hidden common factor) for all projection errors (or idiosyncratic risks) does not necessarily imply the omitted factor is non-diversifiable.

It is the persistency of these cross-sectional memories for the idiosyncratic risk that may indicate the need for further elaboration on the asset pricing models. In the following section, an alternative method for assessing the non-diversifiability of the hidden factor in the approximate factor structure of asset returns is considered where cross-sectional cumulative sums of residuals are applied.[15]

4.3.2 *The Need for a Sequential Model Search*

To reduce the complexity of discussion, we first assume the hidden factor (or component) whether diversifiable or not is asymptotically orthogonal to all preselected proxies for factors. In the following Assumption A6, it is assumed that the error terms of each stage of the model search is asymptotically orthogonal to the already included proxies for factors. In this case, it is feasible to consider many estimation methods for the factor loadings of the preselected proxy variables for factors.

On the other hand, since the model search for empirical asset pricing models is of interest, inclusion of the proxies for the hidden factors in the error terms provides the steps to expand the models. This in turn introduces the necessity to orthogonalize sequentially the additional candidate proxies with the already included variables to expand the dimension of the empirical asset pricing models. Hence, certain orthogonalization schemes will be devised before the expansion of the models. A detailed algorithm for the model search is stated later on.

Assumption A8 Let $\lim_{T\to\infty} \frac{1}{T}\sum_{t=1}^{T} E|X_t\epsilon_{it}| = \tilde{\mathbf{o}}_p(1)$, for each asset i, $i = 1, 2, \ldots, n, \ldots$, as $T \to \infty$, where $\tilde{\mathbf{o}}_p(1)$ is a $(k+q+1)\times 1$ vector of zeros, $1 \le k \le p$, $1 \le q \le u$, where p and u are as defined in Assumptions A1 and A2, and

$$X_t = \left(1, \widetilde{x_{1t}}, \ldots, \widetilde{x_{qt}}, f_t^{(1)}, \ldots, f_t^{(k)}\right)'$$

represents the $(k+q+1)\times 1$ vector of included known common factors at time t. In addition, let $\lim_{T\to\infty}\frac{1}{T}\sum_{t=1}^{T}X_tX_t' = M$, where M is a $(k+q+1)\times(k+q+1)$ positive definite matrix. In addition, let $\lim_{T\to\infty}\frac{1}{T}\sum_{t=1}^{T}\epsilon_{it} = o_p(1)$, $\lim_{T\to\infty}\frac{1}{T}\sum_{t=1}^{T}f_{ht}^2 < \infty$, and $\lim_{T\to\infty}\frac{1}{T}\sum_{t=1}^{T}E|f_{ht}v_{it}| = o_p(1)$ for each asset i, $i = 1, 2, \ldots n, \ldots$.

Notice that in Assumption A8, the matrix M can be of lower rank than $k+q+1$ where the generalized inverse of the matrix exists. However, the current context assumes the full rank for simplicity. In addition, the idiosyncratic risks (including the hidden factor) are assumed as asymptotically orthogonal to the preselected variables $X_t = \left(1, \widetilde{x_{1t}}, \ldots, \widetilde{x_{qt}}, f_t^{(1)}, \ldots, f_t^{(k)}\right)'$ for simplicity. For further extensions, we may allow the chosen factors to be asymptotically correlated with the idiosyncratic risk (or hidden factor). However, in that case, the usual least-squares estimates will be biased and inconsistent for the factor loadings for each asset. Furthermore, for the purpose of a robust model search, some orthogonalization schemes (via projection) can be applied to the variable selection at each stage of the search. Also for the model search for factor(s) of empirical asset pricing models, it is feasible to assume that $k \geq 1$, and $q \geq 1$.

In particular, although the common correlated effects (CCE) estimator proposed by Pesaran (2006) for the coefficients of individual-effect regressors is applicable for the large panel data with a hidden factor structure, it can be shown that even the application of CCE may not necessarily provide consistent estimates for factor loadings when the hidden factor (in idiosyncratic risk) is non-diversifiable even though the asymptotic orthogonality condition (for the hidden factor and idiosyncratic risk) holds. Details of the arguments are shown later in this chapter.

Similarly, Bai (2003) also assumes the asymptotic orthogonality conditions among the included factors and idiosyncratic risk. Notice that the assumption does not assume the other proxies excluded from X_t are orthogonal to X_t; all these proxies for factors may be mutually correlated. However, the hidden factor f_{ht} is assumed to be asymptotically orthogonal to the set of tentatively included variables and factors in X_t. When the hidden unobservable factor is not orthogonal to all prespecified factors or proxies, a sequential regression with a model search method should be applied to obtain consistent estimates for the parameters of interest.

In fact, any researcher in finance (as well as all empiricists for empirical asset pricing models) will strive to search for all plausible approaches to discover any regularity in asset returns. It is rarely feasible that some included regressors are still related to some unknown common factors that may explain the security returns. If so, then the empiricist on searching the asset pricing models that suffer from omitted residual risk should perform some model misspecification tests on the data and correct their specification, instead.

Proposition 4.6 *Given Assumption A8 where the idiosyncratic risk that contains the hidden unobservable factor of stochastic factor loadings is asymptotically orthogonal to all preselected factors, the least-squares estimates for parameters on the preselected factors of each individual asset's rate of return in Eq. (4.1.1) are consistent, regardless of whether the hidden unobservable factor is diversifiable or not.*

In addition, if the hidden unobservable factor is not orthogonal to the preselected variables and a sequential orthogonalization is applied to additional variables versus preselected variables, the factor loadings can be consistently identified.

Proof

(1) When the unobservable factor is asymptotically orthogonal to all preselected factors or variables, the argument is easy. A simple least-squares method will suffice to provide the consistent estimates, following the arguments of Bai and Ng (2002) and Bai (2003).
(2) When the unobservable factor is not orthogonal to all preselected factors or explanatory variables, the estimation should perform some sequential regressions on the model(s) prescribed. The reasoning can be demonstrated by the following setting.

Let the k-th stage ($k \geq 1$) model search successfully and end up with the empirical asset pricing model such that, in compact matrix form, for each asset i, $i = 1, 2, \ldots, n$,

$$\underline{r}_i = X\beta_i + \underline{\epsilon}_i, \tag{4.3.7}$$

where there is a possible hidden factor (either diversifiable or non-diversifiable) in the error term so that for the scalar factor loading β_i^h

for asset i, $i = 1, 2, \ldots, n$,

$$\underline{\epsilon}_i = \beta_i^h f_h + \underline{\upsilon}_i, \tag{4.3.8}$$

where $\underline{r}_i = (r_{i1}, \ldots, r_{iT})'$, $X = (X_1', X_2', \ldots, X_T')'$, $f_h = (f_{h1}, f_{h2}, \ldots, f_{hT})'$, $\beta_i = (\alpha_i, \beta_{i1}, \ldots, \beta_{ik})'$, and $\underline{\epsilon}_i$, $\underline{\upsilon}_i$ are both *T-by-1* vectors of noises. In addition, let $E[\underline{\epsilon}_i|X] = \underline{0}$, $E[f_h|X] = \underline{0}$, $E[\underline{\upsilon}_i|X] = \underline{0}$. Given these conditions, we can have the consistency of least-squares estimates for the coefficients in β_i.

However, when expanding the model such that there exists a proxy X_e (possibly related to the already included variables and proxies for factors, X) for the unobservable hidden factor f_{ht}, it is shown that

$$X_e = X\gamma^\star + a_h f_h, \tag{4.3.9}$$

where X_e is a *T-by-1* vector of proxy variable, $\gamma^\star$ is a non-null $(k + q + 1) \times 1$ vector, and $a_h \neq 0$ is a scalar.[16] Then, this implies that the new proxy is related to the already included proxies and can be used to approximate the hidden factor. Hence, from the above setting, it is easy to see that, if we directly substitute the X_e into Eq. (4.1.3), this will show that

$$\begin{aligned} \underline{r}_i &= X\beta_i + \frac{\beta_i^h}{a_h}(X_e - X\gamma^\star) + \underline{\upsilon}_i \\ &= X\beta_i + \frac{\beta_i^h}{a_h}X_e + \left(\underline{\upsilon}_i - X\frac{\beta_i^h}{a_h}\gamma^\star\right) \\ &= X\beta_i + \frac{\beta_i^h}{a_h}X_e + \underline{\xi}_i. \end{aligned} \tag{4.3.10}$$

In fact, it seems like one can directly estimate the empirical asset pricing models with both X and X_e as the proxy variables for factors. Unfortunately, X and X_e are correlated, and the model may be subject to collinearity problems. Furthermore, the noise vector $\underline{\xi}_i$ is also correlated with explanatory variables X. A consistent estimate of the coefficient for X_e is not feasible.

To deal with that, a sequential procedure for estimation in the model search is needed. For simplicity and explanation, the dimensional setting for regression is considered in a "per-asset" manner where the matrix operations are confined to the "per-asset" case. The entire setting can be extended to the panel-data framework with matrices for both cross-sectional and time-series dimensions.

The steps for sequential settings are as follows. (1) Regress $\underline{r_i}$ on X then save its residuals and denote them as $\underline{e_i}$. (2) Regress X_e on X and denote its residuals as $\underline{\eta_e}$. (3) Perform the regression of $\underline{e_i}$ on $\underline{\eta_e}$, which will provide the consistent estimates for $\frac{\beta_i^h}{a_h}$.

The derivation can be shown in the following. In the first step, when regressing $\underline{r_i}$ on X, the residual $\underline{e_i} = M\epsilon_i$, where $M = I - X(X'X)^{-1}X$. It is straightforward to see that, given Assumption A8, the least-squares estimate $\hat{\beta}_i$ is consistent, while in the second step, when regressing X_e on X, the residual $\underline{\eta_e} = MX_e$. This implies $\underline{\eta_e} = M(X\gamma^\star + a_h f_h) = a_h M f_h$. On the other hand, $\underline{e_i} = M\epsilon_i = \beta_i^h M f_h + M\underline{\upsilon_i}$. Let the coefficient when regressing $\underline{e_i}$ on $\underline{\eta_e}$ be denoted as $\widetilde{\gamma}_i$. Then, using substitution, it can be shown that[17]

$$\widetilde{\gamma}_i = \beta_i^h \left(X_e'MX_e\right)^{-1} X_e'Mf_h + \left(X_e'MX_e\right)^{-1} X_e'M\underline{\upsilon}_i \tag{4.3.11}$$

Now

$$\begin{aligned}\left(X_e'MX_e\right)^{-1} X_e'M\underline{\upsilon}_i &= \left(X_e'MX_e\right)^{-1} \left[X_e'\underline{\upsilon}_i - X_e'X(X'X)^{-1}X'\underline{\upsilon}_i\right] \\ &= \left(\frac{X_e'MX_e}{T}\right)^{-1} \left[\left(\frac{X_e'\underline{\upsilon}_i}{T}\right) - \left(\frac{X_e'X}{T}\right)\left(\frac{X'X}{T}\right)^{-1}\left(\frac{X'\underline{\upsilon}_i}{T}\right)\right] \\ &= o_p(1),\end{aligned} \tag{4.3.12}$$

following the weak law of large numbers as $T \to \infty$. On the other hand,

$$\begin{aligned}\beta_i^h \left(X_e'MX_e\right)^{-1} X_e'Mf_h &= \beta_i^h \left(X_e'MX_e\right)^{-1} X_e'f_h \\ &\quad - \beta_i^h \left(\frac{X_e'MX_e}{T}\right)^{-1}\left(\frac{X_e'X}{T}\right)\left(\frac{X'X}{T}\right)^{-1}\left(\frac{X'f_h}{T}\right) \\ &= \beta_i^h \left(X_e'MX_e\right)^{-1} X_e'f_h - o_p(1).\end{aligned} \tag{4.3.13}$$

It is straightforward to see when assuming $\frac{1}{T}\sum_{t=1}^{T} f_{ht}^2 \xrightarrow{p} \sigma_h^2$,

$$\begin{aligned}\frac{1}{T}X_e'f_h &= \gamma^{*\prime}\left(\frac{X'f_h}{T}\right) + a_h\left(\frac{f_h'f_h}{T}\right) \\ &= a_h\sigma_h^2.\end{aligned} \tag{4.3.14}$$

In addition, it can be shown that as $T \to \infty$,

$$\begin{aligned}\left(\frac{X_e'MX_e}{T}\right) &= \frac{a_h^2 f_h' M f_h}{T} \\ &= a_h^2\left(\frac{f_h'f_h}{T}\right) - a_h^2\left(\frac{f_h'X}{T}\right)\left(\frac{X'X}{T}\right)^{-1}\left(\frac{X'f_h}{T}\right) \\ &= a_h^2\sigma_h^2 - o_p(1).\end{aligned} \tag{4.3.15}$$

Hence, as $T \to \infty$,

$$\widetilde{\gamma}_i = \beta_i^h\left(\frac{a_h\sigma_h^2}{a_h^2\sigma_h^2}\right) + o_p(1) = \frac{\beta_i^h}{a_h} + o_p(1). \tag{4.3.16}$$

This shows that the sequential estimate for the coefficient of additional proxy X_e is consistent. In addition, the new proxy for the hidden factor is no longer X_e. Instead, the next proxy should be η_e, the residuals when regressing X_e on X.

Notice that the above proposition only provides the arguments for estimating the factor loadings on additional proxies when projecting the security returns on some hypothesized common factor structures. A sequential scheme is suggested in which one should cautiously identify the common regressors for security returns when performing empirical asset pricing models. Although the contemporaneous methods with various robust procedures in the literature are applicable for identifying possible explanatory variables for security returns, further statistical inferences are required to identify that the added proxy (or proxies) really contributes to the explainability and non-diversifiability of the systematic components of security returns after consistently estimating the parameters. Furthermore, although the above arguments are based on the asymptotic approach as $T \to \infty$, recursive estimation can be developed such that for each subperiod $T^* < T$, $T^* \to \infty$, the sequential orthogonalization can still be implemented for the added variables.

In addition, although there are concerns over the possible time-varying coefficients and cross-sectional correlations of the return series, the sequential procedures with orthogonalization will assist the reduction of the impacts from these possibilities of empirical modeling when the regressions are performed on each individual stock returns separately.

4.3.3 The Nonidentifiability of the CCE Estimator for a Hidden Non-diversifiable Factor

Pesaran (2006) provides a general framework for large panel data with possibly unknown common factors. The work also introduces a new method where the individual-specific regressors are filtered through the cross-sectional average to eliminate the effect of unobserved common factors. In fact, the unknown hidden factor can be approximated by the linear combination of the cross-sectional averages of dependent variables and individual regressors filtered through the known common factors/variables.

However, the framework may not prevail since (1) the unknown common factors (in idiosyncratic risk) may not be properly approximated with the cross-sectional weighted average of dependent variables and known individual-specific regressors if the unknown factors are non-diversifiable as defined in Definition D3; (2) the CCE estimator may not provide any consistent estimates for the factor loadings of the hidden factor and individual-specific regressor if non-diversifiable factors are present in the idiosyncratic risk.

More specifically, if the hidden factor is non-diversifiable, then the cross-sectional weighting scheme (random or not) will not be able to eliminate the possible stochastic variation of the hidden factor. In other words, there is a possibility that the cross-sectional weighted averages of individual-specific regressors and security returns after being filtered through common regressors in the panel data will still contain a non-diversifiable stochastic component whose L^2-norm will not vanish to zero. In that case, the CCE estimator, which applies the cross-sectional weighted averages of individual-specific regressors and stock returns (after being filtered through common regressors in the panel data) as the proxy for the hidden unobservable factor, will not be immune from possible correlations with the factor loadings of a hidden non-diversifiable factor. Hence, it is not feasible when using the CCE to identify the genuine impact of a hidden non-diversifiable factor.

A simplified univariate version of Pesaran's (2006) work (with an individual-specific regressor, a univariate common regressor, and a single hidden factor f_h) can be shown as follows.

$$\begin{aligned} r_{it} &= \beta_i x_t + \theta_i \mathring{a}_{it} + \epsilon_{it}, \\ \epsilon_{it} &= \beta_i^h f_{ht} + \nu_{it}, \\ \mathring{a}_{it} &= \breve{\alpha}_i x_t + \overline{b_i} f_{ht} + \varsigma_{it} \end{aligned} \tag{4.3.17}$$

for $i = 1, 2, \ldots, n$, where x_t is the known common regressor preselected, $\mathring{a}_i$ is a known individual-specific regressor for security return i, $\{\beta_i^h\}_{i=1,2,\ldots,n}$ are stochastic factor loadings for the unknown factor, and $\{\beta_i, \theta_i\}_{i=1,2,\ldots,n}$ are the nonstochastic coefficients for the common variable and individual-specific regressor, respectively.

In particular, $\{\overline{b_i}\}_{i=1,2,\ldots,n}$ are the nonzero stochastic parameters that describe the relationship between hidden factor f_h and $\{\mathring{a}_{it}\}_{i=1,2\ldots,n}$, and $\{\overline{b_i}\}_{i=1,2,\ldots,n}$ are uncorrelated with the other variables or parameters in (4.0.19), $\{\breve{\alpha}_i\}_{i=1,2,\ldots,n}$ are nonstochastic parameters that show the correlation between individual-specific regressors $\{\mathring{a}_{it}\}_{i=1,2\ldots,n}$ and known common regressor x_t, $\{\nu_{it}\}_{i=1,2,\ldots,n}$ and $\{\varsigma_{it}\}_{i=1,2,\ldots,n}$ are mutually independent random noises.[18]

Following Pesaran (2006), the randomly varying coefficient models for the factor loadings $\{\beta_i^h, b_i\}_{i=1,2,\ldots,n}$ are assumed to have

$$\begin{aligned} \beta_i^h &= \widetilde{\beta} + \ddot{\tau}_i \\ \overline{b_i} &= \overline{b} + \ddot{\pi}_i \end{aligned}, \tag{4.3.18}$$

where $\widetilde{\beta}$ and $\overline{b}$ are the means of β_i^h and $\overline{b_i}$ for all $i = 1, 2, \ldots, n$, respectively. By stacking up both r_{it} and $\mathring{a}_{it}$, the system of equations can be shown as

$$\begin{aligned} r_{it} &= \beta_i x_t + \theta_i \mathring{a}_{it} + \beta_i^h f_{ht} + \nu_{it} = (\beta_i + \theta_i \breve{\alpha}_i) x_t + (\theta_i \overline{b_i} + \beta_i^h) f_{ht} + \theta_i \varsigma_{it} + \nu_{it}, \\ \mathring{a}_{it} &= \breve{\alpha}_i x_t + \overline{b_i} f_{ht} + \varsigma_{it}. \end{aligned} \tag{4.3.19}$$

What Pesaran (2006) proposes to do is to form a cross-sectional weighted average such that

$$\sum_{i=1}^{n} \omega_i r_{it} = \left(\sum_{i=1}^{n} \omega_i(\beta_i + \theta_i \breve{\alpha}_i)\right) x_t + \left(\sum_{i=1}^{n} \omega_i(\theta_i \overline{b_i} + \beta_i^h)\right) f_{ht} + \sum_{i=1}^{n} \omega_i(\theta_i \varsigma_{it} + \nu_{it}), \tag{4.3.20}$$

$$\sum_{i=1}^{n} \omega_i \mathring{a}_{it} = \left(\sum_{i=1}^{n} \omega_i \breve{\alpha}_i\right) x_t + \left(\sum_{i=1}^{n} \omega_i \overline{b_i}\right) f_{ht} + \sum_{i=1}^{n} \omega_i \varsigma_{it}.$$

Or, in a more compact form, let $\overline{r_t} = \sum_{i=1}^{n} \omega_i r_{it}$, and $\bar{\mathring{a}}_t = \sum_{i=1}^{n} \omega_i \mathring{a}_{it}$,

$$\begin{aligned} \overline{r_t} &= \widetilde{w} x_t + \bar{\theta} f_{ht} + \overline{u}_t, \\ \bar{\mathring{a}}_t &= \overline{\alpha} x_t + \overline{b} f_{ht} + \overline{\varsigma}_t, \end{aligned} \tag{4.3.21}$$

where $\widetilde{w} = \sum_{i=1}^{n} \omega_i(\beta_i + \theta_i \breve{\alpha}_i)$, since $\sum_{i=1}^{n} \omega_i = 1$, and $\sum_{i=1}^{n} \omega_i \ddot{\tau}_i = \sum_{i=1}^{n} \omega_i \ddot{\pi}_i = o_p(1)$, Hence, it is easy to see that

$$\sum_{i=1}^{n} \omega_i \overline{b_i} = \sum_{i=1}^{n} \omega_i(\overline{b} + \ddot{\pi}_i) = \overline{b}$$

where $\overline{\alpha} = \sum_{i=1}^{n} \omega_i \breve{\alpha}_i$, and $\overline{u}_t = \sum_{i=1}^{n} \omega_i(\theta_i \varsigma_{it} + \nu_{it}), \overline{\varsigma}_t = \sum_{i=1}^{n} \omega_i \varsigma_{it}$,

$$\begin{aligned} \bar{\theta} &= \sum_{i=1}^{n} \omega_i(\theta_i \overline{b_i} + \beta_i^h) \\ &= \sum_{i=1}^{n} \omega_i(\theta_i(\overline{b} + \ddot{\pi}_i) + (\widetilde{\beta} + \ddot{\tau}_i)) \\ &= \overline{b}\left(\sum_{i=1}^{n} \omega_i \theta_i\right) + \widetilde{\beta}\left(\sum_{i=1}^{n} \omega_i\right) \\ &= \overline{b}\left(\sum_{i=1}^{n} \omega_i \theta_i\right) + \widetilde{\beta} \\ &= \overline{b}\theta_w + \widetilde{\beta}. \end{aligned}$$

If, under the assumption that the cross-sectional weighted averages for the random noises converge as $n \longrightarrow \infty$, where $\overline{u}_t \longrightarrow o_p(1)$, and $\overline{\varsigma}_t \longrightarrow o_p(1)$ since they are considered random noises, it is straightforward to have as $n \longrightarrow \infty$,

$$\begin{aligned} \overline{r_t} &= \widetilde{w}x_t + \bar{\theta}f_{ht} + o_p(1) \\ \overline{\mathring{a}}_t &= \overline{\alpha}x_t + \overline{b}f_{ht} + o_p(1). \end{aligned} \tag{4.3.22}$$

Given that the cross-sectional weighted averages of $\left(\beta_i^h, \overline{b_i}\right)_{i=1,2,\ldots,n}$ will converge to the nonstochastic means $\left(\widetilde{\beta}, \overline{b}\right)$, the coefficients in Eq. (4.3.21) are also nonstochastic. Hence, the unknown hidden common factor f_{ht} can be approximated by the linear combinations of cross-sectionally weighted averages $\overline{r_t}$ and $\overline{\mathring{a}}_t$ after filtering through the common known variable x_t. That is, through simple algebra,

$$\begin{aligned} f_{ht} &= \frac{1}{\left(\bar{\theta}^2 + \overline{b}^2\right)}\left[\left(\bar{\theta}\overline{r_t} + \overline{b}\overline{\mathring{a}}_t\right) - \left(\bar{\theta}\widetilde{w} + \overline{b}\overline{\alpha}\right)x_t\right] + o_p(1), \\ &= \frac{1}{\left(\bar{\theta}^2 + \overline{b}^2\right)}\left[\bar{\theta}\left(\overline{r_t} - \widetilde{w}x_t\right) + \overline{b}\left(\overline{\mathring{a}}_t - \overline{\alpha}x_t\right)\right] + o_p(1). \end{aligned} \tag{4.3.23}$$

As a result, it is feasible to approximate the hidden factor f_{ht} by using the cross-sectional weighted averages as $\overline{r_t}$ and $\overline{\mathring{a}}_t$ filtered through the common regressor x_t if the coefficients in Eq. (4.3.21) are either nonstochastic or uncorrelated with $\left\{\beta_i^h\right\}_{i=1,2,\ldots,n}$. In other words, if using the linear combinations of error terms when regressing the cross-sectional weighted averages as $\overline{r_t}$ and $\overline{\mathring{a}}_t$ on common regressor x_t, the unknown factor can be approximated by using the known variables as long as the coefficients in Eq. (4.3.21) are all nonstochastic (which implies that all the stochastic components or noises are eliminated by the cross-sectional weighted averages as $\overline{r_t}$ and $\overline{\mathring{a}}_t$ and their projections on common regressor x_t).

However, this condition may be violated if the hidden factor is non-diversifiable as defined in Definition D3 and with Assumption A5. The

Assumption A5 sets the non-diversifiable factor in the L^2-norm. Therefore, if the hidden factor is non-diversifiable, the cross-sectionally weighted averages of $\left(\beta_i^h, \overline{b_i}\right)_{i=1,2,\ldots,n}$ cannot converge to some nonstochastic means as $\left(\widetilde{\beta}, \overline{b}\right)$. Otherwise, their L^2-norms will be equal to zero.

For example, if the hidden factor f_{ht} is non-diversifiable and following the additive-form setting in Eq. (4.3.21), the coefficients of $\overline{\theta}$ may (for instance) still contain a nondegenerated stochastic component such as ϑ_ω^n (and $0 < E|\vartheta_\omega^n|^2 < \infty$) where $\lim_{n\to\infty} \sum_{i=1}^n \omega_i \beta_i^h = \widetilde{\beta}. + \lim_{n\to\infty} \sum_{i=1}^n \omega_i \ddot{\tau}_i \xrightarrow{p} \widetilde{\beta}. + \vartheta_\omega^n$, and the weighted average of the stochastic components $\{\ddot{\tau}_i\}_{i=1,2,\ldots,n}$ in $\left\{\beta_i^h\right\}_{i=1,2,\ldots,n}$ will not converge to zero as $n \to \infty$. In other words, the weighted average of $\left\{\theta_i \overline{b_i} + \beta_i^h\right\}_{i=1,2,\ldots,n}$(denoted as $\overline{\theta} = \overline{b}\theta_w + \widetilde{\beta} + \vartheta_\omega^n$,) is (at least) correlated with some $\left\{\beta_i^h\right\}_{i=1,2,\ldots,n}$.

Therefore, the approximation of f_{ht} by using linear combinations of cross-sectionally weighted averages $\overline{r_t}$ and $\mathring{\overline{a}}_t$ when filtered through the common regressor x_t may possibly make the factor loadings $\left\{\beta_i^h\right\}_{i=1,2,\ldots,n}$ of f_{ht} unidentifiable when the proxy as Eq. (4.3.21) is substituted into the system of equations in (4.3.16). This is so since $\overline{\theta}$ may still be correlated with $\left\{\beta_i^h\right\}_{i=1,2,\ldots,n}$ given that the stochastic component or noise as $\vartheta_\omega^n = \sum_{i=1}^n \omega_i \ddot{\tau}_i$ is correlated with (some of) $\left\{\beta_i^h\right\}_{i=1,2,\ldots,n}$ where $\sum_{i=1}^n \omega_i \beta_i^h \overset{p}{\nrightarrow} \widetilde{\beta}$.

As a result, when the proxy for f_{ht} is substituted into the system of Eqs. (4.3.16) and (4.3.20), the conventional ordinary least-squares estimators will not necessarily provide consistent estimates for the factor loadings $\left\{\beta_i^h\right\}_{i=1,2,\ldots,n}$ of the hidden factor f_{ht}. Therefore, the (asymptotic) statistical inferences for the importance of the hidden factor is not entirely feasible.[19]

In fact, the setting in Eq. (4.3.17) with the conditions that $\sum_{i=1}^n \omega_i \ddot{\tau}_i = \sum_{i=1}^n \omega_i \ddot{\pi}_i = o_p(1)$, already precludes the non-diversifiability of the hidden factor of Definition D3 in the idiosyncratic risk of Eq. (4.3.21). Specifically, if the hidden factor is subject to randomly varying coefficient(s) and is non-diversifiable, then the CCE method may not obtain the consistent estimates for factor loadings of the security returns.

On the other hand, if following the CCE method with auxiliary regression by projecting $\{\mathring{a}_{it}\}_{i=1,2\ldots,n}$ on $\overline{r_t}$, $\overline{\mathring{a}}_t$ and x_t, it can be shown that

$$\begin{aligned}
\mathring{a}_{it} &= \widetilde{\mathring{a}_{it}} + \varsigma_{it} \\
&= \ddot{\alpha}_i x_t + \overline{b_i}\left[\frac{\bar{\theta}}{\left(\bar{\theta}^2 + \overline{b}^2\right)}(\overline{r_t} - \widetilde{w}x_t) + \frac{\overline{b}}{\left(\bar{\theta}^2 + \overline{b}^2\right)}\left(\overline{\mathring{a}}_t - \overline{\alpha}x_t\right)\right] + \varsigma_{it}, \\
&= \left(\ddot{\alpha}_i - \frac{\overline{b_i}\bar{\theta}\widetilde{w}}{\left(\bar{\theta}^2 + \overline{b}^2\right)} - \frac{\overline{bb_i}}{\left(\bar{\theta}^2 + \overline{b}^2\right)}\overline{\alpha}\right)x_t + \left[\frac{\overline{b_i}\bar{\theta}}{\left(\bar{\theta}^2 + \overline{b}^2\right)}\right]\overline{r_t} \\
&\quad + \left[\frac{\overline{b_i b}}{\left(\bar{\theta}^2 + \overline{b}^2\right)}\right]\overline{\mathring{a}}_t.
\end{aligned}$$

Therefore, if $\bar{\theta}$ is nonstochastic given that $\sum_{i=1}^{n}\omega_i\tau_i = \sum_{i=1}^{\ddot{n}}\omega_i\ddot{\pi}_i = o_p(1)$ with a diversifiable unknown factor f_{ht}, the projection error of $\{\mathring{a}_{it}\}_{i=1,2\ldots,n}$ on $\overline{r_t}$, $\overline{\mathring{a}}_t$ and x_t (denoted as $\widetilde{\mathring{a}_{it}}$) can be used to replace the individual-specific regressor $\mathring{a}_{it}$ in Eq. (4.3.17) to obtain consistent estimates for $\{\theta_i\}_{i=1,2,\ldots,n}$ even though $\{\overline{b_i}\}_{i=1,2,\ldots,n}$ are stochastic since $\{\overline{b_i}\}_{i=1,2,\ldots,n}$ are orthogonal to all other variables and parameters.

However, it is easy to ascertain that when f_{ht} is non-diversifiable (where only $\sum_{i=1}^{n}\omega_i\ddot{\pi}_i = o_p(1)$), the coefficients on $\overline{r_t}$, $\overline{\mathring{a}}_t$ and x_t all include the non-diversifiable stochastic components ϑ_ω^n given that $\overline{\theta} = \overline{b}\theta_w + \widetilde{\beta} + \vartheta_\omega^n$ where ϑ_ω^n is correlated with $\{\beta_i^h\}_{i=1,2,\ldots,n}$. Thus, the projection error of regressing $\{\mathring{a}_{it}\}$ on $\overline{r_t}$, $\overline{\mathring{a}}_t$ and x_t (without considering the possible non-diversifiable components ϑ_ω^n) will contain some random non-diversifiable errors which cannot be eliminated through increasing samples of time-series observations.

Therefore, the attempt by substituting the projection error of $\{\mathring{a}_{it}\}_{i=1,2\ldots,n}$ on $\overline{r_t}$, $\overline{\mathring{a}}_t$ and x_t in Eq. (4.3.21) to replace the impact from the unknown hidden factor may not necessarily provide consistent estimates for $\{\theta_i\}_{i=1,2,\ldots,n}$ of individual-specific regressor x_t since the projection will still contain an additional non-diversifiable component ϑ_ω^n in all coefficients of $\overline{r}_t$, $\overline{\mathring{a}}_t$ and x_t by substituting $\overline{\theta} = \overline{b}\theta_w + \widetilde{\beta} + \vartheta_\omega^n$ into the above equation and placing it in Eq. (4.3.21).

Notice that the CCE method of Pesaran (2006) provides the consistency of estimates for individual-specific effects, the $\{\theta_i\}_{i=1,2,\ldots,n}$ in Eq. (4.3.16) when the hidden unknown factor is diversifiable. The focus is not on estimating the coefficients associated with the known and preselected variables and common factor per se or to identify the impact from the non-diversifiability of the hidden factor to the security returns when both the security returns and individual-specific regressors are related to the hidden factor. Given this, it is straightforward to state that if the focus of study is to search and identify the impact of the non-diversifiable (hidden) factors for asset returns, a sequential model search as stated in Proposition 4.6 is needed.

4.4 Intensity of Non-diversifiability of Hidden Factors

4.4.1 *The Sum of the CUSUMs*

In this section, we first propose a new measure of the intensity of non-diversifiability by locating the number of non-diversifiable factor(s) in the asset-pricing models. The analysis considers that the partial sums of the CUSUMs of weighted idiosyncratic risks are not automatically finite even though the underlying (hidden) factor is diversifiable. Specifically, these partial sums all require certain exponentially decaying weights to become finite—except for some extreme cases. It is also noticeable that the statistics of CUSUMs are related to the non-diversifiability of factors of the presumed asset pricing models through the magnitude of the convergence rates of these weighted partial sums when suitable sequences of weights (such as an equally weighted scheme, for instance) are applied. Specifically, the argument leads to a more general alternative statistical inference versus the applications of the rescaled-variance test in Sect. 4.2 of this chapter. In particular, the test statistics developed here do not directly apply the cross-sectional memory condition of presumed idiosyncratic risk because the study of the intensity of non-diversifiability is related to statistical inferences based on the Hurst exponent.

In particular, the convergence rate for these (weighted) cross-sectional partial sums coincides with the Hurst exponent in the fractional Brownian motion if the fractional invariance principle is applied to these CUSUMs. Similar to the time-series analysis, these findings show that the higher the intensity of non-diversifiability of the (hidden) factor, the higher the Hurst exponent. This in turn leads to the statistical inferences based on the Hurst exponent to identify the extent of non-diversifiability of (proxies for) factors when the empirical search for asset pricing models is of interest.

Although various statistical tests for long dependence (such as adjusted range-scale statistics, the rescaled-variance test, and the KPSS test)[20] in time-series data are available, there are very few works that connect the existence of the non-diversifiable factor (in idiosyncratic risk) with these tests. One commonality of these tests is that they are somewhat based on the CUSUMs of the underlying data streams. In the following, the justification of these tests with the intensity of non-diversifiability on the hidden factor (in idiosyncratic risk) is provided.

A few definitions and assumptions are needed to provide the prerequisites. At first, under the null hypothesis of short-term cross-sectional memory, the estimation of the underlying panel data regressions needs to be shown with consistency. Furthermore, since the equally weighted scheme in diversification also satisfies the conditions of a well-diversified portfolio, we shall focus on an equally weighted scheme for simplicity.

In the following, a possible cross-sectional argument for non-diversifiability is considered. The notion is to develop an alternative measurement of the intensity of non-diversifiability of the hidden factor in the empirical asset pricing models. Notice that since the equally weighted portfolio also satisfies the properties of well-diversified portfolios according to Definition D2, it suffices to provide an example of a hidden factor by using an equally weighted portfolio.[21]

Since under the null hypothesis that there is no non-diversifiable hidden factor in $\{\epsilon_{it}\}_{i=1,2,...}$, where the equally weighted portfolio will diversify all hidden factors away, let σ_{it}^2 be the variance of ϵ_{it}, where $E\left[\frac{1}{n}\sum_{i=1}^{n}\epsilon_{it}\right]^2 \to 0$ as $n \to \infty$. Then it is straightforward to see that at any time t, $t \geq T$, $T \to \infty$,

$$\lim_{n\to\infty} E\left[\frac{1}{n}\sum_{i=1}^{n}\epsilon_{it}\right]^2 = \lim_{n\to\infty}\frac{1}{n^2}\left(\sum_{i=1}^{n}\sigma_{it}^2 + 2\sum_{i=1}^{n}\sum_{\substack{j=1\\ i\neq j}}^{n}\text{Cov}(\epsilon_{it},\epsilon_{jt})\right) \longrightarrow 0. \tag{4.4.1}$$

In other words, under the null hypothesis, a diversifiable factor will imply that $E\left[\frac{1}{n}\sum_{i=1}^{n}\epsilon_{it}\right]^2$ (which is the L^2-norm of $\frac{1}{n}\sum_{i=1}^{n}\epsilon_{it}$) will converge to zero as the number of assets n grows. However, the sum of these m subseries or the so-called sum of cumulative sums may not necessarily be finite as $n\to\infty$ even if the underlying hidden factor may (to some extent) have the item such as $E\left[\frac{1}{n}\sum_{i=1}^{m}\epsilon_{it}\right]^2\to 0$ for some $1\le m\le n$. We may use a simple example to demonstrate this intuition. Let $\sigma_{it}^2=\sigma_t^2$, for all $i=1,2,\ldots,n$, without loss of generality. For n assets, the L^2-norm of each m subseries, $1\le m\le n$ will be

$$E\left[\frac{1}{n}\sum_{i=1}^{m}\epsilon_{it}\right]^2=\frac{1}{n^2}\left(m\sigma_t^2+2\sum_{i=1}^{m}\sum_{j=i+1}^{m}\sigma_{ij}\right). \tag{4.4.2}$$

Since the hidden factor is diversifiable, it can be shown that $\lim_{n\to\infty}\frac{1}{n^2}\left(m\sigma_t^2+2\sum_{i=1}^{m}\sum_{j=i+1}^{m}\sigma_{ij}\right)=0$ uniformly for all $1\le m\le n$, which also implies that $\lim_{n\to\infty}\frac{2}{n^2}\sum_{i=1}^{m}\sum_{j=i+1}^{m}\sigma_{ij}=0$. However, the partial sums of these m subseries in Eq. (4.4.2) across all m's (or so-called cumulative sums) will become

$$\sum_{m=1}^{n}E\left[\frac{1}{n}\sum_{i=1}^{m}\epsilon_{it}\right]^2=\frac{n(n+1)}{2n^2}\sigma_t^2+\frac{2}{n^2}\sum_{m=2}^{n}\left(\sum_{i=1}^{m-1}\sum_{j=i+1}^{m}\sigma_{ij}\right). \tag{4.4.3}$$

It is easy to see that the firm term in Eq. (4.4.3) will be finite. However, we may expand the second term in Eq. (4.4.3) and show that

$$\frac{2}{n^2}\sum_{m=2}^{n}\left(\sum_{i=1}^{m-1}\sum_{j=i+1}^{m}\sigma_{ij}\right)=\frac{2}{n^2}\left\{\sum_{i=1}^{n}(n-i)\sigma_{1,i+1}\right.$$
$$\left.+\sum_{i=2}^{n}(n-i)\sigma_{2,i+1}+\cdots+\sigma_{n-1,n}\right\}. \tag{4.4.4}$$

Notice that in Eq. (4.4.1), regardless of whether the hidden factor is diversifiable, the entire weighted sum may be growing with n since the numbers of items in the series are increasing with n also, unless these covariances converge to zero at a really fast pace.

In other words, every term in Eq. (4.4.1) may be converging to zero, yet their sum in Eq. (4.4.1) doesn't necessarily have a finite converging limit. This is straightforward to see even under the cross-sectional mixing or other short-memory conditions of $\{\epsilon_{it}\}_{i=1,2,...}$. Notice that the variance of $\frac{1}{n}\sum_{i=1}^{n}\epsilon_{it}$ grows with the number of asset returns n. However, they may grow at a different rate over the various memory conditions of $\{\epsilon_{it}\}_{i=1,2,...}$.

Hence, the infinite sums in Eq. (4.4.1) may or may not be finite depending on the growth rates. Instead, without loss of generality, the infinite sum in (4.4.1) could grow at an exponential rate such as n^{α}, where $0 \leq \alpha < 1$. The result is obvious if the underlying hidden factor is non-diversifiable. Therefore, in order to have the infinite sum in Eq. (4.4.1) converge, it might be necessary to normalize it with the power law as $n^{-\alpha}$.

More specifically, the less diversifiable the hidden factor is, the higher the value of α is. More explicitly, whether the infinite series will converge (to zero) or not depends on the speed of convergence of the weighted cumulative sum $\frac{1}{n}\sum_{i=1}^{m}\epsilon_{it}$ over different m, $m \leq n$, $n \longrightarrow \infty$.

If the hidden factor is strongly diversifiable such that each component in the series of Eq. (4.4.1) converges to zero rapidly enough, the entire sum in Eq. (4.4.1) may also converge to zero as well when $n \longrightarrow \infty$. Otherwise, the implication is that a missing factor is needed for the model specification. In addition, if $\epsilon_{it} = \eta_{it} + \nu_{it} = \beta_i^h f_{ht} + \nu_{it}$, where the factor loadings $\{\beta_i^h\}_{i=1,2,...,n}$ are nonstochastic, it can be shown that the partial sum of the L^2-norm of the equally weighted idiosyncratic risk is easily separable from the weighted partial sum of the hidden factor loadings and the variance of the hidden factor such that

$$
\begin{aligned}
\sum_{m=1}^{n} E\left[\frac{1}{n}\sum_{i=1}^{m}\epsilon_{it}\right]^2 &= \sum_{m=1}^{n} E\left[\frac{1}{n}\sum_{i=1}^{m}(\beta_i^h f_{ht} + \nu_{it})\right]^2 \\
&= \sum_{m=1}^{n}\left(\frac{1}{n}\sum_{i=1}^{m}\beta_i^h\right)^2 E[f_{ht}^2] + o_p(1) \qquad (4.4.5) \\
&= \sum_{m=1}^{n}\left(\frac{1}{n}\sum_{i=1}^{m}\beta_i^h\right)^2 \sigma_{ht}^2.
\end{aligned}
$$

For simplicity, if $\{\epsilon_{it}\}_{i=1,2,...}$ contains only a hidden factor, and assuming the weak law of large numbers holds such that $\frac{1}{T}\sum_{t=1}^{T}(f_{ht}^2 - E[f_{ht}^2]) = o_p(1)$, and letting the factor loadings of the hidden factor be nonstochastic, we can also derive the following equality such that

$$\begin{aligned}
&\frac{1}{n^2}\sum_{m=1}^{n}\left[\frac{1}{T}\sum_{t=1}^{T}\left[\left(\sum_{i=1}^{m}\epsilon_{it}\right)^2 - E\left(\sum_{i=1}^{m}\epsilon_{it}\right)^2\right]\right]\\
&= \sum_{m=1}^{n}\left[\frac{1}{T}\sum_{t=1}^{T}\left(\left(\frac{1}{n}\sum_{i=1}^{m}\epsilon_{it}\right)^2 - E\left[\frac{1}{n}\sum_{i=1}^{m}\epsilon_{it}\right]^2\right)\right],\\
&= \frac{1}{T}\sum_{t=1}^{T}\sum_{m=1}^{n}\left[\frac{1}{n^2}\left(\sum_{i=1}^{m}\beta_i^h\right)^2 (f_{ht}^2 - E[f_{ht}^2])\right] + o_p(1),\\
&= \left(\sum_{m=1}^{n}\left(\frac{1}{n}\sum_{i=1}^{m}\beta_i^h\right)^2\right)\left(\frac{1}{T}\sum_{t=1}^{T}(f_{ht}^2 - E[f_{ht}^2])\right),
\end{aligned} \tag{4.4.6}$$

uniformly for all n, $n = 1, 2, \ldots$, as $n \to \infty, T \to \infty$. These equations hold even if the hidden factor is non-diversifiable.

For instance, if the term $\sum_{m=1}^{n}\left(\frac{1}{n}\sum_{i=1}^{m}\beta_i^h\right)^2 = O(n^\alpha)$, $0 \leq \alpha < 1$, then $\sum_{m=1}^{n}\left(\frac{1}{n}\sum_{i=1}^{m}\beta_i^h\right)^2$ may not be bounded even if the hidden factor is moderately diversifiable as $n \to \infty$. Instead, we may need to multiply another $n^{-\alpha}$ to make it finite. Furthermore, due to the factor structure, the partial sums of cumulative weighted sums for factor loadings is factored out from the term, $\frac{1}{T}\sum_{t=1}^{T}(f_{ht}^2 - E[f_{ht}^2])$.

Given that the cross-sectional sample size n and the time-series horizon T may grow jointly, with or without any further conditions, these arguments still hold since both the cross-sectional sample size and that of the time series can increase jointly. We may also see that these partial sums of the cross-sectional CUSUMs of the weighted idiosyncratic risks are subject to different exponential growth rates with respect to n, such as n^α, depending on the factor loadings associated with the hidden factor.

Notice that even though $\frac{1}{T}\sum_{t=1}^{T}(f_{ht}^2 - E[f_{ht}^2]) = o_p(1)$, if the partial sum $\sum_{m=1}^{n}\left(\frac{1}{n}\sum_{i=1}^{m}\beta_i^h\right)^2 = O(n^\alpha)$, then from Eq. (4.4.6), it is obvious that

$\left(\sum_{m=1}^{n}\left(\frac{1}{n}\sum_{i=1}^{m}\beta_i^h\right)^2\right)\left(\frac{1}{T}\sum_{t=1}^{T}(f_{ht}^2 - E[f_{ht}^2])\right) = o(n^{\alpha})$. That is, the product of the partial sums of the squared weighted CUSUMs of idiosyncratic risks and $\frac{1}{T}\sum_{t=1}^{T}(f_{ht}^2 - E[f_{ht}^2])$ will converge to zero only if multiplied by $n^{-\alpha}$.

If $\alpha > 0$, and $\frac{1}{T}\sum_{t=1}^{T}(f_{ht}^2 - E[f_{ht}^2]) = o_p(1)$, these weighted CUSUMs do not converge to zero as $\frac{1}{T}\sum_{t=1}^{T}\left(\sum_{m=1}^{n}\left[\left(\frac{1}{n}\sum_{i=1}^{m}\epsilon_{it}\right)^2 - E\left(\frac{1}{n}\sum_{i=1}^{m}\epsilon_{it}\right)^2\right]\right) \neq o(1)$ even when $n \to \infty$, $T \to \infty$. In the extreme case when $\alpha = 0$, the implication is that the partial sums of the weighted CUSUMs of the factor loadings in the hidden factor are finite when $n \to \infty$ without any additional weighting or normalization. That is $\sum_{m=1}^{n}\left(\frac{1}{n}\sum_{i=1}^{m}\beta_i^h\right)^2 = o(1)$.

In other words, if the hidden factor is completely diversifiable, it is necessary that the partial sum $E\left[\frac{1}{n}\sum_{i=1}^{m}\epsilon_{it}\right]^2$ (which is the L^2-norm of $\frac{1}{n}\sum_{i=1}^{m}\epsilon_{it}$) should be equal to $o(1)$ uniformly for all m and $1 \leq m \leq n$ when $n \to \infty$. The converse, however, is not necessarily true. Hence, this implies that the hidden factor is well-diversifiable only if the components of these partial sums diminish to zero very rapidly. Thus, no further normalization or weighting scheme is needed.

Likewise, we may develop an index for the intensity of non-diversifiability of the hidden factor in idiosyncratic risks (and the already included factors) by considering the need for additional normalization of these partial sums of the weighted cumulative sum of the idiosyncratic risk to converge to zero. Hence, the higher the coefficient α is, the less diversifiable the hidden factor is. In the following, a few definitions are provided for the analysis of diversifiability.

Definition D6 Given the partial sums of idiosyncratic risks as $\sum_{m=1}^{n}E\left(\frac{1}{n}\sum_{i=1}^{m}\epsilon_{it}\right)^2$ for any date t, $t \geq T$, $T \to \infty$, and for the slowly varying function $L(n)$, the coefficient $\alpha \in R$,

$$\alpha = \inf_{\tilde{a}\geq 0}\left[\tilde{a}|n^{-\tilde{a}}L(n)\sum_{m=1}^{n}E\left(\frac{1}{n}\sum_{i=1}^{m}\epsilon_{it}\right)^2 = O(1)\right],$$

as $n \to \infty$ is denoted as the intensity of non-diversifiability of the hidden factor in idiosyncratic risks, $\{\epsilon_{it}\}_{i=1,2,}$. Or alternatively, for the nonequally weighted schemes, the intensity of non-diversifiability α is defined as

$$\alpha = \inf_{\tilde{a}\in[0,1]} \left[\tilde{a} | n^{-\tilde{a}} L(n) \sum_{m=1}^{n} E\left(\sum_{i=1}^{m} \omega_i \epsilon_{it} \right)^2 = O(1) \right]$$

when $n \to \infty$.

Since the equally weighted scheme also belongs to the set of well-diversified portfolios, the definition will use an equally weighted scheme for simplicity from now on. Given the above results, it is straightforward to assess the intensity of the non-diversifiability of the hidden factor by using the moment conditions. That is, if the sample sizes of both the time horizon and the cross-sectional observations can expand asymptotically, a variance-type estimation similar to Giraitis et al. (2003) for the intensity of the non-diversifiability of the hidden factor is available—even though the approach of these authors assumes Gaussian processes.

Incidentally, the above definition of the intensity of the non-diversifiability of the idiosyncratic risk is similar to that of Berenguer-Rico and Gonzalo (2014) in defining the summability of stochastic processes. Their definition shows that the summability of stochastic processes $\{X_m\}_{m=1,2,\ldots,}$ can be measured as $\alpha = \inf_{\tilde{a}\geq 0}\left[\tilde{a}|n^{-\tilde{a}}L(n)\sum_{i=1}^{n} X_i = O_p(1)\right]$, as $n \to \infty$. The condition applied in our context (especially on the cumulative sums of idiosyncratic risk), however, is of a stronger condition as convergence in second-order moments. Berenguer-Rico and Gonzalo (2014) define the summability of the stochastic processes in terms of a probability limit. Their goal of study, however, is to extend the notion of cointegration to a nonlinear setting.

Notice that, in the above Definition D6, the summability of $\sum_{m=1}^{n} E\left(\frac{1}{n}\sum_{i=1}^{m}\epsilon_{it}\right)^2$ depends critically on the convergence rate of the item $E\left(\frac{1}{n}\sum_{i=1}^{m}\epsilon_{it}\right)^2$ for all $m = 1, 2, \ldots, n$. In other words, the speed at which these terms converge will determine the intensity of the non-diversifiability α defined in Definition D6. The empirical testing for the intensity of non-diversifiability when using the exponent α is equivalent to considering the growing rate of the moments of the cumulative sums of the idiosyncratic risk. Hence, alternatively, since convergence in second-order moments implies convergence in probability, a weaker condition for this can also be made.

4.4.2 A Simple Cross-Sectional Approach

In extending the above framework, an alternative approach with weak convergence in distribution is considered here. Notice that if $n^{-\alpha}\sum_{m=1}^{n} E\left(\frac{1}{n}\sum_{i=1}^{m}\epsilon_{it}\right)^2 = O(1)$, $t \geq T$, $T \to \infty$, it follows that

$$n^{-\alpha}E\left|\sum_{m=1}^{n}\left(\frac{1}{n}\sum_{i=1}^{m}\epsilon_{it}\right)\right|^2 = O(1)$$

with a dominated convergence property of infinite series since $E\left(\frac{1}{n}\sum_{i=1}^{m}\epsilon_{it}\right)^2 \geq \left(E\left|\frac{1}{n}\sum_{i=1}^{m}\epsilon_{it}\right|\right)^2$ for all n and m, where $n \geq m$. Since convergence to an (absolute) mean-square norm implies convergence in probability (and in distribution), the following Assumption A8 can be provided without loss of generality.

Explicitly, a test statistic can be formed if additional assumptions for the possible weak convergence of these cumulative sums are provided. Given the additional weak convergence condition, the test statistic can be formed at a point t in time, where $t = T + 1, T + 2, \ldots$, and T is the time frame (or training sample) for estimation of the empirical asset pricing models where $T \to \infty$. In other words, a sequential detection scheme to find an additional hidden non-diversifiable factor can be devised. Specifically, the following test statistics can be applied as diagnostic tests for empirical asset pricing models and as the rejection rule of model selection in constructing the model confidence sets.[22]

If the weak convergence is established, the test statistic for the intensity of non-diversifiability can be developed when the (normalized) partial sum of these squared cumulative sums of idiosyncratic risk converges to a square integral of a Brownian bridge provided that the null hypothesis of no hidden non-diversifiable factor holds. Given the two Definitions D4 and D5 are provided for the self-similar processes and fractional Brownian motion, development for the intensity of non-diversifiability can be associated with the Hurst exponent where the invariance principle for the partial sums of the long-dependent random variables can be applied.

More extensively, we also discover that the intensity of non-diversifiability for the hidden factor is related to the Hurst exponent if the fractional invariance principle for the idiosyncratic risks holds. The intensity of non-diversifiability of the hidden factor (or convergence rate of the partial sums of cross-sectional CUSUMs of idiosyncratic risks) is related to the Hurst exponent of a fractional Brownian motion if the following invariance principle holds. In particular, the notion of intensity of non-diversifiability when related to the Hurst exponent greater than $\frac{1}{2}$, also concurs with the result in Theorem 4.1 where cross-sectional long dependence may be present if the hidden factor is non-diversifiable.

Notice that the following invariance principle actually includes the usual cases when the cumulative sums converge to a standard Brownian motion under various mixing conditions when the Hurst exponent is equal to $\frac{1}{2}$.

In addition, the weak convergence in the cross-sectional CUSUMs includes the cases where the hidden factor can be either diversifiable or non-diversifiable. Hence, based on the results in Theorem 4.1, it is feasible to consider the following Assumption A9 where cross-sectional long dependence is included in the possible weak convergence in distribution for these cross-sectional cumulative sums of idiosyncratic risk.

Assumption A9 Let the (presumed) idiosyncratic risk $\{\epsilon_{it}\}_{i=1,2,...}$ for each time t, $t \geq T$, $T \rightarrow \infty$, and for cross-sectional sample size n, $n \longrightarrow \infty$, follow the fractional invariance principle such that[23]

$$\frac{1}{n^H \sigma_H} \sum_{i=1}^{[nz]} \epsilon_{it} \xrightarrow{d} B_H(z), \tag{4.4.7}$$

where $0 < z \leq 1$, $[x]$ stands for the largest integer that is less than x, $x \in R^\dagger$, $B_H(z)$ is a fractional Brownian motion with the Hurst exponent H, $0 < H < 1$, $\sigma_H^2 = \lim\limits_{n\rightarrow\infty} \frac{1}{n} E\left(\sum_{i=1}^{n} \epsilon_{it}\right)^2$, and the notation $\xrightarrow{d}$ stands for the convergence in distribution. In particular, with the definition of fractional Brownian motion, when $0 < H < \frac{1}{2}$, the stochastic process is antipersistent; when $H = \frac{1}{2}$, it becomes the standard Brownian motion; and when $H > \frac{1}{2}$, the stochastic process will have long dependence.

Proposition 4.4 *Given Definitions D4, D5, D6, and Assumption A9, for any date t, $t \geq T$, $T \rightarrow \infty$, the weighted partial sums of the CUSUMs of the idiosyncratic risks, $n^{-\alpha} \sum_{m=1}^{n} \left(\frac{1}{n} \sum_{i=1}^{m} \epsilon_{it}\right)^2$ will converge in distribution to the square integral of fractional Brownian motion such that*

$$n^{-\alpha} \sum_{m=1}^{n} \left(\frac{1}{n\sigma_H} \sum_{i=1}^{m} \epsilon_{it}\right)^2 \xrightarrow{d} \int_o^1 (B_H(z))^2 dz, \tag{4.4.8}$$

if $n \to \infty$, *where* $H = \frac{\alpha+1}{2}$. *In particular, when* $\alpha = 0$, *the weak convergence will result in*

$$\sum_{m=1}^{n}\left(\frac{1}{n\sigma}\sum_{i=1}^{m}\epsilon_{it}\right)^2 \xrightarrow{d} \int_o^1 (B(z))^2 dz, \tag{4.4.9}$$

where $B(z)$ is the standard Brownian motion.

Proof Based on Assumption A9, it is feasible, by applying the continuous mapping property for weak convergence, and setting $H = \frac{\alpha+1}{2}$,

$$n^{-\alpha}\sum_{m=1}^{n}\left(\frac{1}{n\sigma_H}\sum_{i=1}^{m}\epsilon_{it}\right)^2 = \frac{1}{n}\sum_{m=1}^{n}\left(\frac{1}{n^H\sigma_H}\sum_{i=1}^{m}\epsilon_{it}\right)^2 \xrightarrow{d} \int_o^1 (B_H(z))^2 dz, \tag{4.4.10}$$

And by setting $\alpha = 0$, it follows that

$$\sum_{m=1}^{n}\left(\frac{1}{n\sigma}\sum_{i=1}^{m}\epsilon_{it}\right)^2 \xrightarrow{d} \int_o^1 (B(z))^2 dz, \tag{4.4.11}$$

since $\alpha = 2H - 1$, this will provide an approach to verify the intensity of non-diversifiability of the hidden factor. In fact, when the hidden factor is completely diversifiable, the Hurst exponent H will be equal to $\frac{1}{2}$ since $\alpha = 0$.

The weak convergence in Eq. (4.4.9) will become a convergence in distribution toward a square integral of Brownian motion. Hence, the statistical test for the null hypothesis as $\alpha = 0$ (or $H = \frac{1}{2}$) may feasibly be used to investigate whether the hidden factor (if there is one) is indeed non-diversifiable or not. We may now devise a test statistic such that, under the null hypothesis of no non-diversifiable hidden factor in ϵ_{it} where $H = \frac{1}{2}$, it will converge in distribution to a square integral of a Brownian bridge where the distribution is available. In particular, the test statistic is derived based on the residuals of the fitted models currently applied to the training sample size n and T, where $n, T \to \infty$. The following Assumption A8 assumes that the weighted partial sums of residuals will approximate to that of the error terms from the presumed empirical asset pricing models.

Assumption A10 $|\frac{1}{n\sigma_H}\sum_{i=1}^{m}\epsilon_{it} - \frac{1}{n\hat{\sigma}_H}\sum_{i=1}^{m}\hat{\epsilon}_{it}| = o_p(1)$ for all $H \in [\frac{1}{2}, 1)$ as $n, T \longrightarrow \infty$.

Notice that, even though the sum of residuals such as $\sum_{t=1}^{T}\hat{\epsilon}_{it} = 0$ for any given time frame T, $T \to \infty$ (for instance, a least-squares estimation), as usual, the cross-sectional sum of these residuals $\sum_{i=1}^{n}\hat{\epsilon}_{it}$ may or may not be equal to zero with a sample size n. Hence, the statistic can be shown that as $n \to \infty$, for any date $t \geq T$, $T \to \infty$ (or, for $t = T+1, T+2, \ldots,$ where T is a time horizon for training samples, $T \to \infty$) and denoting $\hat{\sigma}_H$ as $\hat{\sigma}$ when assuming $H = \frac{1}{2}$ for simplicity,

$$
\begin{aligned}
\xi_n &= \sum_{m=1}^{n}\left(\frac{1}{n\hat{\sigma}}\sum_{i=1}^{m}(\hat{\epsilon}_{it} - \bar{\hat{\epsilon}})\right)^2 \\
&= \sum_{m=1}^{n}\left(\frac{1}{n\hat{\sigma}}\sum_{i=1}^{m}\left(\hat{\epsilon}_{it} - \frac{1}{n}\sum_{i=1}^{n}\hat{\epsilon}_{it}\right)\right)^2 \\
&= \frac{1}{n}\sum_{m=1}^{n}\left[\frac{1}{\sqrt{n}\hat{\sigma}}\sum_{i=1}^{m}\left(\hat{\epsilon}_{it} - \frac{1}{n}\sum_{i=1}^{n}\hat{\epsilon}_{it}\right)\right]^2 \\
&= \frac{1}{n}\sum_{m=1}^{n}\left[\frac{1}{\sqrt{n}\hat{\sigma}}\sum_{i=1}^{m}\hat{\epsilon}_{it} - \frac{m}{n}\left(\frac{1}{\sqrt{n}\hat{\sigma}}\sum_{i=1}^{n}\hat{\epsilon}_{it}\right)\right]^2 \\
&\xrightarrow{d} \int_0^1 (B(z) - zB(1))^2 dz, \\
&\xrightarrow{d} \int_0^1 \widetilde{B}(z)^2 dz
\end{aligned}
\tag{4.4.12}
$$

where $B(z)$ is a standard Brownian motion for $z \in [0, 1]$. Hence, the statistic ξ_n will converge in distribution to a square integral of a Brownian bridge $\widetilde{B}(z)$. One advantage of the test statistic is that, although we base the convergence rate on the moments for cumulative sums, it does not consider the finiteness of the moments of these cumulative sums.

In fact, for any given finite sample size n, these sample moments are always finite. Although there are many articles that develop various tests for the factor structures or number of factors, these tests either ignore the verification of non-diversifiability of the identified factor(s) or the tests simply fail to consider the convergence rates of moment conditions of these factors and their factor loadings. Instead, the test statistic here is to consider the convergence rate of the moments of these cumulative sums, and the coefficient such as the Hurst exponent is used to construct the test where asymptotic distribution is available when the null hypothesis (of no hidden non-diversifiable factor) holds.

In other words, the test for the existence of a hidden non-diversifiable factor becomes the test of whether the Hurst exponent is greater than $\frac{1}{2}$ or not when using the distribution of the square integral of a Brownian bridge. In fact, Eq. (4.4.12) can be considered as a cross-sectional KPSS test for long dependence (see Beran et al. 2013).

Kiefer (1959) and the recent development in Tolmatz (2002) have shown the distribution of the square integral of a Brownian bridge, where Tolmatz provides more accurate values for the table of distribution. In fact, Smirnov's (1936) ω^2-goodness of fit test which coincides with a square integral of a Brownian bridge on [0, 1] has the distribution function as

$$F(\lambda) = 1 - \frac{2}{\pi}\sum_{k=1}^{\infty}\int_{(2k-1)\pi}^{2k\pi}\frac{e^{-x^2\lambda/2}}{\sqrt{-x\sin x}}dx, \tag{4.4.13}$$

where λ is the level of the square integral of a Brownian bridge as in Eq. (4.4.12). With the tables of distribution provided in Kiefer (1959) and Tolmatz (2002, 2003), it is straightforward to assess the p-values of the test statistics in Eq. (4.4.12) where the sum of the squared cumulative sums of the mean deviations for the idiosyncratic risk is calculated.

More explicitly, it is feasible to form the hypothesis testing as:

$$H_o : \alpha = 0,$$

$$H_a : \alpha > 0,$$

where $\alpha = 0$ is equivalent to setting the Hurst exponent as $H = \frac{1}{2}$ when the hidden factor is diversifiable, and the alternative hypothesis is when $H > \frac{1}{2}$ where cross-sectional long dependence may prevail. If one finds the statistic in Eq. (4.4.12) tends to have the probability $\Pr(\xi_n > \lambda|\alpha = 0) < 1 - F(\lambda)$, this shows that there is a high likelihood that there is a hidden non-diversifiable factor in the idiosyncratic risk of the prespecified asset pricing models.

On the other hand, given that $n^{-\alpha}\sum_{m=1}^{n} E|\frac{1}{n}\sum_{i=1}^{m}\epsilon_{it}|^2 = n^{-\alpha}\sum_{m=1}^{n} ||\frac{1}{n}\sum_{i=1}^{m}\epsilon_{it}||^2 = O(1)$ is a summable infinite series as $n \longrightarrow \infty$, and since the expectation is unconditional, it is feasible to argue that the series is summable for all $t \geq T$ as $T \to \infty$, if and only if

$$n^{-\alpha}\sum_{m=1}^{n}\left[||\frac{1}{n}\sum_{i=1}^{m+1}\epsilon_{it}||^2 - ||\frac{1}{n}\sum_{i=1}^{m}\epsilon_{it}||^2\right] < O(1), \tag{4.4.14}$$

where the notation $||.||$ stands for the L^2-norm. Notice that, in using the Cauchy-Schwarz inequality for L^2-norm, it can be shown that

$$\sum_{m=1}^{n}||\left(\frac{1}{n}\sum_{i=1}^{m+1}\epsilon_{it}\right)-\left(\frac{1}{n}\sum_{i=1}^{m}\epsilon_{it}\right)||^2 \geq \sum_{m=1}^{n}\left[||\frac{1}{n}\sum_{i=1}^{m+1}\epsilon_{it}||^2 - ||\frac{1}{n}\sum_{i=1}^{m}\epsilon_{it}||^2\right]. \tag{4.4.15}$$

Therefore, if one can verify that for all $t \geq T$ as $T \to \infty$,

$$\begin{aligned} n^{-\alpha}E&\left(\sum_{m=1}^{n}\left(\frac{1}{n}\sum_{i=1}^{m+1}\epsilon_{it}\right)-\sum_{m=1}^{n}\left(\frac{1}{n}\sum_{i=1}^{m}\epsilon_{it}\right)\right)^2 \\ &= n^{-\alpha}E\left(\sum_{m=1}^{n}\left(\left(\frac{1}{n}\sum_{i=1}^{m+1}\epsilon_{it}\right)-\left(\frac{1}{n}\sum_{i=1}^{m}\epsilon_{it}\right)\right)^2\right) \\ &\leq n^{-\alpha}\left(\sum_{m=1}^{n}E\left|\left(\frac{1}{n}\sum_{i=1}^{m+1}\epsilon_{it}\right)-\left(\frac{1}{n}\sum_{i=1}^{m}\epsilon_{it}\right)\right|^2\right) \\ &\leq O(1), \end{aligned} \tag{4.4.16}$$

this will show that $n^{-\alpha}\sum_{m=1}^{n} E|\frac{1}{n}\sum_{i=1}^{m}\epsilon_{it}|^2 = n^{-\alpha}E\left(\sum_{m=1}^{n}|\frac{1}{n}\sum_{i=1}^{m}\epsilon_{it}|^2\right) \leq O(1)$.

Since convergence in moments implies convergence in probability (and hence in distribution), a weaker necessary condition such as $n^{-\alpha}\sum_{m=1}^{n}|\frac{1}{n}\sum_{i=1}^{m}\epsilon_{it}|^2 = O_p(1)$ is feasible. This in turn implies that $n^{-\alpha}\left(\sum_{m=1}^{n}\left((\frac{1}{n}\sum_{i=1}^{m+1}\epsilon_{it})-(\frac{1}{n}\sum_{i=1}^{m}\epsilon_{it})\right)^2\right) \leq O_p(1)$. Hence, it also possible to consider another alternative statistic ς_n based on a quadratic variation of fractional Brownian motion.

4.4.2.1 *Quadratic Variation of Cross-Sectional Blocks of Presumed Idiosyncratic Risk*

Let $j = 1, 2, \ldots, l$ be the index for cross-sectional blocks of "presumed" idiosyncratic risk in a model search of empirical asset pricing models, and let $n_j = r_j n$, where r_j is a positive integer. That is, divide the cross-sectional number of asset returns into several blocks where each block contains n asset returns, then define the statistic $\varsigma_n(j)$ as

$$\begin{aligned}
\varsigma_n(j) &= n_j^{-\alpha} \sum_{m=1}^{n_j} \left((\frac{1}{n_j} \sum_{i=1}^{m+1} \epsilon_{it}) - (\frac{1}{n_j} \sum_{i=1}^{m} \epsilon_{it}) \right)^2 \\
&= n_j^{-(2H-1)} \sum_{m=1}^{n_j} \left((\frac{1}{n_j} \sum_{i=1}^{m+1} \epsilon_{it}) - (\frac{1}{n_j} \sum_{i=1}^{m} \epsilon_{it}) \right)^2 \\
&= \frac{1}{n_j} \sigma_H^2 \sum_{m=1}^{n_j} \left(\left(\frac{1}{n_j^H \sigma_H} \sum_{i=1}^{m+1} \epsilon_{it} \right) - \left(\frac{1}{n_j^H \sigma_H} \sum_{i=1}^{m} \epsilon_{it} \right) \right)^2 \\
&= \Delta_\epsilon + \widetilde{\eta_j}
\end{aligned} \tag{4.4.17}$$

for each block j, where Δ_ϵ is a small constant, and $\widetilde{\eta_j}$ is a zero-mean random noise. Then, since $n^{-\alpha} \sum_{m=1}^{n} |\frac{1}{n} \sum_{i=1}^{m} \epsilon_{it}|^2 = O_p(1)$, it is feasible to see that for $j = 1, 2, \ldots, l$, Eq. (4.4.17) will hold for all blocks when the intensity of non-diversifiability is defined as α. In other words, for each block j,

$$\ln \left(\sum_{m=1}^{n_j} \left(\left(\frac{1}{n_j} \sum_{i=1}^{m+1} \epsilon_{it} \right) - \left(\frac{1}{n_j} \sum_{i=1}^{m} \epsilon_{it} \right) \right)^2 \right) - (2H-1)(\ln(n_j)) - \ln(\Delta_\epsilon) = o_p(1). \tag{4.4.18}$$

Hence, for $j = 1, 2, \ldots, l$, and letting

$$\begin{aligned}
Z_n(j) &= \sum_{m=1}^{n_j} \left(\left(\frac{1}{n_j} \sum_{i=1}^{m+1} \epsilon_{it} \right) - \left(\frac{1}{n_j} \sum_{i=1}^{m} \epsilon_{it} \right) \right)^2 \\
&= \frac{1}{n_j} \sum_{m=1}^{n_j} \left(\left(\frac{1}{\sqrt{n_j}} \sum_{i=1}^{m+1} \epsilon_{it} \right) - \left(\frac{1}{\sqrt{n_j}} \sum_{i=1}^{m} \epsilon_{it} \right) \right)^2
\end{aligned}$$

then it is shown that

$$\ln\left(Z_n(j)\right) \approx \mu_\theta + (2H-1)\ln(n_j) + \nu_j. \tag{4.4.19}$$

Therefore, in using the regression of the above equation, it is feasible to obtain an estimate for the intensity of non-diversifiability. That is, given that $\overline{\ln(n)} = \frac{1}{l}\sum_{j=1}^{l}\ln(n_j)$ and $n_j = r_j n$,

$$\begin{aligned}\hat{\alpha} &= \frac{\sum_{j=1}^{l}\left(\ln(n_j)-\overline{\ln(n)}\right)\left(\ln\left(Z_n(j)\right)\right)}{\sum_{j=1}^{l}\left(\ln(n_j)-\overline{\ln(n)}\right)^2} \\ &= \frac{\sum_{j=1}^{l} y_j\left(\ln\left(Z_n(j)\right)\right)}{\sum_{j=1}^{l} y_j^2},\end{aligned} \tag{4.4.20}$$

where $y_j = \ln(r_j) - \frac{1}{l}\sum_{j=1}^{l}\ln(r_j)$.

Notice that $Z_n(j) = n_j^{2H-1}\left(\frac{1}{n_j}\sigma_H^2\sum_{m=1}^{n_j}\left(\left(\frac{1}{n_j^H\sigma_H}\sum_{i=1}^{m+1}\epsilon_{it}\right)\right.\right.$ $\left.\left.-\left(\frac{1}{n_j^H\sigma_H}\sum_{i=1}^{m}\epsilon_{it}\right)\right)^2\right)$. Hence, it is feasible to have

$$\begin{aligned}\ln\left(Z_n(j)\right) &= \ln\left(n_j^{2H-1}\right) + \ln\left(\frac{1}{n_j}\sigma_H^2\sum_{m=1}^{n_j}\left(\left(\frac{1}{n_j^H\sigma_H}\sum_{i=1}^{m+1}\epsilon_{it}\right)\right.\right. \\ &\qquad \left.\left.-\left(\frac{1}{n_j^H\sigma_H}\sum_{i=1}^{m}\epsilon_{it}\right)\right)^2\right) \\ &= (2H-1)\ln(n_j) + \ln(\varsigma_n(j)).\end{aligned}$$

Substituting the above term into Eq. (4.4.20), it is easy to see that

$$\begin{aligned}\hat{\alpha} &= \frac{\sum_{j=1}^{l}\left(\ln(n_j)-\overline{\ln(n)}\right)\left((2H-1)\ln(n_j)+\ln\left(\varsigma_n(j)\right)\right)}{\sum_{j=1}^{l}\left(\ln(n_j)-\overline{\ln(n)}\right)^2} \\ &= (2H-1) + \frac{\sum_{j=1}^{l}\left(\ln(n_j)-\overline{\ln(n)}\right)\left(\ln\left(\varsigma_n(j)\right)\right)}{\sum_{j=1}^{l}\left(\ln(n_j)-\overline{\ln(n)}\right)^2} \\ &= \alpha + \frac{\sum_{j=1}^{l} y_j\left(\ln\left(\varsigma_n(j)\right)\right)}{\sum_{j=1}^{l} y_j^2},\end{aligned} \tag{4.4.21}$$

since $\sum_{j=1}^{l}\left(\ln(n_j)-\overline{\ln(n)}\right)\ln(n_j) = \sum_{j=1}^{l}\left(\ln(n_j)-\overline{\ln(n)}\right)^2$. Now $\varsigma_n(j) = \Delta_\epsilon + \widetilde{\eta_j}$, and $\Delta_\epsilon\left(\sum_{j=1}^{l}\left(\ln(n_j)-\overline{\ln(n)}\right)\right) = o_p(1)$ so if the idiosyncratic risk is subject to intensity α such that the cumulative sums are eliminated when $n^{-\alpha}$ is applied, it is easy to see that $\frac{\sum_{j=1}^{l} y_j(\ln(\varsigma_n(j)))}{\sum_{j=1}^{l} y_j{}^2}$ is bounded from above.

In addition, since $\varsigma_n(j)$ is relatively small, it is feasible to have a Taylor expansion for its logarithm such that

$$
\begin{aligned}
\ln\left(\varsigma_n(j)\right) &= \ln\left(\varsigma_n(j)=1\right) + \left(\frac{1}{\varsigma_n(j)}\right)\bigg|_{\varsigma_n(j)=1}\left(\varsigma_n(j)-1\right) + R_\xi \\
&= \left(\varsigma_n(j)-1\right) + R_\xi \\
&\approx \left(\varsigma_n(j)-1\right) + o_p(1),
\end{aligned}
$$

where R_ξ is a negligible remainder term. Substituting this expression into Eq. (4.4.21) and using $\sum_{j=1}^{l} y_j = 0$, it is easy to see that

$$
\hat{\alpha} = \alpha + \frac{\sum_{j=1}^{l} y_j \varsigma_n(j)}{\sum_{j=1}^{l} y_j{}^2} + o_p(1), \tag{4.4.22}
$$

Proposition 4.5 *Given the estimate for the intensity of non-diversifiability in Eq. (4.4.22), it can be shown that $\hat{\alpha}-\alpha$ will converge to zero in probability as $n \to \infty$ with a sufficient number of blocks of cross-sectional asset returns. In addition, the estimate $\hat{\alpha}$ is also unbiased in the sense that $E(\hat{\alpha}) = \alpha$.*

Proof Given that $\varsigma_n(j) = \Delta_\epsilon + \widetilde{\eta_j}$, it is easy to see that for a sufficient number of blocks of cross-sectional asset returns, since $\sum_{j=1}^{l} y_j = 0$,

$$
\frac{\sum_{j=1}^{l} y_j \varsigma_n(j)}{\sum_{j=1}^{l} y_j{}^2} = \Delta_\epsilon\left(\frac{\sum_{j=1}^{l} y_j}{\sum_{j=1}^{l} y_j{}^2}\right) + \frac{\sum_{j=1}^{l} y_j}{\sum_{j=1}^{l} y_j{}^2}\widetilde{\eta_j} = 0 + o_p(1).
$$

In addition, since $\sum_{j=1}^{l} y_j = 0$, and $E\left(\widetilde{\eta_j}\right) = 0$ for all $j = 1, 2, \ldots, l$, it is also feasible to see that $E(\hat{\alpha}) = \alpha$.

Applying Assumptions A9 and A10, it can be shown that as $n \to \infty$ for all $t \geq T$ as T is sufficiently large, and letting $H = \frac{\alpha+1}{2}$, $|\hat{\varsigma}_n(j) - \varsigma_n(j)| = o_p(1)$,

$$\hat{\varsigma}_n(j) = \frac{1}{n_j}\left(\sum_{m=1}^{n_j}\left(\left(\frac{1}{n_j^{(\frac{\alpha+1}{2})}\sigma_H}\sum_{i=1}^{m+1}\hat{\epsilon}_{it}\right) - \left(\frac{1}{n_j^{(\frac{\alpha+1}{2})}\sigma_H}\sum_{i=1}^{m}\hat{\epsilon}_{it}\right)\right)\right)^2$$

$$\xrightarrow{d} \frac{1}{n_j}\sum_{m=1}^{n_j}(B_H(z_{m+1}) - B_H(z_m))^2 \tag{4.4.23}$$

In other words, the above statistic $\hat{\varsigma}_n(j)$ will converge in distribution to the quadratic variation of the fractional Brownian motion $B_H(z)$, $0 \leq z_m \leq 1$ for all $0 < m \leq n$, and all blocks $j = 1, 2, \ldots, l$.[24] Based on Berzin et al. (2014), the quadratic variation of the fractional Brownian motion (where $0 < H < 1$) converges almost certainly to a diminishing term as $n \to \infty$ such that

$$\frac{1}{n}\sum_{m=1}^{n}(B_H(z_{m+1}) - B_H(z_m))^2 \xrightarrow{a.s.} n^{-2H}\sigma_{2H}||Z||^2,$$

where $||Z||^2$ represents the second-order moment of a standardized normal variable. Replacing the term of $\varsigma_n(j)$ in Eq. (4.4.22) with the above expression, it can be shown that as $n \to \infty$, the second term in Eq. (4.4.22) will vanish. Hence, the above estimate for the intensity of non-diversifiability is consistent such that $\hat{\alpha} = 2H - 1 + o_p(1) = \alpha + o_p(1)$ as $n \to \infty$.

Hence, given Assumption A10, it can be stated that for all cross-sectional blocks of asset returns,

$$\hat{\varsigma}_n(j) = \frac{1}{n}\left(\sum_{m=1}^{n}\left(\left(\frac{1}{n^{(\frac{\alpha+1}{2})}\hat{\sigma}_H}\sum_{i=1}^{m+1}\hat{\epsilon}_{it}\right) - \left(\frac{1}{n^{(\frac{\alpha+1}{2})}\hat{\sigma}_H}\sum_{i=1}^{m}\hat{\epsilon}_{it}\right)\right)\right)^2.$$

$$\xrightarrow{d} \frac{1}{n}\sum_{m=1}^{n}(B_H(z_{m+1}) - B_H(z_m))^2. \tag{4.4.24}$$

Namely, in using the residuals from the regressions, the quadratic differences from the CUSUMs of residuals will converge in distribution to the quadratic variation of the fractional Brownian motion. Again, if the null hypothesis assumes that there is no hidden factor such that $\alpha = 0$, it is easy to see that this statistic simply converges in distribution to the quadratic variation of the Brownian motion. Thus, if the asymptotic distribution of statistics in using the power variation of the fractional Brownian motion is available, it is feasible to consider the asymptotic distribution of $\hat{\alpha}$.

Notice that Berzin et al. (2014) show that for the fractional Brownian motion with the Hurst exponent H, $0 < H < 1$, it is possible to obtain a consistent estimate for the Hurst exponent when using the power variations from the discrete sample path of the stochastic process. The asymptotic normal distribution for estimates of the Hurst exponent is also given in Berzin et al. (2014). However, the asymptotic distribution of H in Berzin et al. (2014) depends on the Hermite expansion which is more difficult to use in practice, and the distribution of $\hat{\alpha}$ requires a transformation such as $\hat{\alpha} = 2\hat{H} - 1$.

In addition, Tudor (2013) shows that if $H \le \frac{3}{4}$, the centered quadratic variation of the fractional Brownian motion will converge in distribution to a standard normal law as $n \to \infty$. And if $H > \frac{3}{4}$, the weighted quadratic variation of the fractional Brownian motion will converge to a non-Gaussian standard Rosenblatt random variable asymptotically when $n \to \infty$. Therefore, if given the null hypothesis as $\alpha = 0$, the Hurst exponent H will become $\frac{1}{2}$. and the centered quadratic variation (which can be approximated with Eq. (4.4.23) is applicable to the test whether there is a hidden non-diversifiable factor in the error terms of the presumed empirical asset pricing model or not.

Given that the interest of study is on whether $\alpha = 0$ versus $\alpha > 0$, it is easier to focus on the asymptotic distribution of $\hat{\alpha} - \alpha$ under the null hypothesis as $\alpha = 0$.

Proposition 4.6 *Given the above setting for the estimate of intensity of non-diversifiability* α *and under the null hypothesis that* $\alpha = 0$, *then* $n^{\frac{3}{2}}(\hat{\alpha} - \alpha)$ *of the estimate for the intensity of non-diversifiability will converge in distribution to a rescaled Gaussian random variable such that*

$$n^{\frac{3}{2}}(\hat{\alpha} - \alpha) \xrightarrow{d} \sum_{j=1}^{l} \left(\frac{y_j}{r_j^{\frac{3}{2}} \sum_{j=1}^{l} y_j^2} \right) \hat{Z}, \tag{4.4.25}$$

as $n \to \infty$ where $\hat{Z}$ is a zero-mean normal random variable with distribution $N(0, C_{\frac{1}{2}}^2)$, $C_{\frac{1}{2}}^2 = \mu_4 - \mu_2^2$, under the null such that $H = \frac{1}{2}$, and equivalently $\alpha = 0$, and y_j is as defined in Eq. (4.4.20).

Proof Notice that, from Nourdin and Réveillac (2009), it is shown that under the null hypothesis $\alpha = 0$ (or $H = \frac{1}{2}$) when $n \to \infty$,

$$\frac{1}{\sqrt{n}} \sum_{m=1}^{n} \left(n(\Delta_m B)^2 - 1 \right) \xrightarrow{d} N(0,\, C_{\frac{1}{2}}^2), \tag{4.4.26}$$

where $\Delta_m B$ represents the increment of Brownian motion, $C_{\frac{1}{2}}^2$ is a constant such that $C_{\frac{1}{2}}^2 = \mu_4 - \mu_2^2$ where μ_κ is the κ-th order moment of a standard Gaussian variable distributed as $N(0, 1)$ and as $\kappa = 2$ for the quadratic variation such that $\mu_2 = 1$, according to Nourdin (2008). Now that $n_j \varsigma_n(j) = \sum_{m=1}^{n_j} (\Delta_m B)^2$, it can be shown that

$$n_j^2 \varsigma_n(j) - 1 = \sum_{m=1}^{n_j} n_j (\Delta_m B)^2 - 1, \tag{4.4.27}$$

and hence,

$$\begin{aligned} n_j^{\frac{3}{2}} \varsigma_n(j) - \frac{1}{\sqrt{n_j}} &= \frac{1}{\sqrt{n_j}} \left(n_j^2 \varsigma_n(j) - 1 \right) \\ &= \frac{1}{\sqrt{n_j}} \left(\sum_{m=1}^{n_j} n_j (\Delta_m B)^2 - 1 \right) \\ &\xrightarrow{d} N(0, C_{\frac{1}{2}}^2). \end{aligned} \tag{4.4.28}$$

Now

$$\begin{aligned} n_j^{\frac{3}{2}} \varsigma_n(j) &= \frac{1}{\sqrt{n_j}} \left(\sum_{m=1}^{n_j} n_j (\Delta_m B)^2 - 1 \right) + \left(\frac{1}{\sqrt{n_j}} \right) \\ &= \frac{1}{\sqrt{n_j}} \left(\sum_{m=1}^{n_j} n_j (\Delta_m B)^2 - 1 \right) + o(1) \\ &\xrightarrow{d} \hat{Z} + o(1), \end{aligned} \tag{4.4.29}$$

as $n \to \infty$ where $\hat{Z}$ is a zero-mean normal random variable with distribution $N(0, C^2_{\frac{1}{2}})$. Hence, it is shown that when $\alpha = 0$ under the null hypothesis,

$$n^{\frac{3}{2}} (\hat{\alpha} - \alpha) = \sum_{j=1}^{l} \left(\frac{y_j}{r_j^{\frac{3}{2}} \sum_{j=1}^{l} y_j^2} \right) n_j^{\frac{3}{2}} \varsigma_n(j)$$
$$\xrightarrow{d} \sum_{j=1}^{l} \left(\frac{y_j}{r_j^{\frac{3}{2}} \sum_{j=1}^{l} y_j^2} \right) \hat{Z}, \tag{4.4.30}$$

since all the components in $\sum_{j=1}^{l} \left(\frac{y_j}{r_j^{\frac{3}{2}} \sum_{j=1}^{l} y_j^2} \right)$ are nonstochastic, where l is the number of blocks in the cross-sectional observations of asset returns.

Hence, based on Eq. (4.4.25), it is feasible to obtain the specification test for the estimate of the intensity of non-diversifiability when using the residuals of fitted models. Therefore, for some number of blocks in the cross-sectional presumed idiosyncratic risk, the test statistic $n^{\frac{3}{2}} (\hat{\alpha} - \alpha)$ of the estimate of the intensity of non-diversifiability will converge in distribution to a rescaled normal variable when the number of cross-sectional observations $n \to \infty$ in each block j under the null hypothesis $\alpha = 0$. Specifically, the test of interest is a one-tailed test where the alternative hypothesis is $\alpha > 0$.

Notice that the conventional arguments for the specification tests usually apply the norming sequence as $n^{\frac{1}{2}}$. However, the current context for asymptotic distribution of the intensity of non-diversifiability requires the norming sequence to be $n^{\frac{3}{2}}$ due to the applications of the quadratic variation (of Brownian motion).

4.4.3 Two-Dimensional Lattice-Process Setting for Idiosyncratic Risk

Given that every empirical study for asset pricing models is based on a collection of finite samples, the verification of the growth rate of these moments may require a large number of cross-sectional/time-series observations since the studies are mostly based on sampled moments. In addition, especially for empirical studies, the framework for the consistent estimates of moments may need to have a sufficiently long time horizon (as $T \longrightarrow \infty$) to detect the hidden non-diversifiable factor. For instance, in order to apply the above definition of non-diversifiability, a condition of a weak law of large numbers is provided to consider the multi-indexed sums over inter-temporal and cross-sectional observations.

Assumption A11 $|\frac{1}{T}\sum_{t=1}^{T}\left(\frac{1}{n}\sum_{i=1}^{m}\hat{\epsilon}_{it}\right)^2 - E\left(\frac{1}{n}\sum_{i=1}^{m}\epsilon_{it}\right)^2| \xrightarrow{p} 0$ as $T \longrightarrow \infty$ for all n's, $1 \leq m \leq n$, $n \rightarrow \infty$.

Given Assumption A11 and Definition D5, we may consider that as $T \longrightarrow \infty$ there exists an N sufficiently large that for all n's, $n > N$, and $1 \leq m \leq n$, and for a slowly varying function $L(n)$ at infinity where for all $a > 0$ $\lim_{n\longrightarrow\infty} \frac{L(an)}{L(n)} = 1$ such that

$$n^{-\alpha}L(n)\frac{1}{T}\sum_{t=1}^{T}\sum_{m=1}^{n}\left(\frac{1}{n}\sum_{i=1}^{m}\epsilon_{it}\right)^2 \approx O_p(1). \tag{4.4.31}$$

In addition, we may also have under Assumption A11

$$n^{-\alpha}\left|\frac{1}{T}\sum_{t=1}^{T}\sum_{m=1}^{n}\left(\frac{1}{n}\sum_{i=1}^{m}\hat{\epsilon}_{it}\right)^2 - \frac{1}{T}\sum_{t=1}^{T}\sum_{m=1}^{n}\left(\frac{1}{n}\sum_{i=1}^{m}\epsilon_{it}\right)^2\right| \approx o_p(1),$$

for sufficiently large time horizon T. However, the condition in Eq. (4.4.31) requires that the growth rates of n and T must be high enough where both $n \rightarrow \infty$, and $T \rightarrow \infty$ to certify the results. Thus, from Eq. (4.4.31) and under Assumption A11, we may develop another test statistic such that

$$\eta_{n,T} = \frac{1}{T}\sum_{t=1}^{T}\sum_{m=1}^{n}\left(\frac{1}{n\hat{\sigma}}\sum_{i=1}^{m}(\hat{\epsilon}_{it} - \bar{\hat{\epsilon}}_t)\right)^2 \tag{4.4.32}$$

where $\bar{\hat{\epsilon}}_t = \frac{1}{n}\sum_{i=1}^{n}\hat{\epsilon}_{it}$ is the cross-sectional mean of the (presumed) idiosyncratic risk at time t, $1 \leq t \leq T$.

When under the null hypothesis $\alpha = 0$ where the idiosyncratic risk is strongly diversifiable (even if there is a hidden factor unidentified) and

Assumption A8 holds, it is straightforward to follow the sequential limit method of Connor and Korajczyk (1993) and show that for any given T as $n \to \infty$ first,

$$\eta_{n,T} \xrightarrow{d} \frac{1}{T} \sum_{t=1}^{T} \left(\int_0^1 (\widetilde{B}_t(z)^2) dz \right), \tag{4.4.33}$$

where $\widetilde{B}_t(z)$, $0 \leq z \leq 1$, for any given T, is a standard Brownian bridge at time t. Thus, we can introduce an alternative method to assess the non-diversifiability of the hidden factor (if any) in the idiosyncratic risk.

Notice that the square integral of the Brownian bridge is still stochastic since it is a random functional defined on the probability space $(\Omega, \mathscr{F}, P)$. In addition, for each time t, the square integral of the Brownian bridge $\widetilde{B}_t(z)$, is identically distributed according to the work of Tolmatz (2002, 2003). Thus, denoting $\int_0^1 (\widetilde{B}_t(z)^2) dz$ as $\ddot{\xi}_t$, which is a random function defined on $(\Omega, \mathscr{F}, P)$, a central limit theorem (for $\eta_{n,T} \approx \frac{1}{T} \sum_{t=1}^{T} \ddot{\xi}_t$ on the function space L^2) can be developed if an independence assumption (for these square integrals) over time horizon T is given.[25] Explicitly, it can be shown that as $T \to \infty$ on Eq. (4.4.33),

$$\frac{\sqrt{T}}{\sigma_\eta} (\eta_{n,T} - \mu_\eta) \xrightarrow{d} N(0, 1), \tag{4.4.34}$$

where μ_η is the mean of $\int_0^1 (\widetilde{B}_t(z)^2) dz$, and σ_η^2 is the variance of $\int_0^1 (\widetilde{B}_t(z)^2) dz$, respectively.[26]

Theorem 4.7 *Given the above setting and Assumption A9, when letting $n \to \infty$ first and letting $T \to \infty$ subsequently, the statistic $\eta_{n,T}$ will have a weak convergence such that under the null hypothesis $\alpha = 0$,*

$$\frac{\sqrt{T}}{\sigma_\eta} (\eta_{n,T} - \mu_\eta) \xrightarrow{d} N(0, 1), \tag{4.4.35}$$

where $\mu_\eta = \frac{1}{6}$, and $\sigma_\eta^2 \approx 0.022222$ according to the table provided by Tolmatz (2002). In addition, the test statistic is consistent in the sense that if $\alpha > 0$ under the alternative, $\sqrt{T}\eta_{n,T} \to \infty$ as $n \to \infty$ for any date T.

Proof Given Assumption A9, when $n \to \infty$ and under the null hypothesis $\alpha = 0$, it is straightforward to see that for each time $t \geq T$,

$$\sum_{m=1}^{n} \left(\frac{1}{n\hat{\sigma}} \sum_{i=1}^{m} (\hat{\epsilon}_{it} - \bar{\hat{\epsilon}}_t) \right)^2 \xrightarrow{d} \int_0^1 (\widetilde{B}_t(z)^2) dz.$$

Hence, it follows that for all given times T,

$$\eta_{n,T} \xrightarrow{d} \frac{1}{T} \sum_{t=1}^{T} \left(\int_0^1 (\widetilde{B}_t(z)^2) dz \right), \qquad (4.4.36)$$

following the continuous mapping theorem. Now that the inter-temporal independence among these square integrals of the Brownian bridge is assumed, applying the central limit theorem for random functionals on probability space $(\Omega, \mathscr{F}, P)$, the weak convergence of $\frac{\sqrt{T}}{\sigma_\eta}(\eta_{n,T} - \mu_\eta)$ to a standardized normal distributed variable can be obtained as $T \to \infty$.

On the other hand, if the alternative hypothesis holds where $\alpha > 0$, from Eq. (4.4.31) the statistic in the equation will grow with n^α, where $\alpha > 0$. Hence as $n \to \infty$ for any given time horizon T, the test statistic $\eta_{n,T}$ in Eq. (4.4.32) will also grow such that $\eta_{n,T} \to \infty$. Therefore, the test is consistent as its power approaches one when the alternative hypothesis holds.

In other words, if the sizes of the cross-sectional observations n and the time horizon T grow, the test statistic in Eq. (4.4.35) will converge to a normal distribution with a mean and variance of $\frac{1}{6}$ and 0.022222, respectively, under the null hypothesis $\alpha = 0$. However, the above statistic is formed when the inter-temporal independence among all the (time-indexed) square integrals of the Brownian bridge is given, even though generalization may be needed if the consistent estimates for their inter-temporal dependence are credible.

Instead, the framework can be extended to consider the asset pricing models on random fields where the omitted hidden factor (which is similar to the dynamic factor structures) may cause both inter-temporal and cross-sectional dependence in idiosyncratic risk. An extended and similar condition for non-diversifiability in random fields is covered in the following where the idiosyncratic risk may contain the hidden factor that possibly is of both inter-temporal and cross-sectional dependence.

To extend the above setting of the intensity of non-diversifiability, we may consider that the idiosyncratic risk $\{\varepsilon_{it}\}_{i=1,\ldots,n}^{t=1,\ldots T}$ is in a two-dimensional random field. In this case, even if there exists a hidden common factor for the risk, the setting may allow both cross-sectional and inter-temporal dependence where the hidden factor may not be serially independent over time. For $t = 1, \ldots T, i = 1, \ldots, n$, let the empirical asset pricing model be shown as

$$\begin{aligned} r_{it} &= E\left[r_{it}|I_t\right] + \epsilon_{it} = \sum_{j=1}^{k} \beta_{ij} X_t^{(j)} + \epsilon_{it}, \\ \epsilon_{it} &= \eta_{it} + \upsilon_{it} = \tilde{B}_i' \mathfrak{F}_{ht} + \upsilon_{it} = \sum_{s=1}^{p} \tilde{b}_{is} \tilde{f}_{st} + \upsilon_{it}, \end{aligned} \tag{4.4.37}$$

where $\underline{X}_t = (X_t^1, X_t^2, \ldots, X_t^k)$ is a $k{\times}1$ vector of known proxies (including the constant one for the intercept) in empirical asset pricing models at the k-th stage of the model search ($k \geq 1$) for empirical asset pricing models (where k can be set to 1 at the initial stage), η_{it} is a two-dimensional isotropic random field which can be decomposed into two components $\{\tilde{B}_i, \mathfrak{F}_{ht}\}\ i = 1, 2, \ldots, n,\ t = 1, 2, \ldots, T$, where $\mathfrak{F}_{ht}$ is a p-by-1 vector of hidden unknown factors $\{\tilde{f}_{st}\}_{s=1,\ldots,p}$ (or lagged factors) with possible temporal dependence, $\{\tilde{B}_i\}_{i=1,2,\ldots,n}$ are $p{\times}1$ vectors of (random) factor loadings of the hidden factors $\mathfrak{F}_{ht}$ for each asset i, where $E[\tilde{B}_i] = \underline{\mathbf{0}}_p, \upsilon_{it}$ is a random noise for all asset $i's$ and t's, $\{\tilde{B}_i\}_{i=1,2,\ldots,n}$ and $\{\mathfrak{F}_{ht}\}_{t=1,2,\ldots,T}$ are mutually independent across all (i, t), $i = 1, 2, \ldots, n, t = 1, 2, \ldots, T$, I_t is the current information set available up to time t for model specification.

Notice that if dynamic factors are of interest, consider $\mathfrak{F}_{ht} = \left[\tilde{f}_t, \tilde{f}_{t-1}, \ldots, \tilde{f}_{t-p}\right]'$ as a $p{\times}1$ vector of lagged hidden factors; hence the factor loadings can be expressed as the coefficients of these lagged factors. Given suitable mixing conditions for the hidden factors, the covariance of the partial sum of these dynamic factors can be shown to be finite. The partial sum of covariances in $\{\epsilon_u\}_{u \in Z^2}$ (where Z^2 represents the two-dimensional lattice with coordinates of positive integers) can be shown as depending on whether some of the hidden factors are diversifiable or not.

The essential issue is what impact will occur if the hidden factors are non-diversifiable (across all assets and time horizons). The following claim will show that if the underlying hidden factors are non-diversifiable, the $\{\eta_u\}_{u\in Z^2}$ (and henceforth, $\{\epsilon_u\}_{u\in Z^2}$) will follow a long-memory two-indexed lattice process).

Theorem 4.8 *Given that the presumed idiosyncratic risk of an empirical asset pricing model follows a two-indexed lattice process as $\{\epsilon_u\}_{u\in Z^2}$ with hidden factor structure as in Eq. (4.4.37), and if there exists (at least) a hidden non-diversifiable factors in $\mathfrak{F}_{ht}$, then for a given $\mathbf{u} \in Z^2$, the absolute sum of covariances of a two-indexed lattice process will not be summable such that*

$$\sum_{A_{\mathbf{u}}(\lambda),\lambda\to\infty} |Cov(\epsilon_{\mathbf{u}}, \epsilon_{\mathbf{v}})| \longrightarrow \infty, \tag{4.4.38}$$

where $A_{\mathbf{u}}(\lambda)$ is an arbitrary two-dimensional area that contains the points $\mathbf{u}, \mathbf{v}$ as $\mathbf{u} = (i_1, t_1)$ and $\mathbf{v} = (i_2, t_2)$ represents the coordinates in the two-dimensional lattice with distance λ-apart and the area $A_{\mathbf{u}}(\lambda)$ is expanding through the distance λ, where $\lambda = \min[|i_1 - i_2|, |t_1 - t_2|], i_1, i_2 = 1, \ldots, n$ and $t_1, t_2 \in [1, \infty)$.

Proof Since the memory condition of ϵ_u depends on η_u in Eq. (4.4.37), it is straightforward to focus on the memory of η_u. From Theorem 4.1, it has already been shown that at any time t, $t = 1, 2, \ldots T$, if (at least) one of the factor loadings $\{\tilde{B}_i\}_{i=1,2,\ldots,n}$ of hidden factors are non-diversifiable, the presumed idiosyncratic risk will have cross-sectional long dependence. Hence, the current work is to show that if the hidden factors of $\mathfrak{F}_{ht}$ in Eq. (4.4.37) are subject to short-term memory (for instance, some mixing conditions), the covariances over $(i, t) \in A_u(\lambda)$ will not be summable where the arbitrary two-dimensional area $A_u(\lambda)$ expands as $\lambda \to \infty$.

Consider that there exists at least one hidden factor in $\mathfrak{F}_{ht}$ (say, $\tilde{f}_{st}$, $s \in [1, p]$) (denoted from now on as $\tilde{f}_t$ for simplicity) which is non-diversifiable such that for any particular asset i_1, $i_1, i_2 \in [1, n]$, where $m = |i_1 - i_2|$ and assuming that $\rho_{it}(m) = \text{Cov}(\tilde{b}_{i_1}, \tilde{b}_{i_2})C_{st} \approx \left(\frac{1}{m}\right)^{\alpha} L(m)C_{st}$ is the covariance function for asset i_1 for distance λ across all assets on this s-th component of $\tilde{B}_{i_1}$ where $0 < \alpha \leq 1$, $L(m)$ is a slowing varying function of m, *then*C_{st} is a positive constant and $\sum_{\lambda=0}^{\infty} |\rho_{it}(m)| = \infty$, without loss of generality. Since the covariance function of η_u can be shown as

$$\begin{aligned}\mathrm{Cov}(\eta_{\mathbf{u}}, \eta_{\mathbf{v}}) &= E\left[\left(\tilde{B}'_{i_1}\mathfrak{F}_{ht_1}\right)'\left(\tilde{B}'_{i_2}\mathfrak{F}_{ht_2}\right)\right] \\ &= E\left[\mathfrak{F}'_{ht_1}\left(\tilde{B}_{i_1}\tilde{B}'_{i_2}\right)\mathfrak{F}_{ht_2}\right],\end{aligned}$$

it is easy to see that matrix multiplication can be done with partitioned matrices. For simplicity, it is assumed that the non-diversifiable factor is stacked up as the first component in vector $\mathfrak{F}_{ht}$, without loss of generality.

Let $\mathfrak{F}_{ht} = \begin{bmatrix}\tilde{f}_t \\ F_t\end{bmatrix}$ where $\tilde{f}_t$ is the particular hidden non-diversifiable factor in $\mathfrak{F}_{ht}$, and let $\tilde{B}_i$ be partitioned accordingly (with similar dimension) as $\tilde{B}_i = \begin{bmatrix}\tilde{b}_i \\ B_i\end{bmatrix}$ for the factor loadings and assuming that $\tilde{b}_i$ and B_i are uncorrelated, for simplicity. Then, the cross products of the covariance function can be denoted as

$$\begin{aligned}\mathrm{Cov}(\eta_{\mathbf{u}}, \eta_{\mathbf{v}}) &= E\left[\mathfrak{F}'_{ht_1}\left(\tilde{B}_{i_1}\tilde{B}'_{i_2}\right)\mathfrak{F}_{ht_2}\right] \\ &= E\left\{\left[\tilde{f}_{t_1}, F'_{t_1}\right]\left(\begin{bmatrix}\tilde{b}_{i_1} \\ B_{i_1}\end{bmatrix}\left[\tilde{b}_{i_2}\ B'_{i_2}\right]\right)\begin{bmatrix}\tilde{f}_{t_2} \\ F_{t_2}\end{bmatrix}\right\} \\ &= E\left\{\tilde{b}_{i_1}\tilde{b}_{i_2}\tilde{f}_{t_1}\tilde{f}_{t_2} + \tilde{b}_{i_2}\tilde{f}_{t_2}F'_{t_1}B_{i_1} + \tilde{f}_{t_1}\tilde{b}_{i_1}B'_{i_2}F_{t_2} + F'_{t_1}B_{i_1}B'_{i_2}F_{t_2}\right\}. \end{aligned} \tag{4.4.39}$$

Hence, by the triangular inequality $|X + Y| \geq |X| - |Y|$, the Cauchy-Schwarz inequality, and the fact that the hidden factors and their random factor loadings are mutually independent, the absolute value of covariance between $\eta_{\mathbf{u}}$ and $\eta_{\mathbf{v}}$ can be shown to be

$$\begin{aligned}|\mathrm{Cov}(\eta_{\mathbf{u}}, \eta_{\mathbf{v}})| &= \left|E\left\{\tilde{b}_{i_1}\tilde{b}_{i_2}\tilde{f}_{t_1}\tilde{f}_{t_2} + \tilde{b}_{i_2}\tilde{f}_{t_2}F'_{t_1}B_{i_1} + \tilde{f}_{t_1}\tilde{b}_{i_1}B'_{i_2}F_{t_2} + F'_{t_1}B_{i_1}B'_{i_2}F_{t_2}\right\}\right| \\ &\geq |E[\tilde{b}_{i_1}\tilde{b}_{i_2}\tilde{f}_{t_1}\tilde{f}_{t_2}]| - |E[\tilde{b}_{i_2}\tilde{f}_{t_2}F'_{t_1}B_{i_1} + \tilde{f}_{t_1}\tilde{b}_{i_1}B'_{i_2}F_{t_2} + F'_{t_1}B_{i_1}B'_{i_2}F_{t_2}]| \\ &= |E[\tilde{b}_{i_1}\tilde{b}_{i_2}]E[\tilde{f}_{t_1}\tilde{f}_{t_2}]| - |E[\tilde{f}_{t_2}F'_{t_1}]E[\tilde{b}_{i_2}B_{i_1}] + E[\tilde{b}_{i_1}B'_{i_2}]E[\tilde{f}_{t_1}F_{t_2}] \\ &\quad + E[F'_{t_1}F_{t_2}]E[B'_{i_2}B_{i_1}]| \\ &\geq |E[\tilde{b}_{i_1}\tilde{b}_{i_2}]E[\tilde{f}_{t_1}\tilde{f}_{t_2}]| - |E[\tilde{f}_{t_2}F'_{t_1}]||E[\tilde{b}_{i_2}B_{i_1}]| - |E[\tilde{b}_{i_1}B'_{i_2}]||E[\tilde{f}_{t_1}F_{t_2}]| \\ &\quad - |E[F'_{t_1}F_{t_2}]||E[B'_{i_2}B_{i_1}]| \\ &= |E[\tilde{b}_{i_1}\tilde{b}_{i_2}]E[\tilde{f}_{t_1}\tilde{f}_{t_2}]| - o_p(1) - o_p(1) - |E[F'_{t_1}F_{t_2}]||E[B'_{i_2}B_{i_1}]|. \end{aligned} \tag{4.4.40}$$

In other words, the absolute value of the covariance between $\eta_{\mathbf{u}}$ and $\eta_{\mathbf{v}}$ is greater than the difference when the absolute value of the product term is $|E[\tilde{b}_{i_1}\tilde{b}_{i_2}]E[\tilde{f}_{t_1}\tilde{f}_{t_2}]|$ (for a non-diversifiable factor) minus that of the diversifiable factors and their factor loadings. Given that the factors in F_t are diversifiable, it can be seen that the factor loadings and these factors are of short memory such that for $\mathbf{u}= (i_1, t_1)$, and $\mathbf{v} = (i_2, t_2)$,

$$\lim_{A_{\mathbf{u}}(\lambda),\lambda\to\infty} \frac{1}{|A_{\mathbf{u}}(\lambda)|} \sum_{0}^{|t_1-t_2|} |E[F'_{t_1}F_{t_2}]| = 0 < \infty,$$

$$\lim_{A_{\mathbf{u}}(\lambda),\lambda\to\infty} \frac{1}{|A_{\mathbf{u}}(\lambda)|,} \sum_{0}^{|i_1-i_2|} |E[B'_{i_1}B_{i_2}]| = 0 < \infty,$$

where $|A_{\mathbf{u}}(\lambda)|$ represents the cardinality of the area surrounding $\mathbf{u}$ with distance λ.

Notice that the short memory conditions imply that the limits of the partial sums of covariances of (B_{t_1}, F_{t_1}) surrounding $\mathbf{u}= (i_1, t_1)$ are finite, respectively. Hence, given that $\Delta_p(1) < \infty, \lambda = \min[|i_1 - i_2|, |t_1 - t_2|]$, $i_1, i_2 = 1, \ldots, n$ and $t_1, t_2 \in [1, \infty)$, the limit of the partial sum of Eq. (4.4.40) for the area $A_{\mathbf{u}}(\lambda)$ can be expressed as

$$\begin{aligned}
&\sum_{A_{\mathbf{u}}(\lambda),\lambda\to\infty} |\mathrm{Cov}(\eta_{\mathbf{u}}, \eta_{\mathbf{v}})| \\
&\quad\geq \sum_{A_{\mathbf{u}}(\lambda),\lambda\to\infty} |E[\tilde{b}_{i_1}\tilde{b}_{i_2}]E[\tilde{f}_{t_1}\tilde{f}_{t_2}]| - \Delta_p(1), \\
&\quad= \lim_{A_{\mathbf{u}}(\lambda),\lambda\to\infty} \sum_{0}^{|i_1-i_2|}\sum_{0}^{|t_1-t_2|} E[\tilde{b}_{i_1}\tilde{b}_{i_2}]|E[\tilde{f}_{t_1}\tilde{f}_{t_2}]| - \Delta_p(1), \\
&\quad= \lim_{A_{\mathbf{u}}(\lambda),\lambda\to\infty} \left(\sum_{0}^{|i_1-i_2|} E[\tilde{b}_{i_1}\tilde{b}_{i_2}]\right)\left(\sum_{0}^{|t_1-t_2|} |E[\tilde{f}_{t_1}\tilde{f}_{t_2}]|\right) - \Delta_p(1), \\
&\quad\approx \lim_{A_{\mathbf{u}}(\lambda),\lambda\to\infty} \left(\sum_{0}^{|i_1-i_2|} \tilde{C}\left(\frac{1}{|i_1-i_2|}\right)^{\alpha} L(|i_1-i_2|)\right)\left(\sum_{0}^{|t_1-t_2|} |G(|t_1-t_2|)|\sigma_{\tilde{f}}^2\right) \\
&\quad\quad -\Delta_p(1), \\
&\longrightarrow \infty,
\end{aligned} \tag{4.4.41}$$

when the hidden non-diversifiable is present as a (cross-sectionally) long-dependent component, regardless of the temporal dependence of the factor $\tilde{f}_t$. In other words, the two-dimensional lattice process of $\{\epsilon_{\mathbf{u}}\}_{\mathbf{u}\in A_{\mathbf{u}}(\lambda)}$ will become a long-memory random field if there is a hidden non-diversifiable factor in the presumed idiosyncratic risk of Eq. (4.4.37) provided that $\{\upsilon_{it}\}$ is only a random noise.

The function $G(|t_1 - t_2|)$ determines the autocovariance function (with $G(0) = 1$) of $\tilde{f}_{t_1}$, since the hidden non-diversifiable factor is assumed to contain some inter-temporal dependence depending on the distance $|t_1 - t_2|$. For instance, $G(|t_1 - t_2|)$ can be expressed as the power function, such as $G(|t_1 - t_2|) = (|t_1 - t_2|)^{-\tau}$, as well as to express the intensity of the temporal dependence of $\tilde{f}_t$. The range of τ will determine the persistence of the autocovariance of $\tilde{f}_{t_1}$.

Also, notice that if $\tilde{f}_t$'s are inter-temporally independent, $E[\tilde{f}_{t_1}\tilde{f}_{t_2}] = 0$ (and hence, for $G(|t_1-t_2|) = 0$) for any $|t_1-t_2| \neq 0$. However, when $t_1-t_2 = 0$, $G(0) = 1$. Hence, the expression $\sum_0^{|t_1-t_2|} |G(|t_1 - t_2|)|\sigma_{\tilde{f}}^2$ will become a single term as $\sigma_{\tilde{f}}^2$ only. This will be the result of Theorem 4.1 when tests for factor structure focus on the cross-sectional dependence. And hence, the finding of Theorem 4.8 can be applied as a necessary property for empirical asset pricing models to verify if there is any need to expand the dimensions of the models for pricing kernels of asset returns.

Notes

1. Notice that we assume the static factor structure here for simplicity. Further extension of the inter-temporal dependence among the factors as in dynamic factor models can be provided if needed. In addition, with this setting, the orderings of the proxies for factors are not necessarily known in advance (see Ouysse 2006). In other words, the conclusion in the following theorems and claims hold true whether the orderings of proxies for factors are known or unknown.
2. See Cochrane (2001) p. 129 for details.
3. Assuming that $E[\beta_i^h] = 0$ for all for all $i = 1, 2, \ldots n$ is for simplicity. The following arguments in Theorem 4.1 will still hold if a more general condition such as $E[\beta_i^h] \neq 0$ for almost all $i = 1, 2, \ldots n$ is introduced.
4. For simplicity, it is assumed that the presumed proxies for factors f_t and hidden factor $\{f_{ht}\}_{i=1,\ldots,T}$ are orthogonal to each other.
5. Specifically, the theoretical asset pricing models with factor structures will need to verify that these factors are compensated with (statistically) significant associated risk premiums. Since no assumption is given on the

a priori existence of a factor structure, as in most theoretical asset pricing models, no further discussion on the second-pass regressions are considered here. The intent of model searching is then the identification of any expansion of proxies for factors within the current context of models. In this perspective, the following analyses are aimed at devising model selection with testing through diagnostic tests.

6. The notation here implies that all elements in the vector β_H are square-integrable in L^2 space.
7. Notice that the result in Theorem 4.1 can also hold true even when the prespecified models are subject to a nonlinear factor structure for the conditional expectation in Eq. (4.1.1).
8. The selection rule as $\ddot{\xi}(\epsilon_{it}) > 0$ is chosen as a simplification. Additional rules can be introduced if more detailed descriptions for sample selection are provided.
9. This means that only the population mean of the random factor loadings is equal to zero. It doesn't state that the hidden factor loadings are equal to zero for all assets of interest.
10. Notice that the notation is only to state that not all factor loadings of the hidden factor are equal to zero.
11. The following section is a modified version of work in Jeng and Liu (2012) which provides details of applications with backward elimination in the model search.
12. In essence, the search is similar to the parsimonious encompassing test.
13. However, a criterion is set that the sampling will only consider the existing firms in the sample periods.
14. One possible reason for using conditional moments is to allow the introduction of a dynamic factor structure when past information is taken into account.
15. Jeng and Liu (2012) provide a cross-sectional long-memory test to verify the possible non-diversifiable hidden factor in the idiosyncratic risk when the Fama-French three-factor model is applied for security returns. The empirical result indicates that the claim of additional hidden factor(s) for the Fama-French model is not confirmed since there is no significant cross-sectional dependence shown in the idiosyncratic risk.
16. Certainly, it will more general to include a random noise u_e in Eq. (4.1.55), where u_e is independent of $\underline{\upsilon}_i, X$, and f_h. However, it is easy to see that if $X_e = X\gamma^\star + a_h f_h + u_e$, the noise can be combined in the hidden factor such that $a_h f_h + u_e = a_h(f_h + \frac{1}{a_h}u_e) = a_h f_h^\star$. then, rewrite Eq. (4) as $\underline{\epsilon_i} =$

$\beta_i^h f_h + \underline{\upsilon}_i = \beta_i^h f_h^\star + (\underline{\upsilon}_i - \frac{1}{a_h} u_e) = \beta_i^h f_h^\star + \underline{\upsilon}_i^\star$. The arguments here will still apply.

17. The following results still hold if the generalized inverse matrices are applied to the matrices $(X'X)$ and $X_e'MX_e$, respectively.
18. In Pesaran (2006), the noises $\underline{\upsilon}_i$ and $\underline{\zeta}_i$ are mutually independent, yet each has serial dependence. For simplicity, we assume they are not of serial dependence here.
19. A possible scenario may also occur when applying Theorem 4.1 that the cross-sectionally weighted average of these long-memory random variables may still contain some long dependence due to the non-diversifiable hidden factor.
20. In fact, it is easy to discover that all these test statistics are all based on the sum of CUSUMs of the underlying variables.
21. The other advantage for the setting is that the test statistics developed here can be applied at times when one is concerned with some possible misspecification errors in the factor structure, as long as the sample size of the cross-sectional observations is sufficiently large.
22. In brief, this cross-sectional detection approach can be applied to out-of-sample statistics for some given time horizons T, $T \to \infty$. Furthermore, if additional decision rules are added, a monitoring scheme can be developed if one is interested in the on-line checking for the hidden non-diversifiable factor.
23. Notice that the setting here provides the conditions even for a sequential detection test with additional observations where $t = T + 1, T + 2, \ldots$, and T is the current time horizon used for training samples to estimate the coefficients in the hypothesized models when T is sufficiently large.
24. Notice that if $H = \frac{1}{2}$, then $Z_n(j)$ will converge in distribution to the quadratic variation of the Brownian motion if Assumption A9 holds.
25. Notice that the central limit theorem for these random functions can be extended to the dependence conditions. For simplicity, an independence condition is assumed here.
26. These two statistics are available according to Tolmatz (2002, 2003).

References

Ang, A., R.J. Hodrick, Y. Xing, and X. Zhang. 2006. The Cross-Section of Volatility and Expected Returns. *Journal of Finance* 61: 259–298.

Bai, J. 2003. Inferential Theory for Factor Models of Large Dimensions. *Econometrica* 71: 135–171.

Bai, J., and S. Ng. 2002. Determining the Numbers of Factors in Approximate Factor Models. *Econometrica* 70: 191–221.

Barber, B.M., and J.D. Lyon. 1997. Firm Size, Book-to-Market Ratio, and Security Returns: A Hold-out Sample of Financial Firms. *Journal of Finance* 52: 875–883.
Beran, J., Y. Feng, S. Ghosh, and R. Kulik. 2013. *Long Memory Processes.* Berlin: Springer.
Berenguer-Rico, V., and J. Gonzalo. 2014. Summability of Stochastic Processes—A Generalization of Integration for Non-Linear Processes. *Journal of Econometrics* 178: 331–341.
Berzin, C., A. Latour, and J.R. León. 2014. *Inference on the Hurst Parameter and the Variance of Diffusions Driven by Fractional Brownian Motion.* Springer.
Brown, B.M. 1994. Grouping Corrections for Circular Goodness-of-Fit Tests. *Journal of Royal Statistical Society B* 56: 275–283.
Campbell, J.Y. 1996. Understanding Risk and Return. Journal of Political Economy 104: 298–345.
Chamberlain, G. 1983. Funds, Factors, and Diversification in Arbitrage Pricing Models, *Econometrica* 51, 1305–1323.
Chamberlain, G., and M. Rothschild. 1983. Arbitrage, Factor Structure, and Mean-Variance Analysis on Large Asset Markets. *Econometrica* 51: 1281–1304.
Chudik, A., M.H. Pesaran, and E. Tosetti. 2011. Weak and Strong Cross-Section Dependence and Estimation of Large Panels. *Econometrics Journal* 14: 45–90.
Cochrane, J.H. 2001. *Asset Pricing.* Princeton: Princeton University Press.
Connor, G., and R. Korajczyk. 1993. A Test for the Number of Factors in an Approximate Factor Model. *Journal of Finance* 48: 1263–1291.
Embrechts, P., and M. Maejima. 2002. *Self-Similar Processes.* Princeton: Princeton University Press.
Fama, E.F., and K.R. French. 1993. Common Risk Factors in the Returns on Stocks and Bonds. *Journal of Financial Economics* 25: 23–49.
Gagliardini, P., E. Ossola, and O. Scaillet. 2016. Time-Varying Risk Premium in Large Cross-Sectional Equity Data Set. *Econometrica* 84: 985–1046.
Giraitis, L., P. Kokoszaka, R. Leipus, and G. Teyssiere. 2003. Rescaled Variance and Related Tests for Long Memory in Volatility and Levels. *Journal of Econometrics* 112: 265–294.
Goyal, A., and P. Santa-Clara. 2003. Idiosyncratic Risk Matters. *Journal of Finance* 58: 975–1008.
Grinblatt, M., and S. Titman. 1985. Approximate Factor Structures: Interpretations and Implications for Empirical Tests. *Journal of Finance* 40: 1367–1373.
Hansen, L.P., and R. Jagannathan. 1991. Implications of Security Market Data for Models of Dynamic Economies. *Journal of Political Economy* 99: 225–262.
Hansen, P.R., A. Lunde, and J. Nason. 2011. The Model Confidence Set. *Econometrica* 79: 453–497

Jagannathan, R., and Z. Wang. 1998. An Asymptotic Theory for Estimating Beta-Pricing Models Using Cross-Sectional Regression. *Journal of Finance* 53: 1285–1309.

Jahn, J. 2007. *Introduction to the Theory of Nonlinear Optimization*. 3rd ed. Berlin: Springer.

Jeng, J.-L., and W. Liu. 2012. Do Idiosyncratic Risks in Multi-Factor Asset Pricing Models Really Contain a Hidden Nondiversifiable Factor? A Diagnostic Testing Approach. *Journal of Mathematical Finance* 2: 251–263.

Jeng, J.-L., and E. Tobing. 2012. Finding Hidden Non-Diversifiable Factors – A Model Search with Cross-Sectional CUSUM Tests. Working Paper.

Kan, R., and G. Zhou. 1999. A Critique of the Stochastic Discount Factor Methodology. *Journal of Finance* 54: 1221–1248.

Kiefer, J. 1959. K-Sample Analogues of Kolmogorov-Smirnov and Cramér-von Mises Tests. *Annals of Mathematical Statistics* 30: 420–447.

Kwiatkowski, D., P.C.B. Phillips, P. Schmidt, and Y. Shin. 1992. Testing the Null Hypothesis of Stationarity Against the Alternative of a Unit Root. *Journal of Econometrics* 54: 159–178.

Li, H., and Y. Xu. 2002. Survival Bias and the Equity Premium Puzzle. *Journal of Finance* 57: 1981–1995.

Li, Y., and W.J. Mayer. 2007. Impact of Correction for Dynamic Selection Bias on Forecast of Retention Behavior. *Journal of Forecasting* 26: 571–582.

Maag, U.R. 1966. A k-sample Analogue of Watson's Statistic. *Biometrika* 53: 579–583.

Nourdin, I. 2008. Asymptotic Behavior of Weighted Quadratic and Cubic Variations of Fractional Brownian Motion. *Annals of Probability* 36: 2159–2175.

Nourdin, I., and A. Réveillac. 2009. Asymptotic Behavior of Weighted Quadratic Variations of Fractional Brownian Motion: The Critical Case H=1/4. *The Annals of Probability* 37: 2200–2230.

Onatski, A. 2009. Testing Hypotheses about the Number of Factors in Large Factor Models. *Econometrica* 77: 1447–1479.

Ouysse, R., 2006, Consistent Variable Selection in Large Panels when Factors are Observable. *Journal of Multivariate Analysis* 97: 946–984.

Pesaran, M.H. 2006. Estimation and Inference in Large Heterogeneous Panels with a Multifactor Error Structure. *Econometrica* 74: 967–1012.

Petkova, R. 2006. Do the Fama-French Factors Proxy for Innovations in Predictive Variables? *Journal of Finance* 61: 581–621.

Ross, S.A. 1976. The Arbitrage Theory of Capital Asset Pricing. *Journal of Economic Theory* 13: 341–360.

Shanken, J. 1992. On the Estimation of Beta-Pricing Models. *Review of Financial Studies* 5: 1–33.

Smirnov, N.V. 1936. Sui la distribution de w^2. *Comptes Rendus (Paris)* 202: 449–452.

Tolmatz, L. 2002. On the Distribution of the Square Integral of the Brownian Bridge. *Annals of Probability* 30: 253–269.

Tolmatz, L. 2003. Addenda: On the Distribution of the Square Integral of the Brownian Bridge. *Annals of Probability* 31: 530–532.

Tudor, C.A. 2013. *Analysis of Variations for Self-Similar Processes*. Berlin: Springer.

Watson, G.S., 1961. Goodness-of-Fit Tests on A Circle. I. *Biometrika* 48, 109–112.

White, H. 2001. Asymptotic Theory for Econometricians. Revised Edition. Cambridge: Academic Press.

CHAPTER 5

Hypothesis Testing with Model Search

This chapter covers the discussions of model selection tests in empirical asset pricing models with the asymptotic properties developed in Chap. 4. In particular, model selection with forward selection for variables in empirical asset pricing models is introduced. The purpose of this chapter is to consider the sequential model search where model selection tests (or criteria) with additional asymptotic properties for common factors of asset returns are used. Differing from the other empirical studies, the emphasis is on the cross-sectional commonality of these presumed variables or factors when the asset returns are projected onto these variables. Given that the underlying intrinsic mechanism of asset returns is unknown, the sequential model search is to pursue the optimality in approximation that the basic requirement for these presumed variables or factors will satisfy the coherence condition where cross-sectional dependence is persistent.

Since sequential model selection tests are applied, the asymptotic properties differ from the usual model specification tests. Given the sequential schemes, the power and size of the test statistics are affected by the sequential procedures applied. Discussions on stopping time and the optimality of sequential searching are needed. Specifically, the procedures are to show that the approach of searching for empirical asset pricing models should be flexible enough to accommodate the possibly time-changing nature of pricing kernels and the varieties of the information sets obtained.

Instead of claiming the superiority of certain models or proxies for factors in the empirical asset pricing models, this chapter will present an

J.-L. Jeng, *Empirical Asset Pricing Models*,
https://doi.org/10.1007/978-3-319-74192-5_5

adaptive approach in which the search for these models can be expanded to some sequential statistical inferences so that more robust results can be obtained when the underlying pricing kernels are possibly evolving over time. The emphasis is not on which model is better. Instead, it is on which approach can provide us with a better way to improve the search for empirical asset pricing models.

There are lots of model selection criteria developed in both the statistic and econometric literature. Although there are various robust data sources, the essence of model selection in empirical asset pricing models is different from applications of these criteria in other fields. As mentioned earlier, selection in these models should consider: (1) the evolving nature of the data source where models are only approximations possibly based on the available information; (2) the purpose of building the models is to identify the possible explanatory variables of security returns and to obtain the systematic components from them.

5.1 Model Selection with Hypothesis Testing

As indicated by Hansen (2005), there are four types of conceptual errors in econometric model selection: parametric vision, the assumption of a true data generating process, evaluation based on fit, and ignoring the impact of model uncertainty on inference. Although a semiparametric vision is suggested by Hansen (2005), the idea is actually more toward the robust version of statistical inferences. For instance, instead of assuming a particular (say) exponential family of distribution functions (and the associated likelihood functions), a semiparametric inference with robust statistics incurs an alternative assumption so as to reduce the a priori requirement on the data generating process.

In addition, Hansen (2005) mentions that the conventional model selection methods assume that the true data generating process concerns the elements of the finite set of potential models. The model selection procedure's consistency is to show that the probability of selecting the true model approaches 1 as the sample size grows. In fact, the models can only be considered as approximations to the data generating process. Likewise, the issue of consistency should be modified to see how much the goodness of the model may approximate to the data generating process.

More likely and especially for financial data, the underlying data generating process may be evolving over time. In other words, the conventional model selection criteria may lose their consistency in selecting the models if the underlying data generating process is evolving where the data may either result in an entirely different scheme or the process now occurs based on the originally assumed set of models.

Given that the models are only considered as approximations to the data generating process, the original development of consistency in model selection criteria (of finite sets of assumed models) is not sufficient to cover econometric model selection. Accordingly, we will need to focus attention on certain dimensions or features that are important to us for our applications.

As stated in Hansen (2005) "often a model is designed and estimated for a purpose. It follows that when we are explicit about the intended purpose, we should design model selection optimally for this purpose." The same emphasis should also apply to the empirical asset pricing models. Specifically, if the purpose of building these models is to identify the essential determinants for asset returns, it must satisfy the requirement that the inclusion of variables (or a particular functional form) fulfills non-diversifiability so as to exhibit the systematic components of asset returns whenever possible.

5.1.1 *Model Confidence Set*

Hansen et al. (2011) introduce the concept of a model confidence set for model selection which does not assume that there is a particular true model for the underlying data generating mechanism. The procedure can be applied to compare many objects including a comparison of models. Ideally, the objective of a model confidence set is to identify the set of models (denoted as $M^{\star}$) that consists of the best model(s) from a collection of models M^{o}, where the *best* is defined in terms of a criterion that is user-specified. The procedure is to produce a model confidence set $M^{\star}$ with a collection of models built to contain the best models with a given level of confidence.

Accordingly, the procedure is about producing a model confidence set $\widehat{M}^{\star}$ (where $\widehat{M}^{\star} \subseteq M^{o}$) with sample information of relative performances such that $\widehat{M}^{\star}$ may include the set of best model(s) with a certain probability (similar to the confidence interval of population parameters in statistical inferences). In other words, the procedure is information-oriented using the data obtained.

Given that $M^{\star}$ may contain more than one best model, we may consider the possibility of more than one model being the best. Two testing procedures are introduced in the model confidence set: one is the equivalence test δ_M; the other is an elimination rule, e_M.

The equivalence test is initially applied to the set $M = M^o$. If δ_M is rejected, the objects in M are not equally "good", and the elimination rule e_M is applied to eliminate those non-equally "good" objects from M. The procedure is repeated until δ_M is "accepted" and the model confidence set consists of the "surviving" objects. Hence, giving the significance α in all tests, the procedure will guarantee that $\lim_{n\to\infty} P(M^{\star} \subseteq \widehat{M}^{\star}_{1-\alpha}) \geq 1 - \alpha$. In particular, when $M^{\star}$ contains only one object, the procedure will have $P(M^{\star} = \widehat{M}^{\star}_{1-\alpha}) = 1$.

The setting of the model confidence set does not require that there exists a "true" model for the data. Instead, the models are selected by using the sample information and the elimination rule for the competitive models. Specifically, let M^o contain a finite number of models (or objects) indexed by $i = 1, \ldots, m_o$, where the objects are evaluated by the loss function $L_{i,t}$ for object i in period t, $t = 1, \ldots, T$.

For instance, the loss function can be the function of the forecast errors, the R-squared, or the other specification test statistics. Define the relative performance variable for all $i, j \in M^o$ as

$$d_{ij,t} = L_{i,t} - L_{j,t},$$

and assume that $\mu_{ij} \equiv E\left(d_{ij,t}\right)$ is finite and does not depend on t for all i, $j \in M^o$. Hence, in terms of expected loss, item i is preferred to alternative j if $\mu_{ij} < 0$. Based on the above setting, we may define the set of superior models (or objects) as the following Definition D1.

Definition D1 The set of superior objects (or models) is defined as

$$M^{\star} \equiv \left\{i \in M^o : \mu_{ij} \leq 0, \forall j \in M^o\right\},$$

where the notation $\forall$ means "for all".

In other words, the objective of the model confidence set is to determine the set $M^{\star}$, where the procedures are through a sequence of significance tests, and objects (or models) that are significantly inferior to other elements in M^o are eliminated. The procedures are enlisted in the following.

The hypothesis that will be tested is

$$H_{o,M} : \mu_{ij} = 0, \forall i, j \in M,$$

where $M \subset M^o$, and the alternative hypothesis is denoted as

$$H_{A,M} : \mu_{ij} \neq 0, \exists i, j \in M,$$

where the notation $\exists$ means "for some". That is, for some $i, j \in M$, $\mu_{ij} \neq 0$. In other words, the null hypothesis $H_{o,M}$ holds true if $M^* \subset M$, and it will be rejected if M contains some elements in M^* and its complement is $M^o \setminus M^*$ according to Hansen et al. (2011). We will now provide the following model confidence set MCS procedures.
The procedures require an equivalence test δ_M and an elimination rule e_M. The equivalence test δ_M is to consider the null hypothesis $H_{o,M}$ for any $M \subset M^o$. The elimination rule e_M is to identify the object (model) in M that will be removed from M when $H_{o,M}$ is rejected. For simplicity, $\delta_M = 0$ and $\delta_M = 1$ are denoted for $H_{o,M}$ as being accepted and rejected, respectively. The details are stated as follows.

Step 0. Set $M = M.^o$
Step 1. Test $H_{o,M}$ using the test δ_M at level α.
Step 2. If $H_{o,M}$ is accepted, define $\widehat{M}^*_{1-\alpha} = M$; otherwise, use e_M to eliminate the object (model) from M and repeat Step 1.

Notice that the procedures do not prespecify what test should be used to test the null hypothesis. This allows flexibility for determination in statistical inference to be applied, which can also be data-dependent. Another feature is that the procedures do not set a particular order or sequence for hypothesis testing as in many model selection criteria or tests.[1] Based on the above description of the MCS procedures, it is easy to see that the procedures start with the largest set or collection of possible models. Then, the equivalence rule and elimination rule are applied to see if further reduction of the contents of the set is necessary. The procedures are repeated until no further reduction is feasible. This algorithm is similar to the top-down approach in model selection such as (parsimonious) encompassing tests and many others.

Assumption A1 For any $M \subset M^o$, (a) $\limsup_{n\to\infty} P(\delta_M = 1|H_{o,M}) \leq \alpha$, (b) $\lim_{n\to\infty} P(\delta_M = 1|H_{A,M}) = 1$, (c) $\lim_{n\to\infty} P(e_M \in M^*|H_{A,M}) = 0$.

Notice that the assumption in (a) is to set the asymptotic level of a type-1 error so that it will not exceed $\alpha\%$. It is actually a "tail" condition since the definition as $\limsup_{n\to\infty}$ applies to the sequence of probabilities of rejecting the null hypotheses (as $P(\delta_M = 1|H_{o,M})$ given that $H_{o,M}$ holds true) infinitely many times when the number of models increases asymptotically. However, it does not assume the condition holds unanimously for all hypotheses and models as the number of models increases asymptotically. On the other hand, condition (b) assumes that the power of the tests is equal to one as $n \to \infty$. Likewise, when the number of models increases, condition (c) assumes that the superior objects (or models) will not be eliminated. Given these assumptions, Hansen et al. (2011) provide the following theorem for asymptotic properties of MCS procedures.

Theorem 5.1 (MCS Properties) *Given the above assumptions, (1)* $\liminf_{n\to\infty} P(M^* \subset \widehat{M}^*_{1-\alpha}) \geq 1 - \alpha$, *and (2)* $\lim_{n\to\infty} P(i \in \widehat{M}^*_{1-\alpha}) = 0$, *for all* $i \notin M^*$.

In other words, following MCS procedures, the sequence of probabilities $P(M^* \subset \widehat{M}^*_{1-\alpha})$ exceeds (or is equal to) $1 - \alpha\%$ all but finitely many times when number of models increases. That is, the procedures will have a confidence level more than $1 - \alpha\%$. In addition, the error rate, as some superior objects (or models) are eliminated, will approach zero as the number of models increases asymptotically.

Corollary 5.2 (MCS Properties) *Suppose the above assumptions hold and* M^* *is a singleton, then* $\lim_{n\to\infty} P(M^* = \widehat{M}^*_{1-\alpha}) = 1$.

More extensively, Hansen et al. (2011) establish the coherency between the test and elimination rules in the MCS procedures.

Theorem 5.3 *Suppose that* $P(\delta_M = 1,\ e_M \in M^*) \leq \alpha$. *Then it follows that* $P\left(M^* \subset \widehat{M}^*_{1-\alpha}\right) \geq 1 - \alpha$.

Applications of the MCS procedures can be seen in (for instance) Barmalzan and Najafabadi (2012) where the concept is used in the extension of Vuong (1989) test for non-nested models. Notice that the application is only for the unknown density function of the data source, the test for non-nested models being sufficient for the purpose of study. Unfortunately, the applications of asset returns in finance (especially for the empirical asset pricing models) need to consider both the nested and non-nested models given the time-varying nature of financial data.

5.2 Sequential Model Search: Forward Selection and Control

In order to justify the necessity of certain explanatory variables or proxies for factors in empirical asset pricing models, the specification test must indicate the feature that inclusion of such variables identifies the essentiality among all asset returns. Hence, the specification test (which will be jointly applied in the model search within the proposed list of variables) must show such features for the models to be meaningful and suitable for purpose. Differing from the MCS procedures described earlier, this section provides a sequential model search method where a forward selection procedure is applied.

For applications in regressions, we substitute $\{\epsilon_{it}\}_{i=1,2,...}$ with the residuals from the fitted regressions $\{\hat{\epsilon}_{it}\}_{i=1,2,...}$ when $\{r_{it}\}_{i=1,2,...,n,,t=1,2,...,T,}$ are regressed on the known proxy (or proxies) in empirical asset pricing models. Furthermore, using the same foundation, another similar statistic can be developed. The following Theorem 5.4 shows that another form of cross-sectional cumulative sum (CUSUM) statistic can also be used as a specification test for empirical asset pricing models to verify a hidden non-diversifiable factor (or component) in projection errors. The tests are extensions of the diagnostic tests provided in Chap. 4 although the tests developed earlier are also applicable to the model search as well. The purpose is to identify the need for further expansion of the model with additional proxies for non-diversifiable factor(s).

The procedures of Khan et al. (2007) in search of a robust linear model with forward selection and stepwise procedures provide an example of model search. Given that the step-by-step methods of model search are computationally efficient, the methods may incur outliers and other contaminations. Their method is to search for an additional explanatory variable (after any arbitrary initial selection) when using pairwise assessments of robust (partial) correlations. The abridged version of their approach can be stated in the following:

(1) Standardize each variable (including the dependent variable);
(2) Choose the initial explanatory variable by checking the variable that has the largest absolute correlation with the dependent variable;
(3) Regress all other explanatory variables (in the information set) on this initial explanatory variable and save the residuals from such regressions;
(4) Calculate the partial correlations of the residuals in step (3) with the dependent variable of the model of interest;
(5) Select the variable with the largest partial correlation with the dependent variable;
(6) Continue the process from step (3) to step (5) until the stopping rule is satisfied.

Notice that the procedures are based on the robust method for finding the association between the dependent variable and independent variables. The procedures can reduce the computational burden when the list of explanatory variables expands. However, their analysis is based on the partial correlations for the selection of variables. The approach in this section is to show that the diagnostic tests we develop here (and those in Chap. 4) can be applied to determine the selection of the explanatory variables of empirical asset pricing models using some similar procedures. In particular, the testing procedures will ensure the inclusion of variables certifies the non-diversifiability of the proxies for factors. Therefore, the variables applied in the empirical asset pricing models are capable of extracting the essential determinants for excess returns of securities.

The following Theorem 5.4 shows an alternative diagnostic test based on the residuals from fitted empirical asset pricing models (in any stage of a model search). In other words, the following test is to identify if the current stage of a model search is sufficient. Hence, the test can be applied as a stopping rule if it fails to reject the null hypothesis.

For simplicity, it is assumed that $\{\widetilde{x_{st}}\}_{s=1,2,\ldots,u}$, $u \geq 1$ only contains a constant term for the following derivations on the diagnostic tests for omitted non-diversifiable factor(s). Specifically, the following test statistics (for variable selection) of Corollary 5.5 can also be applied to the choice of variables in $\{\widetilde{x_{st}}\}_{s=1,2,\ldots,u}$, $u \geq 1$ for their explanatory roles as non-diversifiable as well.

Theorem 5.4 *Under the null hypothesis that the projection errors* $\{\epsilon_{it}\}_{i=1,2,\ldots}$ *from the presumed empirical asset pricing model (at the k-th stage of model search) as shown in Eq. (4.1.1) in Chap. 4 do not contain a hidden non-diversifiable factor (or component), let* $\{\hat{\epsilon}_{it}\}_{i=1,2,\ldots}$ *be the residuals of fitted regressions for asset returns at time t and* $\{\epsilon_{it}\}_{i=1,2,\ldots}$ *follow the invariance principle of (cross-sectional) short-memory stochastic processes, and let* $\hat{s}^2_{n,T} = \frac{1}{n}\sum_{i=1}^{n}\hat{\epsilon}^2_{it} + 2\sum_{l=1}^{n-1}\theta(\frac{l}{q})\hat{\gamma}_t(l)$ *be the heteroskedasticity and autocorrelation consistent estimate for the cross-sectional asymptotic variance* σ_t^2 *at time t,* $t \geq T$, *for sufficiently large T, where* $\hat{\gamma}_t(l) = \frac{1}{n}\sum_{i=1}^{n-l}\hat{\epsilon}_{it}\hat{\epsilon}_{i+l,t}$, *and* $\theta(\cdot)$ *is the kernel function with bandwidth q,* $q \to \infty$, $\frac{q}{n} \to 0$, *and assume that* $\frac{1}{T}\sum_{t=1}^{T}\hat{s}_{n,T} = \frac{1}{T}\sum_{t=1}^{T}\sigma_t + o_p(1) \xrightarrow{p} \ddot{\sigma} > 0$, *the panel CUSUM statistic* $\hat{\Psi}^{\epsilon}_{n,T}$ *such that*

$$\hat{\Psi}^{\epsilon}_{n,T} = \frac{1}{T}\sum_{t=1}^{T}\left[n^{-1}\sum_{m=1}^{n}\left(\frac{1}{\sqrt{n}}\left|\sum_{i=1}^{m}(\hat{\epsilon}_{it} - \bar{\hat{\epsilon}}_t)\right|\right)\right], \tag{5.2.1}$$

will show that for sufficiently large T, $t \geq T$,

$$\frac{\hat{\Psi}^{\epsilon}_{n,T}}{\left(\frac{1}{T}\sum_{t=1}^{T}\hat{s}_{n,T}\right)} \xrightarrow{d} \int_o^1 |\widetilde{B}_t(z)|dz \tag{5.2.2}$$

provided that $\left(\frac{1}{\sqrt{n}}\sum_{i=1}^{m}\epsilon_{it}\right) \xrightarrow{d} \sigma_t B_t(z)$, $0 < z \leq 1$, $1 \leq m \leq n$, as $n \to \infty$, for each $t \geq T$, where $\widetilde{B_t}(z)$=$B_t(z) - zB_t(1)$ is a Brownian bridge and $B_t(z)$, is a standard Brownian motion defined on [0, 1], where $z \in [0, 1]$.

The statistic $\hat{\Psi}^{\epsilon}_{n,T}$ is consistent in the sense that $\frac{\hat{\Psi}^{\epsilon}_{n,T}}{(\frac{1}{T}\sum_{t=1}^{T}\hat{s}_{n,T})} \to \infty$ as $n \to \infty$, $T \to \infty$ if there is a hidden non-diversifiable factor in $\{\epsilon_{it}\}_{i=1,2,\ldots}$ under the alternative hypothesis such that $n^{-H}\sum_{i=1}^{[nz]}\epsilon_{it} \xrightarrow{d} \gamma B_H(z)$, $z \in [0, 1]$, $H > \frac{1}{2}$, σ^2_{Ht} is the long-run variance of $\{\epsilon_{it}\}_{i=1,2,\ldots}$ when $\{\epsilon_{it}\}_{i=1,2,\ldots}$ are of cross-sectional long memory, $\gamma > 0$, γ is a scalar, and $W_H(z)$ is a fractional Brownian motion. The distribution for $\int_o^1 |\widetilde{B}_t(z)|dz|$ can be found in Johnson and Killeen (1983) (where tabulated critical values for different significance levels are provided) as

$$\Pr\left(\int_o^1 |\widetilde{W}_t(z)|dz \le b\right) = \left(\frac{\varpi}{2}\right)^{\frac{1}{2}} \sum_{s=1}^{\infty} \left(\frac{1}{\delta_s^{\frac{3}{2}}}\right) \zeta\left(\frac{b}{\delta_s^{\frac{3}{2}}}\right), \tag{5.2.3}$$

$$\zeta(x) = \frac{3^{\frac{3}{2}} e^{\frac{-2}{27x^2}}}{x^{\frac{1}{3}}} A_i((3x)^{-\frac{4}{3}}, \tag{5.2.4}$$

$$\delta_s = \frac{-a_s'}{2^{\frac{1}{3}}}, \tag{5.2.5}$$

where A_i is the Airy function and a_s' is the s-th zero of A_i'.

Proof Notice that the hidden factor is assumed to be inter-temporal independent. Hence, for each time t, the test statistics depend crucially on the estimates of the long-run cross-sectional variance. Since the estimate (say) $\widehat{s}_{nt}^2 = \frac{1}{n}\sum_{i=1}^{n}(\epsilon_{it} - \overline{\epsilon}_{nt})^2 + 2\sum_{j=1}^{q}\varpi_j(q)\hat{\gamma}_{jt}$ is a consistent estimate for the long-run cross-sectional variance $\widetilde{\sigma}_t^2$ as $n \to \infty$, given the memory condition $\{\epsilon_{it}\}_{i=1,2...}$ in Assumption A7 of Chap. 4,[2] and by the continuous mapping theorem, the statistic

$$\hat{\Psi}_{n,T}^{\epsilon} = \frac{1}{T}\sum_{t=1}^{T}\left[n^{-1}\sum_{m=1}^{n}\left(\frac{1}{\sqrt{n}}\left|\sum_{i=1}^{m}(\hat{\epsilon}_{it} - \widehat{\overline{\epsilon}}_t)\right|\right)\right],$$

will converge to a functional of a Brownian bridge such that

$$\frac{\hat{\Psi}_{n,T}^{\epsilon}}{\left(\frac{1}{T}\sum_{t=1}^{T}\hat{s}_{n,T}\right)} \xrightarrow{d} \int_o^1 |\widetilde{B}_t(z)|dz.$$

In addition, if there is a non-diversifiable hidden factor in the idiosyncratic risk as in Assumption A6 of Chap. 4, and assuming that for each time t, $q^{2H-1}\hat{s}_{nt}^2 \xrightarrow{p} \ddot{\sigma}_t^2$, (where $\ddot{\sigma}_t^2$ is the long-run cross-sectional variance of $\{\epsilon_{it}\}_{i=1,2...}$ when under cross-sectional long memory.) Then the test statistic will converge in distribution as

$$\left(\frac{q}{n}\right)^{2H-1}\frac{\hat{\Psi}_{n,T}^{\epsilon}}{\left(\frac{1}{T}\sum_{t=1}^{T}\hat{s}_{n,T}\right)} \xrightarrow{d} \int_o^1 |\widetilde{B}_H(z)|dz,$$

where $\widetilde{B}_{H_t}$ is a fractional Brownian bridge at date t with Hurst exponent H, $\frac{1}{2} < H < 1$. Since the rescaled variance is positive, $\frac{q}{n} \to 0$ as $n \to \infty$, and $2H - 1 > 0$, $\frac{\hat{\Psi}^{\epsilon}_{n,T}}{(\frac{1}{T}\sum_{t=1}^{T} \hat{s}_{n,T})} \to \infty$ when $n \to \infty$, hence the test is consistent.

In particular, Johnson and Killeen (1983) also provide a table of probability distribution with respect to different critical values for the distribution of L^1- norm of a Brownian bridge. Thus, the model search can be obtained through diagnostic checking. If the null hypothesis of no non-diversifiable hidden factor in the error term is rejected, it shows that we may then consider a possible model expansion with other proxies for factors.

Following the reasoning of Theorem 4.1 and Corollary 4.2, we have an additional condition to ensure that the selected proxies are of non-diversifiable factor loadings. An alternative method suggested is to perform a sequential model search with forward selection by expanding the dimension of the model for non-diversifiable loadings with specification tests.

In other words, the model search will begin with forward selection by using two steps: (1) verifying the included proxy is non-diversifiable and (2) checking to see if the error terms still contain some hidden non-diversifiable factor(s). Therefore, the model search is to obtain the most parsimonious model of relevant variables. In addition, we identify the model by selecting the proxies that most likely represent the non-diversifiable components of excess returns.

Essentially, it is necessary to pick up the variables or proxies for factors that ensure the non-diversifiability of their factor loadings to specify the non-diversifiable or "systematic" components in excess returns. Moreover, given that the model search with all different possible permutations of variables may be too computation-intensive, a sequential approach may reduce the number of searches needed.

For instance, if we perform the model search with model selection criteria for all possible variables to be included, we will need to search around 2^p models just for p variables. Instead, the following forward-selection sequential model search approach only needs to check for $\frac{p(p+1)}{2}$ models. Although the difference is relatively small when the number of variables is small, the difference increases dramatically when the number of variables increases asymptotically.[3]

Although the above $\hat{\Psi}^{\epsilon}_{n,T}$ is devised for projection errors, we may also introduce the $\hat{\Psi}^{f(j)}_{n,T}$ statistics in the fitted values of the empirical asset pricing model to establish the sequential model search such that $\hat{\Psi}^{f(j)}_{n,T} = \frac{1}{T}\sum_{t=1}^{T}\left[n^{-1}\sum_{m=1}^{n}\left(\frac{1}{\sqrt{n}}|\sum_{i=1}^{m}(\hat{h}^{(j)}_{it} - \overline{\hat{h}^{(j)}_{t}})|\right)\right]$, where $\hat{h}^{(j)}_{it} = \hat{\beta}^{(j)}_{i} f^{(j)}_{t} = \beta^{(j)}_{i} f^{(j)}_{t} + o_p(1)$, is the fitted value of the j-th proxy in the empirical asset pricing model. The intuition for sequential model selection tests is simple.

In the following Corollary 5.5, it is shown that if the k-th proxy is indeed needed and has non-diversifiable factor loadings, the $\hat{\Psi}^{f(j)}_{n,T}$ for the fitted values of this proxy will be statistically significant and increasing with n and T due to cross-sectional long dependence. In particular, the higher the $\hat{\Psi}^{f(j)}_{n,T}$ is, the more essential the variable is for describing the non-diversifiable component of excess returns.

Many model selection tests or criteria are to obtain the optimal model(s) of the relevant variables where the "true" model is assumed in the data generating process. Unfortunately, in empirical asset pricing models, it very likely that any model can only be considered as an approximation. Given that, the assessment of the goodness of models is not simply based on the statistical significance such as p-values of the t-statistics (or others) to justify the inclusion.

Instead, locating relevant variables in the model search for empirical asset pricing models should consider that the fundamental purpose is to search for a model with non-diversifiable factors (or proxies) to explain the essential (common) features of asset returns. It is not merely to verify whether certain variables are statistically significant in the conventional hypothesis testing using the t (or Z)-statistics and χ^2-statistics. As stated earlier, if the cross-sectional long dependence (induced by non-diversifiability) prevails, the conventional test statistics based on cross-sectional data or properties of asset returns may not have the stated asymptotic distributions which follow from the typical central limit theorem.

More explicitly, locating some models with statistically significant diversifiable variables or proxies may not necessarily improve the model specification since the findings do not necessarily identify the "systematic" "non-diversifiable" components for excess returns within finite samples. Thus, we may devise a sequential search for the model of excess returns using the above model selection tests and all specification tests developed in Sects. 4.4.2 and 4.4.3.

Let the upper bound of the number of proxies (in the information set) be denoted as p, and the maximum number of proxies currently selected as k, where $1 \leq k \leq p$. The setting here simply includes the situation where the choices of variables are possibly prescreened (using sample information and economics/finance theories) so that the maximum number of proxies considered is less than the entirety of all feasible explanatory variables.

The following test statistic in Corollary 5.5 can also be considered as the elimination/equivalence rule in the MCS procedures where if the included proxies are already non-diversifiable, then the tests will reject the null hypothesis and show that these proxies should remain in the models and further verifications or expansions may be considered. The elimination rule, however, will consider whether these test statistics are subject to ignorable differences (over the addition of variables) or not. If the difference is minor and if the test statistics for omitted non-diversifiable factor(s) in using the residuals of fitted models are insignificant, that will terminate the need to consider the other possible models, which is the stopping rule in the following algorithm.

In other words, the following test statistics can be applied to the MCS algorithm if the setting of forward selection is changed to the same bootstrapping approach as in Hansen et al. (2011). Given that the bootstrapping approach is more computation-intensive, the current work proposes a forward selection method similar to the concept of Khan et al. (2007) without using the partial correlations.

Nevertheless, the entire algorithm proposed here is similar to that of Hansen et al. (2011) such that the identification of models is only to search for the "better" approximations where the essentiality of proxies for systematic/non-diversifiable risk is satisfied. In particular, there is no a priori assumption that there is a true model (or models) for the asset returns of interest. The following test statistic assumes that the search is at the j-th stage ($1 \leq j \leq k$) where $j-1$ proxies are already identified.

Corollary 5.5 *Given Theorem 5.4, let the test statistics of a candidate variable for the j-th proxy (where $1 \leq j \leq k$) $\hat{\Psi}^{f(j)}_{n,T}$ be defined as*

$$\hat{\Psi}^{f(j)}_{n,T} = \frac{1}{T}\sum_{t=1}^{T}\left[n^{-1}\sum_{m=1}^{n}\left(\frac{1}{\sqrt{n}}\left|\sum_{i=1}^{m}(\hat{h}^{(j)}_{it} - \overline{\hat{h}^{(j)}_{t}})\right|\right)\right], \tag{5.2.6}$$

where $h_{it}^{(j)} = \beta_i^{(j)} f_t^{(j)}$, *and* $\hat{h}_{it}^{(j)} = \hat{\beta}_i^{(j)} f_t^{(j)} = h_{it}^{(j)} + o_p(1)$ *is the fitted value of the j-th proxy in the empirical asset pricing model and* $\overline{\hat{h}_t^{(j)}}$ *is their cross-sectional average. Then if this candidate variable concerns diversifiable loadings, it follows that if* $T \to \infty, t \geq T$,

$$\frac{\hat{\Psi}_{n,T}^{f(j)}}{\left(\frac{1}{T}\sum_{t=1}^{T}\hat{s}_{n,T}^{(j)}\right)} \xrightarrow{d} \int_o^1 |\widetilde{B}_t(z)|dz, \tag{5.2.7}$$

provided that $\left(\frac{1}{\sqrt{n}}\sum_{i=1}^{m} h_{it}^{(j)}\right) \xrightarrow{d} \sigma_t B_t(z)$, $0 < z \leq 1$, $1 \leq m \leq n$, as $n \to \infty$, where $\widetilde{B}_t(z)$=$B_t(z) - zB_t(1)$ is a Brownian bridge and $B_t(z)$ is a standard Brownian motion defined on the interval $[0, 1]$, where $z \in [0, 1]$. Let $\hat{s}_{n,T}^{(j)2} = \frac{1}{n}\sum_{i=1}^{n}\hat{h}_{it}^{(j)2} + 2\sum_{l=1}^{n-1}\theta(\frac{j}{q})\hat{\gamma}_t^{(j)}(l)$ be the heteroskedasticity and autocorrelation consistent estimate for the cross-sectional asymptotic variance $\sigma_t^{(j)2}$ of $\left\{h_{it}^{(j)}\right\}_{i=1,2,\ldots}$ at time t, $t \geq T$, where $\hat{\gamma}_t^{(j)}(l) = \frac{1}{n}\sum_{i=1}^{n-l}\hat{h}_{it}^{(j)}\hat{h}_{i+l,t}^{(j)}$, and $\theta(\cdot)$ is the kernel function with bandwidth q, $q \to \infty$, $\frac{q}{n} \to 0$, and assume that $\frac{1}{T}\sum_{t=1}^{T}\hat{s}_{n,T}^{(j)} = \frac{1}{T}\sum_{t=1}^{T}\sigma_t^{(j)} + o_p(1) \xrightarrow{p} \ddot{\sigma} > 0$.

The statistic $\hat{\Psi}_{n,T}^{f(j)}$ is consistent with $\frac{\hat{\Psi}_{n,T}^{f(j)}}{\left(\frac{1}{T}\sum_{t=1}^{T}\hat{s}_{n,T}^{(j)}\right)} \to \infty$ as $n \to \infty, T \to \infty$ if $\left\{h_{it}^{(j)}\right\}_{i=1,2,\ldots}$ follows the alternative hypothesis such that $n^{-H}\sum_{i=1}^{[nz]} h_{it}^{(j)} \xrightarrow{d} \gamma W_H(z)$, $z \in [0, 1]$, $H > \frac{1}{2}$, σ_{Ht}^2 is the long-run variance of $\left\{h_{it}^{(j)}\right\}_{i=1,2,\ldots}$ when $\left\{h_{it}^{(j)}\right\}_{i=1,2,\ldots}$ are of cross-sectional long memory, $\gamma > 0$, γ is a scalar, and $\mathcal{B}_H(z)$ is a fractional Brownian motion.

Proof Similar to Theorem 5.4, since the test statistic is a continuous functional of $\left\{h_{it}^{(j)}\right\}_{i=1,2,\ldots}$ and these variables follow the invariance principle under dependence, the convergence in distribution as

$$\frac{\hat{\Psi}_{n,T}^{f(j)}}{\left(\frac{1}{T}\sum_{t=1}^{T}\hat{s}_{n,T}^{(j)}\right)} \xrightarrow{d} \int_o^1 |\widetilde{B}_t(z)|dz,$$

will hold true when using the continuous mapping theorem under the null hypothesis of there being no non-diversifiable factor in the asset returns. On the other hand, if the factor is non-diversifiable then, applying Assumption A7 of Chap. 4, the test statistic $\hat{\Psi}^{f(j)}_{n,T}$ is consistent since

$$\frac{\hat{\Psi}^{f(j)}_{n,T}}{\left(\frac{1}{T}\sum_{t=1}^{T}\hat{s}^{(j)}_{n,T}\right)} \rightarrow \infty,$$

as $n \rightarrow \infty$, $T \rightarrow \infty$.

For the arguments of the (forward-selection) sequential model search, the following Assumption A1 implies that (after the j-th stage of the model search, $j \geq 1$) the modeler has (at least) already included some $j-1$ proxies that may partially approximate to the non-diversifiable components of the excess returns. That is, at the k-th stage of the model search, some $j-1$ relevant proxies with non-diversifiable factor loadings should have been identified. Applications of the new model selection test are to verify if further expansion of the model is needed.

Otherwise, if these factor loadings are diversifiable, it is implied that the modeler has simply included some diversifiable proxies at first, even though they could be statistically significant. For instance, if the capital asset pricing model (CAPM) is valid for the first stage of the model search, the best candidate proxy will be some rates of returns of market indices. The factor loadings of all excess returns projected on this proxy should be non-diversifiable if these market indices are closely associated with the market portfolio.

In the following, the above test statistics in Theorem 5.4 and Corollary 5.5 can be incorporated into the model search with forward selection. Given that the forward selection starts from the most parsimonious model, it initiates the search with the most conservative view where the ambiguity of essentiality of the included variables/proxies is minimized. Similarly, these tests can also be included in the MCS procedures for the equivalence and elimination rules, hence the model search can start with the set that includes all possible models of variables of interest where a randomization scheme is applied for the different combinations. An earlier version of the procedures is also discussed in Jeng (2015) where the search for explanations in the systematic components of asset returns is critical before the application of abnormal returns in the event studies of corporate finance.

Particularly since the initial step incurs the maximum of the test statistics among all possible proxies, there is no immediate need to consider the orderings or sequences of these preselected proxies. One advantage is that although MCS procedures can identify the set of models with certain confidence levels, some randomization schemes such as a bootstrapping method may be required to cover all possible combinations/orders of model specifications when a set of candidate models is assumed to start with.

Instead, the following algorithm provides the selection of the models with the maximization of test statistics (for non-diversifiability) at each stage of the model search, which is not subject to any orders or sequences for the hypotheses to be assessed. Nor is any stage of the model search based on the partial R^2 approach as in Ouysse (2006) given that the R^2 statistics can be misleading in identifying the essentiality of proxies for factors. In particular, all the specification tests for the missing non-diversifiable factor can be applied to each stage of the model search by substituting the model selection test statistic $\frac{\hat{\Psi}^{f(\tau)}_{n,T}}{\left(\frac{1}{T}\sum_{t=1}^{T}\hat{s}^{(j)}_{n,T}\right)}$ with the test statistics developed in Sects. 4.4.2 and 4.4.3.

The detailed algorithm is stated as follows:

(1) Select one proxy variable $f_{\tau t}$, $\tau = 1, 2, \ldots, k$ initially from $\{f_{\tau t}\}_{j=1,2,\ldots,k} \in \underline{\mathbf{f}}_t$, where $\underline{\mathbf{f}}_t$ is the set of all presumed k proxy variables for factors at time t. Run the univariate regressions of $\{r_{it}\}_{i=1,2,\ldots,n}$ on the $f_{\tau t}$ for each $i = 1, 2, \ldots, n$ to obtain the factor loadings $\hat{\beta}_{ij}$. Select those proxies where $\frac{\hat{\Psi}^{f(\tau)}_{n,T}}{\left(\frac{1}{T}\sum_{t=1}^{T}\hat{s}^{(j)}_{n,T}\right)}$ are statistically significant. Choose the proxy variable among these significant proxies when using maximum $\frac{\hat{\Psi}^{f(\tau)}_{n,T}}{\left(\frac{1}{T}\sum_{t=1}^{T}\hat{s}^{(j)}_{n,T}\right)}$ and denote it as $f_t^{(1)}$ for the first stage of the model search as $j = 1$.

(2) Apply the diagnostic test on the residuals to see if further expansions are needed when the residuals $\left\{\hat{\epsilon}^{(j)}_{it}\right\}$ may still contain some non-diversifiable hidden factors.

(3) Pursue a further model search at the $(j + 1)$-th step, where $j = 1, \ldots, s, s \leq k$. Let $\hat{\epsilon}^{(j)}_{it} = r_{it} - \hat{\alpha}_i - \hat{\beta}_{i1} f_t^{(1)} - \cdots - \hat{\beta}_{i(j)} f_t^{(j)}$,

which represents the residual after the j-th step of the search. Select and obtain the orthogonalized $(j+1)$-th stage regressor $\hat{\lambda}_t^{(j+1)}$, where $\hat{\lambda}_t^{(j+1)}$ is the residual after regressing each candidate variable f_t^* in $\hat{\Pi}_t = \underline{f_t}/\left\{f_t^{(1)}, f_t^{(2)}, \ldots, f_t^{(j)}\right\}$ on the already selected proxies $\left\{f_t^{(1)}, f_t^{(2)}, \ldots, f_t^{(j)}\right\}$, and $\hat{\Pi}_t = \underline{f_t}/\left\{f_t^{(1)}, f_t^{(2)}, \ldots, f_t^{(j)}\right\}$ represents the subset of $\underline{f_t}$ that excludes the already chosen proxies $\left\{f_t^{(1)}, f_t^{(2)}, \ldots, f_t^{(j)}\right\}$.[4]

(4) Perform univariate regressions of $\left\{\hat{\epsilon}_{it}^{(j)}\right\}_{i=1,2,\ldots}$ on the orthogonalized $(j+1)$-th stage regressor $\hat{\lambda}_t^{(j+1)}$ for factor loading $\left\{\hat{\beta}_{i,(j+1)}\right\}_{i=1,2,\ldots}$. Construct the new residual at stage $j+1$ as $\hat{\epsilon}_{it}^{(j+1)} = r_{it} - \hat{\alpha} - \hat{\beta}_{i1} f_t^{(1)} - \cdots - \hat{\beta}_{i,(j)} f_t^{(j)} - \hat{\beta}_{i,(j+1)} \hat{\lambda}_t^{(j+1)}$ for the $(j+1)$-th step. Select the proxy $\hat{\lambda}_t^{(k+1)}$ (across all f_t^* where $f_t^* \in \hat{\Pi}_t$) maximizes over $\frac{\hat{\Psi}_{n,T}^{f(j+1)}}{\left(\frac{1}{T}\sum_{t=1}^{T} \hat{s}_{n,T}^{*}\right)}$ which are statistically significant, and denote it as $f_t^{(j+1)}$. Continue step (2).

(5) If for some sufficiently small $\delta \in R$, $\delta > 0$, $\left|\frac{\hat{\Psi}_{n,T}^{f(j+1)}}{\left(\frac{1}{T}\sum_{t=1}^{T} \hat{s}_{n,T}^{(k)}\right)} - \frac{\hat{\Psi}_{n,T}^{f(j)}}{\left(\frac{1}{T}\sum_{t=1}^{T} \hat{s}_{n,T}^{(k-1)}\right)}\right| < \delta$, check to see if $\frac{\hat{\Psi}_{n,T}^{\epsilon}}{\left(\frac{1}{T}\sum_{t=1}^{T} \hat{s}_{n,T}\right)}$ (that is, the diagnostic test for the residual at the $(j+1)$-th stage) is still significant in the asymptotic distribution of $\int_o^1 |\widetilde{W}(z)|dz$. If so, continue step (2). If not, the search stops.

In other words, the procedures start with a variables search on the proxy variable(s) by fitting the returns with univariate linear regressions. We then perform the model search by expanding the model with more proxies using sequential model selection tests.

Therefore, for model searching among empirical asset pricing models, the above procedures simply begin with the univariate regressions for the excess returns against any possible variable selected for the first proxy of the factor. Using the derived statistics above, the procedure selects the proxy by choosing the one that is both significant and is the maximum of all test statistics of these variables in the first step.

After selecting the first proxy, apply the diagnostic test to see if the residuals may still contain some non-diversifiable hidden factors. If the test shows significance, further expansions may be needed. Now project the residuals on the other not-yet-selected proxies of factors to obtain the orthogonalized regressors. Choose the one with the maximum test statistics as the next proxy for the factor. Continue these steps until the stopping rule is satisfied as in step (5).

The above procedures emphasize using the specification test(s) to verify the non-diversifiability of any proxies that are used to approximate the presumed factor structure. As stated earlier, the studies of empirical asset pricing models should begin with the verification of the "essentiality" of the proxies before any further statistical inferences are made from the factor premiums. Conventional studies using the second-pass cross-sectional regressions may suffer problems such as data snooping issues (in sampling errors) and over-fittedness when using proxies to confirm the necessary factor premiums of these proxies. The procedures provided here perform the identification of these proxies at the outset when the model search begins.

In other words, instead of lumping together all presumed variables in regressions and then verifying the factor premiums (of these variables) to confirm their explanatory role in risk premiums, the study should begin with the exploratory data analysis to identify the role of non-diversifiability in explanatory variables in return processes. Otherwise, without considering model selections for these proxies on their non-diversifiability, the verification of factor premiums in the presumed regressions may be making up a story even though there's nothing to tell.

5.3 Epilogue

The work on empirical asset pricing models is enormous. Regardless of how ambitious the researcher (or any enchanted graduate student) may be, it is impossible for anyone to cover the entire scope of the research done on these models. For instance, for the discussion on the predictability of stock returns alone, various empirical and rigorous studies are abundant in the literature. Even so, inquiry into (un)predictability is merely one perspective of empirical studies. The remaining questions, such as "What causes it?" and "How may these findings relate to the determinants of stock returns?", demand further critical research. What is essential for anyone who is interested in empirical finance to know is that these works are only the *fundāmenta* accomplished so far. Reflections from the past do help. However, the steps needed for future development are far more immensely important.

For instance, the specifications of asset pricing models devise certain paradigms for understanding the forming of the risk premiums of asset returns. Rigorous work on the theoretical foundations, econometrics, and time-series analysis is provided for a main purpose. Namely, to understand the underlying determinants of the data generating mechanism. It is not difficult to learn that all these theoretical/empirical works in asset returns, such as the CAPM, the arbitrage pricing theory (APT), the multifactor models, and the stochastic discount factor (including contemporaneous research) do not suffice to finalize the schemes of studies. A time-evolving system in the capital markets requires further vision to improve the analytical framework.

Further work in the extension of random fields may become a promising field of study since both the time-series dynamic (that may encompass the inter-temporal dependence) of stock returns and the cross-sectional (or even locational) inter-dependence among all the assets can be taken into account simultaneously. Further work in extending the current theoretical research of asset pricing theories to these higher-dimensional settings will become more essential for both econometrics and time-series verification.

In addition, given that the underlying "true" systems of asset return processes are unknown, it is useful to consider the model search (at least) from the empirical perspectives. All models may only be considered as approximations to the underlying data generating mechanism. How to obtain the legitimate model selections for the time-evolving systems to improve understanding of the determining components of the system remains a challenging and continuing task for research into empirical asset pricing models.

Notes

1. Likewise, Hansen et al. (2011) provide the bootstrap applications of MCS procedures since they don't depend on the orders or sequences of hypothesis tests.
2. Notice that this is only one candidate estimator for the long-run variance. Many other estimates can also be applied and the same convergence in distribution still holds.
3. Notice that the forward-selection sequential model search is not identical to the forward search proposed by Atkinson and Riani (2002). Their approach is based on the increasing subsets of all observations to verify the model.

4. One reason for the orthogonalization is to obtain the estimate of the factor loadings of the newly included proxy—given that these proxies are possibly correlated. This approach is similar to Forsythe et al. (1973) and Billings and Wei (2005).

References

Atkinson, A.C., and M. Riani. 2002. Forward Search Added-Variable t-Tests and the Effect of Masked Outliers on Model Selection. *Biometrika* 89: 939–946.

Barmalzan, G., and A.T.P. Najafabadi. 2012. Model Confidence Set based on Kullback-Leibler Divergence Distance. *Journal of Statistical Research, Iran* 9: 179–193.

Billings, S., and H.-L. Wei. 2005. A Multiple Sequential Orthogonal Least Squares Algorithm for Feature Ranking and Subset Selection. *ACSE Research Report* No. 908.

Forsythe, A.B., L. Engelman, R. Jennrich, and P.R.A. May. 1973. A Stopping Rule for Variable Selection in Multiple Regression. *Journal of the American Statistical Association* 68: 75–77.

Hansen, B. 2005. Challenges for Econometric Model Selection. *Econometric Theory* 21: 60–68.

Hansen, P.R., A. Lunde, and J. Nason. 2011. The Model Confidence Set. *Econometrica* 79: 453–497.

Jeng, J.-L. 2015. *Analyzing Event Statistics in Corporate Finance: Methodologies, Evidences, and Critiques.* Basingstoke: Palgrave Macmillan.

Johnson, B. McK., and T. Killeen. 1983. An Explicit Formula for the C.D. F. of the L_1 Norm of the Brownian Bridge. *Annals of Probability* 11: 807–808.

Khan, J.A., S.V. Aelst, and R.H. Zamar. 2007. Building and Robust Linear Model with Forward Selection and Stepwise Procedures. *Computational Statistics and Data Analysis* 52: 239–248.

Ouysse, R. 2006. Consistent Variable Selection in Large Panels when Factors are Observable. *Journal of Multivariate Analysis* 97: 946–984.

Vuong, Q.H. 1989. Likelihood Ratio Test for Model Selection and Non-Nested Hypotheses. Econometrica 57: 307–333.

BIBLIOGRAPHY

Ang, A., and G. Bekaert. 2007. Stock Return Predictability: Is it There? *Review of Financial Studies* 20: 651–707.

Berzin, C., and J. León. 2007. Estimating the Hurst Parameter. *Statistical Inference for Stochastic Processes* 10: 49–73.

Dedecker, J., P. Doukhan, G. Lang, J. LeonR, S. Louhichi, and C. Prieur. 2007. *Weak Dependence with Examples and Applications.* New York: Springer.

He, L.-Y., and W.-B. Qian. 2012. A Monte Carlo Simulation to the Performance of the R/S and V/S Methods- Statistical Revisit and Real World Application. *Physica A* 39: 3770–3782.

Sommer, S., and R.M. Huggins. 1996. Variable Selection using the Wald Test and a Robust C_p. *Applied Statistics* 45: 15–29.

Trzcinka, C. 1986. On the Number of Factors in the Arbitrage Pricing Model. *Journal of Finance* 41: 347–368.

Westerlund, J. 2005. A Panel CUSUM Test of the Null of Cointegration. *Oxford Bulletin of Economics and Statistics* 67: 231–262.

White, H., and J. Wooldridge. 1988. Some Invariance Principles and Central Limit Theorems for Dependent Heterogeneous Processes. *Econometric Theory* 4: 210–230.

J.-L. Jeng, *Empirical Asset Pricing Models*,
https://doi.org/10.1007/978-3-319-74192-5

INDEX

Note: Page numbers followed by 'n' refer to notes.

J.-L. Jeng, *Empirical Asset Pricing Models*,
https://doi.org/10.1007/978-3-319-74192-5

FSC
www.fsc.org
MIX
Papier | Fördert gute Waldnutzung
FSC® C083411

Kolibri 360 GmbH
Ferdinand-Jühlke-Straße 7
99095 Erfurt, Deutschland
produktsicherheit@kolibri360.de